THE DISENCHANTED SELF

THE
DISENCHANTED SELF

Representing the Subject in the
Canterbury Tales

H. Marshall Leicester, Jr.

University of California Press
Berkeley • *Los Angeles* • *Oxford*

University of California Press
Berkeley and Los Angeles, California

University of California Press, Ltd.
Oxford, England

© 1990 by
The Regents of the University of California

Library of Congress Cataloging-in-Publication Data

Leicester, H. Marshall (Henry Marshall), 1942–
    The disenchanted self: representing the subject in the
Canterbury tales / H. Marshall Leicester, Jr.
        p.   cm.
    Bibliography: p.
    Includes index.
    ISBN 0-520-06760-6 (alk. paper).—ISBN 0-520-06833-5
(pbk. : alk. paper)
    1. Chaucer, Geoffrey, d. 1400. Canterbury tales.   2. Self-
consciousness in literature.   3. Subjectivity in
literature.   4. Point-of-view (Literature)   5. Persona
(Literature)   6. Self in literature.   I. Title.
PR1875.S45L45   1990
821'.1—dc20   89-5143
                                                                CIP

Printed in the United States of America
1   2   3   4   5   6   7   8   9

The paper used in this publication meets the minimum
requirements of American National Standard for Information
Sciences—Permanence of Paper for Printed Library Materials,
ANSI Z39.48–1984. ♾

For Nan and Harry
Sine quibus, non

Contents

Acknowledgments

About the only thing to be said for the length of time it has taken me to write this book is that it has provided me with the help, generosity, and encouragement of so many friends, whose virtues, not the least of which was patience, have meant so much. Indeed, I fear I will not thank all who deserve it, and I am sure I cannot thank any as much as they deserve. But if mention here cannot suffice, it will have to do, and with all its limits it is a glad task.

First, to those who taught me. Thanks to my father, for all the usual role-model reasons, with the added bonus of a sense of humor and the fun of thinking, and to my mother for, among other things, some lessons in feeling for, with, and against others that have kept coming back to me. Thanks to Marie Borroff, who introduced me to the study of Chaucer and later directed my dissertation, and who encouraged me from the very beginning to do what I wanted and follow the thought where it led. Alvin Kernan and Martin Price had more to do with the beginnings of this project than they will remember, and so did A. Dwight Culler. Leo Braudy, Billy Hamilton, Ralph Hanna, Diane Janeau, Frank McConnell, Harry Schroeder, and Suzie Wood Leicester Urbick kept those times interesting in complicated ways that have lasted.

Of E. Talbot Donaldson what shall I say? I heard his voice in the notes to *Chaucer's Poetry* long before I met him, and I hear it still now that he is gone. His skepticism and taste have measured my intemperance for years, and the thought of his horselaugh has kept me from more and greater excesses than he would credit. I regret that he did not live to read this book, and I would gladly settle for having him with us still if he never read it.

My colleagues past and present at the University of California at Santa Cruz have put up with listening to me work things out for twenty years, though I am bound to say that they have often given at least as good as they got. There are turns in my thoughts and my prose that would not be there without Sara Mack Amis, P. Reyner Banham, Murray Baumgarten, Jim Clifford, Teresa de Lauretis, Bob Durling, John Ellis, Floyd Estess, Angus Fletcher, Mary-Kay Gamel, John Halverson, Donna Haraway, Virginia Jansen, John Jordan, John Lynch, Paul Mann, Doug McClellan, Bob Meister, Gary Miles, Seth Schein, Tom Vogler, Michael Warren, and Hayden White. Kristine Brightenback and Cécile Schreiber didn't know that they were teaching me Old French in addition to everything else. George Amis and Tilly Shaw have read and talked about gender with me for years now, and though I may never forgive them for seeing less use in Lacan than I do (since both are stylists of extraordinary elegance), they have been the best of colleagues and the best of friends.

This book has been researched and written in a number of places around the country and outside it, and I have received shelter and sustenance for both body and mind from many friends and helpers. The John Simon Guggenheim Foundation provided support for a year's leave; I have had a sabbatical from UCSC; and the Research Committee of the Academic Senate at UCSC has dependably paid for research assistance and copying. Congenial surroundings in which to write in New York were provided by Virginia Clifford, Andrée Hayum, Richard Howard (who threw in what Stephen Koch calls the best library south of Fourteenth Street, to say nothing of giving us all Roland Barthes and the rest of it), Anne Lauterbach, Helen Rosenthal, and Lenore Rosenthal. Rosalind Krauss loaned me books no one else had when I needed them badly; Annette Michelson said things I kept remembering; and they both kept *October* coming out. I don't think Yvonne Rainer knows how much her wit, her seriousness, her work, and her friendship have meant to me, though she may be able to measure something of what I've learned from her by her knowledge of how much I needed to learn.

My students in Chaucer seminars over the years have done their best to keep me honest for the moment without suspecting how much I was stealing for the future, and Tom Cartelli, David Ehrman, Barbara Gottfried, Marina Leslie, Diane Manning, and Lori Nelson are in for a shock or two. Those of my students who have also been my research assistants know all too well where the bodies are buried—luckily they are too well mannered and too good friends to tell: Sylvia Huot, Rennie Coit, Beth Pittenger, and Ward Risvold have all given me far more than bulging file cabinets. Wallie Romig, head of the Cowell steno pool and the best administrator of anything anywhere I have ever seen, kept daily life and the manuscript moving; Dan Wenger led me through UNIX with patience and elegance; and Marianna Alves and Sara Silva typed the book into the machine, Middle English and all, with preternatural accuracy.

Colleagues around the country have provided me with opportunities to try out preliminary versions and shorter forms of much that appears here: C. David Benson, Mary Carruthers, Carolyn Dinshaw, Avrom Fleishman, Alan Gaylord, Tom Hahn, David Lawton, Al Shoaf, and their colleagues have offered, listened, and responded with generosity. Earlier versions of material included here have appeared in *PMLA, Studies in the Age of Chaucer,* and *Women's Studies.* I am grateful to them for permission to reprint, and to D. S. Brewer Press.

And so I come to those who have read, commented on, shaped, and improved the manuscript. Thanks are due to Ralph Hanna, Constance Jordan, Bonnie Krueger, Laura Slatkin, and two anonymous readers for the University of California Press, for sympathetic and critical commentary of extraordinary intelligence and helpfulness; to Ted Irving, whose unreasonably testy refusal to believe that Palamon and Arcite "really" want to rape and/or kill Emelye forced me to think harder and more carefully about the relation of psychological structures to social ones; to Carolyn Dinshaw for innumerable good conversations, for showing me her work and reading mine, and for giving the book its final title; to John Fyler for his enormous learning, his unerring sense of the ridiculous even in his best friends, and for suggesting, at a crucial early stage, the book's present order and overall plan; to Bob Hanning for countless kindnesses, personal and professional, over the years, not least the welcome he gave me into his National Endowment for the Humanities seminar on Chaucer in the summer of 1985, when most of Part II was written out of the stimulation of the group. Judith Ferster, besides writing the best book to date on Chaucer and contemporary theory, and besides her elegant lucidity in print and in person, was also the third reader for the press and wrote a report so sympathetic, intelligent, and penetrating that I was able to use it as an outline for my revisions: she is more responsible than I am altogether comfortable admitting for a lot of what I like about the book. Doris Kretschmer shepherded the manuscript through the University of California Press with just the right blend of patience and

xii   Acknowledgments

enthusiasm; she has gotten out of me more of the book I was trying to write (as opposed to the one I first wrote) than I would have believed possible. Rose Vekony and Richard Miller have socialized the text expertly and tactfully. Finally, thanks are due to Dan Kempton, my best student, my best reader, and my best critic, who understood what I was trying to do even when I didn't, showed me what could be done with *The Pleasure of the Text,* and on more than one occasion has helped me to know how to "go on."

I thank Walton T. Roth for "services, warious," as Sam Weller might have said. Though there is no German verb *werken,* the verb *wirken* (I looked it up) means to produce works, as in the cognate English expression *to work a miracle.* If much of the work (and the love) has been my own, there is enough of the feeling of the miraculous left here for gratitude to draw on and keep drawing. My daughter Elizabeth deserves gratitude for her lucidity and enthusiasm and for her ability to pick up what's essential in an argument about material she doesn't know and help the old man figure it out. The fact that I love her has nothing to do with these things, he said, and so I get to be grateful for that too. And thank you to Billie Harris for being around when I needed it and for being beautiful, funny, and smart whether I need it or not.

Concerning the two to whom this book is dedicated, I had hoped that the fact of the dedication would absolve me from having to say why, since there is no end to that saying. Readers who encounter them and their works only here should know that their names are Nan Rosenthal and Harry Berger, Jr., that they have been to me teachers, colleagues, friends, my significant others, and my other selves, that they have helped me to think and to feel and to love and to work as well as I am able, and that the dedication means what it says.

Introduction

Nec illud minus attendendum esse arbitror, utrum . . . magis secundum aliorum opinionem quam secundum propriam dixerint sententiam, sicut in plerisque Ecclesiastes dissonas diversorum inducit sententias, imo ut tumultu-ator interpretatur, beato in quarto dialogorum attestante Gregorio.

In my judgment it is no less necessary to decide whether sayings found [in the sacred writings and the Fathers] are quotations from the opinions of others rather than the writer's own authoritative pronouncements. On many topics the author of Ecclesiastes brings in so many conflicting proverbs that we have to take him as impersonating the tumult of the mob, as Gregory points out in his fourth dialogue.

Abelard, *Sic et Non, Prologus*

THE PROBLEM: VOICE, TEXTUALITY, IMPERSONATION

In *The Idea of the Canterbury Tales* Donald R. Howard identified a perennial strain in the Chaucer criticism of the last thirty years or more—isolated it, defined it clearly, and gave it a name. Discussing the *Knight's Tale,* he remarks:

> Chaucer . . . introduced a jocular and exaggerated element that seems to call the Knight's convictions into question. For example, while the two heroes are fighting he says "in this wise I let hem fighting dwelle" and turns his attention to Theseus:

> > The destinee, ministre general,
> > That executeth in the world over all
> > The purveiaunce that God hath seen biforn,
> > So strong it is that, though the world had
> > sworn
> > The contrary of a thing by ye or nay,
> > Yet sometime it shall fallen on a day
> > That falleth nat eft within a thousand yeer.
> > For certainly, our appetites here,
> > Be it of wer, or pees, or hate, or love,
> > All is this ruled by the sight above.

I

> This mene I now by mighty Theseus,
> That for to hunten is so desirous,
> And namely at the grete hert in May,
> That in his bed there daweth him no day
> That he nis clad, and redy for to ride
> With hunt and horn and houndes him
>   beside.
> For in his hunting hath he swich delit
> That it is all his joy and appetit
> To been himself the grete hertes bane.
> For after Mars he serveth now Diane.
>   (1663–82)

All this machinery is intended to let us know that on a certain day Theseus took it in mind to go hunting. It is impossible not to see a mock-epic quality in such a passage, and hard not to conclude that its purpose is ironic, that it is meant to put us at a distance from the Knight's grandiose ideas of destiny and make us think about them. This humorous element in the Knight's Tale is the most controversial aspect of the tale: where one critic writes it off as an "antidote" to tragedy another puts it at the center of things, but no one denies it is there. It introduces a feature which we will experience in many a tale: we read the tale as a dramatic monologue spoken by its teller but understand that some of Chaucer's attitudes spill into it. This feature gives the tale an artistry which we cannot realistically attribute to the teller: I am going to call this *unimpersonated artistry*. In its simplest form it is the contingency that a tale not memorized but told impromptu is in verse. The artistry is the author's, though selected features of the pilgrim's dialect, argot, or manner may still be impersonated. In its more subtle uses it allows a gross or "low" character to use language, rhetoric, or wit above his capabilities. (Sometimes it is coupled with an impersonated *lack* of art, an artlessness or gaucherie which causes a character to tell a bad tale, as in *Sir Thopas,* or to violate literary conventions or proprieties, as in the Knight's Tale.) The effect is that of irony or parody, but this effect is Chaucer's accomplishment, not an impersonated skill for which the pilgrim who tells the tale deserves any compliments.

> (Howard, *Idea of the Canterbury*
> *Tales,* 230–31)

Having generated this principle, Howard goes on to apply it, at various points in the book, to the tales of the Miller, the Summoner, the Merchant, the Squire, and the Manciple. He is in good and numerous company. One thinks of Charles Muscatine's characterization of certain central monologues in *Troilus and Criseyde:* "The speeches must be taken as impersonal comments on the action, Chaucer's formulation, not his characters' "; of Robert M. Jordan, who, having presented an impressive array of evidence for a complicated Merchant in the *Merchant's Tale,* argues from it, like Dryden's Panther, "that he's not there at all"; of Anne Middleton's exemption of selected passages of the *Physician's Tale* from the pilgrim's voicing; of Robert B. Burlin's praise of the *Summoner's Tale* despite its being "beyond the genius of the Summoner"; and of many other commentators on the *Knight's Tale,* some of whom I will return to later.[1]

In my view this "unimpersonated artistry" is a problem, and a useful one. Howard's formulation—an attempt to describe an aspect of Chaucer's general practice—is valuable because it brings into the sharp relief of a critical and theoretical principle something that is more diffusely present in the practical criticism of a great many Chaucerians: the conviction, often unspoken, that at some point it becomes necessary to move beyond or away from the pilgrim narrators of the *Canterbury Tales* and to identify the poet himself as the source of meaning. If the assumption is stated this broadly, I probably agree with it myself; but Howard's way of putting it does seem to me to reflect a tendency, common among Chaucer critics, to invoke the poet's authority much too quickly. Howard helps me to focus my own discontent, not with his criticism (much of which I admire), but with a more general situation in the profession at large. If we consider "unimpersonated artistry" as a theoretical proposition, it seems open to question on both general and specific grounds; that is, it seems both to imply a rather peculiar set of assumptions to bring to the reading of any text and, at least to me, to be an inaccurate reflection of the experience of reading Chaucer in particular.

1. Muscatine, *Chaucer and the French Tradition,* 264–65. In a more general statement on the *Canterbury Tales,* Muscatine observes: "No medieval poet would have sacrificed all the rich technical means at his disposal merely to make a story sound as if such and such a character were actually telling it. The *Miller's Tale,* to name but one of many, would have been thus impossible" (171–72). See also Lawlor, *Chaucer,* chap. 5, and Jordan, *Shape of Creation.* Jordan is, on theoretical and historical grounds, the most thoroughgoing and principled opponent of the notion of consistent impersonation in Chaucer's work. In this connection his book deserves to be read in its entirety; see also Jordan, "Chaucer's Sense of Illusion." Middleton, "*Physician's Tale* and Love's Martyrs." Burlin, *Chaucerian Fiction,* 165. Elizabeth Salter's reading of the *Knight's Tale,* in her introduction to Chaucer, *The Knight's Tale and the Clerk's Tale,* is perhaps the most consistently developed in terms of the "two voices" of the poet. See also Thurston, *Artistic Ambivalence.*

"Unimpersonated artistry" implies a technique, or perhaps an experience, of reading something like this: we assume that the *Canterbury Tales* are, as they say, "fitted to their tellers," that they are potentially dramatic monologues, or, to adopt what I hope is a less loaded term, that they are instances of *impersonated* artistry, the utterances of particular pilgrims. After all, we like to read Chaucer this way, to point out the suitability of the tales to their fictional tellers, and most of us, even Robert Jordan, would agree that at least some of the tales, and certainly the Canterbury frame, encourage this sort of interpretation.[2] We read along, then, with this assumption in mind until it seems to break down, until we come across a passage that we have difficulty reconciling with the sensibility—the temperament, training, or intelligence—of the pilgrim in question. At that point, alas, I think we too often give up. This passage, we say, must be the work of Chaucer the poet, speaking over the head or from behind the mask of the Knight or the Miller or the Physician, creating ironies, setting us straight on doctrine, pointing us "the righte weye." Unfortunately, these occasions are seldom as unequivocal as the one case of genuine broken impersonation I know of in the tales, the general narrator's "quod she" in the middle of a stanza of the *Prioress's Tale* (VII, 1771). Different critics find the poet in different passages of the same tale, and they often have great difficulty in deciphering his message once they *have* found him—a difficulty that seems odd if Chaucer thought the message worth disrupting the fiction.

Thus Howard, whose observations on the critical disagreement over the humorous element in the *Knight's Tale* are well taken, offers an interpretation of "The destinee, ministre general" that is in fact uncommon. His account of the ironic tone of these lines in context is at least more attentive to the effect of the language than are the numerous readings that take the passage relatively straight. Even within this group, however, the range of proposed answers to the question, Who's talking here? is sufficiently various to raise the issue I am interested in. To mention only those who discuss this particular passage, the work of William Frost, Paul G. Ruggiers, and P. M. Kean is representative of the large body of criticism that remains relatively inattentive to the whole question of voicing in the tale.[3] They share a

---

2. Howard states the position admirably (*Idea of the Canterbury Tales*, 123–24).
3. Frost, "Interpretation of Chaucer's Knight's Tale"; Ruggiers, "Some Philosophi-

view of the passage as a piece of the poem's doctrine, to be taken seriously as part of an argument about man's place in the cosmos. Of those who, like Howard, find something odd about the passage, Burlin thinks that the speaker is Chaucer, who intends to suggest by it that Theseus is a man superior to Fortune but unaware of Providence (*Chaucerian Fiction*, 108), whereas Richard Neuse, the only critic to attribute the speech unequivocally to the Knight, maintains that it differentiates the latter's implicitly Christian view of the story from Theseus's more limited vision.[4] Who *is* talking here, and to what end? What are the consequences for interpretation if we concede both that the passage makes gentle fun of the machinery of destiny, at least as applied to so trivial an event, and that it is the Knight himself who is interested in obtaining this effect? Howard's suggestion notwithstanding, the passage is not really directed at Theseus's hunting but at the improbably fortuitous meeting in the glade of Theseus, Palamon, and Arcite described in the lines that immediately follow (I, 1683–1713).[5] This encounter is one of many features in the first half of the tale that show that most of the plot, far from being the product of portentous cosmic forces (Palamon and Arcite are consistently made to look silly for taking this view), is generated by human actions and choices, not least by those of the narrating Knight in conspicuously rigging events and manipulating coincidences. The Knight, as Neuse points out ("The Knight," 300), is adapting an "olde storie" for the present occasion, and the irony here reflects his opinion of the style of those "olde bookes." To him that style embodies a dangerous evasion of human responsibility for maintaining order in self and society by unconsciously projecting the responsibility onto gods and destinies.

The point is that a notion like unimpersonated artistry, by dividing speakers into parts and denying them the full import of their speaking, puts us in the difficult position of trying to decide which parts of a single narrative are to be assigned to the pilgrim teller and which to the "author"; in these circumstances it is not surprising that different

---

cal Aspects"; Kean, "The *Knight's Tale*," in Kean, *Chaucer and the Making of English Poetry*, 2:1–52.

4. Neuse, "The Knight," 312–13.

5. References to Chaucer are from Benson, ed., *The Riverside Chaucer*, 3d ed., which is based on Robinson, ed., *The Works of Geoffrey Chaucer*, 2d ed. References to the *Canterbury Tales* give fragment number and line numbers.

critics make the cut in different places. All such formulations involve finding or creating two speakers (or even more) in a narrative situation where it would appear simpler to deal with only one.[6] The procedure seems to me theoretically questionable because it is unparsimonious or inelegant logically: it creates extra work and it leads to distraction. Narrative entities are multiplied to the point where they become subjects of concern in their own right and require some sort of systematic or historical justification such as unimpersonated artistry or the deficiency of medieval ideas of personality;[7] before long we are so busy trying to save the appearances of the epicyclic constructs we ourselves have created that we are no longer attending to the poems that the constructs were originally intended to explain. Therefore I would like to preface my more detailed opposition to unimpersonated artistry with a general caveat. I call it Leicester's razor: *narratores non sunt multiplicandi sine absolute necessitate.*

Naturally I do not intend to let the matter rest with this general and essentially negative formula, though I think its application clears up a lot of difficulties. I want to use the space my principle gives me to argue that the Canterbury tales are individually voiced, and radically so—that each of the tales is primarily (in the sense of "first," that is, the place where one starts) an expression of its teller's personality and outlook as embodied in the unfolding "now" of the telling. I am aware

6. See, for example, Jordan, *Shape of Creation,* 181, where what is apparently envisioned is Chaucer the poet projecting Chaucer the pilgrim as the (intermittent?) narrator of the Knight's story. For an instance of how far this sort of thing can go, see Campbell, "Chaucer's 'Retraction.' "

7. Jordan once again provides the clearest example of this historicist form of argument, but D. W. Robertson also uses it, as in the introduction to his *Chaucer's London,* 1–11, where he both specifies and generalizes statements he made previously in his *Preface to Chaucer* such as the following: "The actions of Duke Theseus in the Knight's Tale are thus, like the actions of the figures we see in the visual arts of the fourteenth century, symbolic actions. They are directed toward the establishment and maintenance of those traditional hierarchies which were dear to the medieval mind. They have nothing to do with 'psychology' or with 'character' in the modern sense, but are instead functions of attributes which are, in this instance, inherited from the traditions of medieval humanistic culture" (265–66; see also the discussion of the *Friar's Tale* that immediately follows). This whole line of argument probably originated with Leo Spitzer's "Note on the Poetic and the Empirical 'I' in Medieval Authors." Spitzer's argument is drawn from particular textual investigations and is relatively tentative about its conclusions. Judging from his remarks on Boccaccio, I am not at all sure that Spitzer would see Chaucer as a representative user of the "poetic 'I,' " but in any case I think his successors, unlike him, are arguing from "history" to texts, not the other way around. Spitzer's formulation has become fossilized in those Chaucerians.

that something like this idea is all too familiar. Going back, in modern times, at least as far as Kittredge's characterization of the *Canterbury Tales* as a human comedy, with the pilgrims as dramatis personae, it reaches its high point in Lumiansky's *Of Sondry Folk* (and apparently its dead end as well: no one since has attempted to apply the concept systematically to the entire poem).[8] Moreover, as I said before, we are all given to this sort of reading now and then. I think one reason the idea has never been pushed as hard or as far as I would like to take it is that the voicing of individual tales has almost always been interpreted on the basis of something external to them, usually either some aspect of the historical background of the poems (what we know from other sources about knights, millers, lawyers, nuns) or the descriptions of the speakers given in the Canterbury frame, especially in the *General Prologue*. Such materials are combined in various ways to construct an image of a given pilgrim outside his or her tale, and each tale is then read as a product of the figure who tells it, a product whose interpretation is constrained by the limitations we conceive the pilgrim to have.

The question of historical presuppositions, the feeling that medieval men and women could not have thought or spoken in certain ways, I will address in a moment; but the problem of the Canterbury frame has been the more immediate obstacle to reading the tales as examples of impersonated artistry. Since I do not mean by that phrase what either the critics or the defenders of similar notions appear to have meant in the past, the topic is worth pausing over. The issue is generally joined concerning the question of verisimilitude, the consistency with which the fiction of the tales sustains a dramatic illusion of real people taking part in real and present interaction with one another. The critic who has most consistently taken this dramatic view of the poem is Lumiansky, who locates both the "reality" of the pilgrims and the "drama" of their relations with one another outside the tales themselves, preeminently in the frame. He ordinarily begins his discussion of a given tale and its dramatic context with a character sketch of the pilgrim drawn from the *General Prologue* (and from any relevant links) and then treats the tale itself as an exemplification and extension of the traits and situations in the frame. He is attentive to such details as direct

---

8. Kittredge, *Chaucer and His Poetry*, chap. 5; the famous phrases are on 154–55.

addresses to the pilgrim audience within a tale (such as the Knight's "lat se now who shal the soper wynne," I, 891) and, to a degree, to the ways tales respond to one another, as in fragment III or the marriage group. This approach leads to an account of the poem as a whole that doubles the overt narrative of the frame and, in effect, allows the frame to tyrannize the individual tales: what does not fit the model of actual, preexisting pilgrims really present to one another is not relevant to the enterprise and is variously ignored or dismissed. Other critics have not been slow to point out that this procedure neglects a great deal.[9]

The objection to this "dramatic" model that I would particularly like to single out is its disregard for the poem's constant and intermittently insistent *textuality,* for the way the work repeatedly breaks the fiction of spoken discourse and the illusion of the frame to call attention to itself as a written thing. Such interruptions as the injunction in the *Miller's Prologue* to "Turne over the leef and chese another tale" (I, 3177) and the moment in the *Knight's Tale* when the supposedly oral narrator remarks, "But of that storie list me nat to write" (I, 1201) not only destroy verisimilitude but draw attention to what Howard has called the *bookness* of the poem (*Idea of the Canterbury Tales,* 63–67), as do, less vibrantly, incipits and explicits, the patently incomplete state of the text, or "the contingency that a tale not memorized but told impromptu is in verse" (*Idea of the Canterbury Tales,* 231). Now this conspicuous textuality (by which I mean that Chaucer not only produces written texts but does so self-consciously and calls attention to his writing) certainly militates strongly against the illusion of drama as living presence. It is no doubt this realization, coupled with the counterperception that some tales do seem "fitted to the teller," that has led Howard and others to adopt formulations like unimpersonated artistry in order to stay responsive to the apparent range of the poem's effects. Such a notion allows the critic to hover between bookness (more commonly called *writing* nowadays), which always implies *absence,* and the logocentrism that Howard calls *voiceness*—the fiction of *presence* we feel when "the author addresses us directly and himself rehearses tales told aloud by others: we seem to hear his and the pilgrims' voices, we presume oral delivery" (*Idea of*

9. Jordan is particularly good at evoking the element of "the girlhood of Shakespeare's heroines" that often finds its way into this sort of interpretation; see "Chaucer's Sense of Illusion," especially 24–26.

the Canterbury Tales, 66). If we cannot have presence fully, we can at least have it partly. But when and where exactly, and, above all, whose? As I have tried to suggest, a notion like unimpersonated art-istry—which is an *intermittent* phenomenon—tries to save the feeling that someone is present at the cost of rendering us permanently uncer-tain about who is speaking at any given moment in (or of) the text: the pilgrim, the poet, or that interesting mediate entity Chaucer the pil-grim.

It seems to me that the roadside-drama approach, the criticisms of that approach, and compromise positions (whether explicitly worked out like Howard's or more intuitive) have in common a central confu-sion: the confusion of *voice* with *presence*.[10] All these views demand that the voice in a text be traceable to a person *behind* the language, an individual controlling and limiting, and thereby guaranteeing, the meaning of what is expressed. The language of a given tale, or indeed of a given moment in a tale, is thus the end point of that person's activity, the point at which he or she delivers a self that existed prior to the text. For this reason all these approaches keep circling back to the ambiguous traces of such an external self—in the frame, in the poet, in the facts of history, or in the "medieval mind." But what I mean by impersonated artistry—and indeed what I mean by voice—does not necessarily involve an external self.

In maintaining that the *Canterbury Tales* is a collection of individu-ally voiced texts, I want rather to begin with the fact of their textuality, to insist that there is nobody there, that there is only the text. But if a written text implies and enforces the absence of the self, the real living person outside the text who may or may not have expressed himself or herself in producing it, the same absence is emphatically not true of the voice *in* the text, which I might also call the voice (or subject) *of* the text. In writing, voice is first of all a function not of persons but of language, of the linguistic codes and conventions that make it possible for an "I" to appear.[11] But this possibility has interpretive conse-

10. In what follows I ought to acknowledge a general obligation to the work of Jacques Derrida, perhaps more to its spirit than to any specific essay or formulation. For a representative discussion of the problem of presence and a typical critique of logocen-tric metaphysics, see "Writing Before the Letter," part 1 of Derrida, *Of Grammatology*, 1–93.

11. See Benveniste, *Problems in General Linguistics*. Chapters 18 and 20 are espe-cially helpful, but the whole section (chaps. 18–23) is of value.

quences that are not always noted since it means that we can assign an "I" to any statement. Because language is positional it is inherently dramatic: it always states or implies a first person, the grammatical subject, not only in grammatical relation but also in potential dramatic relation to the other grammatical persons, and it does so structurally—as language—and regardless of the presence or absence of any actual speaking person. Thus any text, by its nature as a linguistic phenomenon, generates its own set of *rhetorical inflections of the grammatical subject,* what in literary texts is often called its speaker. The speaker is a subject created by the text itself as a structure of linguistic and semantic relationships, and the character, or subjectivity, of the speaker is a function of the specific deployment of those relationships in a particular case to produce the voice of the text. This kind of voiceness is a property of any text, and it is therefore theoretically possible to read any text in a way that elicits its particular voice, its individual first-person subject. Such a reading would, for example, try to attend consistently to the "I" of the text, expressed or implied, and would make the referential aspects of the discourse functions of the "I." To put it another way, a voice-oriented reading would treat the second and third persons of a discourse (respectively the audience and the world), expressed or implied, primarily as indications of what the speaker maintains about audience and world and would examine how these elements are reflexively constituted as evidence of the character of this particular subject. It would ask what sort of first person notices these details rather than others and what sort conceives of an audience in such a way that he or she addresses it in this particular tone, and so forth.

Although any text can be read in a way that elicits its voice, some texts actively engage the phenomenon of voice, exploit it, make it the center of their discourse—in fact, make it their content. This sort of text is *about* its speaker, and I contend that the *Canterbury Tales,* especially the individual tales, is such a text. The tales are examples of impersonated artistry because they concentrate not on the way preexisting persons create language but on the way language creates people.[12] They detail how a fictional teller's text im-personates him or her

---

12. A number of tales, including the Prioress's and the Shipman's, suggest how this happens regardless of whether the speaker intends it.

by creating a personality, that is, a textual subject that acts like, rather than is, a person. What this textual impersonation implies for the concrete interpretation of the poem is that the relation I have been questioning between the tales and the frame, or between the tales and their historical or social background, needs to be reversed. The voicing of any tale—the personality of any pilgrim—is not given in advance by the prologue portrait or the facts of history, nor is it dependent on them. The personality has to be worked out by analyzing and defining the voice created by each tale. It is this personality in the foreground, in his or her intensive and detailed textual life, that supplies a guide to the weighting of details and emphasis, the *interpretation,* of the background, whether portrait or history. To say, for example, that the *Miller's Tale* is not fitted to its teller because it is "too good" for him, because a miller would not be educated enough or intelligent enough to produce it, is to move in exactly the wrong direction. In fact, it is just this sort of social typing that irritates and troubles the Miller himself, especially since both the Host and the general narrator typed him long before any Chaucer critic did (I, 3128–31, 3167–69, 3182). The characters in his tale repeatedly indulge in social typing, as does the Miller.[13] The Miller's handling of this practice makes it an issue in the tale, something he has opinions and feelings about. The end of the tale demonstrates how the maimed, uncomfortably sympathetic carpenter is sacrificed to the mirth of the townsfolk and the pilgrims; he is shouted down by the class solidarity of Nicholas's brethren: "For every clerk anonright heeld with oother" (I, 3847). One could go on to show how the representation of the Miller's sensibility in the tale retrospectively and decisively revises the portrait of him in the *General Prologue* into something quite different from what it appears to be in prospect, but the same point can be suggested more economically concerning the Physician. When we read in the *General Prologue* that "His studie was but litel on the Bible" (I, 438), the line sounds condemnatory in an absolute, moral way. Reconsidered from the perspective of the tale, however, the detail takes on a new and more intensive individual life in the light of the Physician's singularly inept use of the

---

13. For example, "A clerk hadde litherly biset his whyle, / But if he koude a carpenter bigyle"; "What! thynk on God, as we doon, men that swynke"; "She was a prymerole, a piggesnye, / For any lord to leggen in his bedde, / Or yet for any good yeman to wedde" (I, 3299–300, 3491, 3268–70).

exemplum of Jephthah's daughter (VI, 238–50). Retrospectively the poet's comment characterizes a man of irreproachable, if conventional, morality, whose profession channels his reading into medical texts rather than sacred ones and who uses such biblical knowledge as he has for pathetic effect at the expense of narrative consistency: he forgets, or at any rate suppresses, that Jephthah's daughter asked for time to bewail her virginity, whereas Virginia is being killed to preserve hers. The situation in the tale is a good deal more complex than this, but I think the general point is clear enough: it is the tale that specifies the portrait, not the other way around.[14]

The technique of impersonation as I am considering it here has no necessary connection with the question of the integration of a given tale in the Canterbury frame. The Knight's mention of writing in his tale is indeed an anomalous detail in the context of the pilgrimage. It is often regarded as a sign of the incomplete revision of the (hypothetical) "Palamon and Arcite," supposedly written before Chaucer had the idea of the Canterbury Tales and afterward inserted in its present position in fragment I. The reference to writing is taken as evidence that the Knight was not the speaker "originally" and, in a reading like Howard's, that sometimes he still isn't.[15] As far as it goes, the argument about the chronology of composition may well be valid, but it has nothing to do with whether the tale is impersonated, a question that can and should be separated, at least initially, from the fiction of the pilgrimage. Details like the Knight's mention of writing are not immediately relevant because they do not affect the intention to create a speaker (they may become relevant at a different level of analysis later). Impersonation, the controlled use of voicing to direct us to what a narrative tells us about its narrator, precedes dramatization of the Canterbury sort in Chaucer, analytically and no doubt sometimes chronologically. The proper method is to ascribe the entire narration, in all its details, to a single speaker (on the authority of Leicester's razor) and use it as evidence in constructing that speaker's subjectivity, keeping the question of the speaker's "identity" open until the analysis is complete. It is convenient and harmless to accept the framing fiction that the Knight's Tale is the tale the Knight tells, as long as we recog-

14. See Kempton, "Physician's Tale."
15. See David, Strumpet Muse, 77–89.

nize that it merely gives us something to call the speaker and tells us nothing reliable about him in advance.

That is the method of reading that will be employed in this book. The first of its leading notions is that the tales must be treated not as the performances of preexisting selves but as texts. They are not written to be spoken, like a play, but written to be read *as if* they were spoken. They are literary imitations of oral performance, in which the medium, writing, makes all the difference.[16] Second, the texts of the tales are to be read with a view to analyzing the individual subject, the voice-of-the-text, that each tale constructs. I will adopt as my central hypothesis the assumption that the speaker of each tale—the pilgrim who tells it—is in both senses the subject of all of its details. I will focus on the world of a given tale as evidence for a characterization of its speaker and examine how that speaker's telling creates him or her in the course of the narration. To find out who each pilgrim "is" is the end point or goal, not the beginning, of the investigation. It can only be approached by looking at what the pilgrim does in telling. In line with these assumptions I will generally refrain from drawing on portraits of the individual pilgrims in the *General Prologue* for advance characterizations of them, though I will occasionally make use of information in the portraits if a given tale seems to authorize it. I will also refrain from drawing on ideas of history and culture taken from outside the poems as a way of preconceiving (or limiting) either the characters of the pilgrims or the nature of their society. This constraint does not mean, however, that I will ignore historical and cultural materials as they are represented in the text. In fact, I am concerned to suggest not only that the pilgrims are the products of their tales, rather than the producers, but also that Chaucer's fiction may explain, rather than be explained by, the "facts" (or, better, the institutions) of the fourteenth century and its social history.

16. Although my assumptions about the relations between literary and oral cultures in Chaucer's poetry start from a position nearly opposite to that of Bertrand H. Bronson (see especially his *In Search of Chaucer*, 25–33), I agree with him that the problem of performance in Chaucer is worth further study; in fact, I think it is a central theme throughout the poet's career. In the *Canterbury Tales* the frame exists precisely to provide a literary representation of the ordinarily extratextual and tacit dimensions of storytelling in writing. The poem presents not merely stories but stories told to an audience that is part of the fiction, and this circumstance allows Chaucer to register the effects of a range of performance conditions.

THE SUBJECT, PRACTICAL CONSCIOUSNESS,
DISENCHANTMENT

The distinction made in the preceding section between self and subject entails a number of further consequences, particularly concerning the kinds of theoretical discourse that I will bring to bear on Chaucer's text. It is common nowadays, not only in linguistics but also in deconstruction, Lacanian psychoanalysis, and certain varieties of social theory, to avoid expressions like *self, person,* and *living character* and to replace them with the term *subject*. One advantage of the substitution is that the term emphasizes those aspects of someone's situation that he or she does not originate or fully control, those aspects of experience to which someone is subject. In modern theory the subject is not conceived as a substantial thing, like a rock, but as a position in a larger structure, a site through which various forces pass. The example I have already used is the grammatical subject, a place in discourse governed from outside itself by the rules of language; but the psychoanalytic subject, as a location of unconscious desire, and the social subject, as an institutional construct—a role, a status, a member of a class—are equally important. The subject as construed by these disciplines is the continually shifting vector product of all the forces in play at the subject site, including unconscious desire, concealed or mystified material and social power, the structures of language, whose relation to consciousness is perhaps less clear, and of course consciousness itself. The essentialist or so-called humanist view of the self as a substance, something permanent and fundamentally unchanging, is from this point of view an illusion. What may seem to consciousness (one's own or another's) a stable and continuous given is in fact a construction and an interpretation, whose character is in large part dependent on who or what is doing the constructing and interpreting.[17] In this book I have tried to use *self* and *subject* consistently to reflect this distinction between the "mystified" and the "modern" notions respectively, though I do not accept the historical implications of those terms.

17. I have chosen here, by way of introduction, from the vast number of accounts of the subject in modern discourse a few that have been particularly influential in my own thinking. Culler, *Structuralist Poetics,* 28–30, is clear and sensible. Freud has a brief and elegant account of the matter from a psychoanalytic perspective in *Civilization and Its Discontents,* 12–13. Nietzsche's discussion in the fragments collected in *The Will to Power,* bk. 3, pars. 481–92, is perhaps the most suggestive of all. For an extremely useful account from the perspective of social theory, see Giddens, *Central Problems,* passim.

What I wish to maintain instead is that both ways of understanding the nature of individuality are already present and at work in the *Canterbury Tales* and that in fact the so-called modern one is the more fundamental for reading the poem: as I have already suggested, and as I will argue in detail in Part I, if we are to take seriously the text's proposition that the tales are told by a series of pilgrim narrators, that proposition cannot mean that the tellers can be treated as preestablished, determinate, and self-certain entities, even when they appear to want to treat themselves that way. The particular revision of the dramatic way of reading the tales that I urge here argues that the poem is a set of texts that are about the subjectivity of their speakers in the technical sense and that Chaucer's subject is the subject, not, or only incidentally, the self.

This thesis in turn entails a relation to the theoretical discourses I make use of that is more complex and in some ways more problematic than a relation of simple acceptance, and this book is not an application of those perspectives to Chaucer, at least not in the sense that it takes Chaucer's text to be simply an instance of their doctrines.[18] I am interested in the light thrown on Chaucer's practice by interpretive methods developed in the work of Roland Barthes, Jacques Derrida, Paul de Man, Jacques Lacan, and others, but only insofar as they illuminate the text's *representation* of the relationships between writing and speech, speakers and hearers, language and subjectivity. Initially this focus allows me to take full advantage of the modern critique of the self and the modern account of the subject and to make full use of the areas of modern theory in which that critique and that account have been centrally pursued. Deconstruction is a procedure for which the undoing (or "disenchantment") of the self and the constructed character (or "re-presentation") of the subject are central preoccupations, and as such it provides a set of powerful tools for evoking certain features of Chaucer's text with a sophistication and especially a concision that would not otherwise be possible. Some indication of this power is the way a deconstructive perspective establishes the connections between topics that otherwise appear to be separate and allows us at once to associate, for example, self with the

---

18. That the same is true of my relation to traditional Chaucer criticism goes (almost) without saying.

various so-called logocentric fictions—presence, live performance (the speaking and hearing of tales represented in the Canterbury frame), and determinate meaning, whereas subject aligns itself with the phenomena of *différance*—absence, textuality (the writing and reading that constitute the actual object we are dealing with), and the indeterminacy of signification. Similarly, Lacanian psychoanalysis focuses on the so-called split subject as it is constituted in the relations of language and desire and thereby allows the unconscious, sexuality, and gender to figure in an account of the subject without requiring us to regard any of them as immutable biological facts. Lacan treats these themes as "the discourse of the Other"—that is, as constructions that are imposed on the subject when it enters into language—and so will I. But I must insist from the outset that I am neither deconstructing nor psychoanalyzing Chaucer's text. Rather, to repeat, I regard these discourses as descriptions, and to a degree as analogues, of Chaucerian practice, and I use them as part of an attempt to describe what the text of the *Canterbury Tales* depicts. In what follows, especially in Part II, I will be concerned to show that not only the poet but also at least one of his characters, the Pardoner, is an active deconstructionist who deliberately mimes official discourses in such a way as to bring out their underlying contradictions. I will be concerned as well to show that these texts do not simply *embody* the workings of desire as Lacan describes it but *represent* sexuality, aggression, and gender in something very like those terms.

I am of course aware that this position represents a departure from the common practice of historically oriented medievalists and Chaucerians, on the one hand, and that of many contemporary theorists, on the other. The first group is likely to feel, as I have already suggested, that I am imputing to the poet and his characters a set of anachronistic understandings and concerns that were historically unavailable to them; the second group might accuse me of stopping short of the full theoretical rigor of the modern critique of the self by imputing a kind and degree of mastery to the subjects I analyze that looks suspiciously humanistic. Convincing answers to these objections, if there are such here, must await the detailed analyses in the body of the book, but it seems appropriate to address them at the beginning provisionally so that the reader has at least some notion of what to expect. I will consider each in turn, beginning with the historicist objection, which I will interpret as a question about what it means to impute certain sorts of intention to the voice of the text. What does it mean, for instance, to say, as I intend to, that the Pardoner is a deconstructor, that the Prioress experiences her *jouissance* beyond the phallus, or that the Knight has a tacit project or enterprise to demystify the ideological elements of his tale as he tells it? What is the nature of the act of tale-telling in the *Canterbury Tales* such that these characterizations are, or could be, applicable to it? To begin to find answers to such questions it is necessary to define in more detail the modalities of consciousness, at least as they seem to present themselves in Chaucer's poem.

We may begin with the distinction between consciousness and the unconscious, where the latter term is understood in fairly strict psychoanalytic fashion as the presumed repository of repressed material of which the subject remains entirely unaware: the drives and desires that "speak" through the gaps in representation and outside the meaning intended in communication. The most important instances of such unconscious material treated in this book are associated with general psychoanalytic concepts of a rather technical kind, such as the Lacanian understanding of castration or the *corps morcelé,* though I contend that at least one of them, *jouissance* (a term I have taken from Lacan as extended by Roland Barthes for a certain sort of ecstatic, erotic pleasure), is represented in a consistent and principled way that is "too interesting not to be deliberate," as de Man once put it (*Blindness and Insight,* 140). Material of this sort is notoriously difficult to ascribe to a specific agent and has become more so of late. I have to posit certain structures of desire to explain at least some aspects of what I hear speaking "besides" in the text. In the Anglo-American tradition of psychoanalytic criticism it would have been usual to assume that such explanations uncovered the unconscious in the text (whether taken to mean the unconscious of its author or of a character) in the mode of mastery and that the critic, or analyst, was in the position of a "subject supposed to know" with respect to it.[19] The increasing familiarity of the Lacanian perspective that locates what

19. *Yale French Studies* 55–56 (1977), the special issue edited by Shoshana Felman entitled *Literature and Psychoanalysis, the Question of Reading: Otherwise,* is probably the starting point of more widespread attention to the so-called new psychoanalysis in literary study in the United States.

might be called the unconscious of the text in the language that text and reader share (that is, that passes through them both) has made this mastery less easy to maintain. It is hard (impossible in principle, I suspect) to know whether the origin of such unconscious structures is in the pilgrim narrator (Chaucer consciously represents what the pilgrim is unconscious of), in Chaucer himself, or in me (why not if there is anything to transference?). These are not mutually exclusive possibilities: I have occasionally tried to register this particular undecidability by noting things I have decided to leave in my own text after I have become aware of meanings I did not intend when I wrote them that still seem in some sense appropriate. It was pointed out by an anonymous reader, for instance, that whatever William of Ockham may have had in mind, Leicester's razor is not an altogether innocent figure for my relation to other critics, though it also seems to me to have something to do with issues of gender, competition, and castration that figure extensively in my analysis of Chaucer.

In any event it is obvious that whatever its provenance, the formulation one gives of this unconscious material will itself be outside the text in the sense that it will be highly self-conscious and analytical as well as remote in terminology and style from the language of the text being described. It will thus be an example of what I will call, following Anthony Giddens, *discursive consciousness,* the kind of reflexive awareness that monitors the ongoing flow of activity so as to be able to give an account or an interpretation of it in so many words.[20] Here too it seems clear that at certain moments the text of the *Canterbury Tales* represents discursive self-consciousness unambiguously—moments like the Knight's reflection on his own tale-telling activity, "I have, God woot, a large feeld to ere" (I, 886), or the Wife of Bath's recovery of the place in her prologue that she has momentarily lost, "But now, sire, lat me se what I shal seyn. / A ha! By God, I have my tale ageyn" (III, 585–86). Now the very fact that a discursive account of unconscious material, of whatever origin, is possible (but always after the fact, retrospectively) suggests that the line between consciousness and the unconscious is not a hard and fast one. There is any amount of evidence in Freud, from the idea of the return of the repressed to the

20. Giddens develops the notion in *Central Problems;* see especially the introduction and chapters 1 and 2, "Structuralism and the Theory of the Subject," and "Agency, Structure," 1–95.

interpretation of dreams and parapraxes and the action of analysis itself, to suggest that the formula of the development of the ego out of the id, *wo es war soll ich werden,* describes a process that is always accompanied by its contrary (many kinds of forgetting, the phenomenon of regression, etc.), and that both processes are continual and ongoing in the life of the subject. Further testimony to the blurred edges of the distinction is in the need Freud felt very early to posit a third, borderline category, the preconscious, to refer to the status of material that is not conscious in the descriptive (or discursive) sense but is not repressed, such as memories that are not immediately conscious but which the subject can recall at will.[21]

Since the distinction between unconscious and preconscious is a function of the operation of memory[22]—if you can remember it, it was preconscious—and since the act of telling a story depends, among other things, on being able to remember it, it is perhaps not surprising that a great many of the effects of Chaucer's text in the *Canterbury Tales* are produced in the undecidable area between conscious and unconscious, where an interpreter finds it difficult to know which side of the division to place them on. Chaucer is representing an activity that takes place in this area and raises these problems by its nature. In part because, for obvious reasons, psychoanalysis is not very interested in the preconscious, the notion has little content and is not well developed. It is more useful at this point to turn again to social theory and employ Giddens's term for the agency of the subject that manifests itself in the area between discursive consciousness and the unconscious—*practical consciousness:* "Practical consciousness consists of all the things which actors know tacitly about how to 'go on' in the contexts of social life without being able to give them direct discursive significance" (*Constitution of Society,* xxii); "[it consists of] tacit knowledge that is skilfully applied in the enactment of courses of conduct, but which the actor is not able to formulate discursively" (*Central Problems,* 57).[23] Practical consciousness is manifested in such

21. See Laplanche and Pontalis, *Language of Psycho-Analysis,* s.v. "Preconscious," 325–27.
22. See the illuminating discussion of memory in Giddens, *Constitution of Society,* 45–51.
23. In relation to language, practical consciousness is obviously related to the notion of competence as developed by Chomsky and others; see Culler, *Structuralist Poetics,* 3–31, for an introduction to the topic with bibliography.

activities as speaking a language: "There is a vital sense in which all of us *do* apply phonological and grammatical laws in speech—as well as all sorts of other practical principles of conduct—even though we could not formulate those laws discursively (let alone hold them in mind throughout discourse)." "But," Giddens adds, "we cannot grasp the significance of such practical knowledge apart from human consciousness and agency" (*Central Problems,* 25)—that is, it makes little sense to call such knowledge unconscious, because it obviously is not repressed. Practical consciousness thus has largely to do with matters of routine and habit, and indeed the other writer who has done the most to develop the idea of practical consciousness, Pierre Bourdieu, calls it habitus, the disposition or way of holding oneself vis-à-vis the social world of institutionalized practices that enables agents to negotiate its vicissitudes and carry out their various conscious and unconscious aims.[24]

From this point of view it is useful to think of telling a story—and certainly everything happens in the *Canterbury Tales* as if Chaucer thought of it this way—as like speaking a language (of which act it is after all a subset). It can also be likened to driving a car, an example that foregrounds the improvisatory and interactive character of practical consciousness. In driving, a set of learned skills is deployed for the most part without self-conscious reflection in a way that is continuously responsive to the unanticipated demands of the flow of conduct: gauging road and weather conditions, making on-the-spot decisions about the best route, etc. On the one hand, the activity is able to express (or at least channel) unconscious motives while it is going on without interfering substantially with its practical aims. Post-Freudian folklore about the phallic meaning of automobiles attests to this ability, as does the irrationally aggressive behavior of other drivers. On the other hand, at the same time "the line between discursive and practical consciousness is fluctuating and permeable" (*Constitution of Society,* 4). As a driver I may become self-conscious about what I am doing if conditions require a particularly demanding exercise of skills (or I may "unconsciously" draw on resources of coordination and muscular

24. Bourdieu, *Outline of a Theory of Practice,* passim, esp. chap. 2, "Structures and the Habitus," 72–95, and chap. 4, "Structures, Habitus, Power: Basis for a Theory of Symbolic Power," 159–97.

memory that, as we say, I did not know I had), and I can explain discursively how to change gears, for instance, to someone who asks.

The interpretive techniques that work best in reading the *Canterbury Tales* model storytelling as an exercise of all three kinds of agency in the subject, with practical consciousness mediating between discursive consciousness and the unconscious. Without such a mediating notion it is relatively easy to prejudge what is possible in the text according to the extreme historicist position that disallows certain kinds of ironic reading, among them the psychoanalytic, on the grounds that people could not have thought this or that back then. Such a position essentially demands that the relation of medieval agents to their institutions be considered only in the mode of discursive consciousness. But as Bourdieu, Giddens, and others have shown, it is necessary to distinguish between institutional *description*, such as a native may produce when asked about his or her kinship system by an anthropologist, and the actual practical *deployment* of that same system, such as a native engages in when looking for the most advantageous marriage for his or her daughter.[25] A lot of what passes for a historical account of Chaucer's world, most obviously perhaps in patristic criticism, seems to me to remain stalled at the level of institutional description without extending to historical interpretation proper because such accounts reduce agency to structure: they content themselves with showing, for example, how the structures of allegorical interpretation discursively formulated by Saint Augustine and others are replicated in Chaucer's text without going on to consider how those structures are deployed there.[26] They thus scant the con-

25. The example is taken from Bourdieu, *Outline of a Theory of Practice*, 30–43. Drawing on his study of the North African Kabyle, he is able to show that in a society where parallel-cousin marriage is the official norm, actual kin relationships are sufficiently complex that they can be figured variously between any two individuals so that kinship can be reinterpreted according to a variety of practical needs: members can find a lineage to legitimate any marriage they make. "The anthropologist is indeed the only person to undertake disinterested research into all possible routes between two points in genealogical space: in practice, the choice of one route rather than another . . . depends on the power relations within the domestic unit and tends to reinforce, by legitimating it, the balance of power which makes the choice possible" (43).

26. There are useful counterexamples in the work of Georges Duby, as in *Three Orders,* where he shows the variety of uses to which the same institution is put in the space of a generation or two, and in W. A. Pantin's classic discussion of the workings of the ecclesiastical patronage system, *The English Church in the Fourteenth Century.*

crete and individual activity of historical agents. The initial reading of the *Pardoner's Tale* offered here addresses this problem and offers a more detailed critique of the historicist position.

By contrast, a modern objection to the kind of reading of Chaucer I propose might refer to the decentering of the subject in such writers as Foucault and Barthes in order to accuse me of reintroducing the very humanistic mystifications I purport to criticize in more traditional dramatic readings of the poem.[27] Such structuralist and poststructuralist perspectives strongly evoked the deep structures of desire and institutional power that move through and constrain individual subjects, and thus they have provided a useful corrective to naturalistic historicism. But the modern critique of the subject has tended to share the reductionism of traditional positivism insofar as it too has not provided a satisfactory account of the *agency* of the subject.[28] If the historicist tendency has been to confine agency to what lies within the discursive consciousness of the historical actors, structuralist analyses like those of Foucault and Althusser have concentrated so intensively on what the actors were "really" doing, as opposed to what they thought they were doing, as to leave themselves open to the accusation of portraying historical agents as "cultural dopes" (Giddens, *Central Problems*, 52):

> The pressing task facing social theory today is not to further the conceptual elimination of the subject, but on the contrary to promote *a recovery of the subject* without lapsing into subjectivism. Such a recovery, I wish to argue, involves a grasp of "what cannot be said" (or thought) as *practice*. . . . It is . . . necessary to insist that the de-centring of the subject must not be made equivalent to its disappearance.

> Institutions do not just work "behind the backs" of the social actors who produce and reproduce them. Every competent member of every society knows a great deal about the institutions of that society: such knowledge is not *incidental* to the operation of society, but is necessarily involved in it.

27. Foucault's "What Is an Author?" and Barthes's "To Write, an Intransitive Verb?" in Richard Macksey and Eugenio Donato, eds., *The Structuralist Controversy* (Baltimore: Johns Hopkins University Press, 1972), 134–45, will do as representative examples.

28. For Foucault, see two essays by Michel de Certeau in his *Heterologies:* "The Black Sun of Language: Foucault," 171–84, and "Micro-Techniques and Panoptic Discourse: A Quid Pro Quo," 185–92.

Every social actor knows a great deal about the conditions of reproduction of the society of which he or she is a member. . . . There are various modes in which such knowledge may figure in practical social conduct. One is in unconscious sources of cognition: there seems no reason to deny that knowledge exists on the level of the unconscious. . . . More significant . . . are the differences between practical consciousness, as tacit stocks of knowledge which actors draw upon in the constitution of social activity, and . . . "discursive consciousness," involving knowledge which actors are able to express on the level of discourse. All actors have some degree of *discursive penetration* of the social systems to whose constitution they contribute.

(Giddens, *Central Problems,*
44–45, 71, 5)

These considerations have led me to attend with special care to the ways the text of the *Canterbury Tales* represents agents who actively engage and deploy the institutions of their culture both practically and discursively. In particular, I have found it most productive to assume that the subject of any tale, as the locus of textual effects, is in some sense in control of those effects unless there is specific evidence (such as an overt expression of uncertainty by the speaker) to the contrary— and even then one must be wary of possible motives the speaker might have for seeming uncertain.

The complexity and sophistication of Chaucer's treatment of agency have led me at points to use his text to explore the limitations of modern theory fully as much as I use the theory to illuminate Chaucer. It was the poet's practice that helped me to see, for instance, that neither Barthes nor Foucault has been able—or at least neither has chosen—to theorize the agency of the subject who decenters the subject: their essays on the topic do not make room for the agents who wrote them. This relative neglect of the reflexive dimension of modern theorizing itself on the part of some of its practitioners has emboldened me in Part II to undertake an investigation of the implications of voicing in texts of Lacan and de Man from the point of view of the gender assumptions they embody.[29] I have done this to get at certain

29. In this book I have chosen Paul de Man as my central instance of deconstructive thinking, both because many of the themes he treats are directly relevant to my concerns here and because the other obvious choice, Jacques Derrida, seems far more aware—at least the voices of his text do—of the implications of his own styles in relation to such things as the discourses of gender and politics. Despite his well-known refusals to

forms of desire active in deconstruction itself, considered as an aspect of what I call the "masculine" imagination. It has seemed to me that this form of gendered imagination is more clearly and deliberately represented in Chaucer's text than it is in the work of modern theorists, so that while they supply the terms for describing it, the more interesting disposition of those terms is provided by the *Canterbury Tales*.

Following Giddens, I have been speaking abstractly here of the relation of subjects to an institutional structure; but what we are always dealing with concretely in the *Canterbury Tales* is the relation of a teller to a tale, which is the crucial instance for Chaucer of the general relation. The entry into the public world that storytelling is in the tales, where no pilgrim tells an "original" story,[30] involves more than an encounter with a particular narrative. It involves as well the confrontation, conscious or not, of the socially constructed and maintained expectations about a story and its meanings that exist prior to any particular telling of it, the institutional character of the story that is usually called its genre. A storyteller has to deal in some way, if only by acceding to them, with the generic expectations an audience will have about the structure and function of an exemplum, fabliau, or miracle tale. Teller and audience know in advance, for example, that a fabliau entails a tacit agreement by both parties to dispense with certain kinds of decorum while the tale is being told, whereas a moral tale ordinarily presupposes a relatively serious and reverent attitude in the teller and a certain sobriety of attention in the audience. Generic expectations of this sort are never, so far as I can tell, maintained or fulfilled unproblematically in the *Canterbury Tales*, but they are always at issue. One way to think about the beginning of the Pardoner's tale, for example, is to see it as a deliberate attempt to subvert the authoritative character of an exemplum by discrediting the conventional probity of the generic speaker of such a story: "For though myself be a ful vicious man, / A moral tale yet I yow telle kan" (VI,

---

pronounce publicly on these topics, Derrida seems much more engaged with them at the level of the sentence, much more literary, therefore much harder to quote in an exemplary fashion. See Norris, "Some Versions of Rhetoric," esp. 191–95.

30. The *Wife of Bath's Prologue* and *pars prima* of the *Canon's Yeoman's Tale* are the closest, and both pilgrims go on to tell narratives that are neither original nor overtly personal.

459–60).[31] Many of the pilgrims betray a sharp awareness of the institutional character of stories: all three of the speakers considered in detail in this book enact in their performances critiques of the ideologies—the tacit, institutionalized assumptions—of the tales they tell, exemplum, romance, and epic.

Such an awareness by no means implies, however, that these subjects are unproblematically free to stand outside the social construction of stories and storytelling in which they participate. One way to describe what happens at the end of the Pardoner's tale would be to say that the Pardoner runs afoul of the relative autonomy and institutional inertia of the exemplum form, the fact that it is difficult to violate genre in such a way as to overcome the social power of generic expectations. He fails, one could say, to get the pilgrims to change their idea of what an exemplum is. In any case, what is represented in the *Canterbury Tales* is the encounter of *subjects,* the narrating pilgrims who are both proposed by the frame and generated as an effect of the texts of the tales, with *institutions,* the stories they tell; put another way, Chaucer conceives and represents the act of storytelling as the encounter of a subject with an institution.

Two further features of this encounter should be noted. The first is that it is conceived temporally. The fiction of performance in the poem is that the telling of a tale unfolds linearly in time for both the audience and the teller. The subject is thus articulated by a pattern of ongoing responses to the act of telling, whether conscious or unconscious, whether directed toward the audience or the tale itself. Apparent contradictions in these responses read as fluctuations in attitude in the subject according to the various contexts and pressures that arise in the course of telling, from the genre of the story to the reactions of the audience to the gender of the speaker, to suggest something of their range. Simply at the level of analysis of the self in the old-fashioned dramatic mode, this temporal dimension needs to be taken into account in detail in constructing the "character" of the speaker. But this rather simple fiction, that the Wife of Bath, to take an obvious example, is seen to digress, lose her place, and change her mind as she goes along, is rendered much more complex when the textuality of the representation is fully taken into account. This is so because the oppor-

31. See the discussion in Leicester, " 'No Vileyn's Word,' " 24–25.

tunity to reread (which is not available to the pilgrim audience) disengages us as readers, as it has already disengaged the poet as writer, from the fiction of linear unfolding and the commitments to presence and determinacy it implies. More intricately yet, the fact that a teller is in a relation to his or her story something like that of a rereader—the teller presumably knows the tale in advance of the telling and is thus always in some sense a reteller—opens up similar textualizing opportunities to the pilgrim narrators themselves. These considerations are first developed in detail in my account of prospective and retrospective reading in relation to the *Wife's Tale* and are generalized thereafter.

Chaucer conceives tale-telling as the interaction of a subject with an institution, a teller with a story. The final feature of this circumstance that I will consider here is a dimension of institutional awareness that is closest, without being confined, to the discursive end of the spectrum unconscious–practical consciousness–discursive consciousness: *disenchantment*. I take the term, with some adjustments, from Max Weber, who gives it a technical meaning that has the advantage of focusing directly on the relation of subjects to institutions. In this sense disenchantment is a function of the process of intellectualization and rationalization of society and the world, the awareness that in dealing with them "there are no mysterious processes that come into play, but rather . . . one can, in principle, master all things by calculation. This means that the world is disenchanted. One need no longer have recourse to magical means in order to master or implore the spirits, as did the savage, for whom such mysterious powers existed. Technical means and calculations perform the service" (Weber, *Science as a Vocation*, 139).

To make the best use of the term for my purposes it is necessary to disengage it, at least initially, from the developmental-historical context of the rise of a scientific worldview that leads Weber to adopt the vocabulary of calculation and technics, in contrast to magic and religion, and to focus instead on the more general issue of human agency. From this perspective disenchantment means the perception that what had been thought to be other-originated, the product of transcendent forces not directly susceptible of human tampering and subversion, is in fact humanly originated, the product of human creation. At the social level disenchantment is thus the perception that what had been taken to be natural, the way things are, is actually institutional, a

construction. In its extreme form it is the suspicion, or even the conviction, that the category of transcendence itself is a human construction
and that there are only institutions. A fully disenchanted perspective
constitutes the world as a tissue of institutions rather than natures and
therefore tends to see experience and social existence as an encounter
between conflicting interpretations rather than the passive reception of
preexisting meanings. This observation is meant to suggest the connections the idea of disenchantment has with textuality, deconstruction,
psychoanalytic suspicions about motives, the decentering of the subject, and the like: all are disenchanted perspectives. It is also meant to
remind the reader that the *Canterbury Tales* can be considered as a
fictional dramatization of conflicting points of view embodied in the
tales of individual pilgrims.[32]

Many gross features of the fourteenth century in Western Europe
and in England suggest that it was a disenchanted epoch in which
people had become not only practically but also consciously and discursively aware of the extent to which matters previously held to be
established and maintained by God had actually been humanly produced and then ascribed to divine agency. One might mention in
passing the Great Schism, Lollardy, the Peasants' Revolt, and the
depositions of Edward II at the beginning of the century and Richard
II in Chaucer's lifetime at its end as examples of the collapse of traditional structures of authority beneath the weight put on them by active and often articulately critical human agents such as caesarean
clergy, Lollards, revolutionary peasants and overmighty barons, and
antipapal political theorists. Such a view of the period is itself traditional, or used to be before the advent of the more pious vision post-
Robertsonian literary history has imposed on Chaucer studies. It even
used to include, as one of the proto-Renaissance characteristics Weber
joined with his friend Burckhardt in recognizing, the rise of the individual, which is not too far from what I call the agency of the subject in
its disenchanted form as the ideology of individuality. I do not intend,
however, to argue a historical justification of this sort for thus reading
Chaucer here, as if the presence of a certain institutional setting were
the historical cause of my reading or the poet's writing. As I have

32. For a forcefully argued instance of this view of the poem's structure, see Patterson, "The 'Parson's Tale.' "

suggested, I think Chaucer's text is among the best primary evidence we have for this reading of the fourteenth century and that it is what best supports such an interpretation of the relevant "facts" of the period. I regard the kind of work I do here as a preliminary contribution to a more properly historical account of the late Middle Ages, and I hope that by the time I am done the reader will have reason to think of the period as one in which not only the structures of the church (such as pardoning) but also gender roles and estates (such as wives and knighthood and, more generally, subjectivity itself) have been deeply affected by a pervasive disenchanted scrutiny.[33] My way to this view of the period through the analysis of voicing in Chaucer's texts puts a new twist on it by allowing me to show not only that these things are going on but also that the actors involved are enacting and producing them, often with a high degree of awareness of what is happening and what they are doing about it. Chaucer, on the evidence of the text, must have been such a disenchanted agent to have portrayed the pilgrims as he did. More important for such a historical view, however, is the fact my reading seeks to establish, namely, that the poet's text portrays many of the pilgrims—central ones for the work as a whole—as themselves disenchanted, the sufferers and agents of a culture whose cover is blown.

AN OUTLINE

This book does not pretend to be either an exhaustive demonstration of its method in all of the tales or an interpretation of the entire poem. The reader who wants an answer to the obvious question, But what about the Parson's tale? will have to wait for another occasion. Rather, the readings of three representative tales given here are intended to suggest how these more ambitious undertakings might be carried out. In the plan of the book I have tried to make things easy for myself (and I hope the reader) by beginning with two easy cases, the Pardoner's and Wife of Bath's tales. I take it that most readers would agree that these tales are patent self-presentations, obviously meant to be dramatic. Part of my concern in this first section will be to show how the

33. See Berger, "Ecology of the Medieval Imagination," and Leicester, "Harmony of Chaucer's *Parlement.*"

method employed is different, and produces different results, from the older, Kittredgean form of dramatic criticism.

The overall direction of the book is from the self to the subject and from the subject to institutions, with disenchantment as the constant thread that runs through its parts. Part I, "Chaucer's Subject," begins with a relatively short preliminary analysis of the *Pardoner's Tale* aimed at evoking the disenchanted perspective of its speaker and the despairing consciousness that drives him. I have made use of Kierkegaard's description of the phenomenology of theological despair in this interpretation because it is the most psychologically oriented discussion in the Western tradition of the sin against the Holy Ghost and is therefore helpful in spelling out the subjective, psychological implications of the Pardoner's performance. The account is preliminary precisely because it conducts the analysis only as far as the elucidation of a specific form of consciousness. This analysis is equivalent to describing the self the Pardoner enacts and suffers in the tale, and stops short of a full treatment of the Pardoner as subject, though it does identify this self as something constructed and maintained in a particular modality of willing.

Part I then turns to the Wife of Bath's prologue and tale, undertaking a more extended reading of the self-presentation that occupies the Wife and dominates her performance, with particular attention to her explicitly disenchanted critique of the male-dominated institutions against which she rebels. This interpretation engages the distinction between self and subject more fully and more directly and attempts to provide an account of the nature and experience of subjectivity out of which the Wife's various selves are constituted.

Part II, "The Subject Engendered," is the most overtly theoretical section of the book. This is in part because I have wanted to emphasize that the theory I use is a set of responses to the particular problems of the texts I read rather than a set of presuppositions for reading them, so that I have placed the theory after the evidence to which it is meant to apply. But it is also because, having considered the Wife and the Pardoner separately in Part I, I undertake to compare them in Part II, which therefore operates at a higher, more theoretical level of generality. Deconstruction and psychoanalysis come into more explicit focus here because a comparison of the two poems inescapably demands consideration of the connection between sexuality and authority, an issue raised with some insistence by each poem separately. This section of the book begins by returning to the Pardoner in order to place him with respect to the fully theorized notion of subjectivity developed in the analysis of the Wife in Part I. A comparison of the Pardoner's *style* of subjectivity with that of the Wife leads directly to the problem of gender and an attempt to generalize about the representation of sexual difference in the poem in terms of what I call the "masculine" and "feminine" imaginations. Part II concludes with a further attempt to sketch how this account of sexual difference might be applied to other gendered subjects in the *Canterbury Tales,* through a brief comparison of the role of *jouissance* in the tales of the Second Nun, the Prioress, and the Nun's Priest.

The long interpretation of the *Knight's Tale* that forms the third part of the book addresses a harder case, a tale that has given rise to theories of unimpersonated artistry precisely because it has not seemed on its face to have a consistent voicing or to lend itself to a thoroughgoing dramatic interpretation. This reading is offered as a demonstration that a voice-oriented method can produce a more coherent and illuminating account of the poem than other methods of interpreting it—that it makes more sense of the tale. The title of Part III, "The Institution of the Subject," is intended to point to the way not only Chaucer but also the Knight have a practical understanding of subjectivity both as something transpersonal, socially constructed, and therefore institutional and as something that has continually to be instituted, kept in existence by the collective activity of individual subjects. This set of concerns arises most immediately, perhaps, in the Knight's treatment of the masculine gaze, the social construction of how the subject sees, in a poem that is fundamentally concerned with the meaning of looking at women.

One reason the tale has seemed less obviously dramatic is that the Knight's activity in the telling often strives to minimize his own considerable disenchantment and its effects on the tale. The Wife of Bath and the Pardoner, because they are relatively marginal figures who overtly contest the official ideological and institutional structures of their worlds and times, emerge more clearly as individuals, or selves, than the Knight. But I also treat institutional questions more explicitly in Part III because they are more central there; it is only in the *Knight's Tale,* of the tales considered in this book, that we confront a subject who, as David Parker suggests, presents himself in institutional terms: "Some [pilgrims] are certainly less individualized: the Knight, the

Parson and the Plowman, for instance; but it would be a mistake, I feel, to say they are idealized without qualifying this as something not irreconcileable with a species of realism. Each in his own way emulates a moral ideal that demands the suppression of individuality, and we ought to give Chaucer and his age the benefit of the doubt by allowing that some people managed to live up to ideals" (Parker, "Trust the Wife of Bath?" 93). Parker's formulation gives a more benign and less effortful impression of what is involved in such emulation than either Chaucer or the Knight, but he is correct to suggest that living up to ideals is an active, even a competitive, pursuit. If it is the case that the project of the *Knight's Tale* is not one of explicit self-presentation as the Wife's and Pardoner's tales are, it is nonetheless also the case that the project it does seem to evince—something like the celebration of chivalry or, in Muscatine's classic formulation, order and the noble life—entails self-presentation because it entails becoming what might ✓ be called the subject of chivalry. The Knight's responses to his tale as he tells it add up to a self-presentation that is also that most Chaucerian of activities, making an example of oneself.

Derrida remarks that a preface or prologue is something written last and put first. Reversing this procedure, my own account of the *General Prologue,* though a version of it was first written fifteen years ago, concludes the book. This arrangement has seemed necessary first because I think too much authority has often been given to the *General Prologue*'s claims to account for the rest of the poem—what I call the prologue's prospective reading. This idea of the prologue has encouraged the kind of interpretation my book is meant to resist and change, and in the interest of that project it has seemed useful to explore how the prologue looks from the standpoint of the tales rather than the reverse, and after reading them rather than before. Second, however, the *General Prologue* is the most extensive *explicit* self-presentation in the *Canterbury Tales* of the figure who claims to have made the work, and it thus supplies an extended opportunity to look at the issues of self and subject as they relate to the figure of the poet. The conclusion, "The Disenchanted Self," looks at that figure, and what he speaks and what is his desire. Since the poet-speaker's voice and subjectivity are, as I see it, the most complex instance of the processes that are represented in the tales, it is appropriate to reserve even the brief suggestion I can manage of how they might work to the end, after the simpler cases have been considered.

I

CHAUCER'S SUBJECT

The Pardoner as Disenchanted
Consciousness and Despairing Self

To my mind the Canterbury tale that responds best to patristic or Augustinian forms of analysis is the Pardoner's. Such studies as that of Robert P. Miller, showing the relevance to the tale of the tradition of the scriptural eunuch and the sin of presumption, or those of Bernard F. Huppé and Lee W. Patterson, demonstrating the even greater importance of the complementary sin of despair, are genuinely helpful in elucidating a narrative so patently, though often so puzzlingly, allegorical.[1] At the same time the tale is one of the most fully dramatized, the most fitted to its teller, of any in the Canterbury collection. It has appealed to dramatically inclined critics since Kittredge as an example of what is freshest and most untraditional in Chaucer's art. It would be disingenuous of me to attempt to conceal my own bias in favor of the latter kind of criticism, but I think there is something to be gained from attending carefully to the typological elements of the tale because they are instructive about the place of the institution of exegetical interpretation in the *Canterbury Tales* and more generally about what it might mean to say that the poem "represents" the time in which it was written.

Though no one can really deny, since Robertson's studies, that Chaucer uses typological methods—at least sometimes—many critics have been reluctant to allow the implications that patristically influenced commentators draw from this fact. I take E. T. Donaldson's comment, first published in 1958, seven years after the appearance of Robertson's "Doctrine of Charity in Medieval Literary Gardens" and four years before his *Preface to Chaucer,* as typical of a dissatisfaction that has continued unabated despite the increasing number of detailed

---

1. R. Miller, "Chaucer's Pardoner"; Huppé, *Reading of the Canterbury Tales,* 209–20; Patterson, "Chaucerian Confession."

and often attractive demonstrations of the presence of typological elements in the poet's work:

> In my criticism I have been reluctant to invoke historical data from outside the poem to explain what is in it. . . . I have therefore eschewed the historical approach used both by the great Chaucerians of the earlier part of this century and by those scholars who have recently been reading Chaucer primarily as an exponent of medieval Christianity. The fact that the difference between what these two historical approaches have attained is absolute—if Chaucer means what the older Chaucerians thought he meant he cannot possibly mean what these newer Chaucerians think he means—has encouraged me to rely on the poems as the principal source of their meaning.[2]

Perhaps one reason for critical hesitation has been the rather illiberal tone of much patristic criticism, which insists that most really interesting human activities are, from a medieval perspective, no more or less than sins. To object to that tone is to risk dismissal as a historically conditioned sentimentalist, but I think what really lies behind the objection is the feeling that if the exegetical critics are right, our ancestors were, in their well-documented distrust of poetry, an impossibly reductive lot who were unable to distinguish clearly between a daisy of the field and the Virgin Mary and who preferred (perhaps rightly) to see the latter whenever they encountered the former.

Still, in the *Pardoner's Tale* these so-called historical elements are stubbornly present. It helps a lot to know something about a tradition of interpretation based on the idea that whereas men make words stand for things, God can make things themselves stand for other things,[3] in dealing with what is being communicated by a passage like the following from the *Pardoner's Prologue*:

> Thanne have I in latoun a sholder-boon
> Which that was of an hooly Jewes sheep.
> "Goode men," I seye, "taak of my wordes keep;
> If that this boon be wasshe in any welle,
> If cow, or calf, or sheep, or oxe swelle

---

2. Donaldson, *Chaucer's Poetry,* vi. See Robertson, "Doctrine of Charity," and *Preface to Chaucer.* Robertson's articles on exegetical criticism and related matters have been collected in his *Essays in Medieval Culture* (Princeton: Princeton University Press, 1980).

3. The locus classicus for this idea is Augustine's *De doctrina christiana,* book 1. My formulation here follows Aquinas's elegant summary in *Summa theologia* 1.1, 10, *resp.*

That any worm hath ete, or worm ystonge,
Taak water of that welle and wassh his tonge,
And it is hool anon; and forthermoore,
Of pokkes and of scabbe, and every soore
Shal every sheep be hool that of this welle
Drynketh a draughte. Taak kep eek what I telle:
If that the good-man that the beestes oweth
Wol every wyke, er that the cok hym croweth,
Fastynge, drynken of this welle a draughte,
As thilke hooly Jew oure eldres taughte,
His beestes and his stoor shal multiplie.

(VI, 350–65)

At the literal level this specimen of the Pardoner's "gaude" is a blatant appeal to the cupidity, or at any rate to the decidedly secular interests, of his "lewed" audience. The bone is a kind of snake oil. Yet the imagery the Pardoner uses about and around the supposed relic—sheep, holy Jews, devouring worms, life-giving wells—seems insistently to imply much more. I do not think it is forcing the passage at all to see in it a persistent typological edge characteristic of his style. The fundamental link the passage takes advantage of is the equation between sheep and Christian souls, the helpless beasts endangered by the worm that dieth not, whom the Good Shepherd has in care. Accordingly, the ancient holy Jew takes on associations perhaps with Jacob (via the well) and almost certainly with the promise made to Abraham echoed in line 365 (Gen. 22.16–18). These associations in turn imply a complex and sophisticated series of interpretations of that promise, originally applied literally to and by the children of Israel under the old law but since figurally fulfilled at a spiritual level under the new law in the care of Christ for his flock. This fulfillment, the outcome of a complex series of, precisely, historical circumstances, is presently embodied in the Pardoner's own profession and act, which is itself a thoroughly historical thing. The Pardoner performs the Holy Spirit's work of the salvation of souls by the mercy of Christ, a divine mission that is mediated through the *plenitudo potestatis* of the papacy as that power came to be understood in the thirteenth century as well as by the delegation of papal authority to the agency of the man before us, who daily completes, or rather debases and frustrates, the divine project begun so long ago.

I am being deliberately impressionistic rather than "textueel" here because what I want to establish is not a particular exegesis but that a spiritual level of meaning is being deliberately and consciously put in play by the speaker behind and around the literal offer of worldly "heele" and enrichment. It seems to me that the passage is overloaded in the direction of this kind of spiritual significance. There is something gratuitous not about the reading itself but about the Pardoner's insistence on packing it in in the very act of mocking and debasing it with his pitch. It is one thing to announce that you are a fraud and that though unrepentant you intend to expose your own fraudulent arts; it is another thing to load those arts themselves with a set of undermeanings that exhibit so complex an awareness of the truth you are abusing. The Pardoner seems to be saying not only, Look how I deceive the ignorant, but also, Look at what an important matter I deceive them about. Whatever his motives, it is at least clear that the effect is achieved by a deliberate forcing of mundane and particular matters into a general and spiritual framework while refusing to let go of the literal level, so that we see both significances at the same time and are unsure to which one to assign priority. Much of the power of the *Pardoner's Tale* derives from a consistent application of this method to the materials of the story. A good deal of the eeriness of the Pardoner's central exemplum comes from the fact that it reverses the invariable order of causes found in all of its analogues, from *The Arabian Nights* to *The Treasure of the Sierra Madre*. In those stories the gold always comes first, and the point is to show that in looking for gold men find death. But in the *Pardoner's Tale* we begin with a search for death and find the gold later. The Pardoner's version thrusts the spiritual implications of the quest into the situation at the outset and juxtaposes them sharply to the extreme, childlike literal-mindedness of the three rioters, who treat death like a bully from the next town.

I intend to argue that such a failure or refusal to distinguish carefully and consistently between literal and spiritual levels of meaning and discourse is at the center of the *Pardoner's Tale*. I will maintain with the patristic critics that the allegorical relation of letter and spirit is the single most important determinant of the tale's meaning. I also want, however, to return to the Pardoner the agency that patristic readings generally deny him and to maintain that he himself is the source of this effect. What exegetical criticism detects in the tale and makes an external doctrinal structure that contains and explains a Pardoner unaware of it is in fact the Pardoner's interpretation of himself, consciously undertaken and offered by him to the pilgrims. The Pardoner is the first exegetical critic of his own tale, obsessed with the spiritual meanings he sees beneath the surface of everyday life. He feels the burden of these meanings himself and attempts, as we shall see, to impose them on others. The Pardoner has long been recognized as the most self-conscious of the Canterbury pilgrims. Part of that self-consciousness involves an awareness of his own condition, and I do not mean simply that he attempts to hide his physical eunuchry—I am not at all sure that he does. The Pardoner's conduct of his tale indicates that among the things he knows about himself and is concerned to make others see are the things Robert P. Miller knows about him: that he is the *eunuchus non dei,* the embodiment of the *vetus homo,* the Old Man whose body is the body of this death and who is guilty of sinning against the Holy Ghost.

From the beginning there is something conspicuous and aggressive about the Pardoner's failure to conceal his various evils and deficiencies, well before he "confesses" some of them in his tale. The general narrator, the Host, and the "gentils" all see through him at once, and it seems likely that they can do so because the Pardoner makes it easy for them. A. C. Spearing has pointed to the obvious fakery of his authorizing bulls from popes and cardinals, and Kellogg and Haselmeyer report that the abuse of carrying *false* relics is "so rare that no contemporary manual even discusses it."[4] Since the relics themselves—pillowcases and pigs' bones—convince no one, it seems fair to say that both the Canterbury frame and the historical background of the tale contribute to the impression the performance also creates that this particular Pardoner goes out of his way to stage his abuses and make them even more blatant than those of most of his historically attested compeers. The same is true of his physical and sexual peculiarities. I take it that such things as his immediate echoing of the Host's "manly" oath "by Seint Ronyan" and his announced preference for jolly wenches in every town though babies starve for it (449–53) have in common the tactic of calling attention to the sexual oddity the *General Prologue* notes so emphatically by deliberately shamming exaggerated virility. This is a form of camp in which the hypermasculinity is as much a put-on as the mock demonism of what

---

4. Spearing, *Pardoner's Prologue and Tale,* 7; Kellogg and Haselmeyer, "Chaucer's Satire of the Pardoner," 228.

Patterson calls his "gross and deliberate parody of sinfulness" ("Chaucerian Confession," 162). The Pardoner's manner *courts* an interpretation that his confession simply confirms and heightens: what interests me most is that the consistent drift of the interpretation he suggests is theological in character. His prologue continually circles back to typologically charged images like the dove sitting on a barn of line 397 or more direct comparisons such as "I wol noon of the apostles countrefete" (447). Although the performance here may be interpreted as a joke, the humor derives from the disproportion between the ultimate issues that are constantly being raised and the cheap faker who raises them—and it is the Pardoner himself who keeps pointing up the discrepancy.

Nor is it clear, even at this early stage, that the Pardoner is only joking. He seems obscurely troubled that his performances can " 'maken oother folk to twynne / From avarice and soore to repente' " (430–31), and, as Patterson has pointed out ("Chaucerian Confession," 164), he insists somewhat too strongly that he does it only for the money. His oddly serious warning about the dangers of false preaching (407–22) reveals how the act has a complexity for him that belies his insistence that he himself preaches only for gain and "al by rote." These more serious aspects of the Pardoner's self-presentation—what he seems to be saying about himself and the world—become clearer in the sermon section of the tale (463–660).

The sermon provides an intense, almost hallucinatory vision of a world dominated and consumed by sin, in which gluttony "Maketh that est and west and north and south, / In erthe, in eir, in water, men to swynke / To gete a glotoun deyntee mete and drynke!" (518–20). The presentation of sin as everywhere, and everywhere having its effect on the world, is heightened by the tendency to assimilate the effects of all sins to each individual sin and to combine sins:

> Hasard is verray mooder of lesynges,
> And of deceite, and cursed forswerynges,
> Blaspheme of Crist, manslaughtre, and wast also
> Of catel and of tyme.
>
> (591–94)

Such passages in isolation might simply be considered exaggeration appropriate to any preacher striving to move his hearers to repentance.

But the Pardoner's way of exaggerating is more complicated. It is one thing to say, as both the Parson (*Parson's Tale* X, 818) and the Pardoner do, that the world was corrupted by gluttony, or to say that original sin contained all other sins in itself potentially; it is another thing to say that the original sin was gluttony (*Pardoner's Tale* VI, 508–11). A standard theological point is turned around here by deliberately overliteralizing the spiritual interrelation of all sins to one another, in keeping with the general tendency of the sermon to treat matter rather than spirit as the root of all evil: "O wombe! O bely! O stynkyng cod, / Fulfilled of dong and of corrupcioun!" (534–35).

The Pardoner consistently and gratuitously forces details that invite disgust at the corruption of the physical, from his description of his reliquaries "Ycrammed ful of cloutes and of bones" (348) to the sheep that need healing "Of pokkes and of scabbe, and every soore" (358) to the brilliant way we are brought too close to the drunkard: "Sour is thy breeth, *foul artow to embrace*" (552, emphasis added). Especially in the description of gluttony, but also elsewhere in the sermon, the Pardoner moves well beyond mere asceticism to an obsessive insistence on the brutal and ugly condition of the flesh, especially of its burden, the sheer labor of keeping this death-bound and filthy bag alive: "How greet labour and cost is thee to fynde!" (537). This kind of thing gives a peculiarly literal (and powerful) emphasis to the frequent and quite orthodox refrain that sin is a living death and that the sinner "Is deed, whil that he lyveth in tho vices" (548, cf. 533, 558).

Though there is evidence here that the Pardoner hates the flesh in general, and no doubt his own body in particular, I do not think that this sense of actual physical corruption, weakness, and impotence is at the root of the Pardoner's character and problem any more than I think that he wishes to conceal his own physical impotence. It should be noted that the ascription of the Fall to gluttony is funny, and deliberately so. It gets its effect from taking the stock rant "Corrupt was al this world for glotonye" (504) and treating it as if it were literally true, and the Pardoner's qualifying asides ("it is no drede," "as I rede") show that he knows this, that he is parodying a certain sort of preaching at the same time as he is preaching. Such parodying of sermon styles is satirical, a mocking condemnation of the inadequacy of literal forms and institutions to contain or even define the reality of sin, and the Pardoner does it throughout his sermon:

Bihoold and se that in the firste table
Of heighe Goddes heestes honurable,
Hou that the seconde heeste of hym is this:
"Take nat my name in ydel or amys."
Lo, rather he forbedeth swich sweryng
Than homycide or many a cursed thyng;
I seye that, as by ordre, thus it stondeth;
This knoweth, that his heestes understondeth,
How that the seconde heeste of God is that.

(639–47)

This passage makes fun of a style of thinking and moralizing whose literalness renders it preposterous. It pursues classification, labeling, and external order at the expense of clear ethical priorities and gives us an image of the preacher as a demented scholastic. A complementary figure is Stilboun, the "wys embassadour," who is himself a moralist and a preacher but also a Johnny-one-note who can only nag over and over that his principals "Shul nat allyen yow with hasardours" (618, cf. 613, 616). I think the Pardoner means these various examples, and the entire sermon, as comments on the kind of preaching, theology, and pastoral care that goes on in the church he represents. Even the snake-oil pitch to the "lewed peple" uses its typological elements to juxtapose and contrast what pardoning ought to be doing with what it actually does. We are perhaps so used to thinking, with the older historical critics, of the Pardoner as an *embodiment* of the notorious abuses of the fourteenth-century church that we tend not to consider that he has *attitudes* toward them—as well he might, for who should know them better?

Patristic criticism, the newer historicism, has been so successful in showing that the Pardoner fits into various typological patterns of sinfulness that it does not consider that he has attitudes toward these as well. But the two historical views need not lead to the contradiction Donaldson deplored if we see that they are both features of the Pardoner's own enterprise in the tale rather than conflicting views from outside it. To put his expert typological practice together with his experienced awareness of the degenerate times in which he lives and works is to uncover the Pardoner's disenchantment. His parodic presentation of doctrinal classification, moral exhortation, and religious institutions like the cult of relics and pardoning itself consistently enforces his contempt for the available instruments of salvation as they are used in the real life of the all-too-corporeal *corpus mysticum* around him. It does so, moreover, by measuring these things against

the spiritual standards of typological meaning, the allegorical truths
that they should, but do not, embody. In every case what ought to be
a manifestation of divine power, mercy, care, and love is shown to be
cheapened and undone by human stupidity or malice, unthinking literalism or calculating self-interest. What the Pardoner is making fun of
is the way the putative transcendence of the institutions of the church
is continually reduced to a set of merely human practices. His disen-
chantment thus makes him a proponent of the older historical view of
the tale as a satire on the corruption of the clergy. The satire is the
Pardoner's, and his own best example is himself.

This last point is important. Though part of what drives the Pardoner's mockery is his outrage that the things of God should be so
cheap, so easily subverted by the merely human, he does not mock—or
preach—as a defense of the divine. One of the unusual rhetorical
features of the sermon is the way it keeps associating the sins it describes with the Pardoner, showing that he is guilty of them. The most
striking instances of this tendency are the passages where the Pardoner
demonstrates his experienced familiarity with the sins he purports to
condemn, as in the description of the drunken dice game (651–55) that
Donaldson calls "so knowingly graphic as to exceed the limits of art"
(*Chaucer's Poetry*, 1093) or the discussion of abuses of the wine trade
and the difficulty of getting an honest drink (562–72). There is nothing
concealed or private about the Pardoner's complicity in these vices;
rather, he brings himself forward as an instance of them, and this
reflexive element gives a particular bite and appropriateness to the
concentration in the sermon on the increased sinfulness and conse-
quentiality of sin in high places. "A capitayn sholde lyve in sobrenesse"
(582), but this one does not, as he shows. Given the context, who else
can the Pardoner be talking about here but himself, and why else is that
remark in the sermon? Similar references to himself lurk in "Redeth
the Bible, and fynde it expresly / Of wyn-yevyng to hem that han
justise" (587), or:

> It is repreeve and contrarie of honour
> For to ben holde a commune hasardour.
> And ever the hyer he is of estaat,
> The moore is he yholden desolaat.
>
> (595–98)

All these images are in effect types and figures of the Pardoner himself,
and he in turn is a type and figure of everything about the church—its

institutions, its preaching, its corrupt ministers—that fails to come to grips with the reality of sin in the world. That reality is, as I have already suggested, very real to the Pardoner. He portrays the wretchedness and misery of the human condition with immediacy and insight. He demonstrates how traditional patterns of classification, description, and exhortation fail to catch or contain the more intimate and existential presence of sin, death, and the burden of the flesh, which he sees in others and feels in himself. He has nothing but contempt, a deeper sense of contempt than we have yet examined, for the consolations of religion, but he takes very seriously the things they are intended to console. "For the letter killeth, but the spirit giveth life" (2 Cor. 3.6). On the one hand there is the horror of existence; on the other there is the church that fails to address or ameliorate that horror—the church that has become a dead letter, and one that kills. Caught between them and embodying them both is the Pardoner:

> "Ther walken manye of whiche yow toold have I—
> I seye it now wepyng, with pitous voys—
> They been enemys of Cristes croys,
> Of whiche the ende is deeth"   (530–33)

The emphasis in the sermon section of the tale divides fairly evenly between these two perspectives (though both are always present), falling on either side of our most immediate and least hyperrhetorical view of him, the passage on the wine of Fish Street and Cheapside. Before that section he primarily develops his heightened view of life's ugliness and the universality of sin. After it he concentrates on the self-condemning mockery of the forms of religious ministry. This division points to and helps explain the development of the Pardoner's consciousness in the tale, the way something *happens* to him here. What happens is that as he manipulates the conventional materials of the sermon to reflect his own obsessions, he becomes more conscious of himself and more aware of both his power and his powerlessness. The power derives from the way he makes himself into a symbol, generalizing his own sinful and death-bound condition to the world around him. He makes the extent and the seriousness of what he stands for (what he makes himself stand for) more explicit as he dramatizes the evil God cannot or will not eliminate. His own presumption, for that is what it is, has the power of making a wasteland of the world. His powerlessness derives from the fact that what he symbolizes (what he makes himself symbolize) is emptiness and privation. His despair, for that is what it is, makes his inability to save others or himself the most salient fact of existence.

Cupiditas, of course, means far more than avarice. In the deep Christian and Augustinian sense in which it is the root of evils and the contrary of *caritas* it refers to a consuming desire for that which one is lacking—it means *wanting* in both senses, or rather, in a particular way. Medieval Christianity understands privation itself as a fundamental fact of the human condition. Saint Augustine images it as the state of a pilgrim far from the blessedness of his home (*De doctrina* 1.4.4). Given this basic lack, two responses are possible. To use (*utor*) the things of this world as a way to get beyond them to God is, paradoxically, to grant them their independence, to open up the possibility of using them in charity, of cherishing them (*De doctrina* 1.33.37). The enjoyment (*fruor*) of the world and others that is *cupiditas* only looks like enjoying them for their own sakes—it really means wanting to enjoy them for oneself, wanting to engulf them and make them the instruments of one's own will. In traditional terms despair is presumption: to say that God cannot forgive you, deliberately and consciously to refuse His forgiveness, is to place limits on His power and mercy, to usurp a judgment that belongs to Him. In its largest sense *cupiditas* is this desire to replace one's lack and one's dependency on the divine with a willed, self-sufficient refusal of them, and the inevitable frustration of this willing produces the heightened, outraged consciousness of dependence and insufficiency and the consequent hatred of God, self, and others that the Pardoner displays. This is the condition that the Pardoner suffers and wills; it is the condition that he half conceals or avoids in the prologue and that he embodies in the sermon. The extent to which his despair breaks loose in the sermon is indicated by the notorious fact that he forgets at the end of it that he has not yet told us how many rioters there were. I interpret this lapse as a sign of the extent to which he has become caught up in the sermon and lost control of the form of his tale in the act of dramatizing his condition, the universality of that condition, and its effects in the world. It is this heightened consciousness that he carries into the exemplum he is at last ready to tell.

The Pardoner's conduct of the exemplum itself demonstrates that it is not well fitted to express his disenchanted sensibility. It is hard to imagine that any exemplum would be since the form itself is an example of the institutionalized literalism he despises. The traditional form of the Pardoner's exemplum argues the proposition, If you are avaricious you will die, in the most literal, and therefore unbelievable, way. It presents a clarified picture of the operations of divine justice that both the Pardoner's experience and his very existence—his continuing success as a fraud, "yeer by yeer"—utterly deny. The exemplum is precisely one of those worthless forms of spiritual teaching, too far removed from the reality of life and sin, that the Pardoner mocks in his sermon. That is one reason he modifies the early parts of the exemplum in an attempt to get the letter of the story to express something about spirit, and the well-attested oddness of the resulting effect shows the inaptness of the form to the purpose.

The peculiarities of the Pardoner's telling are gathered around, and focus on, the Old Man. The first part of the tale is in fact designed to prepare a context for him, and that is why it brings death into the foreground. It has become fairly commonplace by now to see the three rioters and the Old Man as aspects of the Pardoner, and I agree with this notion in general.[5] The problem remains, however, of situating this division in the activity of the Pardoner himself and seeing how he uses it and what he uses it to say. The feeling of miasma in the opening scene arises, as I have previously suggested, from the semiallegorical treatment of an ordinary tavern scene so as to stress its spiritual overtones:

> "Sire," quod this boy, "it nedeth never-a-deel;
> It was me toold er ye cam heer two houres.
> He was, pardee, *an old felawe of youres,*
> And sodeynly he was yslayn to-nyght,
> Fordronke, as he sat on his bench upright.
> Ther cam a privee theef men clepeth Deeth,
> That *in this contree* al the peple sleeth,
> And with his spere he smoot his herte atwo,
> And wente his wey withouten wordes mo.
> He hath a thousand slayn this pestilence.
> And, maister, *er ye come in his presence,*

5. See, for example, Howard, *Idea of the Canterbury Tales,* 357–58; Condren, "Pardoner's Bid for Existence," 200.

> *Me thynketh that it were necessarie*
> *For to be war of swich an adversarie.*
> *Beth redy for to meete him everemoore;*
> Thus taughte me my dame; I sey namoore."
> (670–84, emphasis added)

The italicized phrases outline points at which the Pardoner's sophisticated typological perspective imposes on the innocent one of the
youth. Because of what is at issue, "felawe" points to the fellowship of
all men in sin and before death, "this contree" moves toward "this
world," and the final warning urges the need for a different kind of
readiness and preparation from what the boy seems to have in mind.
And who is "my dame"? Nature? The church? The child speaks more
than he knows.

At one level these characters are an image of the Pardoner's audience, of the "lewed peple" who live in ignorant literal-mindedness in a
world that is more charged with spiritual significance and consequence
than they can imagine. They treat reality as if it were an exemplum and
respond to the offense against human integrity, self-sufficiency, and
community that death is ("Er that he dide a man a dishonour," 691) as
to an external threat, an isolated event, something merely physical. It
has also become common to point out that the rioters' quest is a
blasphemous parody of Christ's sacrifice, which slew spiritual death
for the faithful once and for all.[6] That is true, and it is another instance
of the typological processing that the Pardoner goes out of his way to
give the tale. But it also seems to me that he regards this aspect of the
rioters with a certain ambivalence, even sympathy. There is something
attractive in the youthful idealism that so confidently forms a band of
brothers to slay death. The rioters do not seem really evil in the early
parts of the tale; they are too innocent for that. A student of mine once
compared them to fraternity boys, as much for their trivial dissipation
as for their idealism, and the Pardoner's earliest characterization of
them is not that they were sinful but that they "haunteden folye" (464).
The Pardoner seems momentarily attracted to their quest because it
does correspond to something in him. A literalized version of a desire
to do "Cristes hooly werk," to slay death and save souls by offering

6. For example, Stockton, "Deadliest Sin," 47; Adelman, " 'Som Wit,' " 97.

them Christ's pardon, is nostalgically revived in the rioters' quest (that is, revived as something lost but still desired) and at the same time is placed as naive and overconfident folly. The rioters, unlike the Pardoner, have no idea what they are up against.

What they are up against is the Old Man, who is, as his name suggests, the truth of the experience of the *vetus homo* as that experience is embodied in the consciousness of the Pardoner. He is what their quest leads to and what they might become if they did not live in an exemplum. The best explication of the psychology behind this figure is Kierkegaard's, who provides, in *The Sickness unto Death*, a phenomenology of despairing consciousness that in its play with the categories of literal and spiritual applies directly to Chaucer's text:

> Literally speaking, there is not the slightest possibility that anyone will die from this sickness or that it will end in physical death. On the contrary, the torment of despair is precisely this inability to die. . . . If a person were to die of despair as one dies of a sickness, then the eternal in him, the self, must be able to die in the same sense as the body dies of sickness. But this is impossible; the dying of despair continually converts itself into a living. The person in despair cannot die; "no more than the dagger can slaughter thoughts" can despair consume the eternal, the self at the root of despair, whose worm does not die and whose fire is not quenched. . . . The inability of despair to consume him is so remote from being any kind of comfort to the person in despair that it is the very opposite. This comfort is precisely the torment, is precisely what keeps the gnawing alive and keeps life in the gnawing . . . : that he cannot consume himself, cannot get rid of himself, cannot reduce himself to nothing.
>
> (Kierkegaard, *Sickness unto Death*, 17–19)

> The proudeste of thise riotoures three
> Answerde agayn, "What, carl, with sory grace!
> Why artow al forwrapped save thy face?
> Why lyvestow so longe in so greet age?"
> This olde man gan looke in his visage,
> And seyde thus: "For I ne kan nat fynde
> A man, though that I walked into Ynde,
> Neither in citee ne in no village,
> That wolde chaunge his youthe for myn age;
> And therfore moot I han myn age stille,
> As longe tyme as it is Goddes wille.
> Ne Deeth, allas, ne wol nat han my lyf.
> Thus walke I, lyk a restelees kaityf,
> And on the ground, which is my moodres gate,

I knokke with my staf, bothe erly and late,
And seye 'Leeve mooder, leet me in!
Lo how I vanysshe, flessh, and blood, and skyn!
Allas, whan shul my bones been at reste?
Mooder, with yow wolde I chaunge my cheste
That in my chambre longe tyme hath be,
Ye, for an heyre clowt to wrappe me!'
But yet to me she wol nat do that grace,
For which ful pale and welked is my face."

(716–38)

The Pardoner uses the Old Man as a spokesman for this sophisticated despair. The Old Man's desire to exchange age for youth (720–
26) points to the Pardoner's envy of the innocence of the rioters and of
his "lewed" congregation and suggests that what he wants to be rid of
is not physical decay but consciousness. Although he sounds suicidal
(727–33), the Old Man is not so in the ordinary sense. Because he feels
himself eternal, physical death is beside the point. What he wants is to
be swallowed up—"Leeve mooder, leet me in!" (731)—to become
nothing, to escape from the restless consciousness of his privation, his
cupiditas. This is that sickness unto death of which Kierkegaard
speaks: "perpetually to be dying, to die and yet not to die, to die
death" (Sickness unto Death, 18).

To wish to exchange a chest of worldly goods for a hair shirt
(734–38) is, in effect and typologically, to wish to be able to pay money
for the gift of repentance, to wish that the literal version of pardoning
were the true one. Besides demonstrating decisively that avarice is not
at issue here, this wish indicates that the Pardoner understands that his
situation is willed. He would have to repent to get any relief, and he
will not, though he knows this intransigence is the source of his
wretchedness. He also knows what his obdurate willing makes him:

"But, sires, to yow it is no curteisye
To speken to an old man vileynye,
But he trespasse in word or elles in dede.
In Hooly Writ ye may yourself wel rede:
'Agayns an oold man, hoor upon his heed,
Ye sholde arise;' wherfore I yeve yow reed,
Ne dooth unto an oold man noon harm now,
Namoore than that ye wolde men did to yow
In age, if that ye so longe abyde."

(739–47)

If the sermon is the place in the tale where the Pardoner most clearly expresses his anger, this passage, like the rest of the Old Man's speech, is the place where he most clearly gives vent to his self-pity. But his language also shows that he understands his condition spiritually and exegetically, that he *interprets himself* in traditional terms as the *vetus homo,* and that he uses the identification to express the self-hatred that is complement to the self-pity. The Pardoner's voicing of the unambiguous passage from Leviticus makes it move toward self-condemnation—from "Respect your elders" to "Rise up against the Old Man."[7] This typological meaning is especially clear if the speech is understood and applied where it belongs, outside the tale and in relation to the Pardoner, who goes so far out of his way to show how he trespasses in word and deed.

The encounter with the Old Man is the place in the tale where the Pardoner most openly discloses his own condition and where his voice is least detached from the surface of the story, least qualified by irony and manipulation. It is the point at which he completes the process of putting himself into his tale, and the apparent result is that he has nowhere to go. The Old Man can point the way to death, but as soon as he does so, he vanishes from the story "thider as I have to go" (749). The rioters cannot hear what the Old Man has to tell them, that physical death is only a figure for the spiritual, for something that is eternally within them and in which they live without knowing it. They can only enact the literal and mechanical poetic justice of an exemplum about avarice—or so it seems. Although there is some truth to the idea that the tale becomes more narrow and limited and loses much of its atmosphere of mystery after the departure of the Old Man, it seems to me that his pointing finger remains to haunt the tale in the "signes and

---

7. Leviticus 19:32. "Coram cano capite consurge, honora personam senis: et time Dominum Deum tuum. Ego sum Dominus" (Vulg.). "You shall rise up before the hoary head, and honor the face of an old man, and you shall fear your God: I am the Lord" (RSV). What allows the play of meaning is the Pardoner's peculiar translation of *coram* as "agayns." The word literally means something like "in the presence of." The older senses of *against* can have such meaning (see *OED,* s.v. *against* 1–5), but *coram* is translated "before" in both versions of the Lollard Bible, which is roughly contemporary with the *Canterbury Tales:* "*Before* the hoor heed arys and onour the persone of the oolde, and drede the Lord thi God; Y am a Lord" (early version, before 1382); "Rise thou *bifor* an hoor heed, and onoure thou the persoone of an eld man, and drede thou thi Lord God; Y am the Lord" (later version) (emphasis added). Forshall and Madden, eds., *Holy Bible,* 1:339–40. Cf. Lindberg, ed., *MS. Bodley 959,* 2:57–58 ad loc.

othere circumstances" the Pardoner imposes on the simple exemplum plot.

On the one hand the Pardoner traces the psychological progress of the rioters. Their idealism quickly turns into its contrary and generates a world of cynicism and suspicion in which "Men wolde seyn that we were theves stronge, / And for oure owene tresor doon us honge" (789–90) and every man's hand is against every other's. Such an image suggests the basic sense of the world that generated the idealism in them, the impulse to kill death, in the first place and thereby identifies the underlying protodespair of the rioters. This sense is most evident in the youngest, whose decision to murder his fellows is presented as an accession of self-consciousness. Like his companions he begins with a heightened awareness of the beauty of the world ("thise floryns newe and bryghte" [839, cf. 773–74]) that distracts him from brotherhood and the quest for death. This unself-conscious pleasure quickly shades into *cupiditas,* the desire to possess the object beheld, in order to complete an existence he suddenly perceives as lacking without it:

> "O Lord!" quod he, "if so were that I myghte
> Have al this tresor to myself allone,
> Ther is no man that lyveth under the trone
> Of God that sholde lyve so murye as I!"
>
> (840–43)

The account of how the fiend suggested to him that he should buy poison is theologically careful, not for the sake of the theological point but to mark a shift from external temptation to an inner motion of the will that discovers the preexisting depravity of the soul: "For-why the feend foond hym in swich lyvynge / That he hadde leve him to sorwe brynge" (847–48). By the time the youngest rioter gets to the apothecary, his imagery has begun to resonate with that despairing sense of wasting away that is the Pardoner's own: "And fayn he wolde wreke hym, if he myghte, / On vermyn that destroyed hym by nyghte" (857–58). The Pardoner seems to try to bring the rioters up to the point at which they might begin to discover the *vetus homo* or outcast old Adam in themselves and so begin to share the consciousness of the Old Man.

On the other hand the Pardoner plays with the imagery and structure of the tale so as to suggest in a different way what is "really" going on. His typological imagination seizes on certain details of the story to allude to the spiritual plot of the tale that its literal unfolding obscures. The "breed and wyn" (797) that ultimately kill the rioters, whatever the precise interpretation put on them, are surely an example of a deliberate introduction of sacramental imagery. Similarly, the apothecàry's description of the poison has the by-now familiar overloaded quality of physical details forced onto a spiritual plane:

> The pothecarie answerde, "And thou shalt have
> A thyng that, also God my soule save,
> In al this world ther is no creature
> That eten or dronken hath of this confiture
> Noght but the montance of a corn of whete,
> That he ne shal his lif anon forlete."
>
> (859–64)

The reference, I take it, is to John 12.24: "Truly, truly, I say to you, unless a grain of wheat falls into the earth and dies, it remains alone; but if it dies, it bears much fruit. He who loves his life loses it, and he who hates his life in this world will keep it for eternal life." The standard commentaries identify the grain as the eucharist by which the faithful soul ought to live and spiritual fruit arise. Similarly, the "large botelles thre" (871, cf. 877) that the youngest rioter fills with his poisoned wine refer to the saying of Jesus: "And no one puts new wine into old wineskins; if he does, the wine will burst the skins, and the wine is lost, and so are the skins; but new wine is for fresh skins (Mark 2.22; cf. Matt. 9.17, Luke 5.37). Jerome takes this verse as referring to the transition from the old law to the new. Until a man is reborn and puts aside the *vetus homo,* he cannot contain the new wine of the gospel precepts. The *Glossa ordinaria,* following Bede, reads the wine as the Holy Spirit that transformed the apostles from old to new men but whose spiritual precepts destroy the scribes and the Pharisees of the old law and the proud generally. Since in the story it is evident that the rioters must be the old bottles that are burst, the pattern of typological action in the tale seems clear and consistent: the new law of salvation, the eucharist as the sacrifice of Christ, is poison to these *veteres homines.* This reading, or something like it, is the Pardoner's exegesis of the tale. The peculiarity of this exegesis—it is hardly usual to present the instruments of Christ's mercy as poison—reflects the Pardoner's own experience of the promise of salvation and his more spiritual sense of himself as the Old Man. What is at stake here can be described in terms of the Kierkegaardian analysis of *offense,* which traces the willed, despairing refusal of divine grace and forgiveness to the insult such free pardon offers to the independence and autonomy of the self. "It takes a singularly high degree of spiritlessness," Kierkegaard points out, "not to be offended at someone's claim to forgive sins. And . . . an equally singular spiritlessness not to be offended at the very idea that sins can be forgiven" (*Sickness unto Death,* 116).[8] Thus the typological action of the tale, like all its other details, must be read on two levels. At the literal level, as it applies to the rioters, the justice of the tale has a certain Old Testament savagery, and what offends the rioters—literal death—is linked to physical punishment meted out by a vengeful God for palpable transgressions. But how much more offensive it is to be offered salvation despite one's worst efforts, and how much worse to alienate oneself from a loving and merciful God whose power is such that He lays down His own life for man's sins. It is this offense that makes what literally poisons the rioters a spiritual poison to the Pardoner: it heightens his sense of what he has cut himself off from.[9]

All this psychological and theological sophistication finally has little effect, however, on the exemplum. If in the course of his tale the Pardoner has embodied his sense of himself and the world and put his "venym under hewe of hoolynesse" (421–22) into literal bottles of poisoned wine—spirituality under hue of venom, as it were—that embodiment remains eccentric, sporadic, and largely veiled, more deeply felt by the Pardoner than argued in the story. The large-scale patterns of spiritual reference that critics have detected in the tale are all there, more or less, and they are there because the Pardoner puts them there; but they remain largely implicit and structural, carried by typological allusions to be caught only by the learned.[10] Indeed, the very fact that the Pardoner makes the tale more typological as he proceeds shows his increasing sense that he cannot get it to say what he

8. For the bread and wine and other eucharistic symbolism in the tale, see Nichols, "Pardoner's Ale and Cake." For John 12:24–25, see *Glossa ordinaria, PL* 114, col. 402, and Aquinas, *Catena aurea,* ad loc. For the synoptic passages, see *Glossa ordinaria,* col. 188; Bede, *In Marci Evangelium Expositio, PL* 92, col. 152; Jerome, *Commentaria in Evangelium S. Matthaei, PL* 26, cols. 57–58.
9. See also Kierkegaard, *Sickness unto Death,* 70–71, 83–87.
10. That is, by the literate: interpreting readers, not listeners.

wants more directly. He seems to be trying to make the story bear more weight than it comfortably can, to push its symbolic significance too far.

It seems likely that the Pardoner feels the futility of this forcing, for when he comes to what should be the rhetorical high point of the exemplum, the description of the death agonies of the rioters, he tosses it away with a "What nedeth it to sermone of it moore?" (879) and a reference to a medical textbook (889–95), which, however lurid its account of the symptoms may be, is not reproduced in the tale.[11] I take the feeling of anticlimax here as an indication of the Pardoner's impatience with the conventional poetic justice of the ending. As it stands, the exemplum does not solve or settle anything he feels to be important. The rioters are gone, but sin, death, and the Pardoner remain:

> O cursed synne of alle cursednesse!
> O traytours homycide, O wikkednesse!
> O glotonye, luxurie, and hasardrye!
> Thou blasphemour of Crist with vileynye
> And othes grete, of usage and of pride!
> Allas, mankynde, how may it bitide
> That to thy creatour, which that the wroghte
> And with his precious herte-blood thee boghte,
> Thou art so fals and so unkynde, allas?
>
> (895–903)

It is notable that this moralization of the exemplum, for all its appropriately heightened rhetorical tone, does not arise directly from the events of the tale and only arrives at the "right" moral ("ware yow fro the synne of avarice!" [905]) after several lines of impassioned condemnation of "mankynde" for the same old tavern vices. These vices are generally appropriate to the occasion in the sense that the rioters are guilty of them, but their introduction here breaks the continuity and focus of the conclusion of the tale, and it is difficult to know what to make of the intensity with which they are denounced after the flat tone of the account of the rioters' demise. It is as if the Pardoner

---

11. Compare the cool dispatch of the account of the murder of the poisoner, "Right so they han hym slayn, and that anon" (881). The oddity is noted by Margaret Hallisy: "Chaucer's cool reference to Avicenna at a crucial point in the Pardoner's Tale seems odd: why this understated allusion rather than a detailed description of the poisoned wretches' sufferings?" ("Poison Lore," 54). She provides a sample of the density of Avicenna's thirty-three-page list of the symptoms of poisoning (55–56).

were looking for something on which to vent strong feelings and casting about for a pretext. What the passage does accomplish is a return of the image of a world pervaded by sin generated in the sermon section of the tale. Juxtaposed to this image, more directly and immediately than before, is the Pardoner's self-presentation, which bitterly and cynically compares his mercenary activity (on which he harps) with what it is supposed to pardon (904–15).

Throughout the tale it has been the Pardoner's explicit project to make an example of himself, to unmask and explain his practices. In the course of the telling, as I have tried to show, his attitude toward himself and his profession, his self-hatred and self-condemnation coupled as always with his hatred and contempt of others, has emerged with increasing clarity and intensity, at least for him. His self-presentation throughout the tale constantly stresses his culpability, and as the tale proceeds he seems to take this culpability with increasing seriousness, to regard himself as truly exemplary and symbolic of the evil, corruption, and sinfulness of the world—finally, perhaps, as a type of the Antichrist. When the action of the tale is understood as such a development, as a psychological progression within the narrating consciousness of a self with a certain structure of character, the epilogue begins to make sense as part of a psychological narrative.

By the end of the story the Pardoner seems dominated by his tale: he rejects it at a literal level but remains racked by the heightened and frustrated consciousness of himself that the experience of telling it generates in him. This frustration leads him to force the issue of sin and spirit—the issue of himself—beyond the tale into the real world of the pilgrimage. The real moral the Pardoner has come to draw from the real exemplum of the tale, himself, emerges as he completes that exemplum:

> And lo, sires, thus I preche.
> And Jhesu Crist, that is oure soules leche,
> So graunte yow his pardoun to receyve,
> For that is best; I wol yow nat deceyve.
>
> (915–18)

These famous lines represent not a "paroxysm of agonized sincerity"[12] suddenly arrived at but a simple and direct statement of half of what

12. The phrase is Kittredge's, *Chaucer and His Poetry,* 117. See also his "Chaucer's Pardoner," esp. 122–23.

the Pardoner has been saying all along. They gain their full energy only after the presentation of the other half that immediately follows, in which he seems to say, What you need is Christ's pardon—what you get is mine:

> But, sires, o word forgat I in my tale:
> I have relikes and pardoun in my male,
> As faire as any man in Engelond,
> Whiche were me yeven by the popes hond.
> If any of yow wole, of devocion,
> Offren and han myn absolucion,
> Com forth anon, and kneleth heere adoun,
> And mekely receyveth my pardoun;
> Or elles taketh pardoun as ye wende,
> Al newe and fressh at every miles ende,
> So that ye offren, alwey newe and newe,
> Nobles or pens, whiche that be goode and trewe.
> It is an honour to everich that is heer
> That ye mowe have a suffisant pardoneer
> T'assoile yow in contree as ye ryde,
> For aventures whiche that may bityde.
> Paraventure ther may fallen oon or two
> Doun of his hors and breke his nekke atwo.
> Looke which a seuretee is it to yow alle
> That I am in youre felaweshipe yfalle,
> That may assoille yow, bothe moore and lasse,
> Whan that the soule shal fro the body passe.
> I rede that oure Hoost heere shal bigynne,
> For he is moost envoluped in synne.
> Com forth, sire Hoost, and offre first anon,
> And thou shalt kisse the relikes everychon,
> Ye, for a grote! Unbokele anon thy purs.
>
> (919–45)

When these lines are read in context, it is hard to match them anywhere in Chaucer for sheer venom. There is direct venom against the pilgrims, to be sure—"Paraventure ther may fallen oon or two" sounds like a wish—but most of the Pardoner's contempt for them arises from their failure to see and respond to what he here says he is. The passage recapitulates in concentrated form all the aggressive methods of dramatized self-condemnation the Pardoner has used throughout the tale—his conspicuous avarice, his ridiculous bulls, his rag-and-bone relics, even the hints of perverse sexuality in the obscene invitation "Unbokele anon thy purs"—and tries to ram them down the pilgrims' throats. In doing so, moreover, it gives greatest stress to the symbolic significance of these offered insults. Over and over the speech says, I am what the pope licenses, what the church supplies for your spiritual needs; I am the instrument of Christ's mercy, the representative of the Holy Ghost among you; I am what you kneel to, whose relics you kiss; I am that *cupiditas* that is the root of evils, the Old Adam, the obscenity of the *eunuchus non dei* that invites to fruitless generation; See what I make of the instruments of salvation—what do *you* make of a church that licenses me, of a world in which I am possible, of a God that allows me to exist?

This message is also what the Pardoner has been expounding all along. As an instance of what Kierkegaard calls the demonic form of despair, the Pardoner posits himself as a malignant objection to God and his creation.[13] He presents himself as a proof against the goodness of existence and wills his own misery and evil as a protest against God; he forces into the open what was before only implicit in his self-dramatization, trying to make the pilgrims see it. This message, finally, is what lies behind the Pardoner's typologizing of himself. His consistent practice is to convert the literal, the everyday, the phenomenal, to a sign for spirit. It is his idealism, in the technical sense, and it accounts for the feeling his tale notoriously gives of a world in which the power of the word over reality is nearly total. Having made these transformations, he then insists that the spiritual meaning of an old man, a bottle, or a pardoner is what these things *are* and how they must be treated. This insistence is, in another sense, his literalism and his delusion. But it is also an expression of his own spiritual state, of his presumption and despair. The Pardoner's greatest self-condemnation is his moment of greatest pride, the moment when he attempts to force on the pil-

13. "Rebelling against all existence, [demonic despair] feels that it has obtained evidence against it, against its goodness. The person in despair believes that he himself is the evidence, and that is what he wants to be, and therefore he wants to be himself, himself in his torment, in order to protest against all existence with this torment. . . . Figuratively speaking, it is as if an error slipped into an author's writing and the error became conscious of itself as an error—perhaps it actually was not a mistake but in a much higher sense an essential part of the whole production—and now this error wants to mutiny against the author, out of hatred toward him, forbidding him to correct it and in maniacal defiance saying to him: No, I refuse to be erased; I will stand as a witness against you, a witness that you are a second-rate author" (Kierkegaard, *Sickness unto Death,* 73–74).

grims his own symbolic, typological vision of himself. What he wants here is to get them to take that vision for reality.

What he gets, however, is a set of responses that measures his excess and places it in a world at once more real and more ordinary than the one he has constructed in the course of telling his tale. The Host's answer to the Pardoner's final speech contains touches that seem to recognize the latter's spiritual perspective and perhaps testify to its immediate rhetorical and emotional power: " 'Nay, nay!' quod he, 'thanne have I Cristes curs!' " (946). But I think that what makes the already angry Pardoner even angrier—and silences him—is not that the Host reveals a sexual defect the Pardoner has been at pains to suggest and exploit but that he responds to a spiritual attack with a merely literal one. The Host's answer is not directed to the *eunuchus non dei*, only to a gelding. This response shows that he has missed the point of the Pardoner's self-presentation. His brutal literalism cuts through the tissue of spiritual allusion and moral self-dramatization in the Pardoner's final speech, reducing the Pardoner, his relics, and his "coillons," if he has them, to mere matter, and matter that is not even blasphemous, only insulting. The Host's explosion begins to restore a perspective that has been largely lost in the course of the tale's development when the Pardoner's voice is the only one before us—the perspective of the ordinary world.

There is a mood that sometimes comes on interpreters of the *Pardoner's Tale* in which the histrionics, pervasive irony, and symbolic pretension of the tale, the way it reaches for deep and ultimate meanings, seem open to the skeptical response, Isn't this tale, after all, just a piece of entertainment? Isn't the end just a joke, isn't the Pardoner just a fund-raiser?[14] This way of viewing the tale is valuable because it pinpoints the distinction the tale as a whole makes between the Pardoner's idea of himself—the way he presents himself—and a more detached view taken by the end of the poem and associated with the community of the pilgrims, namely, society. The Host may not know exactly what the Pardoner is doing, but he can tell that it is more than a joke. At first he responds in kind to its aggressive violence, what he rightly calls its anger: he can feel that the Pardoner is imposing some-

14. See John Halverson's levelheaded and persuasive summary of this strand in the criticism, "Chaucer's Pardoner," 191.

thing on him. After his initial outburst, however, the Host begins to put the situation in perspective. Perhaps he is a little shaken by his own reaction and the extent to which he has been drawn into the Pardoner's mood. At any rate he begins to back off: "I wol no lenger pleye / With thee, ne with noon oother angry man" (958–59). At this point other social forces intervene to break the mood further and contain it, as the Knight, observing that "al the peple lough" (961), urges a reconciliation: " 'And, as we diden, lat us laughe and pleye.' / Anon they kiste, and ryden forth hir weye" (967–68).

The conclusion of the tale frames the Pardoner's performance as a social gaffe, a joke in bad taste that has gotten out of hand. It does so by showing how society closes ranks to repair the breach in decorum, the violation of the tale-telling contract the Pardoner has committed. The kiss of peace at the end is, of course, hollow, a mere social form that lets things move forward smoothly. It allows the group to pretend that nothing seriously untoward has happened and leaves the Pardoner in frustrated possession of his unhappy consciousness. This ending may well increase our sympathy for him, but the group is nonetheless correct in its assessment of the situation, for the most effective criticism of the Pardoner's presumption is precisely that it is presumptuous in an ordinary sense. It is preposterous that any man should carry the symbolic weight the Pardoner gives himself. If he takes all our sins on his shoulders by committing them and scapegoats himself like Christ to dramatize the pervasive presence of spirit in ordinary life, his behavior is likely to make us reflect that Christ did not sacrifice himself out of self-hatred and that not everyone who climbs up on a cross is a Christ or a type of Christ, or even a type of the Antichrist. Even the New Testament seems to indicate that two out of three such people are likely to be common thieves.

The way the end of the tale is framed so as to bring the Pardoner's typological consciousness into contact with an actuality that contains him and reveals his limitations suggests that, far from being an example of Chaucer's belief in, and commitment to, typological methods, the tale represents a critique of typology as a way of thinking about the world. We need to make a distinction between typological *methods*, which in the poem are simply one set of rhetorical techniques among many, open to anyone who has a use for them, and a typological *imagination*. Chaucer uses the former occasionally (in fact rather rarely in his own voice in the *Canterbury Tales*), and he has various pilgrims use them for particular purposes in their tales. Unlike Dante, however, he does not seem to have the latter. The Pardoner is the one pilgrim who really does seem to have a typological imagination, a mind that habitually views the smallest details of life in the world *sub specie aeternitatis,* and the text's presentation identifies the violence this cast of mind does to experience. Because the Pardoner demands that the world must be more "perfect" in his own terms than it is, he is constrained to see and suffer it "out of alle charitee" as worse than it is, simpler, blacker, and less flexible. From this perspective what a historically contextualized voice-oriented reading actually finds in the *Pardoner's Tale* is a representation of the temptation to pride and the illusion of power that typological thinking encourages. The tale shows how such thinking may all too easily neglect that it is only God who makes things into signs for other things at the level of eternal truth. The critique that the text conducts identifies typology as a potentially defective form of metaphor or image making that can be led to collapse the necessary distinctions between symbol and referent, literal and spiritual, mind and world. Less abstractly put, the text's framing shows that as a tale the *Pardoner's Tale* is bad because the Pardoner fails to see and sustain the crucial difference between fiction and reality, between a tale and the world in which it is told, and tries to force something he has made onto the world. The end of the tale shows that the typological imagination, by taking a God's-eye view, can all too easily deceive itself into playing God—a form of presumption that does not require divine intervention to discover its limitations.

The Pardoner is, as I have already suggested, the first exegetical critic of his own tale. He distorts his own sermon and exemplum by allegorizing and literalizing them beyond what they will bear. There is in this distortion, perhaps, a lesson for much subsequent exegetical criticism, which, like the Pardoner himself, is too frequently docetist in tendency. That is, this kind of criticism often implies that doctrine is more important than people, that the living temporal-historical experience of real souls has nothing to say for itself, or, typologically and symbolically put, that Christ could not really have deigned to sully his spirit, his divinity, by incarnating it in a real human person. This view is ultimately as unfair to Saint Augustine and the Middle Ages as it is to Chaucer. It can become a form of historical and critical pride, and it seems to me to be no accident that in its purest form exegetical criticism is associated with an attempt to cut off medieval consciousness from our common humanity, to say, as does Robertson, for example, that medieval man (the generic gender reference is telling in this context) had no personality because "he" talked about it differently from the way we do.[15] By neglecting, as it often does, the agency of the historical actors who used the institutionalized historical discourse of typology and by making them its unreflective agents, such a view runs the risk of historical irresponsibility: it makes our ancestors simpler and purer, and therefore less human, than we are—and than they were. But I am beginning to sound like the Pardoner myself, and since I do not plan to burn Professor Robertson at the stake, let me say rather that exegetical criticism, if it loses its sense of proportion, can, like the Pardoner, get a little rude.

I have meant this preliminary interpretation of the *Pardoner's Tale* to exemplify a certain way of reading the text, and now that it is completed, it can perhaps be summarized so as to differentiate more clearly between the kind of voice-oriented methods I propose and a more traditional Kittredgean dramatic reading. So far my interpretation of the Pardoner is based on taking the things he states or implies about himself in the course of his performance as elements in a deliberate self-presentation rather than as things he inadvertently gives away about himself while concentrating on telling a story. In the tradition of dramatic criticism of the tale it has been common to ascribe various "natural" or psychological motives to the Pardoner, such as a desire for recognition of his intellectual superiority, for acceptance in the community from which his physical lack appears to exclude him, for pity, for revenge, and even for death.[16] All these and many other simple or complex combinations of motive that have been suggested seem to me to be functional equivalents or particular expressions of the fundamental dialectical relation between presumption and despair. There has been a problem for a long time about integrating psychological explanations of the Pardoner's character and performance with exegetical interpretation and the theology of the tale. Where the theol-

---

15. Robertson, *Chaucer's London*, 1–11. For a less temperate comment on this position, see Kierkegaard, *Sickness unto Death*, 131.
16. See especially the excellent treatment in Howard, *Idea*, 357–80.

ogy has seemed relatively clear (only two explanations of the Pardoner's spiritual state have been brought forward, and both of them, presumption and despair, are right), the Pardoner's motives have received a broad range of interpretations, most of which, as characterizations of the sort of person who might be imagined to tell this tale, seem attractive and plausible even when they appear to contradict one another. What ails the Pardoner spiritually has been a lot clearer than what he is trying to do in his tale. I think one reason for this problem is that the Pardoner's psychology is theological and is presented and enacted as such by him in the tale.

Halverson and Howard have argued convincingly that the Pardoner's sexuality is his secret, that we do not know that he is a homosexual or even a eunuch, only that some features of his appearance and performance suggest those possibilities.[17] It is precisely such ambiguous features that the Pardoner manipulates for effect; we only get to know them as part of his deliberate self-presentation and self-interpretation. I think the same is true of his "real" motives. Though it is tempting, suggestive, and often valuable to speculate about such things as his feelings of alienation or intellectual superiority, his deformity, or his self-deception, it is unproductive and misleading to treat them, individually or in combination, as if they were *causes* of his performance. He himself does not treat them thus, and we have no access in the text to privileged information (such as, in a different way, exegetical criticism attempts to provide) that is somehow apart from what he actually does and says, for which our only evidence is precisely the text. Such naturalistic explanations, psychological or psychosomatic, are really only typologies of behavior based on different systems of classification from the one the Pardoner uses, and at best they suggest what the human consequences of the psychology of despair might be outside the poem. Inside the poem, however, the details of self-presentation are controlled by a prior structure, an interpretation that is the Pardoner's own. His categories are something like literal and allegorical, or carnal and spiritual, and they take precedence. Other kinds of motivation may be present somewhere in the Pardoner, but if they are, they too remain his secret. Whatever they may be, he transposes them to, and presents them as, spiritual types. His attitude

17. Halverson, "Chaucer's Pardoner," 195–96; Howard, *Idea*, pp. 343–45.

toward "ordinary" human motives, including his own, is the same as his attitude toward metaphor, and toward fiction generally: all such things are the chaff whose phenomenality both conceals and can be made to reveal the poisonous kernel of spiritual truth that is at the center of his world.[18]

Even if the patterns of presumption and despair do control what happens in the unfolding of the tale insofar as they give an accurate description of it, and even if those patterns are in some sense the self the Pardoner enacts, they do not necessarily constitute an essence. What we have in the tale is the representation not of an entity but of an activity, whose agent retires behind his own self-representation and keeps his secrets. The psychological speculations of dramatic criticism are responses to this sense of motive withheld behind the Pardoner's self-presentation. There is always an excess, something left over that establishes a gap between the subject, conceived as the position from which the activity emerges, and the self, which is, so to speak, its content. In this sense the analysis conducted here is preliminary. Though I have tried to give an accurate account of the self the Pardoner presents and the terms in which he presents it, I have not yet attempted to characterize the Pardoner's subjectivity, the structure of the space within which his self-representation occurs and of which it is a subset. Eventually I will argue that that subjectivity is best described as a form of disenchantment, which I will try to explain as the general structure one of whose historical contents, in the era from Saint Augustine to Kierkegaard, is sometimes called despair. But before we reach that point in Part II, we must first examine the self–subject split in the *Wife of Bath's Tale,* in part because features of that text make the topic more accessible there, but in part as well because the issue of gender difference has an important bearing on the development of the argument. For the time being it will suffice to have established the importance and relevance of disenchantment in the limited sense I have given it so far as the perspective that allows the Pardoner as agent to emerge from behind the more general institutional and historical framework of exegetical interpretation. It is, I have argued, his disenchanted deployment of that framework that makes him stand out as the teller of

18. In this he is oddly like Kierkegaard, who in *The Sickness unto Death* exhibits a similar programmatic tendency to interpret the psychological as an epiphenomenal and particular case of the spiritual. I will have more to say about this in Part II.

his tale. His insistence that there is no such thing as disinterested language and that even—or especially—doctrine, as it is encountered in concrete life, did not fall from the sky but is always being used by someone, mostly for ends like his, is what brings him forward in all his pride and despair, questioning and mocking in a voice of his own that disquiets us yet.

2

Self-Presentation and Disenchantment in the *Wife of Bath's Prologue*
A Prospective View

If the pilgrimage is dated April, 1387, then the Squire, who was twenty years old, was conceived in July, 1366. At that time the Knight was in the Middle East. I once drew the consequences of these facts and submitted my parody to a learned journal. The editors returned it, not because it wasn't funny, as perhaps it wasn't, but because it was, they said, "too speculative." I would have called it an illegitimate inference.

James Sledd, "The *Clerk's Tale:*
The Monsters and the Critics"

Supposing truth is a woman—what then? Are there not grounds for the suspicion that all the philosophers, insofar as they were dogmatists, have been very inexpert about women? That the gruesome seriousness, the clumsy obtrusiveness with which they have usually approached truth so far have been awkward and very improper methods for winning a woman's heart? What is certain is that she has not allowed herself to be won.

Nietzsche, *Beyond Good and Evil*

The Pardoner is one of two pilgrims whose tales have been almost universally recognized as being "about" their tellers, as inviting and necessitating some form of dramatic interpretation, whatever that term is taken to mean. The other is the Wife of Bath, and in her case as well even iconographically inclined critics have recognized that it is the teller of the tale rather than, say, its characters, whose iconography needs to be explained. It seems to me that this conviction of the appropriateness of dramatic explanation arises from the obvious fact that these are the only two fictional performances in the *Canterbury Tales* in which self-presentation is the announced and primary aim of the fictional speaker. The Pardoner and the Wife both say that they intend to talk about themselves and then proceed to do so. These two pilgrims explicitly connect their tales proper with their own careers and projects: the Pardoner's is an example of how he preaches, and the

Wife's is an illustration of her thesis, also illustrated in her life, about female sovereignty in marriage. These tales are dramatic because their narrators say they are; and these are pilgrims whose theme is the self.

But this fact poses a problem, touched on at the end of Chapter 1, about the nature of dramatic interpretation and the status of its results. Dramatically oriented critics frequently assume a distinction between what might be called *self-presentation*, the offering of an interpretation of the self and its significance, and *self-revelation*—the manifestation, conscious or not, of some truth about the self:

> We shall find that the Wife's outstanding traits are aggressiveness and amorousness, and that the two combine to produce her militant feminism, which leads her to argue strongly for female sovereignty. Obviously, the tale she tells is aimed at illustrating this tenet; and her tale fits into the context of her antagonism toward antifeminist clerics, such as the Nun's Priest, who has just completed his tale, and towards recalcitrant husbands, such as Harry Bailly. But we shall also see that in the course of her performance Chaucer causes her to make clear certain unfavorable aspects of her character which she does not intend to reveal; she no doubt would look upon such revelation as a source of embarrassment.
>
> (Lumiansky, *Of Sondry Folk*, 119)

The statement is fairly representative of critical practice in the dramatic mode, both in its confident distinctions between conscious and unconscious material and in its assigning of the former to the Wife and the latter to "Chaucer." But how can Lumiansky be so sure which is which? The Wife of Bath's performance, even more obviously than the Pardoner's, invites an attempt to construct a career for her that will explain who she is by explaining how she became what we see before us; but as with the Pardoner, what most invites such a proceeding is also what most puts it in question, the circumstance that the Wife herself announces this project in her prologue, beating the critics to it. It is tempting, no doubt, to treat perceived contradictions in the text as revelations about the Wife that she is unaware of or wishes to conceal, and to use such "slips" as a way of constructing her character from the "facts" thus arrived at. The trouble is that the text does not—in principle cannot—offer any certainty about what has the revelatory status of fact in the Wife's performance precisely because the text is explicitly framed as self-presentation. The speaker may therefore always be construed as having her own opinions, attitudes, and intentions concerning what she reports and her own strategic or tactical reasons even for contradicting herself.

This objection is more than an epistemological quibble. The way we decide to make the distinction between presentation and revelation in effect constructs or creates the Wife of Bath for us, and it has done so in the past with distressingly varied results. Consider, for instance, as relatively uncontroversial a matter as the Wife's horoscope, which not only the scholars who have studied it but also the Wife herself agree is a significant fact about her:

> For certes, I am al Venerien
> In feelynge, and myn herte is Marcien.
> Venus me yaf my lust, my likerousnesse,
> And Mars yaf me my sturdy hardynesse;
> Myn ascendent was Taur, and Mars therinne.
> Allas, allas! That evere love was synne!
>
> (III, 609–14)

Leaving aside for the moment what the Wife makes of this horoscope, we can identify Walter Clyde Curry's reading in *Chaucer and the Medieval Sciences* (91–118) as essentially iconographic. Since he knows that astrology is a fact for the culture and the poet he is studying, he views the Wife as a deliberately created instantiation of medieval belief and ascribes her behavior to her stars. She is a type of her horoscope in much the way a Robertsonian might see her as a type of the Samaritan woman, and Curry's treatment amounts to an explanation of how such a constellation might produce such a life. But Curry also sees that in this reading the Wife's horoscope is a *fate* of which she is conscious, and this circumstance, for him, makes her moving, a woman tragically driven by her stars. By contrast Chauncey Wood, in *Chaucer and the Country of the Stars* (172–80), sees the Wife less iconographically and more dramatically. That is, he presents her as a free individual, a person who misunderstands and misuses her horoscope by ignoring her own freedom in playing the hand the stars have dealt her: "[She says] that she followed her 'constellation' and did not refrain from lechery. . . . this suggests that some value judgment should be made about the Wife: no one had to follow the inclination set forth by the stars, but she seems not to take note of this" (173). The

Wife comes out differently depending on whether a tension or contradiction—here between fate and will—is conceived as consciously un-
dergone and presented (Curry's tragic figure) or unconsciously revealed (Wood's woman in bad faith). When we turn to the criticism at
large, not only tensions and contradictions but also actual uncertainties about the Wife multiply. For example, we do not know for certain
whether she has had children, whether Janekyn is dead, and whether
she committed adultery in her fourth marriage or before it.[1] All this
makes constructing a career and character for the Wife a distinctly
risky business, as the range of those characters and careers in the
critical literature—from sociopathic murderess to tragic heroine to
comic embodiment of the life force—testifies.[2]

Since they contradict one another, at least some of these inferences
must be illegitimate; but I am going to argue that there is a sense in
which they all are. What they all have in common, it seems to me, is a
drive to the reification of the Wife's character. Interpreters try to stand
apart from the Wife and above her, to assume a position of analytical
superiority that is in possession of the "facts" about her, whatever
those facts are held to be. In practice, for example, Wood's analysis is
not so different from Curry's: it gives the Wife her freedom only to
take it away again in the same gesture. It ends, as character-oriented,
dramatic approaches often seem to, by positing a Wife who is fixed,
understood, and dismissable.[3] Each of these competing interpretations
seeks to establish its decoding of the Wife as the discovery of what I
have been calling a self: an essence, however complex, that is the key
to her permanent and prior real nature, who she is, whether that
identity is seen as the result of her iconographic meaning or her past.
The Wife sometimes appears to be surrounded by critics who are
trying to get her to fit a definitive shape, or, as we say, to put her in a

1. See, for example, Biggins, "O Jankyn, Be Ye There?"; Sands, "Non-Comic Wife";
Carruthers, "Painting of Lions."
2. For the murderess and sociopath, see Rowland, "Wife of Bath's Fourth Husband"; Palomo, " 'Bad Husbands' "; Sands, "Non-Comic Wife." For intimations of
tragedy, see, among others, Salter, "Tragic Figure of the Wife of Bath." For the life force,
see the fine article by Rose A. Zimbardo, "Unity and Duality in the *Wife of Bath's
Prologue and Tale*."
3. Wood's tone is in fact rather less attractive than Curry's. The latter at least
sympathizes with the hard fate the Wife's horoscope imposes, whereas Wood, oddly,
seems more certain what to think of her and more certain of his right to judge her.

box. She might well respond, as she does to a husband (which one is not certain), "I trowe thou woldest loke me in thy chiste!" (317). I would like to begin instead by concentrating on the way the Wife herself tries to deal with this constraining impulse in others and with what is not contained or resolved at the beginning of her performance.

One of the first things the text leaves unspecified about the Wife of Bath is why she begins to tell her tale when she does—in fact we do not even know when that is. The *Wife of Bath's Prologue* is a text that begins in indeterminacy, because its context is underdetermined. The fragment that starts with the *Wife of Bath's Prologue* occurs in a number of different positions in the order of the tales in different manuscripts of the *Canterbury Tales*. In no case, however, is there a headlink for it. If we put aside all speculations about what Chaucer might have done had he finished the poem or how the Wife's performance might be viewed as a response to the Man of Law or the Pardoner (in the Ellesmere and Chaucer Society orders respectively)[4] or to fragment I (Hengwrt)—all tales and fragments that break off inconclusively—what we have in all the extant versions is a text that springs from a gap in the poem and a blank on the page, a voice that begins to speak out of nowhere,[5] apparently without antecedents in the immediate situation and as if in the middle of a continuing argument:

> Experience, though noon auctoritee
> Were in this world, is right ynogh for me
> To speke of wo that is in mariage;
> For, lordynges, sith I twelve yeer was of age,
> Thonked be God that is eterne on lyve,
> Housbondes at chirche dore I have had fyve—
> If I so ofte myghte have ywedded bee—
> And alle were worthy men in hir degree.
> But me was toold, certeyn, nat longe agoon is,
> That sith that Crist ne wente nevere but onis
> To weddyng, in the Cane of Galilee,
> That by the same ensample taughte he me

4. It is interesting that Lumiansky sees the Wife as responding to the Nun's Priest. He apparently follows the Bradshaw Shift but assumes that the Wife ignores the tales of fragment C to hark back to the end of B² (*Of Sondry Folk*, 116–17). One wonders what this assumption makes of Pertelote's speech at VII, 2908–17, that is, what if anything does it mean for the Wife to quote the chicken rather than the other way around?

5. See Muscatine's discussion, *Chaucer and the French Tradition*, 207: "It begins in a vacuum."

> That I ne sholde wedded be but ones.
> Herkne eek, lo, which a sharp word for the nones . . .
>
> (1–14)

It is precisely the lack of context here, the fact that the Wife appears to be speaking to no one in particular on the pilgrimage and in response to no specific stimulus from the group, that stresses how much the situation and the speaker are dominated by a larger and more threatening context that has preempted her possibilities of expression. If the Wife wishes to assert the claims of experience, she finds herself doing so in a world in which the experiential immediacy of the moment of speaking appears to be always already conditioned and dominated by the past and a hostile masculine authority. It is perhaps not entirely fortuitous that as the prologue opens, the Wife is confronted by a situation in the fiction very like the one I have described outside it. She might be said to be a victim of textual harassment, in Robert Hanning's splendid phrase,[6] facing an array of critics who have decided notions of what a woman is and how she ought to behave.

If the first of these harassers is the oddly carnal literalist who recently tried to force the Wife to fit the measure of his preposterous application of the story of the Samaritan woman,[7] the others are more formidable and even harder to talk to because they are both absent and present in an even more absolute way. The preexisting structure of institutional antifeminism that presses on the Wife is experienced and responded to by her here in its most abstract, impersonal, and relatively unmediated form as the patriarchal law and the words of Christ, Saint Paul, and Saint Jerome in all their authoritative and authoritarian rigor. These voices are as unsituated here as the Wife's own, and they are treated precisely as texts, at least in the understanding of text that makes of it a permanent record of an unalterable decision. Since it is the Wife herself who cites these voices and brings these issues up, since there is no one else speaking and no one she is speaking to, it seems that she is somehow impelled or forced to situate *herself* in the world constituted by authority—the world of doctrine, official texts, and the patriarchal law. Surely one of the tones at work in the opening lines is something like, We all know I am a problem before anyone says a word; here is my reply to what I know you are thinking, to what men

---

6. See Hanning, "Textual Harassment in Chaucer's *Canterbury Tales*."
7. See Howard, *Idea*, 248–51.

always think. The Wife's method of arguing submits to the law in the very act of combating it and thereby constitutes it all the more as an unsituated absolute, the way things are, an authoritative framework that is everywhere at once and nowhere in particular. She seems to feel that her only recourse is to appropriate the techniques of scriptural gloss and the manipulation of sacred texts that are used against her, and she does so in a voice that is often nervous, hostile, and hairsplitting. She is given to niggling formalities of evidence and citation, and the literalistic quoting of texts and countertexts that conspicuously and ungenerously ignores the spirit (none too generous itself) of her opponents:

> Whan myn housbonde is fro the world ygon,
> Som Cristen man shal wedde me anon,
> For thanne th'apostle seith that I am free
> To wedde, a Goddes half, where it liketh me.
> He seith that to be wedded is no synne;
> Bet is to be wedded than to brynne.
>
> (47–52)

> Wher kan ye seye, in any manere age,
> That hye God defended mariage
> By expres word? I pray yow, telleth me.
> Or where comanded he virginitee?
>
> (59–62)

Where does it say I can't? is scarcely a strong defense, and the Wife seems similarly ill served by many of the other texts and images she tries to invoke in her own behalf in the first part of the prologue. The best she can find is "leve / Of indulgence" (83–84) to marry again, and there seems to be no available version of wifehood that does not end up making her a second-class citizen, a vessel of "tree" rather than of gold, or barley bread in contrast to bread of "pured whete-seed" (99–101; 139–140). The Wife is consistently rendered marginal by the authorities she tries to appropriate, cut off by her "freletee" from the rigorous perfection they hold up.

One way to read the Wife's performance, and one way she herself presents it, is to see the prologue and tale as parts of a process that is intended to counter the situation I have just described by turning the Wife herself into an authority. Not liking the exempla (such as that of the Samaritan woman) offered to her by the male world, the Wife sets out, like the Pardoner, to make an example of herself. In this reading, her experience in marriage leads to a thesis and a demonstration about marriage in general. The necessity of feminine 'maistrye' or sovereignty in marriage, the Wife seems to be saying, is what my life proves, and so does the story I am about to tell. That is, her life adds up to a final meaning that the tale then confirms. Publicly and explicitly the Wife sets out to anticipate her later critics by providing an interpretation of her life. Insofar as that interpretation requires that she constitute her past *as past,* as something that is over and done with and can therefore be generalized from, the Wife herself sets out with the *intention* to reify herself, to turn herself into a counterexemplum in opposition to those in Janekyn's book of wicked wives and the male misogynist tradition.

As I have already suggested, the form the Wife's conduct of this project takes is that of the *appropriation* of the instruments and institutions of masculine authority. Throughout her performance the Wife may be said to womanhandle the traditional instruments of male domination in the interests of her feminist message. The entire second section of the *Wife of Bath's Prologue,* for example (235–378), in which she details how she chided her old husbands "spitously" (223), is presented as a set of slanders that the Wife accused her old husbands of directing at her. The passage is a tissue of clichés drawn from antifeminist sources and put into the mouths of the old husbands: "Thou seist to me it is a greet mischief / To wedde a povre womman, for costage" (248–49). But, the Wife tells us, "al was fals" (382): the old men never said these things, and her accusations were made to intimidate and control them. The compendia of antifeminist lore, like the *Miroir de Mariage* and the other sources of Janekyn's book of wicked wives from which this material is in fact drawn, are meant to provide men with ammunition against women. But there is a sense in which by characterizing women in these ways, men give them license and permission to make what they can of the image for their own purposes; and by citing them here in a context that produces a reversal of their ordinary use, the Wife is pointing to her ability to appropriate even antifeminist characterization and turn it back on men to gain the mastery.[8] A more general example of the same technique is the sover-

8. The strategy is exemplified and illuminated in the "Hers" column of the *New York Times,* July 18, 1985, C2, where Susan Schnur relates the history of her responses to the rabbi of her childhood yeshiva in Trenton, N.J., who "wrapped an enormous

eignty argument itself, which is obviously a reversal of ordinary male-
female power relations and an aggressively polemical appropriation of
all those dreary (and nervous?) arguments about the proper hierarchical subordination of women to men in medieval discussions of the
subject.

Other aspects and implications of this appropriative stance come
out more clearly in the tone of particular passages, as when the Wife
cites the libertine Solomon ostensibly as an example of Old Testament
sanction for multiple marriages:

> Lo, heere the wise kyng, daun Salomon;
> I trowe he hadde wyves mo than oon.
> As wolde God it leveful were unto me
> To be refresshed half so ofte as he!
> Which yifte of God hadde he for alle his wyvys!
> No man hath swich that in this world alyve is.
> God woot, this noble kyng, as to my wit,
> The firste nyght had many a myrie fit
> With ech of hem, so wel was hym on lyve.
> Yblessed be God that I have wedded fyve!
> [Of whiche I have pyked out the beste,
> Bothe of here nether purs and of here cheste.]
>   (35–44b)

If only the justification of "bigamye" were at stake, the example could
have been as economically cited as the immediately following ones of

---

bandage up one wrist so that he would not, God forbid, ever have to shake a woman's
hand. Our rabbi did not touch women":

> At first, as a child, I regarded the rabbi's hand as a simple cootie fetish, like my
> brother Danny's. My girlfriend and I used to chase Danny through the house—
> him shrieking like a figure out of Edvard Munch—while we ran after him with a
> hobbyhorse upon whose head swung a pair of girl's underpants. My guess was
> the rabbi, if we'd ever touched his hand, would have reacted about the same as
> Danny, who was then six years old. . . . In college, the implications of being the
> object of a cootie fetish tickled me. It meant that I had power: I was the Great
> Unscatheable Cootie. I could walk between two men ("the devitalizing estrous
> promenade") while menstruating, and cause death. Being a cootie was strong
> ammunition against that Armageddonish day of feminist rout.

As an early example of the Great Unscatheable Cootie, the Wife of Bath derives power
from similarly flaunting the signs of her impropriety. I am grateful to Professor Sandra
Pierson Prior for pointing out both this reference and its relevance to the Wife of Bath.
See also Giddens, *Central Problems*, 72, and the section entitled "Power, Control,
Subordination," 145–50.

Abraham and Jacob (55–58). Here the Wife's voicing suggests that she identifies with Solomon and envies the license for promiscuity granted to him, and her concentration on "the firste nyght," as if the individual wives were used up and discarded in one merry fit apiece, creates a somewhat edgy and exploitative image of sexuality, which is further reinforced by "nether purs." The implication is that men are to be similarly used up, sexually rifled, as it were, in the same way that they are to be exploited economically.

This exploitative and frequently disparaging attitude toward masculine sexuality is reinforced at various points in the prologue, at times in contemptuous characterizations of male equipment ("thynges smale," "sely instrument," 121, 132) or the performance of her old husbands (198–202, 410–419), perhaps most chillingly just before the Pardoner's interruption:

> In swich estaat as God hath cleped us
> I wol persevere; I nam nat precius.
> In wyfhod I wol use myn instrument
> as frely as my Makere hath it sent.
> If I be daungerous, God yeve me sorwe!
> My housbonde shal it have bothe eve and morwe,
> Whan that hym list come forth and paye his dette.
> An housbonde I wol have—I wol nat lette—
> Which shal be bothe my dettour and my thral,
> And have his tribulacion withal
> Upon his flessh, whil that I am his wyf.
> I have the power durynge al my lyf
> Upon his propre body, and noght he.
> Right thus the Apostel tolde it unto me,
> And bad oure housbondes for to love us weel.
> Al this sentence me liketh every deel—
>
> (147–62)

The Wife's appropriation of the doctrines of the *debitum* and the relative perfection of the married state here shifts from using the authority of the sacred text as an excuse for sexual indulgence—"as frely as my Makere hath it sent"—to invoking the same authority to justify the use of sexuality as a pretext for aggression in a way that brings out more clearly the implications of the earlier passage about Solomon: I'll use it more freely than you might like, she says; I'll wear you out. Though it is certainly true that all this manipulation and threat is scarcely a proper use of authority, one cannot help noticing that it does not present a very satisfying or attractive image of experience either.[9]

An appropriative stance of the sort the Wife adopts, as David Aers has seen with particular clarity, is necessarily reactive, a form of counterpunching, and therefore it can only recapitulate and perpetuate in reverse, like a mirror image, the structure and logic of the institutional order it attempts to refute.[10] Because the Wife's public position in her prologue and tale is founded in the masculine-controlled and economically dominated idea of marriage that pervades the society in which she lives, she is driven by the logic of opposition to adopt a stance that competes with, and therefore reproduces, the exploitation, both economic and sexual, to which women are ordinarily subjected by the masculine world.[11] If marriage in the Wife's society is an institution that reduces women to commodities and subordinates feminine sexuality and individuality to the requirements of economic exchange, a woman who wants to defend herself has only the option of using the assets she possesses to play the game herself, as the Wife makes clear in the theory of marriage she enunciates early in the prologue:

> They had me yeven hir lond and hir tresoor;
> Me neded nat do lenger diligence
> To wynne hir love, or doon hem reverence.
> They loved me so wel, by God above,
> That I ne tolde no deyntee of hir love!
> A wys womman wol bisye hire evere in oon
> To gete hire love, ye, ther as she hath noon.
> But sith I hadde hem hooly in myn hond,
> And sith they hadde me yeven al hir lond,
> What sholde I taken keep hem for to plese,
> But it were for my profit and myn ese?
>
> (204–14)

9. On marriage and the *debitum*, see Cotter, "Conjugal Debt," and Mogen, "*Bona Matrimonii.*" On justifying sexuality as aggression, see Kernan, "Archwife and the Eunuch," 1–2.

10. Aers, *Creative Imagination,* 147–48. See also David, *Strumpet Muse,* 143–47, 153, and Gottfried, "Conflict and Relationship," 203–4.

11. Excellent accounts of the institutional structure and support of this exploitation in the late fourteenth century are given in Aers, *Creative Imagination,* chaps. 5 and 6, 117–173, and Carruthers, "Painting of Lions." See also Bourdieu, *Theory of Practice,* 92 and 164–65.

Aers notes that the Wife rejects "the role of the passive and devotedly servile wife (her rebellion), but only to take on the traditional and culturally celebrated role of the domineering, egotistic husband (her affirmation of the culture)." In doing so, she accepts "the reduction of self and body to the status of a commodity to be bought by males, by accepting the reduction of female sexuality to an instrument of manipulation, control, and punishment" (*Creative Imagination*, 148).

Indeed she does, and the explicitness with which the Wife identifies the economic and power functions of sexual attractiveness sometimes shocks my students when they identify this version of marriage— correctly—as a form of prostitution. It is perhaps worth insisting that the Wife sees marriage in that way here, and that she does not appear at all fazed by it, nor does she consider any alternative model of potential relations between the sexes. She demystifies affection as a weakness to be exploited in economic transactions, something that gives a woman an edge over the man who lets himself be affected. That is to say that her understanding of marriage as a functioning institution, and of the place of affection in it, is as thoroughly disenchanted as the Pardoner's view of preaching. The Wife's very marginality puts her in a position to understand the official cultural account of the "nature" of women and marriage as a human construction because she continually experiences it practically as something done to her by men. Therefore she can identify traditional masculine characterizations of women, negative or positive, as ideological weapons in a struggle for dominance. One advantage of this disenchanted point of view lies precisely in the way it identifies authority as something that is subject to ideological use. It is a lot easier to deal with a man who appropriates scripture—"And yet—with sorwe!—thou most enforce thee, / And seye thise wordes in the Apostles name" (340–41)—than it is to confront the apostle directly. One can more easily say to the husband, "After *thy* text, ne after *thy* rubriche, / I wol nat wirche as muchel as a gnat" (346–47, emphasis added).[12]

We can trace this disenchanted economic view of sexuality and society—"Wynne whoso may, for al is for to selle" (414)—throughout the poem as something the Wife uses to make sense of both the world at large and her own life. Consider, for example, the moment at which

---

12. The point has been seen by Haller, "Three Estates," 51.

she reports with some puzzlement an apparent contradiction in her relationship with Janekyn:

> And yet was he to me the mooste shrewe;
> That feele I on my ribbes al by rewe,
> And evere shal unto myn endyng day.
> But in oure bed he was so fressh and gay,
> And therwithal so wel koude he me glose,
> Whan that he wolde han my *bele chose;*
> That thogh he hadde me bete on every bon,
> He koude wynne agayn my love anon.
> I trowe I loved hym best, for that he
> Was of his love daungerous to me.
> We wommen han, if that I shal nat lye,
> In this matere a queynte fantasye;
> Wayte what thyng we may nat lightly have,
> Therafter wol we crie al day and crave.
> Forbede us thyng, and that desiren we;
> Preesse on us faste, and thanne wol we fle.
> With daunger oute we al oure chaffare;
> Greet prees at market maketh deere ware,
> And to greet cheep is holde at litel prys:
> This knoweth every womman that is wys.
>
> (505–24)

What is striking here is how the working through of the contradiction (he beat her but could always sweet-talk her back into bed when he wanted to) moves simultaneously in the course of the passage toward the highest degree of generalization—this is what all women are like, and the wise ones know it—and the most thoroughly economic form of explanation: all affection including the Wife's own is subject to the law of supply and demand. As Max Weber remarks, there are no mysterious processes that come into play; one can in principle master all things by calculation. The economic account is presented as a kind of key that makes sense of the details of the Wife's biography and at the same time renders her exemplary. The particulars are finally subordinated to, and transcended by, the general truth. This passage is characteristic of the way the disenchanted economic, appropriative, and competitive perspective functions throughout the poem, even in the tale's concluding curse on "olde and angry nygardes of dispence" (1263). In effect the Wife deliberately reduces herself and the meaning of her experience to these terms in order to give that experience au-

thority and the status of a counterexemplum that challenges the masculine mystifications of conventional authority. After all, if a woman is
going to have this sort of thing done to her anyway, it is better for her
to have something to say about the terms in which it is done.

This project has its effect on—that is, it can be used to explain—
certain large-scale features of style and structure in the *Wife of Bath's
Prologue*. The entire account of how the Wife dealt with her first three
husbands, for example (193–451), can be read as another instance of
the tendency, already exemplified above, to employ memory primarily
in the service of generalization. The three men and the marriages they
were involved in are reduced to a single long speech to a nameless
"thou," who is accused of various misdeeds to show "wise wyves"
how to maintain control over their husbands.[13] No distinction is made
among husbands or times—the account is in effect, like the gospels and
Saint Paul, out of time—and as a result the specificity of the passage
seems merely rhetorical, a kind of allusion to concreteness for the sake
of effect rather than actual memories of specific occasions. Because so
much of the speech is made up of lists of antifeminist proverbs attributed to the generalized "thou" ("Thou seyst that droppyng houses,
and eek smoke, / And chidyng wyves maken men to flee / Out of hir
owene houses;" [278–80]), the more specific characterizations ("Thus
seistow, lorel, whan thou goost to bedde" [273, cf. 235, 242, 253,
276–77, 302]) seem tacked on to produce a kind of general fiction of
experiential detail in a context that remains primarily exemplary and
typical. When read as elements in the argument the Wife is constructing—"hou I baar me proprely"—exhibited to show wise wives "Thus
shulde ye speke, and bere hem wrong on honde" (224–26), the various
particular elements do not seem important for their specific content,
and even less so for the particular occasions in the Wife's past when
she used them. The Wife's project here is to make herself into a
textbook, a *miroir de mariage*.

To read the *Wife of Bath's Prologue* in this way is precisely to read
it as an argument, that is, to read it for its conclusions. Such a reading
is fundamentally linear and goal-oriented, or what might be called
prospective in the sense that it looks forward to a conclusion. It is
aimed at producing a narrative of the Wife's life in chronological

13. See Pratt, "Development of the Wife of Bath," 57.

order, husband by husband, that adds up to something. It generates a set of insights about feminine nature (for example, "we wommen konne no thyng hele" [950]), and ends with a general conclusion that subsumes what has gone before, such as "Wommen desiren to have sovereynetee / As wel over hir housbond as hir love" (1038–39). Read thus, the consistent direction of the poem, in its parts and as a whole, is from experience to authority, albeit a disenchanted authority. So the text presents itself, and so the Wife intends her performance to be taken.

Almost everything I have said thus far about the poem, however, I regard as preliminary. This reading, as I have been careful to call it, of the Wife's disenchanted perspective is not so much wrong as incomplete, a place to start in thinking about the tale rather than the last word. Indeed, as I have just argued, a form of this reading is the Wife's own public project (her word is *apert*) in the tale. It is the place from which she starts in the sense that it is her plan for the performance, and I have sketched some of the ways in which she carries it out. But this project, with its doctrinaire feminism and oppositional stance, has something a little too static and structural about it, something other critics besides me have found uncomfortable. My point is that the Wife finds it uncomfortable too. Her public project does not really do justice to the complex and dynamic character of the now of speaking and remembering, the sense of ongoing life and discovery that cannot be totally reduced to an order or an argument, shut up in forms, or completely subjected to authority, even the Wife's own. There is at least one other way to read the Wife's performance, or rather, to reread it.

The kinds of meaning, such as the sovereignty argument, that the Wife proposes publicly are not intrinsic properties of her life. Rather they are an attempt to constitute that life so that only certain sorts of meaning are possible: meaning that is general, stable, authoritative, competitive, countermasculine, economic, and so on. I might note that this sort of public meaning is appropriate to the fictional situation on the pilgrimage because it is precisely the sort of meaning that can be grasped on a single hearing in a face-to-face situation where the audience experiences the performance once only and in order.[14] This is in

14. Roland Barthes has enunciated with particular clarity the way the conditions of speech, as opposed to writing, range it on the side of the law to make it an instrument of

fact the impression of the Wife's meaning that the Clerk and Merchant seem to have gotten since it is essentially this version of her that eventually surfaces in their tales. For actual readers rather than listeners, this kind of reading is prospective or forward-looking in the sense that however many times we actually read the text in this mode, we always do so as if it had a dramatic order of beginning, middle, and end, which we establish to get through the text, that is, to find out what it all adds up to, how it comes out, its so-called final meaning. In this mode we assume that there is a correct reading, even if we have to read repeatedly to discover it, or indeed never discover it. Such a reading in effect doubles the Wife's public project even when it does not agree with her conclusions because it does agree that the meaning of the narration is a proposition of the order, if not the content, of "Wommen desiren to have sovereynetee." In other words, it agrees that the speaker is a self, an entity whose preexistent being can be defined in principle by some such proposition or propositions, however complex they might turn out to be in practice, and therefore that her performance delivers that essence in principle even if we have not yet completely discovered it.

For the Wife, however, such a reading of her life is only possible because she has already lived through it. The reason she can edit her account so as to offer an interpretation that preempts and forestalls other such readings, especially masculine ones, is that, for her, her experience is no longer, as it is for the pilgrim listeners, a prospective unfolding that necessarily occurs in narrative order; it is more like a text that she has already "read" at least once, and her performance on the pilgrimage is a retrospective rereading of that text.[15] She can, to be sure, attempt to naturalize the account and conceal its interpretive bias by presenting her interpretation as an immanent meaning, and so she does in her public self-presentation. But she can also rework and reexamine the events of her life for herself—in effect *rearrange* the text by altering the stress given to its elements. She can disregard or play

---

authority and the dominant ideology. See Barthes, "Writers, Intellectuals, Teachers," esp. 191.

15. The distinction between prospective and retrospective reading is taken from Ferdinand de Saussure, *Course in General Linguistics,* 90. See my "Dialectic of Romantic Historiography."

down mere sequence and one-way cause and effect in favor of more textual principles of organization and meaning, such as patterns of imagery that emerge from points widely scattered in time, and she can allocate significance to past events in terms of their importance to her now, whatever she may have thought they meant when they occurred—and so can we.[16]

Because we are readers and have the Wife as absence and as text, we can follow the traces of her rereadings in a way that the pilgrims, who had her only as a speaking presence, could not: we can reread too. To do so is to attend to certain forms of displacement in the text that lead away from narrative sequence and deductive argument. If the Wife does have a public feminist agenda in the performance, she may also, like the Pardoner, have attitudes about the role she plays to carry out that agenda, and those attitudes can be elicited from her voicing of the message, from the ways she comments on, revises, ignores, or otherwise deploys the events of her life and the elements of her tale. Such a reading allows another text to emerge that is in dialectical tension with the public one. If the Wife's public use of experience is intended to convert it into authority, the private text (her word is *privy*) stands this model on its head, though it is equally disenchanted in the importance it attaches to human agency. It attends, as we will see, to the primacy of individual action over institutional coercion and to the variety of institutionally unintended uses—not just oppositional ones—that experience can make of authority. As its associations with textuality and indeterminacy may suggest, this way of reading is much better suited to evoking the Wife as subject because it continually undoes and reconstitutes, for her as for us, the very self whose stability and permanence she continually puts in question even as she constructs it.

16. Compare Barthes's brief remarks at the beginning of *S/Z*, 15–16. It is perhaps worth stressing from the beginning that the *Wife's Prologue* is a patently *digressive* text that gets out of order from time to time—that is, it bears the traces of the destructuring force of the Wife's own rereading.

3

Retrospective Revision and the Emergence of the Subject in the *Wife of Bath's Prologue*

The Wife of Bath's project to make use of her life as an example emerges in the text out of her response to the Pardoner's interruption. It is not clear until that point that an autobiography is really what she has in mind, but I find it significant that her reminiscence gets started as a result of talking to someone who responds to her:

> "Now, dame," quod he, "by God and by Seint John!
> Ye been a noble prechour in this cas.
> I was aboute to wedde a wyf; allas!
> What sholde I bye it on my flessh so deere?
> Yet hadde I levere wedde no wif to-yeere!"
>
> (III, 164–68)

Whatever one makes of the Pardoner's tone here—since it is unlikely that he is really planning to marry, some sort of irony is presumably intended[1]—it is at least clear that he does not sound much like Saint Jerome or Saint Paul; he does not take up an overtly oppositional and authoritarian stance. Nor does the Wife respond to this interruption and to the Pardoner's "teche us yonge men of youre praktike" (187) as hostile or mocking comments. Rather she appears to take them as an opportunity to moderate her earlier tone and even, perhaps, to apologize for it:

> "Gladly," quod she, "sith it may yow like;
> But yet I praye to al this compaignye,
> If that I speke after my fantasye,
> As taketh not agrief of that I seye,
> For myn entente nys but for to pleye."
>
> (188–92)

---

1. See below, chap. 6.

It looks as if the Pardoner's interruption helps the Wife to extricate herself from the abstract and unsituated debate with authority into which she falls at the beginning of the prologue. He makes her aware of the actual situation of the pilgrimage and shifts her attention somewhat away from the confrontational mode that has dominated her performance thus far. She shows more sensitivity to the everyday social implications of her tirade and to the feelings of the audience and identifies her earlier projection of a Solomon-like vengeful exploitation of men for her own pleasure and anger as what it is, a "fantasye." She seems to become more conscious of herself as a performer and realize that she does not have to take on the whole antifeminist tradition issue by issue. She has only to speak of the woe that is in marriage, and for that task she has a role ready to hand: "This is to seyn, myself have been the whippe" (175). In adopting the role of marital whip for the edification of the audience, the Wife moves explictly into the mode of deliberate self-presentation, a move that gives her, so to speak, a certain distance on herself and that allows the possibility of a somewhat different relationship with the audience to emerge.

This shift in tone in reaction to an external stimulus allows us to see the possibility of speaking about the *Wife of Bath's Prologue* less as a preplanned theoretical argument that has to move through a certain number of points to a conclusion and more as something practical that happens and alters as it goes along in response to a set of more immediate and unstructured contingencies. The most important of these contingencies is not, of course, the response of the audience, though the Wife's sensitivity to them may indeed have something to do with the number of times she is interrupted. Rather, the most important practical determinant of the poem's unfolding is the vagaries of memory as it doubles and redoubles on itself. We, like the Wife, must concern ourselves less with the plot she remembers than with *the plot of her remembering* in the now of narration.[2]

This distinction between the event as it was and as it is remembered emerges as a possibility in the prologue (though admittedly unclearly), perhaps as early as the fifth line, in what could be interpreted as a response in the now of speaking to the memory of five husbands' worth

2. The distinction is that posited by Russian formalism between *fabula* and *siuzhet* and by Benveniste and the French narratologists between *histoire* and *discours* or *récit*. There is a clear, brief account with basic bibliography in Brooks, *Reading for the Plot,* 12–14.

of marital woe: "Thonked be God that is eterne on lyve" (5). It emerges much more clearly as the Wife begins to tell of how she dealt with her three rich old husbands, "As help me God, I laughe whan I thynke / How pitously a-nyght I made hem swynke!" (201–2), because these lines catch the way something that was unpleasant or uncomfortable to live through may not be so to recall. But the first really striking example of the distinction emerges at the end—or what seems meant to be the end—of that same account of her chiding:

> O Lord! the peyne I dide hem and the wo,
> Ful giltelees, by Goddes sweete pyne!
> For as an hors I koude byte and whyne.
> I koude pleyne, and yit was in the gilt,
> Or elles often tyme hadde I been spilt.
> Whoso that first to mille comth, first grynt;
> I pleyned first, so was oure werre ystynt.
> They were ful glade to excuse hem blyve
> Of thyng of which they nevere agilte hire lyve.
> Of wenches wolde I beren hem on honde,
> Whan that for syk unnethes myghte they stonde.
>   Yet tikled I his herte, for that he
> Wende that I hadde of hym so greet chiertee!
> I swoor that al my walkynge out by nyghte
> Was for t'espye wenches that he dighte;
> Under that colour hadde I many a myrthe.
> For al swich wit is yeven us in oure byrthe;
> Deceite, wepyng, spynning God hath yive
> To wommen kyndely, whil that they may lyve.
>
> (384–402)

On the surface this passage is yet another instance of the pattern of working experience into general examples that I have already discussed. The Wife's behavior toward her old husbands is summed up in the proverbs about coming first to the mill and God's gifts to women. The most striking stylistic feature of the passage, however, is the shift from plural to singular pronouns at line 395, "Yet tikled I *his* herte, for that *he* / Wende . . . " (emphasis added), because it suggests a counter-attraction to the particular at the very moment when the conclusion is being drawn. "He" marks a shift from the generalized "thou" and the generalizing "they" of the preceding one hundred fifty lines because it seems to single out an individual and implies that this memory, if no other, is of a particular husband, perhaps even of a particular occasion.

This apparent sharpening of memory would mean little in isolation, but the second time it occurs, in the lines immediately following, the shift in pronoun number takes on increased particularity of reference. The Wife is concluding her summary of how she always bested her old husbands "Atte ende I hadde the bettre in ech degree, / By sleighte, or force, or by som maner thyng" (404–5), when she suddenly, and a little awkwardly, decides to give one more example:

> Namely abedde hadden they meschaunce:
> Ther wolde I chide and do hem no plesaunce;
> I wolde no lenger in the bed abyde,
> If that I felte *his* arm over my syde,
> Til he had maad his raunson unto me;
> Thanne wolde I suffre hym do his nycetee.
> And therfore every man this tale I telle,
> Wynne whoso may, for al is for to selle;
> With empty hand men may none haukes lure.
> For wynnyng wolde I al his lust endure,
> And make me a feyned appetit;
> And yet in bacon hadde I nevere delit.
> That made me that evere I wolde hem chide.
>   (407–19, emphasis added)

The shift to a memory of a single individual signaled by the pronoun shift in line 410 is accompanied by a number of negative features of the experience being remembered. "Thanne wolde I suffre hym do his nycetee" does not make the Wife sound impressed with the act or the actor, and neither do her remarks about enduring his pleasure and making a "feyned appetit."

What is really extraordinary about this memory is the way it mediates a complete reversal in the Wife's explanation of her own behavior in the course of thirteen lines. The passage begins by characterizing her chiding as a deliberate tactic for gaining an advantage ("raunson"), but it ends by making it a *response* to the unsatisfactory nature of the sexual act when she did let him do it; and it seems clearly to be the increasingly specific recollection of just how unpleasant the act was that leads to the change. I take this passage to be a response to the general presentation of the uses of sexuality in the prologue previously, and especially to the Wife's earlier account of her sexual dealings with her first three husbands. Those three, as we know, were good and rich and old (197), and what was good about them was that they gave in to her: she could dominate them and get their riches, and she did not need to care about them. In this context the old men's sexuality, such as it was, was part of the Wife's spoils and a source of amusement to her ("As help me God, I laughe whan I thynke / How pitously a-nyght I made hem swynke!"):

> I sette hem so a-werke, by my fey,
> That many a nyght they songen "Weilawey!"
> The bacon was nat fet for hem, I trowe,
> That som men han in Essex at Dunmowe.
>
>   (215–18)

In its original form this attitude is connected to the Solomon fantasy of men as mere "sely instruments" to be exploited for one's own pleasure and discarded at will, but in the passage under consideration that fantasy is reworked into something more complex.

What clinches the connection between the two moments is bacon. The first time around the reference is to the Dunmow flitch, awarded in that village "to any married couple who lived a year [and a day] without quarreling or repenting of their union," as Robinson says (*Riverside Chaucer*, 867). The reference is thus a humorous and hyperbolic way of stressing her power over her husbands, how successfully, as she goes on to add, she governed them whether they liked it or not (219–23). The second time it occurs, however, bacon means old meat, and it is once again used in an image that juxtaposes sexuality and marital disharmony: "And yet in bacon hadde I nevere delit. / *That made me that evere I wolde hem chide*" (418–19, emphasis added). What the Wife does to the word *bacon,* extending and altering its significance, may be taken as a model for what she does to the meaning of her sexual relations with her first three husbands generally. The development of the image registers the Wife's underlying dissatisfaction with a situation that was, from another point of view, thoroughly satisfactory. Successful as her manipulation of sex was as economics, it was not much fun as sex. That gave an extra edge to her chiding and helps to explain in retrospect why "They were ful glad whan I spak to hem faire, / For, God it woot, I chidde hem spitously" (222–23). The passage embodies the Wife's awareness of another motive coming to the fore, and that awareness of the inadequacy and incompleteness of the first explanation is owing to the more precise memory, indicated by the pronoun shifts, of what those sexual relations were like. The memory develops in the course of the telling, in the now of narration, according to the model of practical consciousness. That is, the treatment of the image of bacon is not discursively singled out for explicit reformulation (as in, When I say *bacon* I really mean . . .), but neither is it the focus of a feeling about sex or men that is clearly unconscious, unavailable to the Wife because it is repressed by her. Rather it is a practical response within the ongoing stream of conduct to a memory that arises from mysterious, and no doubt unconscious, sources, but a response that is itself a practical judgment. It makes use of the bacon image to clarify the meaning of the memory within the framework of already established and ongoing discourse. This phenomenon of *retrospective revision,* the way a later moment in the text simultaneously extends, alters, and undoes an earlier one, is characteristic of the Wife's performance and pervasive in it. Over and over, as we shall see, she reworks something she tells in the act of telling it, rereading the text of her life as she goes along in a way that transforms the meaning of the past in the light of the present.

The section of the prologue in which the Wife's narrative of her life moves from her first three husbands through her fourth shows memory increasingly disrupting the chronological surface of the narrative. Her assertion that she is even with the three old men, "Though I right now sholde make my testament, / I ne owe hem nat a word that it nys quit" (424–25), leads to yet a third specific memory, marked again by a shift in pronouns, of how she dealt with a moment of husbandly anger:

> I broghte it so aboute by my wit
> That *they* moste yeve it up, as for the beste,
> Or elles hadde we nevere been in reste;
> For thogh *he* looked as a wood leon,
> Yet sholde he faille of his conclusion.
> (426–30, emphasis added)

This time the remembered moment is fleshed out by a vivid, complexly toned speech that contains, among other matter, the Wife's brilliant appropriation of the stock theological analogy that takes man as the equivalent of the rational element in the soul and in marriage, and woman as some lower element, will, body, or the like:

> Thanne wolde I seye, "Goode lief, taak keep
> How mekely looketh Wilkyn, oure sheep!
> Com neer, my spouse, lat me ba thy cheke!
> Ye sholde been al pacient and meke,
> And han a sweete spiced conscience,
> Sith ye so preche of Jobes pacience.
> Suffreth alwey, syn ye so wel kan preche;
> And but ye do, certein we shal yow teche
> That it is fair to have a wyf in pees.
> Oon of us two moste bowen, doutelees;
> And sith a man is moore resonable
> Than womman is, ye moste been suffrable."
>
> (431–42)

The Wife's voice is fully engaged in this speech. The mock sweetness, the sudden threat ("And but ye do . . ."), and the final bland and infuriating appeal to the logic of masculine hierarchies make this performance strikingly different from her earlier rehearsal of what she said to her old husbands. Whatever else it may be, it is no list of proverbs. It has the complexity and coherence of a particular, though richly obscure, occasion, and I can understand why the man on the other end of it might have felt like a "wood leon."

In the next moment of the Wife's performance this vividness of memory escapes altogether from her organizing chronological framework. The instances we have been examining so far might be regarded as covert digressions from a relatively straightforward narrative, but what happens next is an open break. The Wife announces that she will speak of her fourth husband and proceeds to inform us, in one brief couplet, that he was a "revelour" and had a mistress (453–54)—and then she drops him:

> And I was yong and ful of ragerye,
> Stibourn and strong, and joly as a pye.
> How koude I daunce to an harpe smale,
> And synge, ywis, as any nyghtyngale,
> Whan I had dronke a draughte of sweete wyn!
>
> (455–59)

As this breakaway digression continues, the mention of wine reminds her, apparently by a logic of simple association, of an anecdote in Valerius about Metellius, who beat his wife to death for drinking wine, which the Wife of Bath reports with indignant defiance: "He sholde nat han daunted me fro drynke!" (463). She observes that "after wyn on Venus moste I thynke" (464), something that is apparently still true of her; at any rate it is reported in the present tense. She concludes, as usual, with a generalization, here about the effects of wine on the feminine libido (460–69).

This time, however, the generalization conspicuously fails to contain or account for the experience, and the Wife seems impelled to try again, in what are perhaps the most famous lines in the prologue:

> But—Lord Crist!—whan that it remembreth me
> Upon my yowthe, and on my jolitee,
> It tikleth me aboute myn herte roote.
> Unto this day it dooth myn herte boote
> That I have had my world as in my tyme.
>
> (469–73)

It is important to see that what is being described here is the direct result of the immediately preceding experience of telling, as "unto this day" suggests. The memory of her youthful energy, stubbornness, and "jolitee" has tickled the Wife in the now of speaking into the expression of feelings more personal and more intense than "In wommen vinolent is no defence" (467) will do justice to. She not only remembers but also *feels* the surge of energy she describes here as what the memory has just done for her. Only after a moment of darker reflection on her present age in comparison to her remembered youth (474–79) does the Wife at last return to the story from which she has moved so far. The fact of digression is underlined by her nearly verbatim repetition of the line with which she began, as if it were necessary to go back and start over: "Now wol I tellen of my fourthe housbonde" (480).

What we are seeing here is a kind of struggle or tension in the Wife between the project of self-presentation, with its need to control, limit, and chronologize experience, to put it behind as something over and done with, and a counterimpulse to acknowledge the increasingly rich and vivid pressure of detailed memories that amounts to a kind of reliving in the present of scattered events and emotions from the past whose connectedness is not temporally organized or discursively unified. It is therefore not surprising that her account of her fourth husband, when at last it does come, partakes of both tendencies. To begin with, it is couched in terms that distinctly recall earlier situations in the prologue and hence revise them in ways that clarify the practical logic of the poem's unfolding:

> I seye, I hadde in herte greet despit
> That he of any oother had delit.
> But he was quit, by God and by Seint Joce!
> I made hym of the same wode a croce;
> Nat of my body, in no foul manere,
> But certeinly, I made folk swich cheere
> That in his owene grece I made hym frye
> For angre, and for verray jalousye.
> By God, in erthe I was his purgatorie,
> For which I hope his soule be in glorie.
> For, God it woot, he sat ful ofte and song,
> Whan that his shoo ful bitterly hym wrong.
> Ther was no wight, save God and he, that wiste,
> In many wise, how soore I hym twiste.
>
> (481–94)

The first thing I want to call attention to here is the stress the passage lays on figures of balance and redress. The husband was repaid, "quit," for the injury he did the Wife by his infidelity; he was made to fry in his own grease to the extent that the Wife was his purgatory. Therefore, as she tells it here, there need remain no hard feelings on either side, and she hopes he is in heaven. This emphasis recalls her remark about the three old husbands earlier: "As helpe me verray God omnipotent, / Though I right now sholde make my testament, / I ne owe hem nat a word that it nys quit" (423–25). That remark, however, immediately precedes the shift of pronouns that carries us into the address to the angry husband (431–450; see above, pp. 87–88), which contains a passage I did not cite before:

> What eyleth yow to grucche thus and grone?
> Is it for ye wolde have my queynte allone?
> Wy, taak it al! Lo, have it every deel!
> Peter! I shrewe yow, but ye love it weel;
> For if I wolde selle my *bele chose,*
> I koude walke as fressh as is a rose;
> But I wol kepe it for youre owene tooth.
> Ye be to blame, by God! I sey yow sooth.
>
> (443–50)

This sounds to me like a bit of making him fry in his own grease, playing as it does with a threat of infidelity that, we may reflect, does not fit the situation with the first three old husbands very well. Those old men are consistently described as cowed and worn down by the Wife's predatory sexuality, as having to endure more of it than they literally can stand. Here, however, we are presented with a speech to a husband who is already looking like a "wood leon" and is being sorely twisted about his desire to possess the Wife exclusively—in short, a man who is being made to fry "for angre and for verray jalousye." What I mean to suggest, of course, is that it is no accident that this speech is immediately followed by "Now wol I speken of my fourthe housbonde" (452) because the Wife has already been speaking of—and to—him before she announces the transition. This interpretation of the passage does not mean that it cannot also be read as addressed to one or all of the first three husbands. In that reading, the apparently affectionate strain sounded by phrases like "Wy, taak it al" or "I wol kepe it for youre owene tooth" is covert aggression of a different sort: it announces the impossibility of escape from the Wife's sexual depredations. Indeed, the passage can also be read as addressed to Janekyn since the threat of infidelity here is allied to the Wife's insistence on her independence, which is more a theme of her fifth than of her fourth marriage, and "Peter! I shrewe yow, but ye love it weel" sounds more probable as addressed to Janekyn than to the unfaithful fourth husband. The point I want to make is not that one of these readings is "right" but that the addressee of the speech is genuinely both multiple and undecidable, equally appropriate or inappropriate to each of three distinct situations. Following the kind of textualized retrospective re-membering the Wife practices here allows and encourages us, like her, to explore the multiplicity of *other* voices and times that emerge from behind the linear project of self-presentation. Once again the surface of narration and example conceals a subtext of memory and experience that emerges only in retrospective rereading.

It is also clear, however, that if the Wife's fourth husband is on her mind before he enters her chronological narrative, and if she covertly relives certain of her dealings with him, her explicit relation of her fourth marriage is quick and dismissive. Having described how she made herself even with him, she moves on at once:

He deyde whan I cam fro Jerusalem,
And lith ygrave under the roode beem,
Al is his tombe noght so curyus
As was the sepulcre of hym Daryus,
Which that Appelles wroghte subtilly;
It nys but wast to burye hym preciously.
Lat hym fare wel; God yeve his soule reste!
He is now in his grave and in his cheste.
Now of my fifthe housbonde wol I telle.

(495–503)

This is the second half of a passage, only twenty-one lines long in all, that the Wife devotes to her fourth marriage, and we might suppose that the brevity of her treatment indicates a lack of interest in it, a desire to get on to the next man and the issue of sovereignty, especially since what we hear about the marriage is inconclusive on that central topic. In terms of "maistrye" it sounds like a rather unsatisfactory draw at best. But from a retrospective vantage the sense of a lack of resolution is the most important thing about the account. I have just suggested that the concerns of the fourth marriage are at work in the text at various points where the surface does not explicitly refer to them; this in turn suggests that the Wife is more concerned with these matters than she lets on publicly.

The fourth was a troubled marriage, and the style of the Wife's avoidance of it suggests how much it still troubles her, even though her presentation does not fully clarify what the trouble was. When she first announces that she will talk about the fourth marriage, the Wife proceeds immediately to digress, as I have already noted. When she comes back to it, in the passage under examination, she tells us something she left out before, something that does not seem to have been the case with her first three marriages—that she cared about what her fourth husband did: "I seye, I hadde in herte greet despit / That he of any oother had delit" (481–82). As Doris Palomo notes, the image the Wife chooses to describe her revenge, "I made him of the same wode a croce" (484), "itself suggests a sorrow that talionic justice could not completely alleviate" (" 'Bad Husbands,' " 308). Moreover, the Wife is concerned to assert her physical fidelity—"Nat of my body, in no foul manere" (485)—in a way she has not previously felt necessary. In her account of the first three marriages she appears content to allow the imputation of infidelity to pass without comment, as in "A wys

wyf, if that she kan hir good, / Shall beren hym on honde the cow is
wood" (231–32, cf. 399), but here she goes out of her way to deny it.
It appears that she not only *was* but also *is* more involved, in some
sense more committed to the fourth marriage, since even now she does
not like to think of herself as open to the charge of having betrayed it.
More of what might be called her self-project, more of what the Wife
feels and wants herself to be, is here somehow bound up with this bad
husband than with the three good old rich ones.

It thus seems likely that the relatively abrupt dismissal of the fourth
husband arises as much from a reluctance or disinclination to deal with
the issues he raises for the Wife as from anything else, and we may
suppose that the businesslike way she moves forward into the account
of her fifth marriage is connected with her desire to have done with the
fourth. Certainly it is notable that she rounds off her initial description
of her life with number five with a return to the public project and its
economic framework. Her explanation of why she loved this husband
best, with its supply-and-demand account of desire and its concluding
proverbial generalization (503–24) comes, after so much vivid remembering, as a real check. It points up by contrast how the fourth marriage has not been integrated into the larger argument.

Yet the Wife's economic interpretation of her sexual experiences
with her fifth husband is reductive, and there are signs that she herself
is aware of that. Her initial characterization of him, "God lete his soule
nevere come in helle!" (504) seems warmer than the subsequent analysis will entirely account for, as does her reaction after the analysis is
completed:

> Greet prees at market maketh deere ware,
> And to greet cheep is holde at litel prys:
> This knoweth every womman that is wys.
>   My fifthe housbonde—God his soule blesse!—
> Which that I took for love, and no richesse . . .
> (522–26)

Indeed, the last line quoted here sounds like a pointed denial, at least
in emotional terms, of the economic analysis, *Nevertheless,* I took him
for love. The sense this response gives of the Wife's dissatisfaction with
the economic explanation, her feeling that at the least it is not enough
to explain her relationship with her fifth husband, is of course confirmed by the extensive account of it that she goes on to give in the rest

of the prologue. But it also appears that she cannot adequately assess the relationship without considering its beginnings, and that need carries her back to the end of her fourth marriage.[3] The tension that is suppressed in the Wife's attempt to dismiss her fourth husband and get on to her fifth resurfaces in her interest in reexamining the transition: there is something there that is still unresolved.

This sense of unresolved complexity increases as the Wife's narration continues. Though her account of her fifth marriage and the circumstances leading up to it is as full of sweeping generalizations as any part of the poem, it is also rich with reexperiencing and the enjoyment of recollection. There are vivid memories of persons ("God have hir soule! Hir name was Alisoun" [530]), of places ("To vigilies and to processiouns, / To prechyng eek, and to thise pilgrimages, / To pleyes of myracles, and to mariages" [556–58]), and even of things. Muscatine long ago noted how full it was of what he thought of as her particular, concrete, "bourgeois" style:

> And wered upon my gaye scarlet gytes.
> Thise wormes, ne thise motthes, ne thise mytes,
> Upon my peril, frete hem never a deel;
> And wostow why? For they were used weel.
>
> (559–62)[4]

Within this context of renewed memory, however, the Wife's account of her dealings with her fifth husband before the death of her fourth is conspicuously and deliberately pitched as an exemplary tale of feminine calculation, manipulation, and deceit. Her initial approach was made "of my purveiance"—just in case, we might say—and the follow-up was engineered by means of a piece of "wifelore" (to adapt an idea of Donald Howard's),[5] a bit of instruction passed down from mother to daughter about how to get men to think and feel what you want them to:

> I bar hym on honde he hadde enchanted me—
> My dame taughte me that soutiltee—
> And eek I seyde I mette of hym al nyght,

3. This point is noted by Rowland, "Untimely Death," 276.
4. Muscatine, *French Tradition*, 205 and 269 n. 57, citing Lowes on the force of "thise."
5. See Howard's discussion of "knightlore," *Idea of the Canterbury Tales*, 228–29.

He wolde han slayn me as I lay upright,
And al my bed was ful of verray blood;
"But yet I hope that ye shal do me good,
For blood bitokeneth gold, as me was taught."
And al was fals; I dremed of it right naught,
But as I folwed ay my dames loore,
As wel of this as of othere thynges moore.

(575–84)

But what are we to do with the carefully vague and uninformative way we are told that the Wife's sense of "purveiance" was awakened when "in the feeldes walked we, / Til trewely we hadde swich daliance, / This clerk and I" (564–66) and that she began to think about the need for another mousehole? Just what did happen out there?[6] What are we to make, in the light of the apparent coolness with which this account is framed, of her reaction at her fourth husband's funeral, a moment when we might expect (as Deschamps does) that calculation and purveyance would especially prevail?

And Jankyn, oure clerk, was oon of tho.
As help me God, whan that I saugh hym go
After the beere, me thoughte he hadde a paire
Of legges and of feet so clene and faire
That al myn herte I yaf unto his hoold.

(595–99)[7]

6. What became, for instance, of the disappearing chaperone, Alys, whose presence, announced at line 548, does not affect subsequent events as much as might be expected?
7. It is a measure of the extent to which the contextualization of her remembering has enabled the Wife to appropriate and revalue the antifeminist topoi on which her self-presentation as the Great Unscatheable Cootie is based that the effect of this passage is utterly unlike that of its source in Deschamps, where the third-person narration and the lack of any extraneous affect stress only the callous calculation attributed to the generic wife:

Du service, obseque et les lays
Oir vouldra parler jamais,
Excepté d'une courte messe;
Et regardera, en la presse
A porter le deffunct en terre,
Quel mari elle pourra querre
Et avoir aprés cesti cy.

She'll never want to hear anything about a funeral service, obsequies and songs, except for a short mass, and she'll be looking out in the crowd that carries the dead man to burial for whatever husband she can find to take after this one.

Eustace Deschamps, *Le Miroir de mariage*, lines 1971–77, quoted in Whiting, "Wife of Bath's Prologue," 220.

What, above all, are we to do with the attention-getting fact that the Wife's narration of the dream she did not dream makes her for once lose her place? "But now, sire, lat me se, what shal I seyn. / A ha! By God, I have my tale ageyn" (585–86).

The critics who detect between the lines of this account a conspiracy of the Wife and Janekyn to murder the fourth husband, followed in some versions by Janekyn's execution for the crime (a scenario that cleans up a number of otherwise uncertain matters in the text), are at least right that something is somehow being displaced here and that there are features of the text that are suspiciously, because conspicuously, unclear, though I am by no means as sure as they are of what the secret is.[8] I begin, however, by noting along with Palomo (" 'Bad Husbands,' " 309) that the Wife's enthusiasm for Janekyn's feet and legs looks like a feint to distract attention from whatever "daliance" went on in the field. Unlike Palomo, however, I go on to note that one of the things this ploy accomplishes is to defer any hint of actual emotional attachment on the Wife's part until after the fourth husband's death and make it sound as if only then she actually fell in love.[9] I connect this deferral in turn with the observations I have already made about the Wife's concern to deny that her "twisting" of her unfaithful husband extended to actual physical infidelity on her part (483–88) and perhaps as well to a certain tone of affection that creeps into her account of husband number four at points. The most telling circumstance in the Wife's account, however, is her casual revelation of her fifth husband's name at the point in the prologue where she tells how they went "into the feeldes" (548–49).

Janekyn is the only one of the Wife's husbands who is named by her, a fact that is itself interesting, and she announces his name at an appropriate point in her chronological account, when he enters on the scene as a potential husband. But of course that is not the first time the name itself occurs in the prologue. A Janekyn is mentioned as a (false)

8. Palomo, " 'Bad Husbands,' " is the best of these. If, as I think, she goes astray, she does so in response to real and important features of the text. She and Rowland, "Timely Death," share a certain cheerful bloodthirstiness and an attractive refusal to subject the Wife's actions to solemn moralizing. This is less true of Sands, "Non-comic Wife." For a sympathetic and sensible criticism of this view, see Hamel, "Contemporary Murder."

9. D. S. Silva takes the bait here: "Only on the day of the funeral did love become real" ("Wife of Bath's Marital State," 9).

witness, along with the Wife's niece, to the things the three old husbands are supposed to have "seyden in hir dronkenesse" (381–83), and
this niece is mentioned again later as one of the people to whom the
Wife was in the habit of betraying her fourth husband's most embarrassing secrets (534–42). This second mention creates a chronological
problem, of course, if we try to fit the Janekyn also mentioned earlier
as "oure apprentice" in the three-old-husbands period into a marital
career that begins when the Wife is twelve and ends twenty-eight years
later by delivering the same Janekyn at the age of twenty into the arms
of the forty-year-old widow.[10] For all I know (and the text refuses to
decide) there were in actual fact two or even three Janekyns in the
Wife's past at different times. But I am too enamored of the variant of
Leicester's razor that runs *Joanniculi non sunt multiplicandi sine ne-*
cessitate to rest in mere chronological probability, and I want to insist
that in the virtual now of the Wife's telling there is only one Janekyn
because the first occasion when the name is mentioned speaks, in
retrospect, with utter precision to the issues and tensions that presently
concern us:

> And yet of oure apprentice Janekyn,
> For his crispe heer, shynyng as gold so fyn,
> And for he squiereth me bothe up and doun,
> Yet hastow caught a fals suspecioun.
> *I wol hym noght, thogh thou were deed tomorwe!*
> (303–7, emphasis added)

Once again what comes later reinterprets what went before. What for
the pilgrim listeners can at most be a matter of vague puzzlement
(Didn't she say something about . . . ?) is for us as (re)readers an
opportunity to trace another strand of the Wife's private reworking of
the text of herself. We can see that this earliest mention of Janekyn,
which first functions as part of an exemplary tirade in the interests of
feminine mastery, is also an address to the fourth husband and another
voice in the Wife's continuing conversation with herself about the
meaning of the end of her fourth marriage.

The Wife remains uneasy about her feelings at this period and
unsure how to interpret them. In the circumstances one cannot give

10. Palomo, " 'Bad Husbands,' " 311, notes the connection but takes it as real,
referring to a subteenage Janekyn who grew up with the Wife.

much weight to the possibility that she is concerned about having her career appear to the pilgrim audience like that of "a respectable woman"—it is a bit late for that—but I do think she wants to respect herself. As Gayatri Spivak remarks, "The will to explain [is] a symptom of the desire to have a self and a world" ("Explanation and Culture," 105), an observation that is true of the *Wife of Bath's Prologue* in numerous ways but here prompts the reflection that so can be the will not to explain. The pattern of the Wife's reticences suggests that she would like to feel that her actions and emotions developed according to a scenario that kept her in control of herself and others: she is trying to minimize the overlaps and ambivalences of disappointment and desire, commitment and self-protection, and thought, word, and deed that arose in the transition from one marriage to another and still arise in telling about it. Like a dramatic-theory critic, the Wife wants to construct an objective and coherent history and personality for herself: she would like to be more of a self and less of a subject than she feels she is. Being somewhat closer to the textual evidence, she finds it harder than other such critics to ride over contradictory evidence in making her interpretation.

The murder theory seems to me to represent a misplaced concretion that strives to find definite events to resolve an uncomfortable emotional tension in the text. This tension is uncomfortable for the Wife first, and her inability or unwillingness to resolve it passes the discomfort along to the critics, who would like to be rid of what she cannot or will not shake: the ambivalence and uncertainty of the relation of events and feelings in her past, the tension between her desire to be quit and her uncertainty about who wronged whom. No one I have read has come up with a fully satisfying interpretation of the Wife's allusion to the *Alexandreis* and the tomb of Darius in relation to the burial of her fourth husband (495–502). I do not understand the full weight of the reference either, but I can offer the following observation. To stop remembering and talking about the fourth husband is, in the present of narrating, a version of what the murder-theory critics are also talking about: it is to put him back in his grave and his chest. From this point of view the allusion briefly delays the very dismissal it is part of to consider how a tomb might be decorated and what is appropriate in a memorial. To raise and dismiss the tomb of Darius is, in this context, to raise a possibility in the present before letting it go; there is perhaps a tinge of regret in "It nys but wast to burye hym preciously" for something that did not work out, that does not deserve, but might have deserved, a better memorial, or that the Wife momentarily wishes might have.

What emerges, then, from behind the explicit, chronological, public project of the prologue is a set of alternative accounts of the Wife's career that she seems to construct privately for herself in the mode of practical consciousness, hovering undecidably between the unconscious and discursive self-consciousness according to an associational, spontaneous, and detemporalized logic.[11] In these accounts chronology and causality are continually being bypassed, subverted, and reinterpreted and questions like, Why did I chide? or, How did (do) I feel about my fourth marriage? are entertained in a mode of genuine uncertainty and exploration. They are thus also accounts in which the Wife's subjectivity emerges because they do not produce a single, "true" private self revealed behind the facade of the public performance. Rather, these readings develop an image of her as a self fragmented, ambivalent, pulled in different directions by different contending forces which the self as such does not originate or entirely control. The voicing of her performance makes the Wife a site of multiple voices, or multiple voicings of the same text, that speak the different roles, projects, desires, and constraints of the divided subject. Both the style of reading/remembering that obtains here and the image of the subject it produces proceed according to the logic of the rhizome as developed by Deleuze and Guattari.[12]

A rhizome is botanically a subterranean stem system, as in tubers, mint, and crabgrass, that performs some of the functions of a root but without the division into central and subordinate units of a branching taproot so that absolute hierarchies of function or importance do not

11. Compare Lee Patterson's description of lines 452–80: "A structural image of dilation, an opening into the subject that is framed by a delayed narrative movement, . . . stands as a paradigm for the rest of the Prologue, which consists of small narrative movements intercalated and retarded with increasingly detailed self-revelations. These digressions are not, as Geoffrey de Vinsauf would say, leaps off to the side of the road, but motivations for the very narrative they retard. Not only, in other words, does the interleaving of digressive meditations within the narrative provide an image of dilation, but the narrative itself is both an opening up and a standing still, a deepening explication of that which is already known" (" 'For the Wyves Love of Bathe,' " 678–79).

12. Deleuze and Guattari, "Introduction: Rhizome," in *Mille Plateaux*, 9–37. Quotations in the next paragraph are from John Johnstone's translation in *On the Line*, 1–65.

exist: "Any point on a rhizome can be connected with any other, and must be" (11). "There are no points or positions in a rhizome, as one finds in a structure, tree, or root. There are only lines" (17). Deleuze and Guattari generalize the properties of rhizomes to a vast array of other systems, including the brain, language, and social organizations, and give the following summary of those properties:

> Unlike trees or their roots, the rhizome connects any point with any other point, and none of its features necessarily refers to features of the same kind. . . . It has neither beginning nor end, but always a middle, through which it pushes and overflows. It constitutes linear multiplicities in n dimensions, without subject or object. . . . In opposition to centered systems (even multicentered), with hierarchical communication and pre-established connections, the rhizome is an a-centered system, non-hierarchical and non-signifying, without a General, without an organizing memory or central autonomy, uniquely defined by a circulation of states.
>
> (47–49)

What comes into focus in the Wife's account is an image of her life as a manifold of this sort, where any point can be connected to any other point in any order according to immediate local (practical) needs and conditions without any privileged center or dominant path.[13] As Deleuze and Guattari point out, the notion of a rhizome is opposed to that of a life or a book "constituted by the interiority of a substance or a subject" (17), by which they mean an author in the traditional romantic sense or what I have been calling a self. Indeed, from this perspective it makes no more sense to speak of *a* life or *a* book than it does to speak of *a* rhizome, as if such a radical heterogeneity were one thing: "They are designated by . . . partitives (*some* crab grass, *some* rhizome . . .)" (17). But if this is an image of the Wife's reading and of

---

13. Deleuze and Guattari's discussion of long-term and short-term memory is relevant here:

> Neurologists and psychophysiologists distinguish between long-term and short-term memory (on the order of a minute). So the difference is not only quantitative: short-term memory is diagrammatic, a kind of rhizome, whereas long-term memory is arborescent and centralized (imprint, engram, trace or photo). Short-term memory is in no way subject to a law of contiguity or immediacy in relation to its object; it can exist at a distance, coming back or returning much later, but always under conditions of discontinuity, rupture, and multiplicity. Furthermore, the two types of memory are not distinguishable as two temporal modes of apprehension of the same thing: what is grasped by the two is not the same, neither the same memory, nor even the same idea.
>
> (*On the Line*, 33–35)

her history, it is also an image of the memory that contains and enables
them: therefore it is an image of her subjectivity, of the kind of thing
she must be to do what she does. I want to conclude this section by
examining two other important examples of this subjectivity in action.
They form two rhizomes that map, respectively, the subject's internal
experience of its own self-undoing and the deconstruction of an external, institutional identity: the Wife's dream and her horoscope. Since
there is no such thing, if the analysis is followed far enough, as an
independent or separate rhizome, the two ultimately turn out to be
interconnected.

Let us begin with the false dream that the Wife used to beguile Janekyn
before her fourth husband's death (575–84). We have already noted
how her narration of this dream leads her to lose the thread of her
discourse, and a plausible interpretation of the stumble is that she
becomes caught up in remembering a dream more important to her
than she wants to admit—that is, that she really did dream it after all.
It may well be so, but since I am less interested in constructing yet
another history for the Wife than in following the ways she does it
herself, I want to put the situation a little differently. Strictly speaking,
the fundamental undecidability between self-presentation and self-
revelation that informs the Wife's discourse applies as much to the
so-called historical facts as to anything else. Since all we have in the
text is the Wife's performance in the virtual now of the pilgrimage, no
item of her reminiscence can be taken unproblematically as fact. She
may always be falsifying, as I fear she is doing here, and the question
of falsification itself is by no means a simple one. What we can say is
that whatever may have happened as experience in the past, in the now
of speaking the prologue the dream takes on importance as a focus of
certain fundamental themes of the text. When the Wife says of the
dream that "al was fals," we perhaps do not entirely believe her, but
we do not thereby simply convict her of lying, especially when we see
that the public assertion that the dream was a deception is not canceled
by the suspected private one that it was evidence of uncontrollable
passion. Nor in fact was either of these two possibilities canceled by
the other in the past when Janekyn got them with the signs reversed.
We do not, after all, suppose the Wife to have been unaware of the
likely effect of telling the dream to Janekyn even if she did dream it, nor
can we assume that she is not inviting the present audience's more or

less conscious complicity in a pretense that she did not.[14] She did not and does not necessarily tell all she knows to Janekyn or the pilgrims, which only shows that authentic experience, if there is such a thing, can be manipulated for effect too. The question of the dream's truth or falsity is genuinely undecidable at a different level: it is the question posed by the Wife's stance to the audience as well as to Janekyn of the *relation* of desire to deception, of the place of sincerity in the struggle for advantage and, of the advantages that accrue to sincerity. The generalized form of this question is precisely what the dream, true or false, is about.

The subtext of the dream is first of all a counterstatement to the commodity view of sexuality that informs both the public argument of the prologue, in general, and the framing of the dream itself as a deception aimed at gaining an advantage, in particular. The pivotal statement in the Wife's account is "blood bitokeneth gold," which can be, and has been, read as a reminder to Janekyn of what he stands to gain by marrying her.[15] The connection of this juncture to other themes of the poem arises through the implications of the dream itself: "He wolde han slayn me as I lay upright, / And al my bed was ful of verray blood" (578–79). Palomo and others have noted how this image takes on meaning in the light of the Wife's career as an evocation of loss of virginity and inflects her mother's lore in the direction of the commodification of sexuality:

> Her mother promoted [the Wife's first] marriage. Years later, the Wife invents a dream for Jankyn's benefit in which she imagines herself slain at night, her bed full of blood. She interprets this dream according to her mother's precepts: "blood bitokeneth gold." Such words to a young girl on the verge of marriage inform her that in exchange for the bloody rupture of the hymen the girl will acquire wealth—exactly the reason comely young virgins like Alisoun and May were married off to fumbling Januaries.[16]

14. We ought not in general to ignore the element of this kind of complicity throughout the prologue, present in such things as the more or less open invitation the Wife offers us to laugh sympathetically with her at the unmerited sufferings of her old husbands—poor things—and the other complicity effects that derive from the basic move she shares with the Pardoner of letting us look behind the scenes.

15. See, for example, Oberembt, "Chaucer's Anti-misogynist Wife of Bath," 293. Here, as elsewhere, this sort of perception sometimes leads to the imputation that Janekyn only married the Wife for her money, as seems to be implied by David, *Strumpet Muse*, 151, and even (oddly, though as usual complexly) by Owen, *Pilgrimage and Storytelling*, 152.

16. Palomo, " 'Bad Husbands,' " 305. See also Shapiro, "Dame Alice."

The other implication of blood, however, is violence—an implication fully registered in the dream—and this dual meaning completes a circuit. Like any other commodity in a relation of exchange, the value of sexuality is fully convertible; that is, gold also betokens blood, and in the dream blood betokens not only loss of virginity but also death. This convergence of gold, sex, and death in the dream is a powerful image in itself, but it becomes still more powerful as it twists and shifts rhizomatically backward and forward through the Wife's text and her life.

One strand of this system winds back into the past and generates a revisionary perspective on the Wife's understanding of the relation between sexuality and economics as forces in play in the institution of marriage. When gold is not being used to trade for blood, it has to be kept somewhere, and the Wife's word for where it is kept, *cheste* or *chiste,* builds up associations with death via her fourth husband:

> It nys but wast to burye hym preciously.
> Lat hym fare wel; God yeve his soule reste!
> He is now in his grave and in his cheste.
>
> (500–502)

> But tel me this: why hydestow, with sorwe,
> The keyes of thy cheste awey fro me?
> It is my good as wel as thyn, pardee!
> What, wenestow make an ydiot of oure dame?
> Now by that lord that called is Seint Jame,
> Thou shalt nat bothe, thogh that thou were wood,
> Be maister of my body and of my good;
> That oon thou shalt forgo, maugree thyne yen.
> What helpith it of me to enquere or spyen?
> *I trowe thou woldest loke me in thy chiste!*
>
> (308–17, emphasis added)[17]

The chance to read textually—to read backward and forward, rhizomatically—lets us see what else the Wife's practical consciousness registers about the commodification of sex in the institution of marriage, counter to her apparent ready acceptance of a disenchanted and competitive view. The sacrifice of pleasure, spontaneity, independence, and affection that the conversion of blood and gold entails is a

17. The connection is first made at line 44b: "Bothe of here nether purs and of here cheste." Besides the lines cited in the text, account should be taken of the request made by the knight in the tale: "Taak al my good and lat my body go" (1061).

bad bargain, not least because it encourages a woman to accept the valuation the system places on her—"to greet chepe is holde at litel prys"—and thus acquiesce in her own dehumanization. The Wife's text embodies her insight that this aspect of the system of marriage, represented in the men who have enacted it, has, like one aspect of Janekyn in the dream, been trying all her life to kill her.

There is still another set of implications to be read out of the knot of tokenings in the dream,[18] a strand that runs forward into the Wife's fifth marriage and the rest of the prologue. This reading of the dream takes a more positive stance toward sexuality and its possibilities and allows us to recuperate those aspects of the Wife's sexual experience that make it more to her than an instrument of exploitation, dehumanization, and murder. We can begin to follow this strand by asking how the dream might function as a projection of the Wife's attitudes toward a potential relationship with Janekyn. As I have already suggested, the dream portrays him as a violent attacker and therefore may be thought to embody a fear that he will turn out to be like all the other men in her life, the agent of a murderous system. Those aspects of the dream that present it as a scene of defloration, however, can have a more positive side if the dream is understood not only as an expression of anxiety but also as a wish. The thought here is something like a desire to start over, to become a virgin again for this man and give oneself "for love, and no richesse," without the taint of commodification that has hitherto marked sexuality for the Wife. It is at least suggestive that shortly after her account of the dream the Wife expresses the warmest feelings about her sexuality in general that she has achieved in the prologue thus far, and she does so in terms that present a more mutual and less exploitative view of it than previously. Part of her pleasure in sex here derives from the fact that others enjoyed it too:

> As help me God, I was a lusty oon,
> And faire, and riche, and yong, and wel bigon,

18. We might think of the dream as the navel of the prologue, somewhat in the way Freud, in a passage that anticipates Deleuze and Guattari's idea of the rhizome, speaks of "the dream's navel, the spot where it reaches down into the unknown. The dream-thoughts to which we are led by interpretation cannot, from the nature of things, have any definite endings; they are bound to branch out in every direction into the intricate network of our world of thought. It is at some point where this meshwork is particularly close that the dream-wish grows up, like a mushroom out of its mycelium" (*Interpretation of Dreams,* 564).

> And trewely, as myne housbondes tolde me,
> I hadde the beste *quoniam* myghte be.
>
> (605–608)[19]

What makes a reading of this sort most convincing to me, however, is that the Wife presents herself as having acted on the wish, so to speak, at the beginning of her marriage to Janekyn:

> What sholde I seye but, at the monthes ende,
> This joly clerk, Jankyn, that was so hende,
> Hath wedded me with greet solempnytee,
> And to hym yaf I al the lond and fee
> That evere was me yeven therbifoore.
>
> (627–31)

The logic of this action is the convertibility of blood and gold: if the appearance of affection is a commodity in the marriage market, then commodities—land and fee—can function in the right circumstances as evidence of affection. After all, that was the way in which the Wife's old husbands sought to manifest their desire for her, and she may well have taken it as an appropriate way to demonstrate love when she came to feel it—especially since there is nothing inherently implausible about the idea. To give what one owns to another need not be a calculated act of exploitation or an attempt to buy the love one can obtain in no other way: it can be a way of giving oneself.

If this logic is what motivated the Wife, however, it quickly emerged in the marriage, and does so even more quickly in the telling, that she made a mistake: "But afterward repented me ful soore" (633). She lost the instruments of control she was accustomed to have over her husbands—"He nolde suffre nothyng of my list" (634)—and she had to put up with *his* chiding. But what is really interesting about this changed situation is the insight it provided, and provides, for the Wife into her own character:

> Stibourn I was as is a leonesse,
> And of my tonge a verray jangleresse,
> And walke I wolde, as I had doon biforn,
> From hous to hous, although he hadde it sworn;
> For which he often tymes wolde preche,
> And me of olde Romayn geestes teche.
>
> (637–42)

19. This passage itself arises from the memory of Janekyn's feet and legs, 596ff.

It should be remembered that even with the fourth husband the Wife's jangling and walking out are understood and presented primarily as a response to something that was done to her first. Certainly her earlier accounts, such as the one that prefaces her dalliance with Janekyn in the field (543–62), register her enjoyment: "For evere yet I loved to be gay" (545). But these pleasures are contaminated by the need to control her husband by gossiping about his intimate secrets and wandering to give the appearance of frying him in his own grease. To put it in a historical frame for a moment, it could be said that what the Wife learned was that marrying Janekyn for love did not change her love of independence, her enthusiasm for gossip, or her interest in gathering new experiences. When those characteristics no longer had to function instrumentally in the system of competition and dominance, they became valuable for their own sakes. When she no longer needed them to make her way in a man's world, the Wife discovered that she also liked them for other reasons.

What is mapped by following out the dream rhizome is a set of undecidable oppositions that are enacted in the events of the Wife's life and embodied in her subjectivity as she tells it. These oppositions manifest themselves at every level, from the generalized relation to the old husbands and the abstract authority of the beginning of the prologue to the complex intimacy with Janekyn and the uncertainties of her relation to the audience. The dream presents in condensed, imaginal form what is opened up by the various moments and events that are connected to it by associative links: the subjective contradictions involved in desiring someone one also deceives and taking advantage of someone for whom one also feels affection, which at the same time engage the wider institutional contradictions inherent both in the economic and affective components of marriage and ultimately, as we shall see, in the social construction of gender. These contradictions are enacted in the Wife's narrated history in a way that suggests increasing self-consciousness about them and even a degree of mastery, but the fact that they continue to be represented in the present of telling stresses that they are not resolved or transcended, only more expertly deployed and better practiced.

Still, it seems accurate to say that a shift in the balance of forces and interpretations takes place as the prologue unfolds. From one point of view the narrative continues to be one in which the Wife follows a line through the rhizome of the "matere" of memory that moves from experience to authority. She presents marriage as competition and strife and picks that thread out of the varied weave of five marriages to arrive at the final and most general moral of "maistrye." It is apparent by now, however, that the unfolding of the narrative is increasingly interrupted by pockets of vivid remembering and feeling engaged in for a variety of reasons that are marginal to the public project. As these pockets accumulate, they decenter the project and create a counter-movement from authority to experience. As this movement comes to dominate the last third of the prologue, it begins to affect the Wife's generalizations themselves more directly. The alternating rhythm of the poem between memory and summary continues, but now the memories more openly question and correct the summaries, and the act of generalizing becomes a more open, ongoing, and explicitly revisionary process. A crucial example of this process is the Wife's dealings with astrology, beginning with her account of her own horo-scope (609–14).

I used the astrology passage earlier as an instance of the way critics of various persuasions about the Wife make use of the same textual evidence to create different but equally reifying versions of her (see above, pp. 67–68). I want now to examine what I put to one side before, the Wife's own interpretation of her horoscope, a matter she is in less of a hurry than the critics to decide. We may conveniently begin with the famous couplet that summarizes her natal constellation, "Myn ascendent was Taur, and Mars therinne. / Allas, allas! That evere love was synne!" (613–14). Its tone is by no means clear. Curry thinks it is a tragic utterance, voiced in repentant bitterness at the life that has been forced on the Wife by an unholy constellation (*Medieval Sciences*, 113), and Wood sees it as something more like a boast, "not an expression of repentance but a comment on an inconvenience" (*Country of the Stars*, 180). But surely what makes the couplet so striking is the way it calls attention to a discrepancy between the *fact* of a certain horoscope and its emotional *meaning* for the speaker. The effect arises precisely from the gap, the failure of connection, between the two perspectives, the descriptive ("Myn ascendent was Taur") and the emotional ("Allas, allas!"). The critics hasten to fill the gap and thereby in their differing readings they enact, rather than describe, the tension the gap creates. But inscribed in that gap is the Wife's discovery of her own uncertainty, her subjecthood. She is using the horoscope to classify and explain herself, just as Curry and Wood are. Classification and explanation are, after all, the most respectably scientific function of astrology in medieval culture, the function that naturalizes it and makes it look ideologically neutral—that is, makes it an *institution*. In the case of the Wife, however, the intrusive line in the couplet betrays her inability or unwillingness to rest in the definition the horoscope offers. She seems to feel a need to comment further:

> I folwed ay myn inclinacioun
> By vertu of my constellacioun;
> That made me I koude noght withdrawe
> My chambre of Venus from a good felawe.
> (615–18)

The Wife does seem to argue as an astrological determinist in this passage. She declares that she followed her "inclinacioun" (here, I take it, a technical term meaning the disposition given by the stars) because of the power ("vertu") of her natal constellation, which made her unable to withhold her planet-dominated "chambre of Venus" from good fellows—"I koude noght" sounds a certain note of helplessness.

Having disposed of the influence of Venus on her life, the Wife turns to that of Mars, or so it appears: "Yet have I Martes mark upon my face, / And also in another privee place" (619–20). The structure of the speech implies some sort of division and distinction—Venus made me do *this*, and Mars made me do *that*—and the influence of the red planet does appear to be similarly conceived as a stamp of character, a mark impressed from outside, like the "prente of seinte Venus seel" earlier (604). The difficulty with this reading is that by the end of the speech the apparent distinction between *this* and *that* breaks down as it becomes evident that Venus and Mars are being invoked to explain not different kinds of behavior but the same phenomenon, namely, the Wife's lack of discretion:

> Yet have I Martes mark upon my face,
> And also in another privee place.
> For God so wys be my savacioun,
> I ne loved nevere by no discrecioun,
> But evere folwede myn appetit,
> Al were he short, or long, or blak, or whit;

I took no kep, so that he liked me,
How poore he was, ne eek of what degree.
(619–26)

This conclusion is a return to the Wife's indiscretions in a more independent and martian spirit. She followed, she says, not a relatively
passive "inclinacioun" but the more active "appetit," and she did so
not helplessly with anyone at all but with anyone she liked "so that he
liked me." The end of the passage gives us a different image of the Wife
as someone who made conditions and exercised choices, who only
gave in to her astrologically conditioned character when she found
someone who appreciated her.[20] As it proceeds, the passage looks less
and less like a single, worked-out explanation of the influence of
various astrological forces on different aspects of the Wife's character
and more like a reworking, a set of alternative explanations of the
same behavior.

Here the astrology rhizome and the dream rhizome begin to connect
because what is at issue in the conflicting claims of Mars and Venus is
a version of the same undecidability manifested in the dream, a question about the conflicting roles of desire and aggression in sexuality
linked to a question about autonomy and involuntary action. It is not
as if the Wife (or Chaucer for that matter) did not believe at all in
astrological influences, and she is surely not wrong to feel that Venus
and Mars have crucially influenced her life. Those names refer to
forces at work in the individual and society, to desire and aggression,
affection and conflict. They exist at the social level in institutions like
marriage and antifeminism that organize and constrain individuals,
and if we moderns are more prone to see them in the psyche as
components of the unconscious rather than as astral impulses beaming
in on us from the heavens, we experience them no less than our
medieval ancestors as *other,* as something that is both part of us and
beyond our conscious originating.

The critics can differ about determinism and freedom in this passage
because the Wife herself sets the critical agenda: she entertains both

20. Since the passage also contains some of the warmth of "trewely, as myne housbondes tolde me, / I hadde the beste *quoniam* myghte be," which immediately precedes
it, and since it expressly excludes poverty as a factor in the choice of a lover, it rejects
economic as well as astrological determinism.

positions in the course of the speech. In shifting from a deterministic position to a more active and independent one, she revises the relative importance of various aspects of her horoscope as well as her own relation to her stars as a cause of her actions, but without simply discarding the element of deterministic constraint in favor of a wholly untrammeled freedom and self-determination. What we have here is not an assertion of a fact about the Wife but an unfolding act of interpretation in which she tries out astrological explanation to see how well it fits her case. The horoscope is less a definition of her character than a means she herself uses to explore the meaning of her life, and by the end of the passage she herself seems to find that means—and that meaning—unsatisfactory. She drops the subject of the stars and proceeds with her story. The horoscope shifts in the Wife's own practice from something general and objective about her to a medium for encountering and articulating the tensions of her subjectivity—something more like a proposition about herself she makes, revises, and then discards. What happens to astrological explanation of human nature in the Wife's text is that both astrology and human nature are called into question. The text portrays an encounter between a subject and an institution whose first outcome here is to render the subject problematic in ways the institution cannot coherently register.

The full implications of this process emerge only later, when the Wife returns to astrology at the end of her first account of Janekyn's book, to explain how the book and Janekyn's horrid delight in its use exemplify the immemorial enmity, decreed by the stars, between women and clerks, the children of Venus and of Mercury:

> He knew of hem mo legendes and lyves
> Than been of goode wyves in the Bible.
> For trusteth wel, it is an impossible
> That any clerk wol speke good of wyves,
> But if it be of hooly seintes lyves,
> Ne of noon oother womman never the mo.
> Who peyntede the leon, tel me who?
> By God, if wommen hadde writen stories,
> As clerkes han withinne hire oratories,
> They wolde han writen of men moore wikkednesse
> Than al the mark of Adam may redresse.

> The children of Mercurie and of Venus
> Been in hir wirkyng ful contrarius;
> Mercurie loveth wysdam and science,
> And Venus loveth ryot and dispence.
> And, for hire diverse disposicioun,
> Ech falleth in otheres exaltacioun.
> And thus, God woot, Mercurie is desolat
> In Pisces, wher Venus is exaltat,
> And Venus falleth ther Mercurie is reysed.
> Therfore no womman of no clerk is preysed.
>   (686–706)

Once again the Wife presents a deterministic image, one that places the causes of clerical disapproval of women above and beyond human tampering or amelioration. As Wood is at pains to point out, this is not an intellectually respectable astrological explanation. He calls it "hilarious" (*Country of the Stars*, 174), and I expect the Wife would agree with him if it did not make her so angry. It seems clear, however, that she is parodying the kind of pretentious explanation we might expect a clerk, like Janekyn, to produce, for once again the Wife goes on to revise the inadequate initial account. She has a better explanation, and she delivers it immediately:

> The clerk, whan he is oold, and may nought do
> Of Venus werkes worth his olde sho,
> Thanne sit he doun, and writ in his dotage
> That wommen kan nat kepe hir mariage!
>   (707–10)

This is a likely enough image of the crabbed astrologer, and part of what gives it its punch and conviction is that it makes the influence of Venus an integral part of the character and experience of the children of Mercury, putting back together what the original distinction had torn asunder. Even more telling is the way this account locates clerkly antifeminism itself in the history of men's frustrations with their own bodies and with women. The Wife suggests that the antifeminist tradition is humanly produced in a way that has little to do with the stars or even with women[21] and identifies astrological explanation itself as a discourse not of matters of fact but of power (or knowledge-power, in

21. See Aers, *Creative Imagination*, 84.

the Foucaultian sense), a use men make of the stars to keep women down.

To follow the somewhat scattered and apparently rather unrelated instances of the Wife's dealings with astrology is to discover an inter-mittent but ongoing encounter, dropped only to be resumed again, whereby the Wife eventually achieves a certain mastery over the insti-tution by coming to understand it more adequately in her own terms. The Wife continues to work on and with astrological explanation until she arrives at a fully disenchanted and demystified understanding of what it is—in other words, how it is used. What enables her to reach this point, and what gives her working out its consistency, is the way she continually subjects abstract astrological formulations to a kind of experiential critique. She puts them in everyday circumstances, presses them to see whether they accord with her own feelings and memories, inquires into the circumstances in which they are used, and imagines (or remembers) the sort of persons who make use of them and their motives. The Wife is as tempted as anyone by the stability and clarity of these explanations; she begins by entertaining them as genuine possibilities for understanding her own behavior and that of others. It is precisely her own experience of doing so and her ongoing dissatisfac-tion with that experience that leads her to resist the temptation and revise the explanations as she proceeds.

The continuity of the Wife's dealings with astrological explanation shows how her experience of herself as a subject and her disenchant-ment, her sense of herself and her view of institutions, are intercon-nected and mutually reinforcing. Out of her practical dissatisfaction with the fit between her experience and her horoscope the Wife in the prologue generates the skeptical tendency of mind that enables her disenchanted deconstruction of astrology as an institution. At the same time the disenchanted point of view itself cannot be said to arise first from her consideration of the horoscope: it was already in operation before it was ever brought to bear on astrology. Neither perspective is founding, neither is prior. Both are, as deconstructionists say, always already in play. The text represents an encounter between a subject and an institution, between the Wife and astrology, an encounter whose outcome is to render both the subject and the institution prob-lematic. In this encounter the Wife progressively becomes more aware that what she and others had taken for a set of facts about her is actually a complex set of interpretations representing and concealing a complex set of social and personal interests. Hence the self posited by the Wife's horoscope, and the self-understanding based on it, was also an interpretation, the product of a complex and largely unwitting collusion or complicity between the Wife and society: she was, becomes, and is a construction, a subject.

4

Janekyn's Book

The Subject as Text

Despite the qualifications made in Chapter 3, it is evident that talking about the Wife's fifth marriage has the effect of making her more self-conscious. As she proceeds, she displays a more complex and assured self-understanding, which is also in certain ways more self-critical and discriminating. Her response to Janekyn's "olde Romayn geestes" (III, 642) and monorhymed proverbs (644–58), for example, is something a bit more complicated than an outright rejection:

> But al for noght, I sette noght an hawe
> Of his proverbes n'of his olde sawe,
> Ne I wolde nat of hym corrected be.
> *I hate hym that my vices telleth me,*
> And so doo mo, God woot, of us than I.
> (659–63, emphasis added)

What is new here is the Wife's willingness to admit that these things are vices, that is, to admit that she felt the pressure and, to a degree, the legitimacy of Janekyn's disapproval—and still feels it since the generalization is in the present tense. The scene of Janekyn preaching to her about her vices is from one point of view a repetition and reversal of the Wife's relation to her first three husbands—the antifeminist lore she used against them he now turns on her—and his book is the embodiment of everything she has been fighting all her life. Yet the differences in the Wife's description of the two situations are far more telling than the similarities, and they generate a significant revision of the earlier instances by the later ones.

What immediately distinguishes the Wife's account of Janekyn's book from her earlier citations of antifeminist lore is the time and detail she spends on contextualizing it as a particular book of a certain determinate makeup, one that was used in specific ways and under

specific conditions. The citations from scripture and the church fathers
in the opening of the prologue are presented as timeless, and often
nameless, authority. Whiting notes that "ten of the fifteen quotations
from Jerome are paralleled in the first one hundred and fifty lines of the
Wife's Prologue,"[1] yet neither the saint nor the name of his book is
mentioned there. The slanderous lore slanderously ascribed to the
three old husbands is similarly presented more or less as if it had fallen
from the sky, as an instance of the sort of things men say about
women. Here, however, we are given a full and even annotated table of
contents that identifies the occupations and other circumstances of
some of the authors:

> And eek ther was somtyme a clerk at Rome,
> A cardinal, that highte Seint Jerome,
> That made a book agayn Jovinian;
> In which book eek ther was Tertulan,
> Crisippus, Trotula, and Helowys,
> That was abbesse nat fer fro Parys.
>
> (673–78)

Not only does this material have sources in particular authors from
particular places and times; it is also used by Janekyn in specific
situations and, so to speak, in a certain tone. The crucial encounter
that led to the Wife's deafness took place "Upon a nyght" when
"Jankyn, that was oure sire, / Redde on his book, as he sat by the fire"
(713–14). The feeling of domestic comfort these lines suggest is supported elsewhere. It is true that Janekyn read often to the Wife, "every
nyght and day" (682), but only "Whan he hadde leyser and vacacioun /
From oother worldly occupacioun" (683–84). It is a leisure activity, a
kind of hobby, not an obsession. What is more, it is conducted in a
mood rather different from, say, the puritanical carping of the nameless interpreter of the Samaritan woman:

> He hadde a book that *gladly,* nyght and day,
> *For his desport* he wolde rede alway;
> He cleped it Valerie and Theofraste,
> *At which book he lough alwey ful faste.*
>
> (669–72, emphasis added)

---

1. That is, before the Pardoner's interruption, which occurs at line 163, Whiting,
"Wife of Bath's Prologue," 208.

What comes through in this description is not only the Wife's continued annoyance but also the fun Janekyn had baiting her. There is
something self-conscious and theatrical about him laughing over his
book in the Wife's presence, as if he read with an eye cocked to observe
the effect he was having; his aim seems at least as much to get a rise out
of her (in which he still succeeds) as to administer serious correction
for her horrid transgressions.

What allows this more nuanced reading to emerge is the accumula-
tion of contextual details that give the account the particularity and
density of experience rather than the abstraction and exemplarity of
authority. Who, how, and when matter here because they matter to the
Wife and press into her memory. This appeal to experience, to contexts
and sources, memories and uses, is one thing the Wife's account of
Janekyn's book and his use of it has in common with her account of
astrology. Identifying the aged, sexually frustrated child of Mercury as
the painter of lions is similar in important ways to identifying the
backgrounds of Saint Jerome and Héloïse, and even more so to identifying and describing Janekyn as the owner and user of the book. As
with astrology, the Wife's relation to the antifeminist tradition has
become more personalized, to the point where she can understand how
she looks to others—"I hate hym that my vices telleth me"—just as
with the impotent clerk she can put herself in a man's place and
understand his predicament.

One thing the disenchanted understanding of astrology and antifeminism does not do, however, is account for the Wife's relationship
to Janekyn and the function of the book in that relationship. The
nature of the relationship itself is something the Wife has also been
working on, at least since the early and inadequate attempt to sum it
up in terms of the economics of desire that led her to begin again with
the end of her fourth marriage (503–24). As she continues to remember, reexamine and redefine her fifth marriage, the meaning of her
relationship with Janekyn becomes for her more and more bound up in
the book of wicked wives. How "I was beten for a book, pardee!"
(712, cf. 634–36, 666–68) is the thread to which she keeps returning as
she moves through the digressive labyrinth of the end of the prologue,
and each time she does so her account of the book is more circumstantial, complex, and impassioned. What the couple made of Janekyn's
book—how it became not only his but also theirs, the symbol and

medium of their mutuality—is the subject of the Wife's final reading of it, to which I now turn.

There are a few brief exempla in the opening sermon section of the *Wife of Bath's Prologue,* none at all in the reported address to the first three husbands, and one (Metellius) set into a digression from the story of the fourth marriage (460–63). Two briefly cited "olde Romayn geestes" (642–49) might also be taken as exemplary, that is, as anecdotes about well-known or important persons that can be used to point up a moral. In the passage before us, however (711–70), there are nine exempla in a row, all on the same theme. No doubt these lives all add up to "Valerie"'s moral, which is also, more briefly, Janekyn's:

> Exemplum harum experimentum cape, quod audax est ad omnia quecunque amat vel odit femina, et artificiosa nocere cum vult, quod est semper; et frequenter cum iuuare parat obest, unde fit ut noceat ut nolens.[2]

> And thus algates housbondes han sorwe.
>
> (756)

Unlike a proverb, however, which has no life of its own beyond its particular applications except as part of the general backdrop of folk wisdom, an exemplum embodies the tension between experience and authority. Exempla can be thought of as selections from individual lives rather than distillations from collective life. Indeed, it is important that an exemplum have some claim to historicity because its authority is in fact empirical: the lives of actual persons prove that the general moral is true. Therefore, even when these lives are being used in an exemplary way, that is, when they are being put to official or collective ideological use, they hold something in reserve.[3] For moralizing purposes this fact about exempla represents something of a danger since the proof-text may not always collapse smoothly into the moral it is supposed to prove. In the case of the first example the Wife cites, this potential danger becomes explicit:

---

2. Walter Map, *Dissuasio Valerii,* iv, iii, 153f., in Whiting, "Wife of Bath's Prologue," 213. "Take example from these experiences how rash is every woman whatsoever to love or hate, both when she wishes by her cunning to do harm (which is always), or when, undertaking to aid, she hinders, so that she does harm without meaning to."

3. See the discussions in my articles " 'No Vileyns Word,' " 24 and passim, and "Oure Tonges *Différance*."

> Of Eva first, that for hir wikkednesse
> Was al mankynde broght to wrecchednesse,
> For which that Jhesu Crist hymself was slayn,
> That boghte us with his herte blood agayn.
> Lo, heere expres of womman may ye fynde
> That womman was the los of al mankynde.
>
> (715–20)

Even without invoking notions like *felix culpa* it is possible to feel that the final couplet of this passage does not exhaust the meaning of Eve; the central couplet, especially "That boghte us with his herte blood agayn," presses a set of consequences of Eve's action that makes the simple antifeminist moral seem more negative and less complex than the universal history to which it supposedly refers. Too much of the story is told to hold the antifeminist line, and this excess of narrative may remind us that there is still more. Though Mary is not explicitly mentioned here or among the daughters of Eve whose stories follow, her absence (like that of Adam, who is similarly suppressed) is conspicuous.

The general point I am arguing here is that the kind of citation involved in using an exemplum sets up with particular clarity the problems of extratextual reference, intertextuality, and the boundlessness of the text that have come to concern modern critical theory. These problems can be focused fairly simply and directly in the following question: Once we have allowed that the text we are reading is crossed by another text, that it has an allusion inserted in it, how do we decide when to stop reading that second text?[4] And what if the second text is itself a member of a body of texts, as is certainly the case with the preponderantly classical legends that make up Janekyn's list? There may not be much to say in favor of Delilah, who betrayed her husband for eleven hundred shekels of silver (Judg. 16), "Thurgh which treson loste he bothe his yen" (723),[5] but Janekyn's account of Dejanira begs a gloss:

---

4. See, for example, J. Hillis Miller, "Critic as Host." The systems of interpretation founded by Saint Augustine in *De doctrina christiana* and resurrected, more or less, by modern exegetical critics are of course addressed to these questions. The *Pardoner's Tale* suggests, however, that they should be seen as increasingly unsuccessful attempts on the part of official culture to set limits to an increasingly unstoppable textual productivity.

5. A longer view of the story of Samson, however, raises some questions. If we take into account the explanation in Judg. 4 of Samson's preference for one inappropriate

> Tho redde he me, if that I shal nat lyen,
> Of Hercules and of his Dianyre,
> That caused hym to sette hymself afyre.
>
> (724–26)

Jean de Meun (or rather li Gilos), in whose part of the *Roman de la Rose* Delilah and Dejanira are juxtaposed like this, is hard on the latter lady. He calls her the thirteenth monster, which Hercules, who "vainqui doze orribles montres," could not overcome, and in this he follows that version of the story that makes her gift of the shirt of Nessus to her husband a witting, jealous, vengeful act.[6] There is, however, another version, of which Ovid's telling in the *Metamorphoses* is a particularly full example. He makes it clear that Dejanira was misinformed by Fama, "quae veris addere falsa gaudet" (*Met.* 9.138–39), that Hercules was besotted with Iole. Dejanira unknowingly ("nescia," 9.155) sent her husband the poisoned shirt of Nessus because that treacherous centaur had told her it had the power to revive a waning love ("munus raptae velut inritamen amoris," 9.133). Similarly, Jerome dismisses Clytemnestra as "[dicitur] occidisse virum ob amorem adulteri"[7]— "for hire lecherye, / That falsly made hire husband for to dye" (737–38). Though she is scarcely an ideal wife, her reasons are not all negligible, including as they do Agamemnon's sacrifice of their daughter Iphigenia (*Met.* 12.28ff) at Aulis to ensure a favorable wind to carry him to his ten-year absence at Troy. Despite Walter Map and Janekyn, motives make a difference: it matters how and why Dejanira "caused" Hercules's immolation, whether lust was Clytemnestra's only passion, and even what God's intentions had to do with Samson's fate. The multiplication of texts of these stories does not make the questions any easier to answer.

Philistine woman—"parentes autem ejus [scil. Samson] nesciebant quod res a Domino fieret, et quaereret occasionem contra Philisthiim" (14:5)—we may wonder about Samson's second choice as well, especially in the light of the outcome, though it is perhaps only an Old Testament perspective that could take what happened to the temple of Dagon as a *fortunate* fall: "multoque plures [Samson] interfecit moriens, quam ante vivus occiderat" (Judg. 16:30).

6. *Roman de la Rose*, 9191–9206, in Whiting, "Wife of Bath's Prologue," 214. The line quoted in the text is 9192.

7. *Adversus Jovinianum*, i 48, col. 280, in Whiting, "Wife of Bath's Prologue," 212.

The next example the Wife cites is that of Eriphyle:

> that for an ouche of gold
> Hath prively unto the Grekes told
> Wher that hir housbonde hidde hym in a place,
> For which he hadde at Thebes sory grace.
>
> (743–46)

Though I am not satisfied that Chaucer's immediate source for the story has been found, Statius's *Thebaid* will suffice to begin to decenter the example and complicate the text. The problem is not so much the wicked wife, on whose perfidy, whatever it is, both Statius and her husband Amphiaraus agree, as the "ouche of gold," which is, whether she knows it or not, no bargain. This is the famous brooch of Thebes, whose possession by Eriphyle is but an episode in a larger career. The "dirum monile Harmoniae" (*Theb.* 2.266–67) was originally made for the wedding of Cadmus and Harmonia by Vulcan at the height of his disillusionment with his own marriage, when he had discovered that even trapping Venus and Mars *flagrante delicto* in bed together did not put a stop to their affair nor gain him the support of the gods: "capto postquam nil obstat amori/poena nec ultrices castigavere catenis" (*Theb.* 2.270–71, cf. *Met.* 4.170ff). Reflecting the mood of its maker, the necklace (as it is in the original and Jerome) is a thoroughly poisonous piece of work. Luctus, Ira, Dolor, and Discordia all aid in its making, and its curse is explicitly blamed (*Theb.* 2.289–305) for the misfortunes of all the women of the house of Thebes: for Harmonia's transformation into a serpent, which in Ovid's account is a result of her love for her husband Cadmus when she sees him transformed before her and asks the gods to join him (*Met.* 4.563–603); for Semele, blasted when Juno tricked her into forcing her lover, Jove, to manifest himself in his full divinity (*Met.* 3.259–309; cf. *Theb.* 2.293, "et fallax intravit limina Iuno"); for Jocasta's marital career with Laius and Oedipus, including the unwittingly incestuous bearing of Eteocles and Polynices, whose quarrel is the story of the *Thebaid* itself (*Theb.* 2.294–96); and for the outcome of the marriage of Argia of Argos to Polynices of Thebes, in part brought about by Eriphyle, who sent Amphiaraus to the war in return for the bauble. Argia gave Eriphyle the brooch willingly because she wanted the expedition to take place for her husband's sake—an interesting example of similar results from apparently different motives, as Polynices and Amphiaraus might testify (*Theb.* 2.297–305, 4.187–213).[8]

Chaucer himself presents us with a bemused reader of the brooch's history in the *Complaint of Mars:*

> The broche of Thebes was of such a kynde,
> So ful of rubies and of stones of Ynde
> That every wight, that sette on hit an ye,
> He wende anon to worthe out of his mynde;
> So sore the beaute wolde his herte bynde.
> Til he hit had, him thoghte he moste dye;
> And whan that hit was his, then shulde he drye
> Such woo for drede, ay while that he hit hadde,
> That wel nygh for the fere he shulde madde.
>
> And whan hit was fro his possessioun,
> Than had he double wo and passioun
> For he so feir a tresor had forgo;
> But yet this broche as in conclusioun
> Was not the cause of his confusioun,
> But he that wroghte hit enfortuned hit so
> That every wight that had hit shulde have wo;
> And therfore in the worcher was the vice,
> And in the covetour that was so nyce.
>
> (*Mars*, 245–62)

Mars's growing uncertainty in this passage about where to lay the blame for the melancholy and terrible events associated with the brooch seems to me an entirely appropriate reaction to the tangle of complicities, complexities, and causalities it knots together, for who could ascribe them all to a single cause? What does it mean for Eri-

---

8. In *Troilus and Criseyde* Criseyde calls upon her mother "that cleped were Argyve" (4.762). Robinson's note to this passage (*Riverside Chaucer,* 830) points out that the name, which does not occur in Boccaccio, turns up again in the Latin summary of the *Thebaid* that is found in the manuscripts of *Troilus and Criseyde* at 5.1494, where it clearly intends Argia, the wife of Polynices (and is translated by Chaucer at 5.1509–10: "Argivam flentem narrat duodenus et ignem"; "And of Argyves wepynge and hire wo; / And how the town was brent"). In Book 3 Criseyde gives Troilus a brooch "gold and azure / In which a rubye set was lyk an herte" (3.1370–71). I would not go so far as to say that Chaucer presents Criseyde as the daughter of Theban Argia and an inheritor of the brooch—there is the problem of a second marriage to Calkas, unattested anywhere, for one thing—but the details are teasing and seem meant to associate Criseyde's experiences in love with the Theban chain of erotic and marital disasters. Should we read the whole of *Troilus and Criseyde* into the list I give in the text?

phyle to possess this brooch? Does it not rather possess her? To see her as one of its owners is to make her a member of an alternate, and indefinitely large, array of women and texts that undoes the consistency and coherence of the list in Janekyn's book and replaces it with an unstoppable play of motives, circumstances, and writings. The brooch of Thebes functions in the Wife's citation of Janekyn's exempla as what Derrida, with weird appropriateness to the Wife's case, calls a hymen that fronts an invagination, that is, the equivocal boundary/ entrance to a pocket in the text that is far larger than the text it is a pocket in.[9] If we pursue our reading of it far enough (in fact, it need not be very far) we arrive at a set of events in a multiplicity of texts—remember that Janekyn's book is itself an anthology from which the Wife is making further excerpts—that not only questions the antifeminist moralizing of the Amphiaraus-Eriphyle exemplum and the list of exempla as a whole but renders any other principle of unification and explanation impossible and undecidable as well. It is as preposterous to say that everything here is the fault of men, or fate, or a cursed ornament, as it is to blame it all on women.

The point is that once the monolithic antifeminist perspective that purports to bind the list of exempla in Janekyn's book is bypassed, the list opens itself to a rhizomatics of intertextuality that can lead in any number of other directions. The brooch of Thebes is a condensation of the list (as the list is a condensation of Janekyn's book, and the book a condensation of the ideology of male domination), much as the dream of gold and blood is a condensation of a whole institutional and personal complex of affective and economic motives. Indeed the two images are linked insofar as the story of Eriphyle is about gold and telling secrets and the connection of both of these to the death of a husband.[10] Pursued far enough, each of these images is part of the same system, which can be traced through the Wife's life, tale, and culture from point to point in a web of implacably relevant connections. If the Wife herself does not make all of these connections equally explicit here (who could?), she certainly does read the list against the grain of its "official" meaning. She seems, for instance, consistently to

9. These notions are discussed in Derrida, "The Double Session," in *Dissemination*, 173–286; idem, "FORS"; idem, "Living On / Border Lines."
10. The Midas exemplum in the tale continues the same themes.

focus on the problem about motives that provides the lever for prying the passage apart, a problem not only at work in the example of Eve at the beginning of the list but also made fully explicit by the paired examples of Livia and Lucy that conclude it—"They bothe made hir housbondes for to dye, / That oon for love, the oother was for hate" (748–49)—in a way that recalls such previous pairs as Delilah and Dejanira and therefore makes them more problematic in retrospect. A close analysis reveals that most of the Wife's attention is directed to a network of intensive and personal meanings, rather than general and exemplary ones, that she constructs from the manifold of Janekyn's text. Though the general points they make about women and marriage may be the reason these stories found their way into the book in the first place, the context of the *Wife of Bath's Prologue* inevitably raises the question of their application to this particular marriage. The materials for an answer are contained in the Wife's manner of telling them, which constitutes precisely such an application. She not only presents these stories, she responds to them, not as instances of authoritative doctrine, but case by case, as if they were reports of individual experiences. She thereby recreates an image of herself in the marriage, an image of her personality as defined in relation to Janekyn and his book.

We might begin this analysis by taking note of the Wife's ability to differentiate herself from certain of these stories, to pick and choose the ways they apply to her and especially the ways they do not. In the case of Pasiphae, for example, she seems genuinely shocked at a kind of sexuality that has no appeal for her:

> Of Pasipha, that was the queene of Crete,
> For shrewednesse, hym thoughte the tale swete;
> Fy! speke namoore—it is a grisly thyng—
> Of hire horrible lust and hir likyng.
>
> (733–36)[11]

Here the Wife reports not only the story but also Janekyn's way of reading it, and she does the same with Clytemnestra: "He redde it with ful good devocioun" (739). These comments can be taken to indicate that Janekyn liked these particular tales because they were particularly good for getting a rise out of the Wife, but if so it was not because they

---

11. Compare the Wife's response to Metellius (460–64) and to Solomon (35–43) and the general reaction at 662, "I hate hym that my vices telleth me."

applied to her but because they did not. They seemed particularly unfair and still do. As in the case of "At which book he lough alwey ful faste" (672), this presentation conveys a sense of the energy that both parties commit to these exchanges and the intensity of their personal involvement in them.

Something else about the quality and character of this involvement emerges in the story of Xanthippe, which evokes an equally decided response from the Wife:

> No thyng forgat he the care and the wo
> That Socrates hadde with his wyves two,
> How Xantippa caste pisse upon his heed.
> This sely man sat stille as he were deed;
> He wiped his heed, namoore dorste he seyn,
> But "Er that thonder stynte, comth a reyn!"
>
> (727–32)

The Wife's care in setting up the punch line here suggests that she finds this story funny and enjoys retelling it herself, but it is also clear that its point for her is not Xanthippe's shrewishness but Socrates's lack of gumption. As the phrases "stille as he were deed," "dorste," and perhaps "sely man"[12] convey here, she feels that any man who cannot defend himself better than that deserves what he gets. This feeling has implications beyond the immediate context, for it provides an occasion to reflect that disagreement is not necessarily a negative thing in a marriage and that if anyone is well positioned to see this, it is the Wife. Her earlier remark, "And yet in bacon hadde I nevere delit," refers not only to her dislike of old meat in the sexual sense but also to the fact that she is not much interested in conventional marital harmony of the sort for which the Dunmow flitch was awarded.[13] There is a good deal of evidence—the whole of the prologue, from one point of view—that the Wife likes a certain amount of resistance from life in general; it

12. *Oxford English Dictionary* (s.v. "seely," cf. "silly") will not admit that the degeneration of Old English *(ge)saelig* from "blessed, therefore innocent" to "innocent, therefore silly" had completed the last stage of its course before the sixteenth century, though it does allow "insignificant, trifling" as early as 1297. Passages like this one and the disparagement of masculine pride in "Now wherwith sholde he make his paiement, / If he ne used his sely instrument?" (131–32) suggest to me that all three stages of the word are present and active in the Middle English of Chaucer's time. In support, see Cooper, " 'Sely John.' "

13. See Hoffman, "Dunmow Bacon."

gives her something to push back at, and something against which to define herself, whether it comes from a horoscope, a book, or a husband. Fighting can be evidence of commitment to a relationship (that is what seems to have been lacking with the fourth husband), and we might view the Wife's marital career as in part a quest for a worthy opponent. It is perhaps this taste for the kind of independence in men that she also values in herself that leads the Wife to try to improve the image of the knight in her tale when, humbled and utterly dependent on the knowledge and judgment of women, he returns to the queen's court to announce what he has discovered about what women most desire: "This knyght ne stood nat *stille as doth a best,* / But to his questioun anon answerde / *With manly voys,* that al the court it herde" (1034–36, emphasis added). At least he is no Socrates.[14]

The Wife of Bath's treatment of these exempla is, as always, an appropriation or womanhandling of them, but in a rather different sense and style from earlier in the prologue. Her more varied, complex, and nuanced response to the stories is evidence of her *appreciation* of them and of Janekyn's book, which is not simply a symbol of oppression and opposition (though it is that too) but also a real source, of which she can make her own uses. On the one hand, these uses may be relatively personal and private, and relatively recessive or even unconscious, as in the case of the story of Eriphyle, which touches on the themes that surround the Wife's continuing ambivalence about her fourth husband. Such "privy" themes especially stress the active character of the Wife's remembering, the way her *choice of these stories to remember* rather than others (of which there must have been many in Janekyn's book) may be dictated more by her present and continuing concerns than by the mere fact that they used to be read to her. On the other hand, the Wife's active remembering may be directed more toward an affirmation of the relationship with Janekyn, as in the case of the story of Latumius, the tenth and last item on the list of exempla. Latumius tells Arrius that he has a tree in his garden on which his three wives have hanged themselves, and Arrius replies, "O leeve brother, . . . / Yif me a plante of thilke blissed tree, / And in my gardyn planted

---

14. Evidence of the sort considered here has occasionally led critics to posit a masochistic streak in the Wife. See Magee, "Problem of Mastery," and Burton, "Ideal Sixth." Once again this seems to me to arise from a desire to convert a tension into a trait.

shal it bee." (762–64). As with Xanthippe, I think the Wife tells this story in part because she too thinks it is funny—she has shown herself ready to appreciate a certain rueful tone in dominated husbands before—and in doing so she affirms her appreciation of Janekyn and his book by affirming the sense of humor they have in common. Once we see the instrumental character of the book, its function as a medium of complex and passionate communication between husband and wife, it becomes clear that Janekyn and Alison are in fact a remarkably compatible couple: they both like to talk, they both like to make love, and they both like to fight.

The passage I have been analyzing forms an introduction to the Wife's narrative of the final battle with Janekyn over the book, but it is itself already a repetition or revival, in the present of telling, of their fights. As it proceeds, the account moves faster and faster, piling up the outrageous things Janekyn said until its energy spills over into the Wife's outraged response, which follows on a list of Janekyn's antifeminist proverbs, as if she had just heard them all from him again:

> And whan I saugh he wolde nevere fyne
> To reden on this cursed book al nyght,
> Al sodeynly thre leves have I plyght
> Out of his book, right as he radde, and eke
> I with my fest so took hym on the cheke
> That in oure fyr he fil bakward adoun.
>
> (788–93)

The vividness and speed of this passage, conveyed in its rapid piling up of actions and reactions and the breathless enjambment that drives the verse, confirm that in recounting her quarrels with Janekyn, the Wife gets angry all over again. Her telling is not a distanced and composed narrative but a passionate reliving. As such, it provides an intensive image of the way they conducted their relationship. Though it is shaped to give a sense of climax and finality to the prologue and prepares for the clinching summation of the Wife's marital philosophy of "maistrye" at the end, it is also continuous with the increasingly vivid memories that precede it, as an image of the ongoing character of the couple's way of being together.

What comes across most vividly about the fight when thus considered is the fun of it. Whatever it was like to have this quarrel, it is clearly a joy to relate now. Its stages, the give-and-take, are much more interesting than the outcome for both the Wife and the reader:

> And he up stirte as dooth a wood leoun,
> And with his fest he smoot me on the heed
> That in the floor I lay as I were deed.
> And whan he saugh how stille that I lay,
> He was agast and wolde han fled his way,
> Til atte laste out of my swogh I breyde.
> "O! hastow slayn me, false theef?" I seyde,
> "And for my land thus hastow mordred me?
> Er I be deed, yet wol I kisse thee."
>
> (794–802)

Notice how little interest the Wife has in the fact of having been hit except as she can use it to prolong the exchange and score points. Her eye remains on Janekyn, and despite her attempt to present the serious-ness of her injury ("Til atte laste out of my swogh I breyde"), the timing of her outcry is keyed to the exact instant when Janekyn, obviously shocked by the violence of his own reaction, is about to flee. Our sense of her distance and calculation affects as well the function and effect of "And for my land thus hastow mordred me?" Though it might be used as evidence for the theory sometimes rather casually put forward that Janekyn only married the Wife for her money,[15] the theatricality of the situation makes the line seem more like a ploy. It is so offhandedly and assumptively dropped here that it sounds like something the couple have argued about before rather than a new accusation, which suggests that this version of their marriage is one the couple are aware of. They both know how it might look to an out-sider—the besotted, rich older woman and the cynical young oppor-tunist—and they use this parody, as the Wife does here, as a pretext. The Wife is *playing a role*—"Er I be deed, yet wol I kisse thee"—to get Janekyn where she can lay her hands on him (ought we to read line 433, "Com neer, my spouse, lat me ba thy cheke!" in its context, as a gloss here? it would give this moment an appropriately more aggres-sive edge), and it is clear that she knows she can trust him to play up. As the man who has been put in the wrong for the moment, he is more

15. See, for example, Oberembt, "Chaucer's Anti-misogynist Wife of Bath," and David, *Strumpet Muse,* 151.

or less obliged to apologize and offer himself for the return blow. That the Wife knows this and can make use of it is evidence that their affection for one another is dependable enough to allow this sort of maneuvering.

Janekyn apologizes, but not abjectly:

> And neer he cam, and kneled faire adoun,
> And seyde, "Deere suster Alisoun,
> As help me God, I shal thee nevere smyte!
> That I have doon, it is thyself to wyte.
> Foryeve it me, and that I thee biseke!"
>
> (803–7)

His mixed feelings come across here as very nuanced. He is sorry, of course, and he apologizes (as he knows he has to, which is not quite the same thing as being sorry). He also knows from the Wife's exaggerated tone that she is not badly hurt (one function of that tone on her part is to reassure him when he is on the point of running away), and that allows him room to keep his own end of the fight up. "It is thyself to wyte" is both an expression of continued annoyance and an attempt to minimize the seriousness of the situation, which may also function as an offer of truce. Of course the Wife will have none of this, and takes her revenge—"And yet eftsoones I hitte hym on the cheke, / And seyde, 'Theef, thus muchel am I wreke'" (808–9)—but she is also careful to keep the situation open. Her final line, "Now wol I dye, I may no lenger speke" (810), has a certain exasperating brilliance since it both forestalls retaliation for her blow and demands further apology and concern, but it also keeps the exchange going because it does demand a response, that is, it gives Janekyn a turn. What that response was we do not know since the Wife here breaks off her account and summarizes the outcome not only of this fight but of the marriage as well. Yet it seems fully appropriate that her remembering, as opposed to her generalizing, does not reach a conclusion but is suspended in a gesture of self-assertion that invites a reply.

The argument that is halted in mid-career at the end of the *Wife of Bath's Prologue* is so intensely presented that it creates something of a problem about its alleged resolution. My colleague Priscilla Shaw pointed out to me that the description of the fight expresses and releases the tension that has been building throughout the prologue in a quasi-sexual way. This feeling of release and completion may have something to do with the warm feelings toward Janekyn the Wife expresses as she concludes:

> God helpe me so, I was to hym as kynde
> As any wyf from Denmark unto Ynde,
> And also trewe, and so was he to me.
> I prey to God, that sit in magestee,
> So blesse his soule for his mercy deere.
>
> (823–27)

Nonetheless, it is not altogether easy to see how we, or the couple, got from the suspended moment of "Now wol I dye, I may no lenger speke" to this:

> But atte laste, with muchel care and wo,
> We fille acorded by us selven two.
> He yaf me al the bridel in myn hond,
> To han the governance of hous and lond,
> And of his tonge, and of his hond also;
> And made hym brenne his book anon right tho.
> And whan that I hadde geten unto me,
> By maistrie, al the soveraynetee,
> And that he seyde, "Myn owene trewe wyf,
> Do as thee lust the terme of al thy lyf;
> Keep thyn honour, and keep eek myn estaat"—
> After that day we hadden never debaat.
>
> (811–22)

"Muchel care and wo" is too vague and summary a characterization of what must have gone on between them to provide a satisfactory—or satisfying—explanation of the suspiciously complete victory the Wife details here. Though "After that day" does not really refer to the day of the argument and in fact covers a thoroughly indefinite amount of time, the closest day in the text we have to refer it to is that of the battle we have just witnessed, and the energy of that description seems somehow to cast doubt on the later assertion. I think it is possible to account for this effect more precisely and show in detail why we should not entirely believe what the Wife says here.

Let us return to the end of the Wife's summary of the contents of Janekyn's book and her description of the way he read it to her:

He spak moore harm than herte may bithynke,
And therwithal he knew of mo proverbes
Than in this world ther growen gras or herbes.
"Bet is," quod he, "thyn habitacioun
Be with a leon or a foul dragoun,
Than with a womman usynge for to chyde.
Bet is," quod he, "hye in the roof abyde,
Than with an angry wyf doun in the hous;
They been so wikked and contrarious,
They haten that hir housbondes loven ay."
He seyde, "A womman cast hir shame away,
Whan she cast of hir smok"; and forthermo,
"A fair womman, but she be chaast also,
Is lyk a gold ryng in a sowes nose."
Who wolde wene, or who wolde suppose,
The wo that in myn herte was, and pyne?
                                        (772–87)

The reader may feel that he or she has seen something like this somewhere before, and the source of that impression is not far to seek. On
rereading the prologue in the context of a knowledge of the Wife's
dealings with her fifth husband and the issues of that marriage, the
relevant passage jumps off the page:

Thou seydest this, that I was lyk a cat;
For whoso wolde senge a cattes skyn,
Thanne wolde the cat wel dwellen in his in;
And if the cattes skyn be slyk and gay,
She wol nat dwelle in house half a day,
But forth she wole, er any day be dawed,
To shewe hir skyn and goon a-caterwawed.
This is to seye, if I be gay, sire shrewe,
I wol renne out my borel for to shewe.
    Sire olde fool, what helpeth thee to spyen?
Thogh thou preye Argus with his hundred yen
To be my warde-cors, as he kan best,
In feith, he shal nat kepe me but me lest;
Yet koude I make his berd, so moot I thee!
    Thou seydest eek that ther been thynges thre,
The whiche thynges troublen al this erthe,
And that no wight may endure the ferthe.
O leeve sire shrewe, Jhesu shorte thy lyf!
Yet prechestow and seyst an hateful wyf
Yrekened is for oon of thise meschances.
Been ther none othere maner resemblances

That ye may likne youre parables to,
But if a sely wyf be oon of tho?
    Thou liknest eek wommenes love to helle,
To bareyne lond, ther water may nat dwelle.
Thou liknest it also to wilde fyr;
The moore it brenneth, the moore it hath desir
To consume every thyng that brent wole be.
Thou seyest, right as wormes shende a tree,
Right so a wyf destroyeth hire housbonde;
This knowe they that been to wyves bonde.
    Lordynges, right thus, as ye have understonde,
Baar I stifly myne olde housbondes on honde
That thus they seyden in hir dronkenesse;
And al was fals, but that I took witnesse
On Janekyn, and on my nece also.

(348–83)

Two of the central concerns of this passage, the question of stepping out (cf. 637–41) and the complaint about incessant citing of antifeminist lore, bring the passage home to Janekyn and the book. When the Wife originally says "al was fals," she is telling the truth about her first three husbands, who did not say these things. But Janekyn did, and once we know about him and his bad habits, this passage takes on a vividness and precision of reference in retrospect that it did not have prospectively, because now we know who "thou" is.

The *Wife of Bath's Prologue*, perhaps uniquely in the *Canterbury Tales*, offers an explanation for the learning of its narrator. The bookishness of almost all of the stories in the collection has been felt to be an argument against dramatic verisimilitude and individual voicing.[16] I think the question needs to be addressed case by case, and I would not deny that sometimes the scholarly surface of the text reminds us that we are getting the stories of the pilgrims as mediated by the retelling of a scholarly poet, nor need it cease to do so here. In the case of the *Wife of Bath's Prologue*, however, historical scholarship has established beyond question that the sources of the poem are almost entirely the works mentioned in it.[17] The crucial step here is less often taken: the

---

16. See, for example, Howard, *Idea of the Canterbury Tales*, 230–31, and Burlin, *Chaucerian Fiction*, 165.

17. See the selections set out in Whiting, "Wife of Bath's Prologue," and especially Pratt, "Development of the Wife of Bath." Pratt argues convincingly (51, 54–55) that Chaucer must have used a version of Janekyn's book rather than assembling the materi-

interpretive meaning in the fiction of this extrafictional and historical fact is that a major source of the Wife of Bath's learning is Janekyn's book of wicked wives.[18] She appears virtually to have memorized it in the course of her encounters with him, and it now forms a kind of basis or medium for much of her discourse on a variety of topics.

The implications are considerable. To begin with, by the time we get to the Wife's account of her fifth marriage in a first reading, we have a richer and more intensive sense of the taste and feel of that marriage than we are probably aware of since not just the passage cited but virtually the whole of the prologue is covertly drawn from materials and experiences that come from it. A retrospective reading gives new meaning to the idea of taking a leaf from someone's book. Furthermore, the problem of the end of the prologue is resolved—or perhaps I should say rendered properly problematic. As the Wife's narrative shows, Janekyn's book was originally experienced by her as an instrument of aggression, a kind of summary of everything men had been trying to do to her all her life, and its mutilation and burning thus represent, from one point of view, the final triumph of feminine "maistrye" and the precondition for a happy marriage. The Wife's *performance* of the narrative, however, demonstrates how the book became the medium through which she and Janekyn carry on their relationship. The Wife's use of Janekyn's book throughout the prologue in the now of speaking constitutes the entire performance as a *continuation* of their debate and of their struggle over that book in the present, long after the supposedly decisive events narrated at the end of the prologue. The Wife, though, is still conducting the debate: what does that say about who has the "maistrye"? Moreover, if we assume for the sake of argument that Janekyn is dead now, the assumption points up with particular poignancy what is clear enough even without it: now, in the present of speaking, without ever losing or denying the component of conflict that is essential to the relationship, the Wife's engagement with Janekyn's book perpetuates Janekyn's memory through the

---

als of the tale directly from the various sources listed in it. The one exception to the rule that a major source of the tale is also mentioned in it by the Wife is the La Vielle section of the *Roman de la Rose*. I am not convinced, however, that that text was not in Janekyn's book: just because the Wife does not list it does not mean it was not there.

18. Though many critics mention it in a relatively unfocused way, such as Kittredge, *Chaucer and His Poetry*, 188.

reexperiencing and the fighting anew of their combats. *Now* that recollection is also a way of keeping the man alive, it is an act of love.

This convergence of Janekyn's book and the text of the *Wife of Bath's Prologue* as a whole establishes the inextricable interinvolvement of the Wife and the book, the fact of the subject as text, as glossed by Roland Barthes:

> *I read the text.* This statement, consonant with the "genius" of the language (subject, verb, complement), is not always true. The more plural the text, the less it is written before I read it; I do not make it undergo a predicative operation, consequent upon its being, an operation known as *reading*, and *I* is not an innocent subject, anterior to the text, one which will subsequently deal with the text as it would an object to dismantle or a site to occupy. This "I" which appears in the text is already itself a plurality of other texts, of codes which are infinite or, more precisely, lost (whose origin is lost).
>
> (*S/Z*, 10)

If there was (as of course there was) a Wife of Bath prior to her fifth marriage,[19] we have her only as mediated and affected, indeed constituted, by the book of that marriage, which now turns out to be prior in the order of narration, the *récit*, to everything prior to it in the order of the narrative, the *histoire*. If both the Wife and Janekyn's anthology, which is itself a textual plurality drawn from countless other texts, are rhizomatic multiplicities, then what I am now describing is the point at which they connect to form a still larger rhizome, the subject-text without an origin, which, it turns out, we and the Wife have always already been reading. I want to conclude this section by reviewing the manifestations of that subject-text as we have encountered them, by way of summing up.

In the first place, because of the unfolding or dramatized character of the Wife's performance, it is particularly evident from the beginning that she *encounters herself* in her telling and that this encounter is more than a *compte rendu* of a preexistent self. In the present of speaking the Wife's ego is an object for consciousness, not conscious-

---

19. And as of course there wasn't, since she is a fictional character. What is interesting here is precisely the way what we must assume to have been Chaucer's actual practice, the deployment of a preexisting text something like Janekyn's book so as to produce an impersonation, is doubled and represented in the text as the activity of the Wife.

ness itself. This facticity comes out most clearly in her experience of herself as *memory* because her memories present themselves to her phenomenologically as spontaneous events in the present, which she does not always control and often does not expect (note that this spontaneous emergence is not, or not necessarily, the same as the manifestation of unconscious symptoms).[20] Moreover, these presentations do not manifest themselves to her as determinate meanings that are recovered from the past. In the case of the Wife's sexual relations with her old husbands, for example (discussed above, pp. 85–87), whatever the specific *events* may have been, their meaning is caught up in the present in a complex knot of antithetical feelings and reversible cause-effect relations whose signifier, perhaps, is "bacon." This word is, so to speak, *a multiple signifier* (the term of art is *aporia* or *undecidable*), which oscillates between systems of signification (successful domination/sexual dissatisfaction; "old meat"/"Dunmow flitch," aggression/desire) without ceasing or coming to rest.

The events of the transition between the Wife's fourth and fifth marriages are similarly invested with both uncertainty and ambivalence, centering perhaps in the question of what happened in the field between the Wife and Janekyn before her fourth husband's death. The question is not really whether they did or did not make love. Though this question presumably has an answer, the Wife does not supply enough information to determine it. What matters is how the character of her feelings (for Janekyn, for the fourth husband, for her own identity as a "married woman") relates to—that is, constitutes—the *meaning* of what happened (for herself at the time and later, for her past and future husbands, for the audience): here the point is that the Wife appears not to have been sure at the time and at any rate is not sure now. Clearly what she did has a bearing for her on who she was, and that in turn has a bearing on who she is, but her uncertainties about the two latter questions keep the determination of the former one in suspension, even for her.

Though moments of this sort, when questions like, Why did I chide? or, How did (do) I feel about my fourth marriage? are instances of genuine uncertainty, when the Wife becomes genuinely problematic to

---

20. See Sartre's commentary on Rimbaud's famous remark, "Je est *un autre*," in *Transcendence of the Ego*, 93–106.

herself, they might perhaps be taken as moments of ambivalence, that is, of conflicting feelings within the same psyche, and so as no necessary threat to fundamental psychic unity: they are moments when one self feels two ways at once. This interpretation is harder to maintain in the case of the dream of blood and gold (see above, pp. 101–6). Again we are faced with an "event" whose historical truth remains problematic, though again the question presumably has an answer that the Wife knows. But the dream functions as an event in the text independently of its historicity, and it does so as another multiple signifier. The aporia here revolves around the nature of sexuality, an enigma that underlies both of the previous examples as well. In context the dream becomes a condensed representation of the multiple and simultaneous systems of positive and negative, affectional and economic, physical and emotional qualities and meanings that sexuality partakes of and participates in.[21] As a fundamental part of her "nature," the Wife's sex is inextricably both personal and social, both a commodity and a source of affectual energy; her sexuality is both a part of herself and alienated from her, a node (like the dream) at which her apparent independence, self-presence, and individuality (what is mine if not my sexuality?) cross her inextricable entanglement in a coercive and defining social network of gender roles and institutional practices. Sexuality has no intrinsic meaning in these terms, only the meaning that is made of it. In the context of her own life and experience the Wife's most common euphemism for her own sexuality—"bele chose," or beautiful thing— is as compact a multiple signifier and as trenchant an expression of this aporia as one could wish.

An equally illuminating example is the Wife's treatment of astrology in the prologue (see above, pp. 107–13), especially because here we have a situation in which the speaker herself is actively attempting to give a description and explanation of her character in relatively formal and abstract terms. She tries not only to tell her experience but also to fit it into a theoretical framework. What happens to astrological explanation of human nature in the Wife's text is that both astrology and human nature are called into question for the speaker herself. As I have suggested, the text portrays an encounter between a subject and an institution, between the Wife and astrology, that undoes both. It is not

---

21. These sets of paired terms are not meant to be parallel.

a question of suddenly discovering or asserting a "real" self as distinguished from a "false" one, as if one version of the self were truer than the other in some absolute sense, any more than it would be accurate to say that the Wife's exploitative and aggressive persona (Mars) is less truly "her" than the more responsive and affectionate one (Venus). Astral influences and their application become a matter of choices, interpretations, and arguments. Who the Wife is in these terms becomes in a strict sense undecidable, and *therefore* a matter about which to make decisions.

In dealing with these forces the *Wife of Bath's Prologue* most fully displays the essential indeterminacy of the subject and the fundamental role of interpretation in its construction. It is a text that consistently works to undermine and render undecidable the distinction between Venus and Mars, eros and aggression, in the Wife's life and consciousness. In my analysis of the prologue I have found numerous instances of the Wife's awareness of the ways Venus can become the servant of Mars, of how, for example, sexuality can become a weapon, an instrument of aggression. But as the poem proceeds, those aspects of it multiply that suggest how Mars may be an agent of Venus and aggression a form of loving, and in the case of the Wife's fifth marriage, at least, the same incidents and behavior exemplify both meanings. The question is indeed about the role of Mercury in the Wife's life, understood less as the planet (though that sense cannot be entirely dismissed) than as learning and overwhelmingly represented in the prologue not as abstract lore but concretely as Janekyn's book. If the book once belonged to Janekyn, it now belongs equally to the Wife, and she uses it to affirm and sustain their relationship. What looked like aggression in the past looks like affection in the present. But was it ever, or is it, simply either one? If an argument in the past was a covert way of expressing commitment, and if that dimension of its meaning emerges more clearly when it is remembered in the present, that does not mean it ceases to register protest and contradiction.

In considering a passage like the one that concludes the sermon to the three old husbands and the retrospective revelation of its source in Janekyn's book (348–83), it does not seem correct merely to say that what we learn in retrospect is the "whole truth" about the passage, in other words, that it is really *only* a covert remembering and continuation of the Wife's engagement with Janekyn. Not only does the text present itself as an account of her dealings with her first three husbands; the details that frame it at the end, where she cites both Janekyn and her niece as evidence "That thus they seyden in hir dronkenesse" (381–83), locate the passage as having been spoken at some point in her fourth marriage and therefore as being addressed to her fourth husband. This flickering among three separate but simultaneous addressees for the same text so as to create chronological impossibilities is absolutely characteristic of the entire chiding section of the prologue and a number of other parts of the text as well. There is no way to settle on a single reference or addressee for such passages. What one can say, however, is that the establishment of Janekyn's book as the fundamental medium of this multitemporal discourse also establishes the causal priority (though not of course the exclusive causality) of the now of performance for *everything that is narrated in the prologue.* Though there is no particular reason to doubt, for example, that the Wife had some such encounters as she describes with her three old husbands, there is every reason to suppose that she did not do so in the exact terms she sets forth in the prologue. Her internalization of Janekyn's book gives the Wife a language and a framework for making sense of her past, and this process is what the entire prologue records. What appears prospectively to be a sequential narrative in which the lines of causality run from past to present turns out in retrospect to be equally, undecidably, a situation where history and its meaning are constructed from the present backward in terms of the current concerns and projects, public and private, unconscious, practical and discursive, of the speaker. However the Wife got to be as she is, in the text it is not only, or perhaps not at all, the past that forms and controls the present but also the present that conditions what is remembered and how it is interpreted. Only by rereading from the end of the prologue can we see how completely this is the case in the Wife's performance.

The temporal indeterminacy of the prologue creates a situation in which the meanings the Wife gives to her experience at any point are always *exceeded* by that experience, as the text always exceeds the readings that are made of it. For example, the entire chiding sermon has one kind of voice and generates one kind of speaker when it is considered as "ensample," as a set of instances of a method. It gets this tone from its place in a certain sort of structure, as what philosophers of language call a second-order utterance, that is, a citation. This tone has nothing to do with any particularities of utterance—one can easily conceive of a passionate and dramatic oral delivery with the clear understanding that the passion was part of the act. The same text, again regardless of the details of its oral voicing, takes on a completely different kind of "voice of the text" when its addressee is understood as Janekyn, or husband number four, or both. The address, the meaning, the place, the temporality, and the *speaker* of the text all become multiple in ways that are at once mutually exclusive and simultaneous.

What we call the Wife of Bath exists in the text as a set of unresolvable tensions between self-revelation and self-presentation, repentance and rebellion, determinism and freedom, the individual and the institution, Venus and Mars, past and present. In each of these cases the opposition is both necessary and unsustainable, and the terms ceaselessly turn into one another. Of course the Wife is a construction, an interpretation. In fact, she is a whole history of interpretations, my own among them. But any text is that, as is any person or any subject. The crux of my argument is that first of all the Wife of Bath is an interpretation for herself, or rather a continuous and ongoing set of interpretations and reinterpretations whose indeterminacies she embodies and hands on to us. And that is what Chaucer's text not only demonstrates but also *proposes* about her.

Quha wait if all that Chaucer wrait was trew? Who knows if the unconscious is structured like a language, as Lacan maintained, or if the self is like a text? The point I have been making throughout this discussion is that whatever the truth of the matter may be, in Chaucer's poem everything happens as if the modern idea of the self as subject were correct. The metaphor of the self as text that I have been using is an image proposed by the poem, at least in the sense that Janekyn's book becomes the model and the medium for the Wife's self-explication. Like that book the Wife's experience, her subjectivity, is constituted in the poem as a manifold or rhizome that lends itself to, or admits of, a multiplicity of articulations, of which the ones analyzed here are simply particular possibilities. The self or selves manifested in the Wife's performance, the voices of that text, might be thought of as like Janekyn's book in being selections from an anthology. This image is intended to recall the quotation from Barthes, which, whether or not it accurately describes the act of reading, does correctly describe what is represented in Chaucer. The Wife of Bath is in effect the first of many readers of her own life, which she gives a voice-oriented reading, like a tale, for the traces of its narrator. Her reading of the text of her life is not the activity or even the discovery of a prior essence but the construction in the present of a posterior and provisional subject under specific conditions of encounter with that text. The Wife does not "know" who she "is"—she has a set of interpretations, for herself and for others, of who she has been, and those interpretations are clearly influenced by the context within which they are made (her sense of her audience, her sense of the task at hand, her intention to propound a theory of marriage, and so on). Those interpretations are also subject to change and open to it; in fact they actually do change in the course of the prologue at various points, and, as I will suggest in analyzing her tale, they can be expected to change in the future. This shifting activity of self-construction is what the Wife's narration and Chaucer's poem are about, both in the sense that they have it as their topic and in the sense that it is what they are doing. At least in this tale Chaucer's subject is the subject, as that term is currently understood.

5

Subjectivity and Disenchantment
The Wife of Bath's Tale
as Institutional Critique

The Friar's brief comment "so have I joye or blis, / This is a long preamble of a tale!" (830–31) and the quarrel between him and the Summoner that develops out of it (832–49) mark the transition from the Wife's prologue to her tale by recalling to us and her the pilgrim audience and the immediate occasion of the telling. The Friar's remark is a reminder of what the Wife herself knows, that her contract with her companions is not satisfied by an account of her life. For both the Wife and the audience, though perhaps in different ways, it is important that her experience engage with, and fulfill itself in, the public sphere. The tale of the loathly lady is traditional; that is to say, it is public property in a way no autobiography can be, and to tell it is to go public, to move beyond a local and idiosyncratic personal history and take one's place in a larger arena. At the same time the interruption reminds us how little of the activity of the Wife's text has been—or could be—available to those who have it only as a live performance and brings back into the foreground the inattention and disinterest in intimacy of the masculine masters of the public world.

The Wife is fully equal to the challenge. However intensely she may have become involved in memory and personal experience in the course of her prologue, she has never really lost sight of the public project of her performance, and she has her tale in readiness as the clinching proof of the position on marriage she has been developing. Indeed, the tale itself is often taken by critics as a mere appendage of the more brilliant prologue, an appendage that restates the main argument about the value of feminine sovereignty or "maistrye" in marriage in a relatively mechanical form. In this view a simple and functional tale is marred (or enlivened, depending on the critic's taste) by some characteristic though irrelevant touches from the Wife, like the

Midas exemplum, and complicated by a windy and dull (or moving and serious) pillow lecture but concludes straightforwardly enough with the QED of the knight's submission and the magical transformation at the end.[1]

There is a lot to be said for this reading. An understanding of the polemical feminist project that underlies the Wife's telling explains much about the form the story takes in her hands, especially in relation to its analogues and its genre. In the case of the Wife's tale the genre is romance, and the fully conscious character of her engagement with romance assumptions and conventions comes out in her deliberate and consistent subversion of them. In its original form the tale the Wife tells is an instrument of the dominant masculine ideology and its values, such as (male) loyalty and courtesy, that demonstrate male superiority. Donaldson's succinct summary of the analogues brings out clearly this ideological bias—and the Wife's subversion of it:

> In the analogues the story is handled in a different style, its real point being to demonstrate the courtesy of the hero, who weds the hag uncomplainingly and treats her as if she were the fairest lady in the land; in two versions the knight is Sir Gawain, the most courteous of Arthur's followers, who promises to marry her not in order to save his own life but his king's. The lady's transformation is thus a reward of virtue. In Chaucer the polite knight becomes a convicted rapist who keeps his vow only under duress and in the sulkiest possible manner.[2]

As in the case of Janekyn's book in the prologue, I take the differences in detail and structure between Chaucer's version of the tale and its analogues as evidence of the speaker's agency, evidence that the Wife knows the traditional version, recognizes its male bias, and deliberately alters it to make her own feminist message more pointed and polemical. The pattern of these alterations is her advance plan for the tale. The fact that only in her version is the knight a rapist means that only in her version is the quest for what women most desire linked specifically and logically to the knight's character and the question of male-female relations. Clearly this particular knight, as a surrogate for

1. See, for example, Kittredge, *Chaucer and His Poetry,* 191; Lumiansky, *Of Sondry Folk,* 117–29; Huppé, *Reading of the Canterbury Tales,* 107–35 (Huppé actually uses the phrase *QED,* 134); and Whittock, *Reading of the Canterbury Tales,* 118–68.

2. Donaldson, *Chaucer's Poetry,* 1077. On the Wife's changes in the traditional story, see also Cary, "Sovereignty and the Old Wife."

men in general, needs to learn more about women, and the plot becomes a device for forcing him to do so. The tale puts him in a position more familiar to women, who ordinarily have to cater to male desires, and gives power to women from the beginning. This is one example of how the Wife's womanhandling appropriation functions in the tale, co-opting traditionally masculine forms for specifically feminine ends. Another example is the "gentilesse" speech, a form of argument that aims at breaking down external hierarchies of power constituted by birth and possessions—"temporel thyng, that man may hurte and mayme" (1132)—in favor of equality before God and individual responsibility for establishing worth and achieving salvation. This argument is traditionally egalitarian but scarcely feminist. It may sometimes be used to urge the right of lowborn men to love and woo noble ladies,[3] but I do not recall it being used before the *Wife of Bath's Tale* to argue that ugly old women are good enough not only to go to the same heaven as knights but even to marry them. Since in no other version of the tale does anything like this speech occur, its function as additional feminist propaganda in the altered tale is clear, and the same is true of the sovereignty argument, with its reversal of the usual male-female hierarchies, which gives the tale its punch line and point.

This summary might be thought of as the straw-man version of the tale. The Wife makes a straw man of the traditional story and its hero, setting up the knight and the old story as images of masculine pretension to knock them over, and obviously she carries out this project.[4] Along the way, as readers have often noticed, she takes advantage of her temporary position as narrator or straw stuffer to enjoy her work. She enjoys the satisfaction in fiction and fantasy of dominating the ill-bred knight and all his kind by making them dependent on feminine wisdom, and she gives herself, in the form of her surrogate the hag, the pleasure of imagining herself magically young and beautiful again,

3. The opportunities the argument affords for aggressive bad faith are already apparent in Andreas Capellanus's fourth dialogue, where a nobleman uses it to try to force his attentions on a woman of a lower class (*Art of Courtly Love*, 62–68).

4. This point has not been altogether lost on critics, though they seldom seem to give the Wife much credit for seeing it too. McCall, *Chaucer Among the Gods*, uses the phrase "straw men" (139) of the Wife's exempla. Schauber and Spolsky, "Consolation of Alison," have shown that the basis of all four of what they identify as the Wife's most common speech acts is the setting up of a proposition that is subsequently denied.

though these pleasures are clearly marginal and incidental to the main message.

The matter of what else the Wife gets out of telling the story, whether fantasies of power or of rejuvenation, begins to touch on a set of effects that arise less from the preconceived manipulation of structure and content in a generic framework than from more properly textual phenomena, the particular stylistic deployment or voicing of the tale as it proceeds. As in the prologue, these effects are often most apparent in digressions from the narrative line and the logic of the argument, and it is here that most of the controversy about the tale arises. Again as in the prologue, it is common among critics to see such features, especially the "gentilesse" speech, as revealing things about the Wife of which she herself is unaware and to use them as a way of establishing her character—that is, her limitations.[5] As before, however, the Wife is not satisfied with the simple appropriation of the instruments of masculine power, an appropriation that can only reproduce the oppression it seeks to combat. In fact, her voicing of her tale subjects it to the same kind of revisionary experiential questioning we saw earlier and enables her to move beyond issues solely of power or mastery to a more searching and wide-ranging critique of the tale's generic assumptions and a more intensive and personal use of its possibilities. The first indication of these concerns in the tale is probably the Wife's relative lack of interest in polemical closure. Having set up the straw knight and sent him on his quest, she is oddly dilatory in knocking him over and getting on with the demonstration. She spends the first one hundred twenty lines, a good quarter of the tale, not telling it. Instead, she pursues what we might call her private interests.

Of the two major digressions in the tale the most assertive is the Midas exemplum, in which the story of the loathly lady vanishes utterly for thirty lines—more if you count the introductory matter—and we find ourselves in the middle of a completely different story about Midas's ass's ears and his wife's inability to keep them secret. The occasion of this digression is the knight's quest to discover what women most desire, and as the Wife lists the variety of opinions he

5. See, for example, Lumiansky, *Of Sondry Folk*, 126–29, whose consistent misogyny is one of the less attractive features of his argument.

encounters on his search, we can see her losing interest in the *quest,* whose outcome is a foregone conclusion, and getting interested in the *question.* The old story and its Arthurian world are dropped in favor of matters of more immediate interest. Just as it is more fun for the Wife to take a shot at the Friar's virility in retaliation for his comment on her prologue than to linger over the romantic world of "fayerie," here it is more interesting to her to consider the variety of possible answers to the question than to give the "right" one. Her voice moves into the present tense; she includes herself among the women whose opinions are being solicited and indicates that she finds some of those opinions better than others: "Somme seyde that oure hertes been moost esed / Whan that we been yflatered and yplesed. / He gooth ful ny the sothe, I wol nat lye" (929–31).

The Midas exemplum itself, though superficially unflattering to women and apparently totally unconnected to the story, is actually a reflection of the Wife's impatience with certain forms of male foolishness, and it has a certain relevance to the development of the romance. It is, after all, not just any secret that the wife of Midas finds herself unable to contain, but one that a great many women, including the Wife of Bath, have had occasion to notice: "Myn housbonde hath longe asses erys two!" (976).[6] Pope, who borrowed the Wife's revision of Ovid for his *Epistle to Arbuthnot,* saw the message clearly:

> Out with it *Dunciad!* let the secret pass,
> That secret to each fool that he's an ass;
> The truth once told (and wherefore should we lie?)
> The queen of Midas slept, and so may I.
>
> (79–82)

This is a secret women have to conceal all the time, especially about their nearest and dearest. The exemplum focuses closely on the genuine anguish of Midas's queen. She is a woman bound by ties of trust and affection—ties she herself acknowledges—to a man who loves her and with whom her own reputation is involved. But he is still a fool:

6. I am indebted to Professor Katherine King, formerly a student in the History of Consciousness Program at the University of California, Santa Cruz, for opening up this line of analysis for me.

He loved hire moost, and trusted hire also;
He preyede hire that to no creature
She sholde tellen of his disfigure.
   She swoor him, "Nay"; for al this world to wynne,
She nolde do that vileynye or synne,
To make hir housbonde han so foul a name.
She nolde nat telle it for hir owene shame.
But nathelees, hir thoughte that she dyde
That she so longe sholde a conseil hyde.

(958–66)

As we have seen in the prologue, this is not the sort of secret the Wife of Bath is used to concealing. We have only to replace Midas's wife with Alison, and Midas himself with the fourth husband or with Janekyn at a moment when he is grinning at her over the top of his book of wicked wives, to see what the experiential sources of the exemplum are and how graphically it records a realistic frustration that the Wife knows well as a daily component of real marriages, even (or especially) good ones. But it is equally interesting to replace Midas's queen with Arthur's, who has to proceed tactfully to rescue the young rapist from vengeful masculine justice so she can set him on the right track. The Wife of Bath puts great stress on the careful courtesy, a style appropriate to a chivalric setting, with which the queen works to get her way. The line "The queene thanketh the kyng with al hir myght" (899) in particular seems deliberately to overstress her courtesy in order to call attention to it. The Midas exemplum is a gloss on this scene, in which the Wife evokes the real strains involved in feminine submission to, and manipulation of, masculine egos that the original scene omits—while reminding us that she herself is considerably less patient than either queen. She reacts critically to something she feels is missing in her original and supplies it, though she does so in a way that does not—at least not yet—directly challenge romance decorum.

Something similar happens with the issue of the quest itself. That the Wife gets involved in the question of what women most desire and drops the history in order to pursue it suggests that the question is hardly settled for her except for polemical purposes; even when the quest has been completed, the "right" answer is always hedged. The hag remarks that there is no woman, however proud, "That *dar seye nay* of that I shal thee teche" (1019, emphasis added), and when the knight announces the answer in court, the ladies who judge him are similarly cagey. They do not say he is right, they just do not say he is wrong: "In al the court ne was ther wyf, ne mayde, / Ne wydwe that *contraried* that he sayde, / But seyden he was worthy han his lyf" (1043–45, emphasis added). In fact, the queen gets exactly what she asks for, "An answere suffisant in this mateere" (910), that is, an answer that suffices, one that will do rather than one that is definitive.[7] The reason for all this hedging is, as the Wife knows and demonstrates by her digressive interest in the "wrong" answers, that the question is an impossible one and the quest for a single answer is a fool's errand anywhere outside a romance. In reality—in experience—different women want different things, and the same woman, like the Wife herself, may want different things at different times. What we are seeing here are the various expressions of a consistent tension between the Wife's disenchanted practical sensibility and the generic character- istics of a tale that is, as she is well aware, not her style. Though at first her reservations are expressed in a relatively covert way and outside the story itself in digressions and asides,[8] as the tale proceeds the Wife confronts what she sees as its deficiencies more directly by introducing a surrogate for herself into the plot in the figure of the hag.

The description that accompanies the entrance of the hag into the tale is a compact portrayal of the Wife's sense of her own career as she has developed it in the prologue and makes most sense when it is read in reference to that development:

> And in his wey it happed hym to ryde,
> In al this care, under a forest syde,
> Wher as he saugh upon a daunce go
> Of ladyes foure and twenty, and yet mo;
> Toward the whiche daunce he drow ful yerne,
> In hope that som wysdom sholde he lerne.
> But certeinly, er he cam fully there,
> Vanysshed was this daunce, he nyste where.
> No creature saugh he that bar lyf,
> Save on the grene he saugh sittynge a wyf—
> A fouler wight ther may no man devyse.
>
> (989–99)

7. See Kaske, "Chaucer's Marriage Group," 52.
8. Note, for instance, her comment on the penalty for rape in Arthurian times,

As I have already suggested, to constitute herself as an authority the Wife has had to give her experience a definitive shape and meaning from which she can generalize; hence she must regard her past as behind her and done with. When she is in this mood, the past disappears as experience, and she feels that her life is finished. Her famous lines on her youth, "But—Lord Crist!—whan that it remembreth me," leading to the reflection "That I have had my world as in my tyme" (469–73), are followed immediately by a meditation that conveys her sharp awareness of the sad difference between now and then:

> But age, allas, that al wole envenyme,
> Hath me biraft my beautee and my pith.
> Lat go. Farewel! The devel go therwith!
> The flour is goon; ther is namoore to telle;
> The bren, as I best kan, now moste I selle.
>
> (474–78)

This pattern, this set of feelings, is recapitulated in the description of the hag. The Wife is sometimes drawn to the symbolist suggestiveness of romance imagery, usually in a mood of nostalgia, even when she is critical of it. The four-and-twenty dancing ladies partake of this mood in their connection with the dance of feminine freedom from the "limitacioun" of friars and other masculine trammels, a freedom associated with the elf queen and her "joly compaignye" at the dawn of time and the beginning of the tale. What gives these associations their power is their connection with the Wife's experience—with her youth ("How koude I daunce to an harpe smale" [457])—and her richly variegated knowledge of life and love, the "olde daunce." Her memory swirls and dances with all the women she has been until they vanish, she knows not where, and leave her all alone as she has become, as she is now. The analogues of the tale often spend time having fun with the comically grotesque ugliness of the hag: "Then there as shold haue stood her mouth, / then there was sett her eye," and so forth.[9] The Wife's more reserved refusal to describe her is also more inward, suggesting not what can be seen but what is felt. I think her words here will bear the inflection: "A fouler wight ther may no *man* devyse," that

---

"Paraventure swich was the statut tho" (893). Whatever it means, it makes us aware of the Wife commenting outside the story.

9. *The Marriage of Sir Gawaine*, quoted in Whiting, "Wife of Bath's Tale," 237.

is, If you, the men who look at me as I speak, think I am decayed, what must I feel, who know what I was? no mere description will do justice to that. No wonder the hag tells the knight, "Sire knyght, heer forth ne lith no wey" (1001).[10]

This is a range of experience with which courtly romance does not deal, and the only answer the form has to the problems of the passing of the "flour," especially in a woman, is magic, that is, fantasy, like the transformation at the end of the *Wife of Bath's Tale*. Those problems are relegated to what happens after stories like this one are over, when, as we all know, they lived happily ever after. Though she may some-times be attracted to it as a form of recreation and momentary escape, the Wife does not believe in magic of this sort any more than she believes that real men deal with the prospect of marrying old and ugly women with the courtesy and equanimity of a Sir Gawain, and her conduct of the story dramatizes that disbelief. Once the knight has won his release, the hag, who obviously does not trust him, pushes forward to remind him publicly of his promise to marry her (1046–57), a promise he acknowledges reluctantly and with a bad grace: "For Goddes love, as chees a newe requeste! / Taak al my good and lat my body go" (1060–61). When the wedding takes place, the Wife delivers herself of an *occupatio* that calls attention to the way her story frus-trates ordinary romance expectations:

> Now wolden som men seye, paraventure,
> That for my necligence I do no cure
> To tellen yow the joye and al th'array
> That at the feeste was that ilke day.
> To which thyng shortly answeren I shal:
> I seye ther nas no joye ne feeste at al;
> Ther nas but hevynesse and muche sorwe.
> For prively he wedded hire on morwe,
> And al day after hidde hym as an owle,
> So wo was hym, his wyf looked so foule.
> (1073–82)

Part of what the Wife is doing in her description of the wedding and the wedding night is to *confront* a genre that has no room for her and other women in her situation with the *fact of herself*. We can feel the glee

10. See Verdonk, " 'Sire Knyght.' "

with which in the person of the hag she appropriates the rhetoric of
courtesy, "smylynge everemo" (1086), and baits the knight (and the
self-gratulatory masculine conventions he stands for so shakily) with a
blank-eyed rehearsal of official ideals:

> Is this the lawe of kyng Arthures hous?
> Is every knyght of his so dangerous?
> I am youre owene love and youre wyf;
> I am she which that saved hath youre lyf,
> And, certes, yet ne dide I yow nevere unright;
> Why fare ye thus with me this firste nyght?
> Ye faren lyk a man had lost his wit.
> What is my gilt? For Goddes love, tel it,
> And it shal been amended, if I may.
>
> (1089–97)

The knight's heartfelt response shows how much the Wife thinks such
chivalric courtesy is worth in the face of real-life decay: "'Amended?'
quod this knyght, 'Allas, nay, nay!/ . . ./ Thou art so loothly, and so
oold also'" (1098–1100).

The hag replies that she could amend all this (and in the story she
can) since she has magical powers. On the one hand, if all the Wife
were interested in was the public and authoritative function of the
story as polemical propaganda, the tale might now proceed to its
conclusion in the proof of the necessity of mastery. But it seems clear
that though the doctrinaire feminist argument of the tale is acceptable
as a position for women in general, and the Wife certainly does not
disagree with it, it is not responsive to the nuance and detail of her own
situation and therefore does not interest her. For one thing, it has little
to do directly with the issues of romance style and convention and their
ideological implications, which have increasingly occupied her as she
narrates. On the other hand, if the Wife were only interested in the
pleasures of fantasy, we would also expect her to get to the end of the
tale since the transformation of the hag as a reward for the knight's
relinquishment of mastery also affords the only opportunity in the
story for such pleasurable imagining. Instead of exercising these options, however, the Wife digresses again. Because she has no urgent
need for argumentative closure and because she does not believe in
magic, she refuses the opportunities to assert mastery and enjoy fantasy that the tale offers, puts them off to a brief moment at the very

end, and proceeds to redirect the tale, to *take it over* and turn it forcibly toward a more tough-minded and realistic examination of her own situation and its potentialities.

The long speech on "gentilesse," "poverte," and "elde" that forms the second major digression in the tale is notable for the consistency with which it presents a diminished image of human possibility and for the constant stress it puts on the inadequacy of earthly hopes and the weakness of earthly power:

> "Ful selde up riseth by his branches smale
> Prowesse of man, for God, of his goodnesse,
> Wole that of hym we clayme oure gentillesse";
> For of oure eldres may we no thyng clayme
> But temporel thyng, that man may hurte and mayme.
>
> (1128–32)

In the face of all this human weakness the speech urges a stoic position. Boethius and Seneca are prominent in it. The burden especially of the account of poverty is, Stop striving for impossible goals and the fulfillment of petty human desires: "He that coveiteth is a povre wight, / For he wolde han that is nat in his myght" (1187–88). Instead, it says, embrace your weakness, understand it, and make of it an occasion of virtue. True "gentilesse" lies not in human glory but in gentle deeds, and the hateful good of poverty leads a man to know his God. The Wife of Bath uses the mask of the hag as an image of her own diminished powers and vanished "flour" to try out this rhetoric, to see what the bran is worth. As a version of the Wife, the hag functions here as a kind of worst-case scenario for her: Suppose I never get married again, suppose I *am* old and ugly and my life *is* essentially over; suppose that the energy of my youth is gone forever and that there is nothing left from now on but the downward slope to death. What resources of self-respect and dignity remain to me, and what ways of living are appropriate to my condition? If all the Wife has left is the wisdom she has gained from her experience, she can at least use it to guide herself into old age, where it may be necessary to adopt a more conventional style of life and attend to the needs of her soul.

If it feels like there is something a little disingenuous about this position, and if a less respectful paraphrase of it might be, Well, I can always get religion, that is probably because we know the Wife too well by now to be entirely convinced by the more pious version. My point is that the Wife feels the same way and that the inadequacies for her of this passive, static, and renunciatory position, this surrender to the values of the patriarchal law, are part of what she discovers in the act of trying it out. The best evidence of this resistance is the emergence of a countermessage in the "gentilesse" digression itself, a "privy" subtext that affirms something different from its "apert" argument and in fact subverts it. This subtext first appears in what I call the torchbearer simile, the rhetorical treatment of a philosophical argument that is in itself clear and easy to make. Boethius does it in a brief sentence: If "gentilesse" were a gift of nature it would always be the same everywhere, "sicut ignis ubique terrarum numquam tamen calere desistit," as fire is always and everywhere hot.[11] Here is the Wife of Bath's version:

> If gentillesse were planted natureely
> Unto a certeyn lynage doun the lyne,
> Pryvee and apert thanne wolde they nevere fyne
> To doon of gentillesse the faire office;
> They myghte do no vileynye or vice.
>   Taak fyr and ber it in the derkeste hous
> Betwix this and the mount of Kaukasous,
> And lat men shette the dores and go thenne;
> Yet wole the fyr as faire lye and brenne
> As twenty thousand men myghte it biholde;
> His office natureel ay wol it holde,
> Up peril of my lyf, til that it dye.
>   Heere may ye se wel how that genterye
> Is nat annexed to possessioun,
> Sith folk ne doon her operacioun
> Alwey, as dooth the fyr, lo, in his kynde.
>
> (1134–49)

Notice how the image of the fire is detached from the argument, slightly displaced from logical sequence and foregrounded in a way that makes the argument itself hard to follow because the image is so detailed and compelling, so much more developed than what surrounds it (or, I might add, than it is in any of its sources). This foregrounding makes the image of the fire flaming out in isolation and

---

11. *Consolatio Philosophiae*, in Boethius, *Theological Tractates*, III pr. 4.

darkness take on a force independent of the place and function of the image in the argument. The bright energy of the fire is affirmed against all the conventional rhetoric of human weakness that surrounds it, and this affirmation is one key to its source and meaning.

Another key is the associations that fire has taken on in the *Wife of Bath's Prologue* and elsewhere in the tale. As in the prologue, the effacement of logical and temporal sequence that textuality and re-reading make possible allows the construction of a system or rhizome of fire imagery that bears on this final instance and decenters it: "For peril is bothe fyr and tow t'assemble; / Ye knowe what this ensample may resemble" (89–90). If fire is initially and fundamentally associated with sexuality for the Wife, it also acquires the aggressive dimension, the intimation of sexual threat, that her free use of her sex sometimes takes on:

> He is to greet a nygard that wolde werne
> A man to lighte a candle at his lanterne;
> He shal have never the lasse light, pardee.
> Have thou ynogh, thee thar nat pleyne thee.
> (333–36)

> Thou liknest [women's love] also to wilde fyr;
> The moore it brenneth, the more it hath desir
> To consume every thyng that brent wole be.
> (373–75)

As the second of these examples suggests, fire comes to be associated with what is uncontrollable, especially by masculine limits and standards. It is something that breaks through and consumes the oppressions of male decorum, as in the case of Midas's wife:

> Hir thoughte it swal so soore aboute hir herte
> That nedely som word hire moste asterte;
> And sith she dorste telle it to no man,
> Doun to a mareys faste by she ran—
> Til she cam there hir herte was afyre—
> (967–71)

Fire has, then, for the Wife far more than conventional connotations of inexhaustible energy, linked not only with sexuality but also with her self-assertion and sense of independence, with everything that makes her most aware of her own vitality. If that vitality is presented in negative and destructive terms earlier in the poem, more as men see it when they try to smother it, here in its more inward and private manifestations it takes on a positive sense as an image of the Wife's freedom even in the midst of constraint. Her private attraction to the image of the torch is an index of her resistance to the darkness and to the message of human weakness and decay that surrounds the fire and the woman. Like the instances in the prologue of surges of energy associated with remembering, with which it is connected, this upsurge of inner fire happens spontaneously and happens now, in the act of speaking.[12] The Wife rediscovers as she speaks what the whole experience of performing the prologue and tale have affirmed: that her resistance, her energy, and her fire are not gone at all, and that they have outlasted the decay of her youth and beauty. This awareness lies behind the reservations she expresses when, in the guise of the hag, she comes to draw the moral consequences of the "gentilesse" argument:

> Yet may the hye God, and so hope I,
> Grante me grace to lyven vertuously.
> Thanne am I gentil, whan that I bigynne
> To lyven vertuously, and weyve synne.
>
> (1173–76)

The conditional mood in which this statement is cast calls attention to the fact that the speaker refrains from identifying herself completely with the position expressed: her hope that God will grant her the grace to live virtuously when she decides to begin carries the implication that that time has not yet arrived.[13]

Thus there is little point to the sort of critical objection that notes how the Wife of Bath cannot qualify as "gentil" under her own definition in the speech and takes this circumstance as an irony of which she is unaware, since this is precisely the point she is affirming triumphantly in her handling of the speech itself.[14] The content or *doctrine* here is neither out of character nor in it for the Wife. Rather it is something that culture (masculine culture at that) makes available and that the Wife is using for her own purposes—here perhaps as a kind of poten-

12. This phenomenon will be considered in a more theoretical framework in Part II under the heading of *jouissance*.
13. See Colmer, "Character and Class," 335.
14. For example, Lumiansky, *Of Sondry Folk;* Ropollo, "Converted Knight," 263–69; Albrecht, "Sermon on 'Gentilesse,' " 459; Slade, "Irony in the Wife of Bath's Tale," 241–47.

tial *remedia amoris* or "remedye of love" (I, 45). What the Wife reaps
in this section of the tale are the real fruits of her experience. External
youth and beauty are and were, she discovers, just as deceptive as the
traditional wisdom has always maintained because they worked to
conceal from her the real inner sources of her vitality, the capacity for
the enjoyment of life and the indomitable spirit that are still with her
now that their conventional physical signs have passed. The external
deprivation, the "poverte," is the condition that makes possible the
discovery of inner fire and inner richness. It is indeed a bringer out of
busyness and an amender of sapience precisely because it "Maketh [a
man] his God *and eek hymself* to knowe" (1202, emphasis added).

By the time she gets to the matter of "elde," the hag is speaking out
clearly for the Wife in words we have heard before:

> Now, sire, of elde ye repreve me;
> And certes, sire, *thogh noon auctoritee*
> *Were in no book,* ye gentils of honour
> Seyn that men sholde an oold wight doon favour
> . . . .
> And auctors shal I fynden, as I gesse.
> (1207–12, emphasis added)

Elde is essentially dismissed, left for the future, because it is not yet
time in the Wife's life—and that time may never come—for her to
lapse into decorum, piety, and silence. No more than Janekyn with his
book can those church fathers and stoic philosophers—men every jack
of them—tame her. The Wife asserts her vitality and her resistance to
the deadening pressure of conventional proprieties in her treatment of
the conclusion of the story—for instance, in the riddle, whose form in
the analogues is a choice between having the hag fair by day and foul
by night or vice versa. The Wife of Bath's version—foul and obedient
or fair and take your chances—reaffirms the sense of her own energy,
independence, and impenitence that has been growing in her during
the latter part of the tale: I'd do it all again, she seems to say, and I will
if I get the chance:

> Or elles ye wol han me yong and fair,
> And take youre aventure of the repair
> That shal be to youre house by cause of me,
> Or in som oother place, may wel be.
> (1223–26)

The extent to which the concerns and the mood that dominate the subtext of the "gentilesse" speech take precedence over the more conventional aspects of the romance is further pointed up by the wife's handling of the final lines of the tale, in which she drops the expected happy ending in the middle of a line and goes out swinging:

> And thus they lyve unto hir lyves ende
> In parfit joye; and Jhesu Crist us sende
> Housbondes meeke, yonge, and fressh abedde,
> And grace t'overabyde hem that we wedde;
> And eek I praye Jhesu shorte hir lyves
> That nought wol be governed by hir wyves;
> And olde and angry nygardes of dispence,
> God sende hem soone verray pestilence!
>
> (1257–64)

This concluding speech reflects both the mood of independence that sustains the Wife and the critique of romance conventions that she has been conducting: the persons of the story may have lived happily ever after, but the Wife doubts the relevance of this ending to real marriages, and she is making no promises about herself. The speech is also a return to the public occasion of the tale in the sense that it presents the Wife in the polemical and oppositional role that is appropriate to the general feminist message and her original battle plan for the story. But that public role and even that message are qualified for us by the private subtext of the telling. The shrew of the end of the tale is a straw woman, a role the Wife plays for tactical reasons that have to do precisely with the inadequacies of the public situation in which she speaks with respect to the complexities of experience. It is clear from both the prologue and the tale that for the Wife "maistrye" is not really a simple mechanical reversal of male domination. In both cases once the woman has been granted sovereignty she refrains from exercising it, and this restraint suggests, on the model of the Wife's fifth marriage, that sovereignty is primarily a tool for achieving feminine independence *within* marriage so that more satisfactory relations between the sexes can have a chance to develop.[15]

15. Once again a number of commentators have recognized the provisional and preliminary—what I would call the public—character of the idea of "maistrye," though once again the Wife herself has not been given much credit for understanding it. Charles A. Owen, in his pioneering and still fundamental study "The Crucial Passages in Five of

"Maistrye" is a way of making room for the possibility of love in the patriarchal world by giving women space to be responsible partners in a relationship. As only an "answere suffisant," it is where everything that is important about marriage begins, not where it ends. If anyone knows that *they lived happily ever after* is no way to talk about the experience of marriage, it is the Wife of Bath. Marriage is where things get harder, though potentially richer and more satisfying. But this aspect of marriage, the opportunity it offers for private fulfillment, is not really appropriate to the situation in which the Wife is performing. In the first place, the experience of real relationships cannot easily be conveyed in a story like this, as the Wife's critique of romance assumptions has made clear. At the end of the tale, consistent with her practice throughout, the Wife makes no real attempt to present the knight as someone who learns something or changes his mind; he is simply coerced and manipulated, as he has been throughout the tale. Those critics who have tried to insist that he is converted by the "gentilesse" speech seem to me to be trying to supply a minimal version of what would be needed to make a conventional happy ending convincing.[16] The conspicuous absence of any such personalization of the knight is part of the Wife's assessment of what the tale, the genre, and the occasion allow. For, in the second place and especially, the experience of real relationships is not something that can be or need be conveyed to a casually assembled group of strangers encountered on a pilgrimage, most of them males, with whom there is little likelihood of, and little reason for, intimacy. As the Friar's interruption may remind us, one reason the personal inflection of the Wife's performance is relatively covert is that there is no one on the pilgrimage as worth talking to as Janekyn.

The unfolding of the prologue and tale in one sense subverts their programmatic statement in that it questions and undermines the Wife's presentation of herself as a definitive, exemplary character who

---

the *Canterbury Tales*," was the first to note the importance of the hag's refusal to exercise domination. Of the several critics who have developed this perception and seen that what the Wife wants—what women want—is some form of mutuality in relationships, particularly fine accounts are given by Howard, *Idea of the Canterbury Tales,* 254–55, and Burton, "Wife of Bath's Fourth and Fifth Husbands," esp. 46–47.

16. The earliest statement of this case is Roppolo, "Converted Knight." See also Cary, "Sovereignty and the Old Wife"; Levy, "Loathly Lady and Dante's Siren"; and Shapiro, "Dame Alice as Deceptive Narrator."

is the completed product of her history. Instead, we come to see that this character is a *role* that she can choose to play or not, depending on the circumstances. The end of the tale shows something of the usefulness of this role. The man-eating monster who appears here and elsewhere may be a caricature of the real Wife of Bath, or at least a partial representation, but as a role it is also a way of making sure that no one will try to take advantage of her: it asserts her independence and keeps it firmly in view. In this sense "maistrye" and the polemical feminism associated with it are practically necessary in the world as a woman finds it, as a defense and a precondition for the mutuality she might prefer. The conditions of the male-dominated public world may be said to have forced this position on the Wife, and its necessity shows just how unsatisfactory the public situation of women is in human terms. That women can find ways to take advantage of the institutional structure that constrains them cannot be construed as an apology or justification for the system. To make the male world into a straw man—to be forced to do so to fight its ubiquitous and dehumanizing public pressures—is still to accept a logic of opposition and appropriation that can only drive someone to constitute herself as a straw woman.[17]

"But lordynges, by youre leve, that am nat I" (112). Beyond and behind the public, necessarily caricatured feminism of the "apert" narration there is a set of "privy" experiences that construct a deeper and more existentially responsible feminism and a more searching critique of male domination. What the Wife responds to intuitively about her tale is less what it includes than what it leaves out. One of the most sexist things about this story and the romance genre it exemplifies is the assumption that women have no consequential interests beyond courtship and marriage. Men may do battle and have adventures, but the stories of women in romance are all love stories. As we have seen, such a story has no way of handling an ugly old woman as heroine—or even an attractive but not classically beautiful middle-aged one—except by magic and no place at all for issues like a

17. This is not to say, however, that there is anything fake about the feminism of the Wife's public position or her commitment to it, even if it does not always express everything she thinks about gender, power, personal relations, and the like. Her position on "maistrye" in marriage is a proposal for real institutional reform in the going system. Her financial dealings, at least what we know of them, are generally consistent with this position and cannot have been easy to sustain.

woman's experience of age and the prospect of death. The Wife's most telling criticism of the tale is that such stories have no room for a Wife of Bath.

The issues of romance—gender and sexual relations, love and marriage—are important to the Wife herself; they have dominated much of her life, and they are fully represented in her prologue and tale. But for us to hold her exclusively to them, or for her to do so herself, does not allow her all the other things in her life and experience, including her humanity before age and death. In fact, in her tale we see the speaker as a woman exercising her "purveyaunce," considering her options in line with her own philosophy: "I holde a mouses herte nat worth a leek / That hath but oon hole for to sterte to" (572–73). She may find her way back into marriage and the dance of relationship that has occupied and engaged her for so long, but she may not. In this open situation the Wife herself remains open. By the end of her tale she has evoked her own energies in the face of what those energies have to contend with and enacted a variety of possible responses to her unknown future. She seems, in part for reasons that will occupy us in Part II, at ease with her subjectivity, which manifests itself to her here as a source of freedom and spontaneity. She finds that her experience has provided her with extensive resources for continuing her *Frauenhandlung* with the authorities—with God the Father, with the masculine world, and with Old Man Death—and that she need not commit or confine herself to any particular role or position except as a tactical move in whatever game she may have occasion to play. The Wife of Bath does not need to define herself once and for all.

2

THE SUBJECT ENGENDERED

6

The Pardoner as Subject
Deconstruction and Practical Consciousness

I want now to return to the question of the Pardoner's subjectivity, beginning in a nontheoretical, practical way by comparing the tone or feel of the Wife's and the Pardoner's performances. Though I know of only one article that attempts a formal comparison of the two figures,[1] readers have always had a general sense, as Lumiansky puts it, of "a kindred spirit between them,"[2] and there are a number of features of the texts that invite putting them together. The two tales are, as I argued in Part I, the only formal and deliberate self-presentations in the poem: each uses a central character as a surrogate for the speaker, and the two pilgrims address each other in the course of the Pardoner's interruption of the *Wife of Bath's Prologue*. One feels the force of Anne Kernan's good question, "Why should it be the Pardoner who interrupts the Wife?" ("Archwife and the Eunuch," 3) even if the answer to it remains uncertain, and a rereading of this moment is a useful place to start making the comparison.[3]

The interruption occurs at a point where the Wife has just summarized her aggressive appropriation of the doctrine of the marriage *debitum*:

> "An housbonde I wol have—I wol nat lette—
> Which shal be bothe my dettour and my thral,
> And have his tribulacion withal
> Upon his flessh, whil that I am his wyf.

1. See Kernan, "Archwife and the Eunuch."
2. Lumiansky, *Of Sondry Folk,* 205. See also Spiers, *Chaucer the Maker,* 137, and, best of all, Patterson, " 'For the Wyves Love of Bathe'," 683.
3. Since this is a rereading, a textual and desequenced retrospective account of the already interpreted text, it will ignore questions like that of the order of the tales, for example, the likelihood that the Wife's tale precedes the Pardoner's in the fictional time of the pilgrimage so that the latter tale has not "happened" yet when they have their encounter. I would like to thank Dan Kempton for nagging me about the importance of this exchange until I was forced to work it out.

> I have the power durynge al my lyf
> Upon his propre body, and noght he.
> Right thus the Apostel tolde it unto me,
> And bad oure housbondes for to love us weel.
> Al this sentence me liketh every deel"—
>   Up stirte the Pardoner, and that anon;
> "Now, dame," quod he, "by God and by Seint John!
> Ye been a noble prechour in this cas.
> I was aboute to wedde a wyf; allas!
> What sholde I bye it on my flessh so deere?
> Yet hadde I levere wedde no wyf to-yeere!"
>
>   (III, 154–68)

After a response by the Wife to the effect, You haven't heard anything yet! (169–83), the Pardoner makes one final comment that leads, as discussed at the beginning of chapter 3, to the Wife's autobiographical continuation:

> "Dame, I wolde praye yow, if youre wyl it were,"
> Seyde this Pardoner, "as ye bigan,
> Telle forth youre tale, spareth for no man,
> And teche us yonge men of youre praktike."
>
>   (184–87)

As Kernan notes, in this "confrontation between the two pilgrims who are apparently polar opposites . . . it seems at first that a quarrel is about to break out between them" ("Archwife and the Eunuch," 25), but an explosion such as takes place at the end of the Pardoner's tale does not occur here. One reason it does not is that from whatever motives, the Wife does not respond to any of the intimations of irony in the Pardoner's intervention—instead she takes him literally, as if there were no mocking or aggressive component in his interruption. Though I am doubtful about Kernan's explanation of the Pardoner's motives, I agree that the Wife *acts as if* "the Pardoner has intended only to express his interest in the idea that Alison has introduced and to encourage her to expand on what she has just said" (ibid.). In a way this behavior is even odder because paradoxically, as I will argue shortly, the Wife is most like the Pardoner in her relation to the masculine law before he interrupts. His comment actually helps her to escape from an essentially fruitless mode of confrontation. Though one could easily imagine her hearing the Pardoner as mocking or patronizing her—as she does the apparently more innocent comment of the Friar later—instead she makes room in her discourse for this other great confessor among the pilgrims. Indeed, it is he who elicits her confession. She responds to his request to "teche us yonge men of youre praktike" as to a genuine request for information and treats the Pardoner as a real partner in dialogue, whose voice makes a contribution to the direction her performance takes. Whatever the particular combination of perceptions and motives that underlies the Wife's reaction here, it is in many ways typical of her and provides an opening for the investigation of how her modes of relation to others and her attitudes toward an experience of self that has much in common with the Pardoner are in contrast to his.

I have already shown in some detail how the Wife's relation to temporality is radically particular and experiential. Even at those moments when she seems most concerned to establish a perspective that is removed from time, she maintains a subtext of her own history. For example, in the chiding speech to the three old husbands, which purports to be a demonstration of how to talk to any husbands at any time, rereading shows that the entire passage can be connected to specific issues and situations in the Wife's fourth and fifth marriages. What appears abstract and atemporal is in fact concrete and historical.[4] Similarly, analysis of the Wife's use of tenses shows how she uses past and present as ways of registering the force, for her in the now of speaking, of various elements of her consciousness: tense is an instrument of experiential nuance. The Pardoner's different attitude toward temporality can be elicited from his different deployment of tense:

> In Flaundres whilom *was* a compaignye
> Of yonge folk that *haunteden* folye,
> As riot, hasard, stywes, and tavernes,
> Where as with harpes, lutes, and gyternes,
> They *daunce* and *pleyen* at dees bothe day and nyght,
> And *eten* also and *drynken* over hir myght,
> Thurgh which they *doon* the devel sacrifise
> Withinne that develes temple in cursed wise
> By superfluytee abhomynable.
> Hir othes *been* so grete and so dampnable
> That it *is* grisly for to heere hem swere.

4. More accurately, insofar as the temporality of the speech is undecidable (see the end of chapter 4), it is multitemporal, that is, applicable in different ways to different *specific* times and situations.

Oure blissed Lordes body they *totere*—
Hem *thoughte* that Jewes rente hym noght ynough—
And ech of hem at otheres synne *lough*.
And right anon thanne *comen* tombesteres . . .
                              (VI, 463–77, emphasis added)

The alternations between past and present tenses in this passage have
a rhetorical force in the now of speaking insofar as they function to
impart varying degrees of vividness and immediacy to the various
elements of the description.[5] The use of the present tense in such things
as "it is grisly for to heere hem swere" or the entry of the dancing girls
serves to make us imaginatively present to what is described: tense is
an instrument of rhetorical nuance. But the overall effect of the passage, especially when read in the context of the Pardoner's performance, is to play down the importance of temporality in favor of a
general effect of timelessness. Since these are not memories but rhetorically enhanced descriptions of various kinds of sinful behavior, the
alternations in tense tend to push the events they affect into a kind of
figural time, a "whenever" or "always." As the passage shows it, sin
occurs continually, so that in a sense it does not matter whether it is
located in the past or the present; in fact the present tense, exactly
contrary to the way the Wife of Bath uses it, is here a marker for the
atemporal or constant.[6] As with the other features of the Pardoner's
sermon the pervasiveness and generality of sin are insisted on at the
expense of the phenomena that happen to embody it at any particular
time or place. This feature is of course in keeping with the exemplary

5. Tense alternation of this sort is of course common in Old French narrative,
especially in the earlier periods, and has collected a large mass of commentary. The
literature is summarized and new ground broken in Fleischman, "Evaluation in Narrative." The one case Fleischman does not consider is the one relevant here, the deliberate
textual representation (rather than the transcription) of what she calls performance
narrative, but her conclusions support my reading of this passage.

6. This opposition suggests the difficulties that arise from Benveniste's analyses of
the functions of tenses in *Problems in General Linguistics,* especially as used by Barthes
in, for example, "To Write: An Intransitive Verb?" or "Structural Analysis of Narratives." Structures like the aorist operate at the level of *langue* as ways of getting something done, as institutions within language, so to speak, for registering *histoire* as
opposed to *discours* in situations where it is more or less appropriate that no one speaks.
At the level of *parole,* however, such "institutions" can be used rhetorically for the
deliberate production by a speaker of *histoire* effects within a particular discourse, as the
Pardoner does here. It seems probable that even at the level of *langue* there is actually
only *discours,* though it sometimes masquerades as *histoire.* See Culler, *Structuralist
Poetics,* 197–200.

thrust of the narrative: the story of the three rioters, told in the past tense, is simply an instance of a more general and timeless set of spiritual conditions that continue to "present" themselves in both inflections of the word. Even those moments when the vividness and detail of the description give the effect of a speaker who knows personally whereof he speaks, such as the passage on the wine of Cheapside or the account of the dice game, employ that experience as a means of associating the speaker with the sins described, of making the Pardoner another example of them.

The same general differences of attitude and procedure characterize the Pardoner and the Wife in their approaches to impersonation—the relation of the self to fictional others. Unlike the Pardoner, the Wife of Bath retains a sense of the difference between one occasion and another, of what is appropriate to a given situation and time and what is not. She retains as well a firm grasp of the practical difference (as opposed to the ontological difference, which may not exist) between fiction and real life: she knows what she can get away with. This sense of differences is manifested in a way that bears on impersonation in the Wife's voicing of the exempla she cites at the end of her prologue (715–70). I have argued at length in chapter 4 that her practice is to make these stories more experiential as she proceeds. In her telling they move toward taking on an independent life of their own and becoming complex historical and existential accounts. In so doing they move away from exemplarity and determinate or paraphrasable meaning, moral or otherwise. In part it is a question of treating these lives as if they had really happened, trying to imagine what it was like to live them, *putting oneself in another's place*. I do not mean to imply that the Wife completely effaces herself, and certainly not that she does not exploit the exempla and the characters in her tale (including the various personae of herself) for her own ends. Insofar as fictional others do become surrogates for the Wife, she treats them, as I have shown, as roles she can play or refuse, and the important thing about a role is that it has a certain autonomy and independence. We think of roles as discrete parts of our repertoire; they are composed of a number of particular routines and address themselves to particular areas of competence. As a story has a plot that can be told in different ways, a role has (or is) a character that can be variously played. (This is not, naturally, an innocent comparison.) The most important example in the Wife's tale is obviously the hag, who is a hypothetical self, a way of examining certain contingencies and trying out certain solutions to them, be they the sobrieties of resigned old age or the fantasies of regained youth. As such, the hag has, as critics have always noticed, a distinctive voice of her own, the voice of the "gentilesse" speech, which is not in any simple sense that of the *Wife of Bath's Prologue*. Moreover, this voice strongly contrasts with that of another role, the Wife as marital whip, which closes the tale by drawing with some firmness the boundary between a fictional happy ending and the ongoing demands of the battle of the sexes in the real world. Another way to describe the Wife's subjecthood would be to say that her self is the enumeration of the roles she is seen to play, the number of other people she can become.

By contrast, the way the Pardoner appears to treat the Wife in her prologue, at least if we take his intervention as to some degree ironic and aggressive, looks like a version of the way he treats the characters in his tale because whatever the interruption means, it works more by calling attention to him than to the Wife's speech. The more ironical the interruption is, the more it seeks to deflect the Wife and the other pilgrims into an engagement with the Pardoner rather than with the meaning of the Wife's discourse. Consider again the speech of the taverner's boy in the *Pardoner's Tale*:

> "Sire," quod this boy, "it nedeth never-a-deel;
> It was me toold er ye cam heer two houres.
> He was, pardee, an old felawe of youres,
> And sodeynly he was yslayn to-nyght,
> Fordronke, as he sat on his bench upright.
> Ther cam a privee theef men clepeth Deeth,
> That in this contree al the peple sleeth,
> And with his spere he smoot his herte atwo,
> And wente his wey withouten wordes mo.
> He hath a thousand slayn this pestilence.
> And, maister, er ye come in his presence,
> Me thynketh that it were necessarie
> For to be war of swich an adversarie.
> Beth redy for to meet hym everemoore;
> Thus taughte me my dame; I sey namoore."
>   (VI, 670–84)

As I pointed out earlier, the speech contains a number of places where the sophisticated typological consciousness of the Pardoner *imposes* on the innocent one of the youth. Insofar as we are being asked to notice a level of spiritual meaning that the character does not intend, we encounter a version of unimpersonated artistry, the Pardoner's meaning, not the character's. In its typologizing drive to reveal the "truth" of the situation, the voice violates impersonation and the integrity of the character in a way that reduces him to an unwitting spokesman for the Pardoner's vision. Similarly, in the case of the three rioters (see above, pp. 48–51) the Pardoner's processing of their speeches and actions not only makes them into pawns of the tale's morality (which any exemplum would do) but also, as I have argued, into deficient or incomplete versions of the Pardoner himself. Though this processing appears to arise in part from the Pardoner's dissatisfaction with the reductive morality of the exemplum, it is itself reductive in that it *appropriates* the tale and its characters, forces them to take on the same meanings that the Pardoner gives himself. The symmetry of the contrast with the Wife is apparent here: the appropriation that is for her the public project of her performance is the subtext of the Pardoner's, which his own public performance ultimately fails to enforce.

The peculiarities of the Pardoner's position emerge most clearly in the epilogue, where it becomes apparent that what he does to his characters he also tries to do to the pilgrims, as indeed he has been doing all along. As with the rioters and the Old Man, though in a different way, in the epilogue the Pardoner undertakes to speak for others—in this case literally to tell them what to do—so as to reveal who they "really" are. As he seems to do less pressingly with the Wife in her prologue, the Pardoner tries to engage the pilgrims in a play of ironies, here in the corrosive ones that are generated by all the possible meanings and inflections of the idea *you take pardon from me*. This forcing of the truth of his falsehood is reductive in the same sense and manner as his other appropriations of the tale and of the occasion of telling because it is controlled by the same contempt for others and the same reduction of their independence. It says to the pilgrims, in effect, You do not see your real spiritual situation, your nothingness; you do not know who you are, that you are like me—and I do. This is one version of the superiority the Pardoner claims, of the presumptuous pride of his despair. His is a sensibility that ultimately makes no distinction between fictional characters and real persons, between a tale and the world it is told in, or between the public and the private realms. The style of the Pardoner's confession is to make the private public in the sense of insisting on the public *significance* of himself, a significance of which others are only versions and extensions. He is, or at least here comes to be, as impatient with fiction as the Parson whose double and contrary the Pardoner strives to be, and he is perhaps even more obsessed than the Parson with the truth behind phenomena, even though he engages that truth in the mode of negation. It is precisely at the moment of the application of the exemplum to real life that the tendency to think of real people as exempla reveals the damage it does to both examples and persons.

It is surely no accident that, as Robinson noticed long ago,[7] the Old Man and the hag cite the same text with respect to themselves, Leviticus 19:32, "Coram cano capite consurge, et honora personam senis":

> In Hooly Writ ye may yourself wel rede:
> "Agayns an oold man, hoor upon his heed,
> Ye sholde arise."
>
> (VI, 742–44)

> And certes, sire, thogh noon auctoritee
> Were in no book, ye gentils of honour
> Seyn that men sholde an oold wight doon favour
> And clepe hym fader, for youre gentillesse;
> And auctours shal I fynden, as I gesse.
>
> (III, 1208–12)

In the *Wife of Bath's Tale* the hag alludes loosely to the text and keeps it in the background. The Wife does not use it as a command or a club; in fact, *she does not use it yet*. It exists for her as a resource, and one that will need further work when the time comes to make it fit her case, as the awkwardness of "clepe hym fader" in the context suggests. Like the hag herself, the text is a *figure of possibility* for the Wife, something she can make use of when the occasion arises. This flexibility, this openness to otherness and possibility within the open-endedness of subjectivity, remains characteristic of the Wife and differentiates her most clearly from the Pardoner.

In the *Pardoner's Tale* the text is presented, both within the fictional world and outside it, as a commandment, which of course it is in Leviticus. As I have argued, the command is ironized by the Pardoner's

7. See his note to III, 1210, in *Riverside Chaucer*, 874.

presentation so as to enter into his characteristic structure of negations, here according to the simultaneous formula *respect your elders /
rise up against the* vetus homo, but without losing the edge of demand
that it carries. In the Pardoner's voicing, the text simultaneously requires one course of action and its opposite and presses this aporia
out of the tale and into the world of the pilgrimage. Like the Old Man
himself, the text is an essential definition of a continuing state of self-
contradiction.

To say so much is to give an account of the Pardoner's irony that is
essentially structural, that is, that describes the functioning of the trope
without reference to the agency and consciousness of the subject. The
central problem of the *Pardoner's Tale* is notoriously the question of
its tone, its *seriousness,* which stems from its relation to the Pardoner's
agency and consciousness. Critics of the tale often feel the need to
distinguish between where the Pardoner is being serious and where he
is being ironic, and each critic gives a different account of the difference.[8] The Pardoner's performance is constituted so as to render this
distinction impossible to make because his language does not distinguish between literal or referential and allegorical or spiritual levels of
meaning in his discourse. Paul de Man, who is himself the master of
deconstruction in this mode and whose account of Rousseau's *Confessions* is extremely valuable for understanding the *Pardoner's Tale,*[9]
speaks of this form of ironization as "the systematic undoing . . . of
understanding" (*Allegories of Reading,* 301), and we might take his
description of the effect of the line "How can we know the dancer from
the dance?" in Yeats's "Among School Children" as a general account
of the Pardoner's discourse. The point at issue is the possibility of
reading any grammatically constituted question as a rhetorical question, that is, one that does not expect an answer, and in the case of the
line from Yeats we face the reverse possibility that what clearly appears to be a rhetorical question may actually be a real one. The
application to the Pardoner emerges if the distinction is transposed to
literal versus spiritual rather than grammatical versus rhetorical:

8. I am indebted to Professor Sandy Feinstein for this observation, made in a National Endowment for the Humanities seminar on Chaucer taught by Robert W. Hanning at Columbia University in the summer of 1985.
9. See especially his discussion of the text as an excuse machine, *Allegories of
Reading,* 278–301.

For it turns out that the entire scheme set up by the first reading [that the question is rhetorical] can be undermined, or deconstructed, in the terms of the second, in which the final line is read literally as meaning that, since the dancer and the dance are not the same, it might be useful, perhaps even desperately necessary, for the question can be given a ring of urgency—"Please tell me, how *can* I know the dancer from the dance"—to tell them apart. . . . Two entirely coherent but entirely incompatible readings can be made to hinge on one line, whose grammatical structure is devoid of ambiguity, but whose rhetorical mode turns the mood as well as the mode of the entire poem upside down. Neither can we say . . . that the poem simply has two meanings that exist side by side. The two readings have to engage each other in direct confrontation, for the one reading is precisely the error denounced by the other and has to be undone by it. Nor can we in any way make a valid decision as to which of the readings can be given priority over the other; none can exist in the other's absence. There can be no dance without a dancer. On the other hand, the authority of the meaning engendered by the grammatical structure is fully obscured by the duplicity of a figure that cries out for the differentiation that it conceals.

(*Allegories of Reading*, 11–12)

This position also has consequences for the subject, the voice of the text. To make determinate meaning or reference disappear in this way is to make a determinate "I" disappear as well. The ironist, like the rhetorical questioner in Yeats's poem, notoriously does not "stand behind" what he says. Because you can never be sure if he is serious or ironic, sincere or rhetorical, his "real meaning" *and his "real self"* are always displaced. They are always something and somewhere else, different and deferred.

An analysis like de Man's produces an account of the place of the self in discourse as always already deconstructed by factors in language that operate in a certain sense before any particular instance, use, or inflection. His account of Yeats, like the famous reading of a passage from Proust that immediately follows it (*Allegories of Reading*, 13–15, cf. 57–58), outlines what he elsewhere calls "a predicament [that] is linguistic rather than ontological or hermeneutic" (*Allegories of Reading*, 300). The absence of a determinate "I" is an effect of the structure of the trope regardless of the intention of the speaker. Language itself reflexively deconstructs the self. The first-person pronoun is what is called, with odd aptness, a shifter, a place in language that can be occupied by any individual. It is the place of a subject that both enacts and is enacted by the play of irony, and the deconstructionist position is that this double dispossession of subject and referent can always be exacted in principle of any text.

So far, then, I have outlined how a deconstruction of the Pardoner as subject in Chaucer's text might proceed, but the question of consciousness can be pursued further. I have argued that we can always interrogate a text as to the attitudes its speaker displays toward the play of language that constitutes it. De Man is also aware that the kind of decentering of the subject he describes can become available to consciousness and that when it does, it has an affective component. For de Man, Rousseau is such a consciousness, and in his analysis of the *Confessions* he points to "the anxiety with which Rousseau acknowledges the lethal quality of all writing. Writing always includes the moment of dispossession in favor of the arbitrary power-play of the signifier and *from the point of view of the subject this can only be experienced as a dismemberment, a beheading or a castration*" (*Allegories of Reading*, 296, emphasis added).

While I am not certain that any subject can experience its *différance* only in this way (would a female subject experience it as castration?), I certainly agree that in the case of the Pardoner this anguished tone or mood is dominant, though with a slightly different inflection. I have argued that the Old Man in the *Pardoner's Tale* is a surrogate for the narrator and in particular a surrogate for, and representation of, the narrator's self-consciousness, his experience of himself. This self-consciousness is, in a manner typical of the tale, allegorically displaced from the spiritual to the literal: we are asked, for instance, to read a literal old man in the story as a figure for the Pardoner as *vetus homo* outside it. From this point of view the Old Man's most direct declaration of his condition, "Lo how I vanysshe, flessh, and blood, and skyn!" (VI, 732; see above, pp. 48–50) must be read, like other details such as the chest and hair shirt, as the ironic literal representation of a spiritual state, a feeling of inner wasting away.[10] The presentation of

10. See the analysis of the presentation of the third rioter above, p. 51. This is not to say that the literal, the physical, is in any way transcended, negated, or left behind: it is precisely because the Pardoner senses himself as spiritual and immortal that he is genuinely horrified and offended by the condition of being embodied, bound to a dying animal. His hatred and contempt of the flesh and its processes is not active only at an allegorical level. Rather, it is precisely *because* the body is an allegory, a sign for spirit, that its carnality is so intolerable.

the Old Man indicates that for the Pardoner the position of the ironist is not that of a superior and undisclosed essence *outside* the system of the trope. What he deploys against others is deployed with equal force against him, and this is painful to him. The Pardoner continually escapes not only us but also himself; he abides in his privation as something he undergoes: "I moot go thider as I have to go" (749). As I have indicated fully, the Pardoner consistently presents himself as the negation of positive terms: the Old Man as the contrary and denial of the *novus homo,* Christ; the *eunuchus* non *dei,* the embodiment of nonnormal sexuality rather than some specific perversion; and so on. He continually makes himself a sign for privation or, as a Lacanian might say, for a lack.[11] The indications are that he experiences this negation in himself as his own nothingness.

Hence *the fundamental experience of the constitution of the subject as an absence is the same* in the cases of the Wife of Bath and the Pardoner. For both, the "I" is what slips away, evades definition, never settles down: only their attitudes toward the alienation and heterogeneity of the self differ. Kierkegaard's skull-numbing initial definition, "The self is a relation that relates itself to itself," out of which *The Sickness unto Death* generates the logic and the phases of despair, is a formulation arising from Hegel's unhappy consciousness and feeding into Heidegger and Sartre; that is, it is a version of the modern concept of the subject as a construction, not a thing, of the self as something separated from itself that must continually make and remake itself. The formula is usefully glossed by his casual remark that "in the life of the spirit, everything is dialectical,"[12] that is, that as in the case of the Wife, any apparent state of self can immediately be understood also as its contrary; hence with the Pardoner the most powerful and insightful is the most miserable, the most physically unimpressive is the most spiritually dangerous, and so on. In effect, the Pardoner's performance—prologue, tale, and epilogue—is a response to, and a flight from, the same fundamental displacement of the subject that is embodied and experienced by the Wife of Bath. What seems for her a set of opportunities is for him an intolerable condition from which he suffers

11. See chapter 7.
12. Kierkegaard, *Sickness unto Death,* 116. It might be remembered that for Kierkegaard spirit is a particular (critical) inflection or extension of Hegel's notion of self-consciousness.

and against which he protests. Both the suffering and the protesting arise from this perception or experience of the self's subjectivity, a perception itself connected to the kind of ironist the Pardoner is, his sexuality, and his disenchanted attack on authority. A brief return to the encounter with the Wife and to its rhizomatic connections with some other areas of the text of the *Canterbury Tales* will help specify these relationships.

The statements that raise the possibility of irony most strongly in the Pardoner's interruption of the Wife are those that refer to his own sexuality, "I was aboute to wedde a wyf" (III, 166) and "teche us yonge men of youre praktike" (III, 187), because they activate the *question* about that sexuality that runs through the text of the poem. The Pardoner's statements to the Wife of course challenge the doubt expressed in the *General Prologue*, "I trowe he were a geldyng or a mare" (I, 691), but they are also related to his own response, in the introduction of his tale, to the oath "by Seint Ronyan!" (VI, 310), which the Host originally addresses to the Physician. In the aftermath of the sad story of Virginia the Host turns to the Pardoner:

> 'Thou beel amy, thou Pardoner,' he seyde,
> 'Telle us som myrthe or japes right anon.'
> 'It shal be doon,' quod he, 'by Seint Ronyon!'
>
> (VI, 318–20)

Critics have been quick to detect a pun on *runnion* (sexual organ),[13] and one is tempted to say that if the pun is not present when Harry Bailly first uses the oath, it comes into being when the Pardoner repeats it. If we needed reminding of the Pardoner's aura of problematic sexuality as established in the *General Prologue*, the slightly equivocal "beel amy," with its mock romance-politesse, helps do the job, as does the Pardoner's iteration, which, so to speak, stops the oath in the flow of discourse, marks it, and singles it out for inspection. The Pardoner has managed with his first phrase to establish his ironic distance in what I will argue is its crucial form, that of a special relation to language.[14]

---

13. See Robinson's note to VI, 310, *Works of Geoffrey Chaucer*, 2d. ed., 728, and *OED*, s.v. "runnion." *Riverside Chaucer* argues against the pun, note to VI, 310, 904.

14. "But I moot thynke / Upon som honest thyng while that I drynke" (VI, 327–28) works the same trick with the "gentils' " protest at 323–26.

If I am right in arguing that all such gestures on the Pardoner's part are deliberate allusions to, and manipulations of, the questionable character of his sexual seeming, then the effect is a conscious one.[15] But even if it is not, whether he presents or reveals himself here, because we do know there is something odd-seeming about him sexually, the Pardoner's citation of the Host still achieves the same effect insofar as he puts himself in *an ironic and negating relation to masculinity* that is at once an imitation and a denial of what it imitates. I shall return to the significance of this move in terms of gender later; for the present it is sufficient to see that the same move is being made in the interruption of the Wife. As Kernan notes, the Pardoner's comment is a response to a topic already raised by the Wife, that of the husband's "tribulacioun . . . / Upon his flessh" (III, 156–57), the aggressive and exploitative possibilities she finds in the marriage *debitum*. The comment thus follows the same pattern as the "Seinte Ronyan" oath, that of repeating and reflecting back to an interlocutor with a twist what he or she has just said, as the echo in "What sholde I bye it on my flessh so deere?" (167) establishes. Because it is an iteration, the Pardoner's remark functions as a *staging* or *miming* of a naive response to the threat the Wife has raised, and the fact that it is the Pardoner who does the iterating supplies the twist and makes the miming conspicuous. As in the exchange with the Host, the Pardoner here plays the masculinity he also suggests he is not.

Though I think the content of this moment, its specific reference to sexuality, is important, I want first to use it as a model of the Pardoner's consistent relation to language and to signifying systems generally. The Pardoner's characteristic activity at all levels is the miming or representation of all signifying relations so as to bring out their inherent contradictions, and that activity makes him not simply an instance of how determinate meaning and the determinate self are deconstructed by the inherent structure of signification but also an active *deconstructor*. As a critic of the established order, like the Wife of Bath, the Pardoner is what de Man calls an "archie Debunker," a questioner of the *arche* or origin, who demonstrates and dramatizes in

15. It is worth noting that "runnion," though perhaps not a primal word, has an antithetical significance since according to *OED* it means "the male sexual organ" and is also an unflattering way to refer to a woman, as in *Macbeth*: "Aroynt thee, Witch, the rumpe-fed Ronyon cryes" (1.3.6).

his own person how the most sacrosanct discourse of the established
order contradicts and undoes itself (*Allegories of Reading*, 9–10). As I
have suggested, his deconstructive weapon is a certain version or
inflection of the trope of irony, the master trope of indetermination.
The Pardoner's use of language, not only in these direct encounters
with other pilgrims but in his entire tale, ironizes the traditional align-
ment of *cortex* with carnal meaning and *nucleus* with spiritual meaning. As he presents it, any term, carnal or spiritual, may occupy a
position at the literal level as a cortex whose allegorical nucleus is its
opposite and negation, and that nucleus can become in turn the cortex
of a further allegorical reading in an unending and uncontainable play
of signification. The text becomes a kind of machine for producing this
play, which is anything but free since it consists of a rigorous structure
of repetitive negations. On the one hand, this language continually
insists that everything we think is physical or literal is actually an
allegory and a sign for spirit: a bottle, a dove on a barn, the shoulder
bone of a sheep, even—especially—a pardoner. On the other hand, at
the same time it insists that everything we think is spiritual is actually
carnal and literal, the corrupt and sinful debasement of the divine by
the merely human: a relic, a sermon, all the institutions of the church,
even—especially—a pardoner. Everything is simultaneously of the
highest importance and urgency and of the utmost triviality.

The Pardoner's iteration of the Wife's statement about the marriage
debitum draws it into the play of reversals that he represents, and
subjects it to his message of the falseness and treachery of the signifier.
That falseness is his de(con)structive truth, or at least what he presents
as the truth, and as always he presents that truth as himself: he is the
ironized signifier par excellence, whose deceptive presence undoes the
possibility of communication in pretending to communicate. What
happens here is that the Pardoner offers the Wife and the pilgrims
entry into the world of nothing-as-it-seems in his own mode of irony
and destructive deconstruction, seeming-as-nothingness. His miming
of the Wife functions as a way of taking her up on her own self-
presentation and asking her to maintain it in the face of his dialectical
challenge: What happens to who you say you are when you try it
with me?

It would make a difference here, as it does in the Pardoner's epilogue, whether the Pardoner thinks he is concealing the equivocation

from everybody,[16] from some members of the audience but not others (does he expect the Wife to catch the irony, as one con artist to another, or is he making fun of her to some or all of the other pilgrims?), or expects everyone to recognize that he is not what he is pretending to be and even that he expects them to know it. But the degree of his self-consciousness is precisely what we cannot tell about the interchange; the cues are too slight and equivocal, the interchange too peripheral and too quickly passed by in the flow of the fictional performance, as is the case in the Pardoner's epilogue as well. Nonetheless I think a little more can be said about the relation of the Pardoner's activity in general to consciousness. It seems apparent that that relation is variable and indeed multiple. In the temporal stream of its unfolding, the text registers various effects it makes most sense to interpret as the teller's active responses, conscious or unconscious or both, to the story as it emerges, but the choice between conscious and unconscious remains indeterminate. The fluctuating use of tenses that I have analyzed as a deployment of tense for rhetorical effect seems more likely to be located toward the conscious end of the spectrum, a monitoring of the details of the narration by its speaker to stress certain points taken to be especially important. But if that fluctuation of tenses is read, as it can be, in the mode of the *Wife of Bath's Prologue* as a reflection of momentary shifts in the speaker's experience of himself, something like memories, then what emerges is a fragmented subject unable to sustain a consistent, linear, lived relationship to temporality, and this experience seems more likely to be involuntary and therefore unconscious, at least at this point in the Pardoner's performance. There is of course no reason why both things cannot be going on at the same time so that a relatively planned rhetorical strategy also expresses an unconscious disposition.

In fact, however, it is most plausible to assume that the majority of these effects are neither unconscious symptoms nor deliberately planned ironic subversions but results of the operation of practical consciousness as it monitors the stream of conduct of the telling, functions of how the teller "goes on," provided we see that the practice in question is that of deconstruction. As Giddens points out, it is in the

16. This is the assumption of Donaldson's reading of the Pardoner's epilogue, *Chaucer's Poetry*, 1092–93.

nature of human action considered prospectively (that is, as irreversible linear unfolding) to resist being broken down into conscious and unconscious components. That determination is a function of retrospective interpretation, what he calls "attention":

> Reasons and intentions are not definite "presences" which lurk behind human social activity, but are routinely and chronically (in the *durée* of day-to-day existence) instantiated in that activity. The intentional character of human actions is: (a) not to be seen as an articulation of discrete and separate "intentions," but a continuous flow of intentionality in time; and (b) not to be treated as a set of conscious states that in some way "accompany" action. *Only in the reflexive act of attention are intentions consciously articulated: normally within discourse.*
>
> (*Central Problems*, 39–40,
> emphasis added)

Intentionality is a function of process; intention is a posterior construction, and *this assertion is as true for the experiencing subject as it is for an outside observer* and as true for a man preaching a sermon as it is for a woman remembering her life. Thus although in the case of both the Wife and the Pardoner there are grounds in the text for saying that they become more self-conscious as they proceed in their tales, that determination is and remains provisional and open to revision depending on different interpretive projects and interests of the reader (or the speaker) at any given point. After all, what is at stake here really only emerges clearly under the conditions of rhizomatic rereading, where its connections with textual situations "before" and "after" it in the fiction of the pilgrimage can be established. Under those conditions, however, what does emerge is precisely the consistency of the Pardoner's deconstructive undoing of signification in the smallest details of his relation to language, others, and himself. Since this effect is achieved however we posit the Pardoner's *intention*, I think we have to say that achieving this effect is his *motive* in the sense of what moves him whether he knows it or not, and regardless of *how* he knows it, at any given point. Practically speaking, it is not a metaphor to say that the Pardoner is a deconstructionist because that is in fact the precise and consistent character of his activity: it is what he knows how—*all* he knows how—to go on doing.

7

From Deconstruction
to Psychoanalysis and Beyond
Disenchantment and the "Masculine"
Imagination

The two sets of terms, or discourses, that I have used up to now to discuss the *Pardoner's Tale,* the traditional discourse of despair and the modern discourse of deconstruction, share a common basic structure with a number of other discourses for which the displacement of the subject is a central concern. That basic structure can be elicited from Jonathan Culler's admirably clear account of Freudian method:

> Freud begins with a series of hierarchical oppositions: normal/pathological, sanity/insanity, real/imaginary, experience/dream, conscious/unconscious, life/death. In each case the first term has been conceived as prior, a plenitude of which the second is a negation or complication. Situated on the margin of the first term, the second term designates an undesirable, dispensable deviation. Freud's investigations deconstruct these oppositions by identifying what is at stake in our desire to repress the second term and *showing that in fact each first term can be seen as a special case of the fundamentals designated by the second term, which in this process is transformed.* Understanding of the marginal or deviant term becomes a condition of understanding the supposedly prior term.
>
> (*On Deconstruction,* 160,
> emphasis added)

The transformation of the second term of which Culler speaks consists in the escape of the term from the dialectical opposition in which it was initially posited. The first term is revealed as a *false contrary* or special case of the second. The second term becomes a term without a contrary, which instead *produces* contraries, including the original false opposition. It should be noted, however, that such master/mistress terms have no determinate content. They are all terms for an undecid-

178

ability or an absence, as the false opposition life/death suggests with a certain mordancy.

There are, however, certain difficulties with both of the discourses in this pattern employed thus far, difficulties that emerge clearly in the attempt to compare the Pardoner with the Wife of Bath. In the case of the traditional discourse of despair Saint Augustine and Kierkegaard establish the pattern, which is that of the Fall, the fundamental deficiency in human existence that gives rise to the contrary states of *caritas* and *cupiditas*. When these states are conceived, as Augustine conceives them, as modes of being in the world or ways of enacting a self, the apparent opposition between the fullness of charity and the lack that occasions *cupiditas* is transformed so that both are now seen as ways of dealing with the fundamental lack, the wanting of God that underlies and constitutes the human condition. The *Pardoner's Tale* at least suggests that Chaucer is aware of this tradition; it is the first depiction in English of the psychology of despair later embodied in Spenser's Despayre, Shakespeare's Richard II, and Milton's Satan, to mention only the most distinguished examples.[1] Despite the availability of some form of this discourse to Chaucer, I hesitate to use *caritas* and *cupiditas* as organizing terms for a number of reasons. To begin with, I am not at all convinced that Chaucer found this dichotomy centrally important for making sense of experience, especially as he found it used around him. The *Pardoner's Tale* itself, though it testifies to the power of the traditional formulation of *cupiditas* and what it makes of the condition of the subject, by its framing suggests that Chaucer is critical of precisely the temptation to moral condemnation that the dichotomy offers. These terms are those of the Pardoner himself, and if his disenchanted critique of them puts in question what they have come to historically, his use of them is itself deeply biased. My suspicion is that Chaucer found this discourse too historically compromised to be useful as a fundamental set of terms *because* it was so current in his own society.

Second, from a practical interpretive point of view it is not so much the uncharitableness of calling the Pardoner cupidinous that bothers me (though it does, a bit) as the complexity and difficulty of working

1. Or perhaps I should say in the English tradition since Grendel belongs in this array but was not available to Chaucer or any other English author until the nineteenth century.

out whether and how it makes sense to call the Wife charitable, though she is at least more open than the Pardoner to the otherness of others. Besides, and more important, even if we could find some metaversion of *caritas* that would include the Wife's practice, this superior Christianity would lose the historical purchase that originally helped to make it attractive since it would be a definition that had to fly in the face of an institutional definition of woman in most Christian societies that lasts well beyond Kierkegaard.[2] It is really its historical inability to give a balanced account of sexual difference that makes this discourse awkward for the present purpose.

We are led, then, to more modern terminologies for elucidating the subjectivity that Chaucer, without the dubious benefit of modern jargon, seems to have conceived in a "modern" way. Deconstruction is obviously a discourse in which this pattern is central, starting perhaps with Derrida's classic undoing of the opposition speech/writing in *Of Grammatology*. As I have already noted, de Man's analyses of Rousseau apply the methods outlined here to the deconstruction of the subject in a way highly relevant to the Pardoner. Both the Pardoner and the Wife of Bath are involved in the structure of the trope of irony that emerges from the false contrary sincerity/irony. Deconstructionist analysis of the sort de Man practices shows how sincerity is just a special case of irony, a particular way of construing or failing to construe the fundamental *différance* of the trace. Concretely, in Chaucer this opposition produces the aporia of self-revelation versus self-presentation and the escape of the subject from itself and others.

Deconstruction, however, has generally not provided a usable account of its own procedures that would explain, once again, the differences between the Wife and the Pardoner. Since from a general theoretical perspective it can be argued that *both* pilgrims are deconstructors, undoers of the representational pretensions of language and enacters of the indeterminacy of the subject, what accounts for the patent opposition between them? It is easier to describe the differences, as I have done in the previous chapter, than it is to find within the discourse of deconstruction ready terms for a principled, theoretical

2. See, for instance, the weird discussion of women's despair, based on the idea that the fundamental character of femininity is "devotedness," in Kierkegaard, *Sickness unto Death*, 50–51. This sort of metaphysical entrapment of woman as the angel in the house is also found in Nietzsche, where, however, it seems more explicitly ironized.

explanation of those differences, which seem to have to do with deconstructive style itself. To identify the two pilgrims as disenchanted, deconstructive ironists goes a certain distance in understanding them, but it eventually requires a further, oppositional classification. It might, indeed, be interesting to play with terms like *aggressive ironist* and *erotic ironist,* but insofar as these terms feel appropriate they suggest the usefulness of shifting to another discourse that shares the common structure but addresses the content of the differences, and sexual difference itself, more directly: psychoanalysis.

In psychoanalysis Jacques Lacan has stressed the structural pattern of false opposition and the subject, particularly, though not exclusively, with respect to the term of lack, castration.[3] Lacan argues that the false contrary of castration is gender. For him the phallus (which is his term for an imaginary construct or fantasy to be distinguished from an actual sexual organ, the penis) is the signifier of the fulfillment of desire, and castration is the signifier of the fact that desire is fundamentally unfulfillable. The genesis of desire is in what is called primary narcissism, the infant's inability to distinguish between itself and the world (as crucially represented by the mother) and its assumption that world (mother) is an extension of self. When this assumption is disproved to the child by the ordinary course of events, far more than the frustration of a particular want is revealed to it:

> Freud describes how the baby can be observed to hallucinate the milk that has been withdrawn from it and the infant to play throwing away games to overcome the trauma of its mother's necessary departures. Lacan uses these instances to show that the object that is longed for only comes into existence *as an object* when it is lost to the baby or infant. Thus any satisfaction that might subsequently be obtained will always contain this loss within it. Lacan refers to this dimension as "desire." The baby's need can be met, its demand responded to, but its desire only exists because of the initial failure of satisfaction. Desire persists as an effect of a primordial absence and it therefore indicates that, in this area, there is something fundamentally impossible about satisfaction itself.[4]

3. It is a pleasure to acknowledge my general dependence in what follows on the enormously lucid and useful presentation of Mitchell and Rose, *Feminine Sexuality.* Their substantial introductions to the volume of Lacanian texts they selected render the difficult clear without simplifying the complex and illuminate the relevance of Lacan to the discourse on gender. Almost as useful, especially for context, has been Clément, *Lives and Legends of Jacques Lacan.*

4. Mitchell, in Mitchell and Rose, *Feminine Sexuality,* 6. See also the discussion of primary and secondary processes in Silverman, *Subject of Semiotics,* 54–86.

In Lacan's account castration stands for this moment of separation, the breaking of the dyadic unity between mother and child. In this economy the phallus is the imaginary solution that the child, aided by its socially constructed surroundings, comes to posit for the lack: it is what the child fantasizes the father has that the mother desires. If the child had that, he or she would recapture the mother's desire and restore the lost unity. But it is a fantasy: the phallus is by definition what the child does *not* have from the beginning, regardless of its particular sexual equipment. The lack is what comes first and is never made up, and it is out of this fundamental sense of lack that the subject is constructed, and constructs itself, as a gendered self.

For Lacan, "male" and "female" are simply different inflections of, and responses to, the prior lack that biological males and females share equally. "Castration" is not a physical reality—the little boy has a penis, and for the girl, as a writer in *Scilicet* remarked, "there is nothing missing in the real."[5] "Castration" is the term without a contrary that generates contraries, the term for what *gives meaning* to the possession or nonpossession of an organ. The act of attaching the fantasy of the fulfillment of desire to an object, making the phallus out of the penis, is what initiates the social construction of gender because for Lacan no such moment is possible outside of language. The entry into desire and the creation of the unconscious (the splitting of the subject into conscious and unconscious), the entry into subjecthood itself, is the entry into language, which Lacan calls the symbolic. The term *symbolic* is in part a way of getting at the broadly extensive view of language that is meant: not just French or English narrowly understood but any institutionalized organization of signs (gestures, facial expressions, kinship systems, economic status, and so on).

The fact that the father is associated by Lacan with the law is first of all a way of indicating the institutionalized and structured character of the symbolic order as well as of saying that the law that language gives to desire is gendered. Lacan calls it the Name-of-the-Father, *le Nom-du-Père*, to stress the connection between reference—naming—and engenderment. The prohibition placed on desire by the entry into language is what creates desire itself by articulating the impossibility of its fulfillment. This situation is expressed in a typically Lacanian pun

5. Anonymous, "Phallic Phase," reprinted in Mitchell and Rose, *Feminine Sexuality,* 113; see Rose's commentary, 42–43.

whereby the Name-of-the-Father is also a prohibition, *le Non-du-Père*. This is essentially the same notion as the Derridian *différance,* the difference and deferral of the signifier in relation to what it signifies, but here set in the context of engenderment and desire.

The fact that the symbolic order is constructed, that it is the entry into the institution of language that initiates the construction of gender out of castration, means that there is a vital but difficult-to-specify component of engenderment and the entry into subjecthood that is contingent and historical. The *content* of gender is a social construction:

> If psychoanalysis is phallocentric, it is because the human social order that it perceives refracted through the individual human subject is patro-centric. To date, the father stands in the position of the third term that *must* break the asocial dyadic unit of mother and child. We can see that this third term will always need to be represented by something or someone.
>
> (Mitchell, in Mitchell and Rose,
> *Feminine Sexuality,* 23)

Lacan's association of the father with the law is thus also a way of identifying the androcentric character of the social arrangements that both precondition and are perpetuated by engenderment. This identification does not mean that the androcentrism of society is founded in biology but that the body is manipulated by (has inscribed in it) a set of sexist arrangements that are potentially alterable. What Lacanian psychoanalysis does in part is describe the mechanisms of this inscription—how socialization, the creation of the gendered social subject, takes place by being written in the body.

A number of implications of this position are relevant to Chaucer. For one thing, literal castration is an issue in the case of the Pardoner, and therefore the *meaning* of castration, whether or not a discursive formulation of it in psychoanalytic terms was available to medieval culture, is also at issue. We might be tempted to psychoanalyze the text, and there are places in it that seem to offer an opening for this kind of interpretation. There is, for instance, the possibility of a psy-choanalytic motive in the plea of the Old Man in the *Pardoner's Tale* to be rejoined with the earth: "Leeve mooder, leet me in!" (VI, 731). In Lacanian terms this plea could be read as a wish to return to a condi-tion before the dyadic union with the mother was broken—that is, to a condition before language—and therefore to escape the division in the subject enforced by language and desire. Psychoanalysis has no difficulty in identifying such a wish to escape castration with the so-called death drive and thus perhaps supplies some confirmation on its own ground of the interpretation already arrived at in other terms.

I do not insist on this interpretation, and I am really no more interested in the details of this sort of reading than I am in those of a typological-patristic one. The detection of unconscious motives of this sort in the text, whether of character, speaker, or author, can too easily take on the appearance of discovering the evidences of a perennial human nature that reproduces itself regardless of its epiphenomenal (historical or institutional) displacements and projections. The result would be the psychoanalytic version of the cortex/nucleus theory, a kind of vulgar Freudianism that imagines it has said something and come to a stopping place in statements like, It's all really the castration complex.[6] The advantage of a Lacanian perspective is that it makes this sort of reading much more difficult, in its insistence that once something has been identified as meaning castration, the question "What does *that* mean?" always remains because that question *is the meaning of castration.* Castration is what poses the question of the meaning of meaning itself, what calls attention to the dependence of meaning on desire and to the fact that meaning, like desire, is not stable.

What is suggestive and useful about the Lacanian version of a psychoanalytic perspective is that it encourages an examination of the link between gender and the law, that is, of the psychosocial *content* of gender. From this point of view it becomes hard to tell whether we ought to think of the Pardoner as occupying the position of analysand or that of analyst since in these terms his activity is an insistent pointing out of castration and a certain debunking of the phallus. The Pardoner may be said to present himself not as a male without an organ but as the embodiment of the lack, a presentation that functions as an *attack* on the paternal establishment and the authority of God the Father. The Pardoner's conspicuous insistence on the fakery of his masculinity functions in tandem with his insistence on the fakery

6. See Wright, *Psychoanalytic Criticism,* esp. 1–6, for a discussion of various ways psychoanalytic criticism may avoid the problems of this kind of reading; see also Jameson, "Pleasure," 7–9.

of his ecclesiastical ministrations through the mediation of symbolic transformations like those embodied in the idea of the *eunuchus non dei*. As such, it is aimed precisely at the symbolic order, at the connection between the phallus and the Name-of-the-Father. The Pardoner's analytical sophistication may suggest the possibility of working out the historical specificity of Lacanian castration in, say, the late Middle Ages. The situation clearly is not one in which the historical agents repress or conceal from themselves the "real meaning"—the sexual causation—of infantile fantasies of power and fears of retaliation embodied in a paternal God. Spiritual lack is imaged by the culture itself as castration, which "means" what Augustine and R. P. Miller say it does. It is not that spiritual eunuchry really means physical castration (a vulgar Freudian view) any more than the reverse: medieval people (indeed medieval men) themselves make the connection between sexuality and authority. Rather, the Pardoner's self-dramatization is founded on the fact that his culture's notions of divine authority are part of the *content* of masculinity for it, and vice versa. That is why he can use each to undermine the other.

Here we rejoin another motif of the general structure we are examining, that of the archie deBunker, the analyst who not only registers the illusory quality of the *arche* but delivers, as Rose says of Lacan, "an *indictment* of the symbolic for the imaginary unity which its most persistent myths continue to promote" (*Feminine Sexuality*, 47, emphasis added). One thing the Pardoner has in common with Lacan is a sometimes strident tone about truth, as summarized here by Rose: "The subject has to recognize that there is desire, or lack, in the place of the Other, that there is no ultimate certainty or truth, and that the status of the phallus is a fraud (this is, for Lacan, the meaning of castration)" (*Feminine Sexuality*, 40). Lacan, de Man, and the Pardoner share more than a common structure of the critique of signification; they also share, at least sometimes, a common way of deploying that critique, which manifests itself as voicing or as a critical tone. To question this tone with any thoroughness in the first two cases is beyond both my purpose and my competence, but the example of the Pardoner does help focus a certain aspect of the tone of the deconstructive-analytical enterprise and perhaps say something about one desire of the deconstructor in a situation where we are concerned less with the subject in or of deconstruction *tout court* and more with a certain version of the deconstructing subject. Precisely because the Pardoner is, so to speak, more single-minded in his debunking enterprise, he provides a situation in which Chaucer's text can help clarify certain tendencies in modern theoretical discourse itself—tendencies I am going to characterize as *"masculine"*—that that discourse often seems to neglect.

As I have already suggested, the Pardoner presents himself not as an independent entity but only in relation to what he undoes. In gender terms he presents himself as the *not-masculine,* or more accurately, in an ironic and negating relation to masculinity that is at once an imitation and a denial of what it imitates. This move is primarily directed at the association of masculinity—the phallus—with authority and the notion of truth. The Pardoner displays a consistent relationship to the idea of the truth in general, whether it be the truth about gender or the truth about language and reference. He mimes them to show their falsity. Kierkegaard suggests that this kind of negating relationship has a stake in what it wants to destroy:

> In hatred toward existence, [demonic despair] wills to be itself, wills to be itself in accordance with its misery. Not even in defiance or defiantly does it want to tear itself loose from the power that established it, but for spite wants to force itself upon it, to obtrude defiantly upon it, wants to adhere to it out of malice—and of course a spiteful denunciation must above all take care to adhere to what it denounces.
>
> (*Sickness unto Death*, 75)

The Pardoner is *against* the idea of truth in such a way that what he is against defines him: he is ultimately supportive of what he tries to undo because he has to constitute it in order to undo it. This bondage to the system one is deconstructing is well recognized in modern theory.[7] In Lacanian terms the Pardoner is an example of another punning extension of the Name-of-the-Father, *les non-dupes errent*—those who are not deceived go astray, for they are those who reproduce most rigorously the structure they have seen through. Psychoanalysis, like deconstruction, is a discourse that does not allot a privileged position to the analyst, who is subject to the same processes he or she analyzes:

> Lacan continually returns to the "subject supposed to know," the claim of a subject to know (the claim to know oneself as subject), and the different forms of discourse that can be organized around this posi-

---

7. See, for example, Spivak, "Translator's Preface," in Derrida, *Of Grammatology*, xiii–xx.

tion. . . . Much of the difficulty of Lacan's work stemmed from his attempt to subvert that position from within his own utterance, to rejoin the place of "non-knowledge" which he designated the unconscious, by the constant slippage or escape of his speech, and thereby to undercut the very mastery which his own position as speaker (master and analyst) necessarily constructs. In fact one can carry out the same operation on the statement "I do not know" as Lacan performed on the utterance "I am lying" . . . —for, if I do not know, then how come I know enough to know that I do not know and if I do know that I do not know, then it is not true that I do not know. Lacan was undoubtedly trapped in this paradox of his own utterance.[8]

Much in Lacan's biography and writing testifies to the frustration and even the pain of this position, as reflected in a tone that is evident to those who study him:

Freud's final writings are often perceived as reflecting an old man's despair. But for Lacan their pessimism indicates a clarification and summation of a theory whose implications are and must be anti-humanist. . . . In the theories of Freud that Lacan redeploys, the distinction between the sexes brought about by the castration complex and the different positions that must subsequently be taken up, confirms that the subject is split and the object is lost. This is the difficulty at the heart of being human to which psychoanalysis and the objects of its enquiry— the unconscious and sexuality—bear witness. To Lacan, a humanist position offers only false hopes on the basis of false theories.[9]

A similar mood or tone is also apparent at times in de Man. It comes out in statements like the one quoted above (p. 171) about the experience of subjectivity as "a dismemberment, a beheading or a castration," and in an analysis by Christopher Norris of the following passage from *Blindness and Insight*:

Whereas the symbol postulates the possibility of an identity or identification, allegory designates primarily a distance in relation to its own origin, and, *renouncing the nostalgia and the desire to coincide*, it establishes its language in the void of this temporal difference. In so doing, it prevents the self from an illusory identification with the non-self, which is now fully, though painfully, recognized as a non-self. It is *this*

8. Rose, in Mitchell and Rose, *Feminine Sexuality*, 50. Neither Rose nor I mean to suggest that Lacan was unaware of the trap.

9. Mitchell, in Mitchell and Rose, *Feminine Sexuality*, 25. Clément, *Lives and Legends*, documents the pain and frustration throughout her book.

> *painful knowledge* that we perceive at the moments when early roman-
> tic literature finds its voice.
>
> (De Man, *Blindness and Insight,* 207,
> emphasis added).
>
> The choice thus posed—"painful" recognition or mystified, evasive
> strategy—is cast in terms of an almost existentialist drive toward au-
> thentic self-knowledge. For de Man the only truth to be grasped through
> language is that "truth" is always non-self-identical, a fugitive knowl-
> edge that nowhere coincides with the moment of its own, self-sufficient
> revelation.
>
> (Norris, *Some Versions of
> Rhetoric,* 201–2)[10]

Painful knowledge: the phrase might stand as the formula of a common element in de Man, Lacan, and the Pardoner, which is less a
function of similar personalities—I am scarcely accusing de Man and
Lacan of despair, which is in any case a version of the phenomenon
that is out of date for them—than of a common structure in the
enterprises in which they are engaged. It is the affective component of
this structure that can sometimes be read in their voices, a tone of
nostalgia for what must be renounced and a certain tragic stoicism, an
odd form of the manliness of enduring what is painful: "I moot go
thider as I have to go" (VI, 749).

This strain of "displaced existential pathos" (Norris, "Some Versions," 204) is a function of the attachment to truth in the mode of
negation. What is sustained by this kind of questioning of the idea of
truth is precisely the idea of truth and its importance even if—
especially if—we cannot have it. A debunker needs bunk, but bunk
only makes sense as a notion in contrast to what would not be bunk.
In all these discourses it is the *categories* of truth and illusion that
remain in place and in play. Each discourse produces a speaker who
may be said to "know" that the ultimate illusion is the illusion that
there is such a thing as truth, but that very knowledge reinstates the
dilemma it attempts to undo. The subject is posited (and enacted) as
something doomed to keep on wanting what it cannot have. We can
easily say of the Pardoner what Rose says of Lacan, that "his own

---

10. Norris contrasts this strain in de Man to the practice of a critic like Geoffrey
Hartman, whom he characterizes as being "at home with the notion of an open-ended
textual 'freeplay' beyond all governance of critical method" as opposed to the " 'perverse' tenacity of argument" found in de Man (195). See also 191–93 and, in the same
volume, articles by Johnson, "Gender Theory," and Foley, "Politics of Deconstruction."

utterance constantly rejoins the mastery which he sought to undermine" (*Feminine Sexuality*, 56). In deconstruction, similarly, the illusory but unavoidable referentiality of language necessitates that it will
go on misrepresenting itself and the subject will go on deceiving itself,
in the same way that for Lacan male subjects are stuck with an organ
that is required to mean and do more than it can—the penis is required
to be the phallus.[11] This same situation seems to inform the Pardoner's
attitude toward the body—carnality and the flesh—in general: we
might say that he is stuck with the phallus even if he does not have a
penis. But in all three cases there is also that displaced existential
pathos that accompanies the structural inevitability of the pattern, and
that is what I maintain is gendered "masculine." Not only a rigorous
itinerary but also a rigorously maintained style runs from the archie
deBunker to the Ol*de Man*.

So far both the deconstructive and the psychoanalytic perspectives
seem more suggestive about the Pardoner than about the Wife of Bath,
and more fully illuminated by him than by her. We might reflect that
psychoanalytic theory has always had trouble with the feminine dating
back to Freud's admission that he had never been able to determine
what a woman wants.[12] For Lacan, especially in his later career, this
problem came to be bound up with what he called the *jouissance* of the
woman, the ecstatic sexual pleasure she experiences mysteriously, not
least because she herself cannot formulate it: "a *jouissance* of the body
which is, if the expression be allowed, *beyond the phallus*" (Lacan,
"God and the *Jouissance* of ~~The~~ Woman," 145). I will return to this
issue shortly, but for Lacan, as for Freud, it remains a difficult and
problematic area.[13] In the present state of affairs *woman* is almost
exclusively a position in the male-dominated symbolic order and is
made to stand for castration, the lack the man feels, fears, and re-
presses. Woman in the symbolic order has been only what men have
made of her and what they have made her be, the other and guarantor
of masculine identity.[14]

11. For example, Lacan's characterization of "the man" as "he who finds himself
male without knowing what to do about it" ("God and the *Jouissance* of ~~The~~ Woman,"
143).

12. Cited in E. Jones, *Sigmund Freud*, 2:421. I am indebted to Teresa de Lauretis for
the reference.

13. See Jameson, "Pleasure," 7.

14. For Lacan, "Woman is not inferior, she is *subjected:* That the woman should be
inscribed in an order of exchange of which she is the object, is what makes for the

Despite this relative impasse, certain advantages of the Lacanian framework remain. It is a perspective that helps to carry us beyond the discourses of despair and deconstruction because of its disenchanted fix on the problem of difference specifically considered as sexual difference. Because it has focused directly on gender not as a biological given but as something that is constructed, albeit largely unconsciously, psychoanalysis has been able to see gender difference as a *capability* rather than merely a fate of the subject. The Lacanian notion that gender is a matter of language means that its syntax, so to speak, is open to any user of the language regardless of his or her biological sex; it means that the subject is bisexual:

> For Lacan, men and women are only ever in language ("Men and women are signifiers bound to the common usage of language"). All speaking beings must line themselves up on one side or the other of this division, but anyone can cross over and inscribe themselves on the opposite side from that to which they are anatomically destined. . . . Note how this simultaneously shifts the concept of bisexuality—not an undifferentiated sexual nature prior to symbolic difference (Freud's earlier sense), but the availability to all subjects of both positions in relation to that difference itself.
>
> (Rose, in Mitchell and Rose,
> *Feminine Sexuality*, 49, 49n)

Such a position makes gender itself a function of a relation to discourse, or, as I now want to put it, *a relation to an institutional structure*. The possibility of bisexuality shows that if gender, like desire, is the discourse of the Other, something from outside the subject that is imposed on it, then gender is an institution, and gender difference is a matter of differing institutional practices. Gender is something with which the subject has to cope, but by the same token it is something—like a law, a role, or a story—that, and with which, the subject can negotiate. I think Chaucer sees gender more or less this way, as simultaneously an institutional construct and a relation to institutions. The *Canterbury Tales* is informed by the practical under-

---

fundamentally conflictual, and I would say, insoluble, character of her position: the symbolic order literally submits her, it transcends her. . . . There is for her something insurmountable, something unacceptable, in the fact of being placed as an object in the symbolic order to which, at the same time, she is subjected just as much as the man." *Seminar II*, quoted in Mitchell and Rose, *Feminine Sexuality*, 44–45.

standing that gender is socially constructed and need have nothing to do with biological sex and therefore that any male or female pilgrim may manifest the institutionalized characteristics, perspectives, and activities of either gender or (more typically) both genders. The poet himself obviously did, or else he could not have represented them in the poem; and as we shall see, the *Knight's Tale* is concerned in important ways with its speaker's male and female identifications, or what seems fair to call his bisexuality. Gender is one more instance that points up the central preoccupation of the *Canterbury Tales,* the representation of the relation of subjects to institutions, and that understanding of gender in turn allows the possibility that gender and gender difference can be subject in the poem to disenchantment.

Disenchantment itself is yet another example of the common pattern I have been tracing, a more explicitly social form of the structure of the subject as the product of a contrary-producing term without a contrary. The apparent secondariness and subordination of the term comes out if the opposition is stated as enchantment/disenchantment since it then appears as no more than the negative version of the first, positive term. In fact, however, calling the first term enchantment is already disenchanted insofar as it posits the first term as an illusion. The opposition is more properly something like transcendence/disenchantment, where in its most radical form, as I said in the Introduction, the second term represents the perception that *the category of transcendence itself is a human construction,* and there are only institutions. Disenchantment is thus a term of absence and *différance,* like irony and gender. A fully disenchanted perspective *constitutes* the world as a tissue of institutions rather than of "natures" and therefore tends to see experience as an encounter between conflicting interpretations rather than as the passive reception of preexisting meanings.

I have consistently argued that both the Pardoner and the Wife of Bath are disenchanted in this first, neutral sense. Each of these pilgrims demystifies those aspects of the world that present themselves as transcendental or authoritative truth, representing them instead as human products. They are agreed about the centrality of male domination in the institutional structure whose claims to transcendence they question. The (male) clerical deployment of the ideology of (male) divine authority to control women, which is the Wife's target, is a version of

the more general conception of ontological meaning not only as plenitude but also as potency, which the Pardoner attacks. The Wife knows
and shows that it is men who own what is called the truth in this
society; the Pardoner elaborates in his own way the fraudulent phallic
pretensions of the church's claim to embody the divine. As I have
suggested, it is neither an accident nor a manifestation of the unconscious that he finds it expedient to put his own masculinity in question
to subvert the authority he represents and hates. But given this similarity, there is still the same question of the differences between them and
the meaning of their contrasting styles of disenchantment. I want to
link these differences to gender and speak of the Pardoner and the Wife
as examples or versions of the "masculine" and "feminine" imaginations as Chaucer conceives that distinction.

It seems appropriate to begin this differentiation, and to finish this
section, by stressing one last time what the Wife has in common with
the Pardoner, as a way of elucidating the "masculine" side of her
bisexuality. From one angle it is striking how alike the two are in their
disenchanted understanding of the society to which, in their different
ways, they are marginal. There is a more emotionally vibrant connota-
tion of disenchantment that links it with the structure of what I have
called painful knowledge, the feeling the word carries that something
has been lost. Disenchantment may generate a hunger for the transcendence it renders absent, so that the world as it is comes to seem
worthless.[15] That is the Pardoner's response, for example, to his own
disenchantment about the church, as an institution whose promise to
transmit the divine has been irremediably sullied by the manipulations
of corrupt human beings like himself. In the case of the Wife her
understanding of the world constructed by male economic and sexual
domination and imposed on her has a strong tendency to generate a

15. "The tension between religion and intellectual knowledge definitely comes to the
fore whenever rational, empirical knowledge has consistently worked through to the
disenchantment of the world and its transformation into a causal mechanism. For then
science encounters the claims of the ethical postulate that the world is a God-ordained,
and hence somehow *meaningfully* and ethically oriented, cosmos. In principle, the
empirical as well as the mathematically oriented view of the world develops refutations
of every intellectual approach which in any way asks for a 'meaning' of inner-worldly
occurrences." Max Weber, "Religious Rejections," 350–51. Once again the relevance of
this perspective (for example, the motivation it provides for despair) is clearer if Weber's
concentration on the rational-empirical-scientific tradition is translated into the operations of human agency in general.

vision of experience that is not merely misandric, a reflex of the misogyny she constantly faces, but actively misanthropic: all persons, men and women alike, are no good because they cannot afford to be. Commodification and competition are the law of existence, and to do unto others before they do unto you is the rule of a world dominated by gold. Something like this is, as we have seen, the public message and the argument of the Wife's prologue and tale.

The most fundamental similarity between the public positions the Wife and the Pardoner take, however, is that both these positions are necessarily committed to the institutional structure they attack, so that the pilgrims who hold them become mirror images of the male domination and the idea of truth that they question. It is this commitment, even in the mode of negation, to the fundamental assumptions of the status quo that I want to identify as the "masculine" imagination. Males, or those who aspire to the masculine position, have an interest (which need not be conscious) in the existing institutional makeup of society because it maintains and perpetuates their dominance. They have also, therefore, an interest in maintaining the mystification of the system as truth, the position that the way things currently are is the way they have always been and the way they must be. Furthermore, they have an interest in maintaining this position to themselves, an interest in self-mystification or *mauvaise foi*. This mystification would be the "masculine" imagination as naive consciousness.

But the commitment that sustains these interests can exist even when the specific individuals involved, males or aspirants to the masculine position, are not personally empowered by the current structure, and it can exist even when they are disenchanted with it. In the latter case disenchantment takes a form that avoids acknowledging the radically constructed character of the world by convicting the status quo of fraudulence in the name of a higher truth. The structure is the same even when the higher truth is that there is no higher truth because the feeling of the fact of fraudulence and the offense it gives are still sustained. Basic to this stance is the idea that current society is a corruption of the truth because, and to the extent that, it is humanly constructed. The dispute is over what constitutes the real truth, not over the category of the transcendent itself, which is left intact in the same gesture in which it is denied. I will call this position *"masculine" disenchantment*. The gender component is particularly clear in the case of the Wife. The "masculine" side of her bisexuality expresses itself in her public project to appropriate male institutions and power in a way that reproduces their exploitative character (see above, pp. 72–76). This is the aspect of the Wife that conforms to the vulgar stereotype of the castrating woman, one who competes for the phallus and its authority, who wants, as we say, to wear the pants, and who exhausts men and reduces them to various forms of real and symbolic impotence.[16] It is also the side of her that engages authority on its own ground and attempts, albeit uncomfortably, to put truth on her side, as she does with the texts of scripture and the church fathers at the beginning of her prologue. As I have suggested, she is in some ways closest to the Pardoner here, before he interrupts her. She finds herself caught up in precisely the sort of mutually negating deconstructive struggle with transcendental meaning that is his specialty. Like the Pardoner, the Wife here enacts herself as the other and the double of the law.

16. "As in every society dominated by male values—and European societies, which assign men to politics, history, or war and women to the hearth, the novel, and psychology, are no exception—the specifically male relation to sexuality [in North African Kabyle society] is that of *sublimation,* the symbolism of honor tending at once to refuse any direct expression of sexuality and to encourage its transfigured manifestation in the form of manly prowess: the men who are neither conscious of nor concerned with the female orgasm but seek the affirmation of their potency in repetition rather than prolongation of the sexual act, are not unaware that, through the intermediary of the female gossip that they both fear and despise, the eyes of the group always threaten their intimacy. As for the women, it is true to say, with Erikson, that male domination tends to 'restrict their verbal consciousness' so long as this is taken to mean not that they are forbidden all talk of sex, but that their discourse is dominated by the male values of virility, so that all reference to specifically female sexual 'interests' is excluded from this aggressive and shame-filled cult of male potency." Bourdieu, *Outline of a Theory of Practice,* 92. Or, as the Wife of Bath says, "wherwith sholde he make his paiement, / If he ne used his sely instrument?" (131–32).

8

The "Feminine" Imagination and *Jouissance*

Skeptics—I am afraid that old women are more skeptical in their most secret heart of hearts than any man: they consider the superficiality of existence its essence, and all virtue and profundity is to them merely a veil over this "truth," a very welcome veil over a pudendum—in other words, a matter of decency and shame, and no more than that.

Nietzsche, The Gay Science

There is no such thing as The woman.
Jacques Lacan, "God and the
Jouissance of <s>The</s> Woman"

THE SECOND NUN

The foregoing analysis suggests that females, or those who find themselves in the feminine position, though they are constrained by the institutional structure that sustains male domination, have no *interest* in it. Any commitments the feminine subject may manifest to the system itself are structurally motivated by the coercion of the system, not its value for the subject, and appear to a disenchanted perspective as arising from fear, self-protection, and the like, whether conscious or not. But from the same perspective it is clear that if a woman cannot escape the domination of the system—which is another way of saying that as woman she is relegated to the private sphere—she has little reason or need to commit herself to its ideas of truth and its public purposes. Because she has no *stake* in the structure that oppresses her publicly, she can use it for private purposes, for whatever ends of her own she may want to pursue, and in whatever way she may find convenient, without regard to its public, masculine meaning.

At this point it is useful to put in play a distinction between *knowledge* and *pleasure,* particularly as developed by Shoshana Felman in

The Literary Speech Act. Comparing the language philosopher J. L. Austin with the seducer Don Juan, she observes:

> It is striking to note that Austin's fundamental gesture, like Don Juan's, consists in substituting, with respect to utterances of the language, the criterion of *satisfaction* for the criterion of *truth*. "Truth and falsity are . . . not names for relations, qualities, . . . but for a dimension of assessment—how the words stand *in respect of satisfactoriness* to the facts . . . to which they refer." Thus, like Don Juan, Austin too introduces into thinking about language the dimension of *pleasure*, quite distinct from that of knowledge; a dimension that is implicit, moreover, in the success/failure criterion of linguistic performance—success or failure that Austin labels, significantly, "felicity" or "infelicity" of action.[1]

Felman points out that this distinction generates a series of others. On the side of "knowledge" we have the *constative* speech act, the term used for the "descriptive utterances, . . . sentences that set forth *statements* of fact, that report a state of affairs, true or false" (*Literary Speech Act*, 15). The parallel speech act on the side of "pleasure" is the *performative*, "expressions whose function is not to inform or describe, but to carry out a 'performance,' to accomplish an *act* through the very process of their enunciation" (ibid.),[2] because it comprises acts that respond to the criteria of success or failure rather than truth or falsehood: they turn out well or badly. Consideration of the kind of aporia or impasse proper to knowledge or pleasure generates the opposition contradiction/scandal: the first term is obviously appropriate to describe the sorts of difficulty that impede the rational and discursive character of knowledge, whereas scandal refers to "unhappy" outcomes of language use that evade or escape purely logical criteria, for example, "statements which, though not false exactly nor yet 'contradictory,' are yet *outrageous*. For instance, statements which refer to something which does not exist as, for example, 'The present King of France is bald,' "[3] or such logical subversions of logic as "And sith a man is moore resonable / Than womman is, ye moste been suffrable" (III, 441–42).

---

1. Felman, *Literary Speech Act*, 61–62. The quotation from Austin is from *How To Do Things with Words*.
2. The classic example, from Austin, is the act of marrying, where the statement "I now pronounce you man and wife" performs the action it describes.
3. Austin, cited in Felman, *Literary Speech Act*, 149.

To these distinctions of Felman's I would add, with respect to Chaucer, on the side of knowledge *public* and *"masculine,"* and on the side of pleasure *private* and *"feminine."* Of the "masculine" collocation, knowledge (or truth)–public (or official)–constative–contradiction, I think enough has been said already. I should also think that the general applicability of the "feminine" collocation, pleasure–private (or personal)–performative–scandal, to the Wife of Bath's performance is clear enough. Crucial here is the attitude taken toward the "masculine" institutional structure and the uses made of it, encapsulated in the Wife's citation of Ptolemy's proverb:

> "Of alle men his wysdom is the hyeste
> That rekketh nevere who hath the world in honde."
> By this proverbe thou shalt understonde,
> Have thou ynogh, what thar thee recche or care
> How myrily that othere folkes fare?
>
> (III, 326–30)

This attitude is no doubt scandalously irresponsible (and since the context is that of the use of the "bele chose," as opposed to its legal ownership, even more so) and cynical—though perhaps in the mood of Nietzsche's old women. Read with a disenchanted eye, it affirms a disinterest in the truth of things in favor of the pleasure they may afford. It scarcely matters who has the world in hand since whoever he is, he is bound to be a man, who will mask his own interest in domination behind knowledge, public truth, and so on. I will call this position *"feminine" disenchantment.* Given this situation, the recommendation for how to use the structure is contained in the Wife's account of how she spent (and spends, one gathers) her leisure time:

> Myn housbonde was at Londoun al that Lente;
> I hadde the bettre leyser for to pleye,
> And for to se, and eek for to be seye
> Of lusty folk. *What wiste I wher my grace*
> *Was shapen for to be, or in what place?*
>
> (III, 550–54, emphasis added)

The "feminine" imagination uses the same institutions and classifications—including self-classifications—as the "masculine" because they are all there is, but it uses them in ways that are more akin to what men call courting, flirting, or even dancing and denigrate as frivolous (and precisely "feminine") than to what men call knowing and reasoning, which belong to them and are serious.[4] For the "feminine" imagination, the given institutional structure is to be, as it were, *cruised*[5] for whatever occasions of private use and private pleasure it may offer, without regard to such proprieties as public meaning or official function. If this characteristic is understood, it is relatively easy to detect the "feminine" imagination at work in the other two tales in the Canterbury collection that are supposed to be told by female narrators.

I have neither the space nor the occasion to present anything like adequate readings of the Prioress's and Second Nun's tales here, but I can at least suggest how such readings might proceed to exemplify the "feminine" imagination in these tales and these pilgrims along the lines I have been following. The fact that the institutions and classifications of gender difference are ideologically established and controlled by male domination means that there is an imbalance in the symmetry of the gender system I have been describing. It means that there is no such thing as "feminine" naive consciousness as opposed to "feminine" disenchantment because any acceptance of the world as it "appears" to naive consciousness is an acceptance of the world as ideologically preprocessed by male domination. In this sense the naive consciousness of a female subject will be "masculine," and this seems to be the case with the Prioress and the Second Nun, at least insofar as they do not explicitly contest male definitions as the disenchanted Wife of Bath does. Both these women have renounced—or never taken up—carnality and competition. They have chosen, agreed, or been forced—who knows?—to eschew the wicked "nature" of women constructed and institutionalized by masculine society (which the Wife appropriates and manipulates), and they signal this avoidance in part by telling tales appropriate to good, pious, and docile women—a saint's life and a miracle of the Virgin—which they do not question or challenge. Far from it: in their relation to gender and sexuality, being neither carnal women nor masculine competitors, they might thus be said, to paraphrase the Second Nun, to be worthy sons of Eve. Both women also extol and identify with Mary, whom they see as the exemplar and

4. At this point I join Lee Patterson's description of medieval "feminine rhetoric." See Patterson, " 'For the Wyves Love of Bathe.' "

5. The term is Roland Barthes's, or his translator's, *Pleasure of the Text*, 4.

original of their own stances. She is the model of what they hope to attain in the next life through perfect humility and submission—the highest recognition from the masculine principle, and the most intimate relations to Him:

> Thow Mayde and Mooder, doghter of thy Sone,
> Thow welle of mercy, synful soules cure,
> In whom that God for bountee chees to wone,
> Thow humble, and heigh over every creature,
> Thow nobledest so ferforth oure nature,
> That no desdeyn the Makere hadde of kynde
> His Sone in blood and flessh to clothe and wynde.
> (VIII, 36–42; cf. VII, 467–73)

> Lady, thy bountee, thy magnificence,
> Thy vertu and thy grete humylitee
> Ther may no tonge expresse in no science;
> For somtyme, Lady, er men praye to thee,
> Thou goost biforn of thy benygnytee,
> And getest us the lyght, of thy prayere,
> To gyden us unto thy Sone so deere.
> (VII, 474–80; cf. VIII, 50–56)

If you remain pure and do not compete, it will all come to you in the end.

The Second Nun is the most articulate spokeswoman for this stance, though critics have generally found her to be the most faceless of the pilgrim narrators. She herself is the first to have made this point, which suggests that *self-effacing* might be a better description:

> Yet preye I yow that reden that I write,
> Foryeve me that I do no diligence
> This ilke storie subtilly to endite,
> For bothe have I the wordes and sentence
> Of hym that at the seintes reverence
> The storie wroot, and folwen hire legende,
> And pray yow that ye wole my werk amende.
> (VIII, 78–84)

This narrator aspires to perfect transparency, subordinating herself as fully as possible to the task of translating her source, the Latin life of Saint Cecilia in the *Golden Legend*. Her desire is the accurate reproduction of the institution: a story about a woman who gave up her life in perfect obedience to the highest law and was the exemplar of the Nun's own ideal of "leveful bisynesse" (5).[6]

Yet the narrator of the life of Saint Cecilia allows that the act of translation does something for her, and perhaps we should believe her when she says that the tale is meant to counter the confusions of idleness. Her presentation of its temptations hovers between the perils of *luxuria* ("delices" [3], "erthely lust and fals affeccioun" [74]) and those of *accidia*, with perhaps more tonal weight given to the latter:

> And though men dradden nevere for to dye,
> Yet seen men wel by resoun, doutelees,
> That ydelnesse is roten slogardye,
> Of which ther nevere comth no good n'encrees;
> And syn that slouthe hire holdeth in a lees
> Oonly to slepe, and for to ete and drynke,
> And to devouren al that othere swynke . . .
>
> (15–21)

The first line of this stanza is peculiar and becomes more so when it is retrospectively reinforced by a line given to Cecilia in the tale, "If this were lyvynge oonly and noon oother" (322).[7] It suggests that even without the fear of judgment in the afterlife, the pains of idleness—a rotten boredom, a feeling of confinement within the sameness of the daily round, and a sense of consuming without producing anything— might be enough to drive one to "bisynesse" out of sheer distraction, a need for something to do. Perhaps even a bride of Christ can suffer from housewife's syndrome. And if there are earthly aspects of the problem, might not the solution have its earthly side as well?

6. The narrator's determination to portray her heroine's "bisynesse" is striking: "She nevere cessed, as I writen fynde, / Of hir prayere" (124–25); "Every seconde and thridde day she faste, / Ay biddynge in hire orisons ful faste" (139–40, where for the second line the Latin source has only "orans"); "Lo, lyk a bisy bee, withouten gile" (195, where the image is in the Latin, but without the adjective); "Tho gan she hym ful bisily to preche" (342); and, at the end of the tale, with her throat cut, "Thre dayes lyved she in this torment, / And nevere cessed hem the feith to teche / That she hadde fostred; hem she gan to preche" (537–39).

7. I do not mean to suggest that there is any twist to Cecilia's straightforward statement that men might fear to lose their lives if there were no other life than this except that the promise of heavenly reward alleviates the fear of martyrdom. But the occurrence of such similar lines in so short and highly crafted a text suggests to the disenchanted voice-oriented reader—me—that this speaker may attach some importance to the issue of the relation between this life and the next one. And then I notice that in both cases the verbal focus is on this life.

Here let me make a few general observations that might guide a more detailed interpretation. Such stylistic criticism as there is of the tale tends to stress, rightly, the closeness of the translation to its source while noting as well the "technical proficiency" (Donaldson, *Chaucer's Poetry*, 1108–9) devoted to the versification of the stanzas, albeit at the expense of narrative subtlety or complexity of character. Commenting on the closeness of the translation, G. H. Gerould remarks that "the differences are as slight as they well could be in a poem of rich tonal beauty compared with a piece of mediocre Latin prose."[8] But it is precisely the resources of poetry, and especially those of stanzaic versification, that are the agents of the transforming "feminine" imagination in the tale. The poetic inversions and the play of sounds that the complex rhyme scheme of the rime-royal stanza demands and encourages are continually exploited for specifically sensuous effect. These techniques are coupled with the exploration of the opportunity, largely denied to continuous prose, to use the final couplet and the sense of point and finality offered by the stanza break to shape punch lines. These and other methods create moments of emphasis that operate alongside the diegetic flow of the narrative and independently of it, establishing a kind of emotional subtext or counterplot. In the first half of the tale, up to the deaths of Tiberius and Valerian, this manipulation of the verse features the occasions of sensuous description that the Latin offers:

> And right so as thise philosophres write
> That hevene is swift and round and eek brennynge,
> Right so was faire Cecilie the white
> Ful swift and bisy evere in good werkynge,
> And round and hool in good perseverynge,
> And brennynge evere in charite ful brighte.
> Now have I yow declared what she highte.
> (VIII, 113–19)[9]

8. Gerould, "Second Nun's Prologue and Tale," 669.
9. The Latin runs as follows. I give the whole etymology from Jacobus to make the difference in the order of etymologies apparent. I have italicized the portion translated in the text:

Cecilia quasi celi lilia vel cecis via vel a celo et lya. Uel Cecilia quasi cecitate carens. Uel dicitur a celo et leos, quod est populus. Fuit enim celeste lilium per virginitatis pudorem. Uel dicitur lilium quia habuit candorem mundicie, uirorem consciencie, odorem bone fame. Fuit enim cecis via per exempli infomacionem, celum per iugem contemplacionem, lya per assiduam operacionem. *Uel dicitur*

With remarkable consistency this stanza employs relatively minute amplifications, word choices that increase the visual or kinetic effect of the language, and a small shift in the order of the etymologies in the Latin original so as to concentrate and focus images of visual beauty and the pleasures of imagined sight with an intensity not present in the source. The slight sense of anticlimax in the last line, which reminds us that this is, after all, only an etymology, points up the involvement of the voice in the description. The stanza is only one small example of the extraordinary extent to which the "translation" savors every pretext the Latin offers for the evocation of garlands, sweet odors of red roses and while lilies, clear light, and the like, to the extent that their

---

celum quia, sicut dicit Ysidorus, celum philosophi volubile, rotundum, et ardens esse dixerunt. Sic et ipsa fuit uolubilis per operacionem sollicitam, rotunda per perseueranciam, ardens per caritatem succensam. Fuit enim cecitate carens per sapiencie splendorem. Fuit et celum populi quia in ipsam tanquam in celum spirituale populus ad imitandum intuetur solem, lunam, et stellas, id est sapiencie perspicacitatem, fide magnanimitatem, et uirtutum uarietatem.

(Jacobus de Voragine, *Legenda Aurea,*
cited in Gerould, "Second Nun's Prologue
and Tale," 671)

Cecilia comes from *coeli lilia,* lily of Heaven, or from *caecis via,* a way unto the blind, or from *coelum,* Heaven, and *lya,* one who works. Or again it is the same *a caecitate carens,* free from blindness, or comes from *coelum* and *leos,* people. For Cecilia was a heavenly lily by her virginity; or she is called a lily because of the whiteness of her purity, the freshness of her conscience, and the sweet odour of her good renown. She was a way unto the blind by her example, a heaven by her unwearying contemplation, a worker by her diligent labour. Or she is called a heaven because, as Isidore says, the heavens are revolving, round, and burning. Thus Cecilia was revolving in that she went around in her good works; she was round in perseverance, and burning with charity. She was also free from blindness by the splendour of her wisdom, and a heaven of the people, because in her, as in a spiritual heaven, the people had Heaven set before their eyes for their imitation; for they saw in her the sun, the moon, and the stars, namely the keenness of her wisdom, the magnanimity of her faith, and the variety of her virtues.

(Jacobus de Voragine, *Golden
Legend,* 689–90)

The Latin primarily stresses a logical, intellectual structure enforced by parallel clauses, whereas Chaucer's English subordinates this structure (without altogether losing it) to the operation of modifiers that stress sensuous experience: "faire," "white," "swift and bisy," "round and hool" (as opposed to the more analytical parallelism of the Latin, "uolubilis per . . . , rotunda per . . ."), "ful brighte," etc. Generally speaking, the more apparent freedoms taken with the translation work to the same effect, as in those noted by Paul E. Beichner: "bath of flambes reed" for "flammis balnearibus" and "confus in thy nycetee" for "necessitate confusum." Beichner, "Confrontation."

function as symbols of spiritual merit is effaced by their sensuous immediacy. The imaginative vision of the speaker lingers on the cortex at the expense of the nucleus.

In the second half of the tale it emerges that the narrator is not so faithful a translator that she sees the need to clutter up the life of Saint Cecilia with the competing exploits of a lot of other—male—martyrs.[10] A long *logomachia* of the usual saint's-life sort between the Roman prefect Almachius and the soon-to-be-martyred Tiberius and Valerian, as well as a number of their conversions of others, is dropped or compressed in the English version, "to tellen shortly" (394), conspicuously foregrounding the lawful busyness of Cecilia and her final confrontation with Almachius. Paul Beichner's analysis of this confrontation remains a classic. He shows in convincing detail how this telling shifts the high point of the story from the death of the martyr to the trial scene and intensifies the clash between Almachius and Cecilia, "creating for each a personality more Chaucerian than traditional; Cecilia had never before been quite so contentious or belligerent, nor had Almachius been so obtuse or stupid" ("Confrontation," 204). I think these effects testify less to the appropriateness and conventionality of a comic perspective in late medieval hagiography[11] than to the enthusiasm of the teller for this part of the tale. She takes advantage of the fact that extremism in the defense of Christianity is no vice, or, as Cecilia herself smugly says when Almachius asks, "Why spekestow so proudly thanne to me?" (473):

> "I speke noght but stedfastly," quod she;
> "Nat proudly, for I seye, as for my syde,
> We haten deedly thilke vice of pryde."
>
> (474–76)

The point is less that what appears to be foolishness from an earthly perspective is actually divine wisdom than that if you are Saint Cecelia or her impersonator, you get to be rude to people without having to ✓

---

10. In a first-rate article, "Laughter in the *Second Nun's Tale*," Anne Eggebroten makes a compelling case for the prevalence of the deliberately contrived image of "the bumbling human vs. God and the saints" (58) throughout the tale. She does not mention—of course it is obvious—that all the bumblers, "the series of three fools who encounter Cecilia and the demands of the divine" (59), are men.

11. See Eggebroten, "Laughter," 59–60.

what about.?
ch version,

answer for it[12]—except of course to God, who approves—just as no blame can attach to the vicarious pleasures that accrue along the way in the exercise of "leveful bisynesse" to describe the beautiful symbols of God's love. Neither of these are pleasures we would expect so humble, so self-effacing, and so sensuously deprived a dweller in the desert (57–63) as this narrator to know much about, but the indications are that it is precisely the tale that both expresses the deprivations and gives imaginative relief to their pressures. There is real insight and energy, as Beichner notes ("Confrontation," 203), in the gleeful and malicious account of Almachius's outraged response to Cecilia's baiting:

> Thise wordes and swiche othere seyde she,
> And he weex wroth, and bad men sholde hir lede
> Hom til hir hous, and "In hire hous," quod he,
> "Brenne hire right in a bath of flambes rede."
>
> (512–15)

There is also, it seems to me, an exact image of the narrator's sense of her own situation, cool and unaffected by all the heat, whether sensual or rancorous, that she has blamelessly generated, in her account of Cecilia in that same bath:

> The longe nyght, and eek a day also,
> For al the fyr and eek the bathes heete
> She sat al coold and feelede no wo.
> It made hire nat a drope for to sweete.
>
> (519–22)

If, as I suggested earlier, the Second Nun's choice of genre posits her as someone who has renounced carnality and competition, her conduct of ✓ the story demonstrates that sensuous imagining and contentiousness

---

12. Eggebroten notes that "the tale is a melodrama, with a struggle between clearly good and bad types; the conclusion is known beforehand, and the theology involved is already accepted by everyone in the audience. The only real interest lies in Valerian's ignorance and surprise at what everyone else already knows. This is how Chaucer chooses to play the story" ("Laughter," 58). "Everyone" includes the Second Nun, and ✓ it is in the space created by the foregone conclusion that she takes her pleasure.

are what she is best at—as long as she does not have to avow them.

Though it is tempting to speculate on the appropriateness of this story told in this way to what we know about the situations of some nuns in the fourteenth century, and especially, perhaps, to what we might guess about a nun who accompanies the Prioress, the text does not supply enough information to carry us very far with any certainty along these lines. Nor does it allow us to reach a decision about the narrator's *consciousness* of what she demonstrably does in her tale. The performance may be said to subvert the divine by dragging it down to earth, by failing to respect the distance between the sacred and its earthly representation. This subversion may well be conscious and may even be a matter of deliberate bad faith. We cannot assume that we are dealing in any simple sense with the speaker's unconscious expression of unconscious drives, and certainly everything happens as if "feminine" disenchantment were the driving force of the tale. What we can say, however, is that the tale clearly does not seem intended by its speaker as a satire. Though the speaker consistently converts the spiritual into the carnal, she does not do so publicly. Her voicing is not directed *against* the tale, as the Pardoner's is, or against the values it purports to express, as the Manciple's is. Rather, she is using the story for her own vicarious imaginative enjoyment. This purpose makes the performance an instance of the "feminine" imagination, exploiting the given institution for its private pleasure without undue concern for the public meaning the story should have. The Second Nun knows what a tale like this one is supposed to do, and she accedes at various points and in various ways to its official function. But she does not let that stop her.

The same might be said for the Prioress, who, perhaps because she is in a social position that commands more independence and power, is rather less cautious about doing what she likes with her tale. Certainly no one has ever missed the distinctiveness of her voice—"This litel child, his litel book lernynge" (VII, 516)—or the ardor of her devotional style. Since there is really a great deal to be said about her tale, and since much of it is not necessary for the present argument, I will confine myself to a single passage. But first I want to return for a moment to the Wife of Bath and the question of *jouissance*, "What thyng is it that wommen moost desiren" (III, 905).

THE WIFE OF BATH AND THE PRIORESS

Something on the order of a subject can be discerned on the recording surface: a strange subject, with no fixed identity, wandering about over the body . . . yet always remaining peripheral . . . being defined by the share of the product it takes for itself, garnering here, there and everywhere a reward, in the form of a becoming or an avatar, being born of the states that it consumes and being reborn with each new state: *"c'est donc moi, c'est donc à moi!"* . . . The subject is produced as a mere residue . . . a conjunctive synthesis of consumption in the form of a wonderstruck: *"c'était donc ça!"*

Deleuze and Guattari, *Anti-Oedipus*

If the reader expects me to do what Freud and Lacan could not and reveal the essence of woman, she has another think coming, and so does he. About all that can be said for sure about what I am calling *jouissance* is that it does not happen where or when it is supposed to, and that may in fact be its definition:

The woman is implicated, of necessity, in phallic sexuality, but at the same time it is "elsewhere that she upholds the question of her own *jouissance,*" that is, the question of her status as desiring subject . . . — what escapes or is left over from the phallic function, and exceeds it. Woman is, therefore, placed *beyond* (beyond the phallus). That "beyond" refers at once to her almost total mystification as absolute Other (and hence nothing other than other), and to a *question,* the question of her own *jouissance,* of her greater or lesser access to the residue of the dialectic to which she is constantly subjected.

(Rose, in Mitchell and Rose,
Feminine Sexuality, 51)

Let me be clear at once that we are not talking about orgasms. We have, I suspect fortunately, no information about the vaginal versus clitoral question in the fourteenth century, not even from Chaucer. What we are talking about is a kind of pleasure that is against the law in the mode of scandal: it is outside the law and shows it up. The treatment of the subject that is most useful for the study of Chaucer is neither by Lacan nor Freud nor Masters and Johnson but by Roland Barthes, his meditations on *jouissance* in *The Pleasure of the Text.*[13]

---

13. The French version was published in 1973, the year after Lacan's Seminar XX had taken up what became *Encore,* and Barthes's book seems to me to be among other things a complex meditation on, and partial critique of, Lacanian concerns. For a

This makes sense if we consider that the *Canterbury Tales* is a representation of a series of encounters with texts broadly conceived. Both the translating Second Nun and the remembering Wife of Bath, for example, deal with narratives that are in some sense preconstructed, and so in fact do all the other pilgrims since none tells an "original" tale. Barthes goes so far as to suggest that *jouissance* ("bliss" in the translation) is easier to come by under these circumstances:

> Many readings are perverse, implying a split, a cleavage. Just as the child knows its mother has no penis and simultaneously believes she has one (an economy whose validity Freud has demonstrated), so the reader can keep saying: *I know these are only words, but all the same . . .* (I am moved as though these words were uttering a reality). Of all readings, that of tragedy is the most perverse: I take pleasure in hearing myself tell a story *whose end I know:* I know and I don't know, I act toward myself as though I did not know: I know perfectly well Oedipus will be unmasked, that Danton will be guillotined, *but all the same . . .* Compared to a dramatic story, which is one whose outcome is unknown, there is here an effacement of [conscious, everyday] pleasure and a progression of bliss (today, in mass culture, there is an enormous consumption of "dramatics" and little bliss).
>
> (Barthes, *Pleasure of the Text*, 48–49)

This passage suggests that this sort of *jouissance,* or at least the opportunity for it, will be familiar in a relatively traditional culture, where it is common to retell the same stories, and that it is often a function of what I have called rereading. It also supports Felman's separation of pleasure from knowledge—unless of course, as Barthes notes, "knowledge itself were *delicious*" (23).

Neither my *jouissance* nor Chaucer's (though both no doubt find their place) is in question here, and no pleasure of the sort under discussion is dependably *transmitted* by the text. Rather, the poem is a representation of the *jouissance* of others and is therefore mediated—at a considerable distance from the fictional experience it constructs. Like all other signifying relations, that between bliss and language is a relation of *différance:* language does not *convey* bliss, it only

---

devastating critique, published the same year, of oppositions of the order vaginal/clitoral, see Luce Irigaray, "Psychoanalytic Theory: Another Look," in *This Sex Which Is Not One,* 34–67, esp. 63ff.

ambiguously marks its traces, where it has been. This circumstance is of course as true for a speaker as for a reader, and it will help us pick up the track of *jouissance* in the text.

There is nothing particularly arcane, and certainly nothing modern, about the manifestation of the unconscious in language. It hides itself, to be sure, but it does so behind the most banal and everyday linguistic occurrences: jokes, slips of the tongue, and so forth. Almost any break in the flow of signification can testify to the force of the subtext that is always covertly in operation: laughter, forgetting—or remembering:

> But—Lord Crist!—whan that it remembreth me
> Upon my yowthe, and on my jolitee,
> It tikleth me aboute myn herte roote.
> Unto this day it dooth myn herte boote
> That I have had my world as in my tyme.
>
> (III, 469–73)

This of course is not *it*. It is testimony after the fact *to* the fact that it was here and that it felt (feels?) good. As I pointed out earlier, the Wife is not primarily characterizing what it was like to be young but rather what it feels like to remember it now. The fictional *experience* to which this passage refers is taking place (fictively) somewhere, somehow, around or behind or through some part of this earlier passage:

> My fourthe housbonde was a revelour—
> This is to seyn, he hadde a paramour—
> And I was yong and ful of ragerye,
> Stibourn and strong, and joly as a pye.
> How koude I daunce to an harpe smale,
> And synge, ywis, as any nyghtyngale,
> Whan I had dronke a draughte of sweete wyn!
> Metellius, the foule cherl, the swyn . . .
>
> (453–60)

The *jouissance* is what is going on besides, and beyond, the narrative, the facts, and the description. It is, so to speak, the punctuation,[14] the

---

14. See the discussion of punctuation as "the moment at which meaning constitutes itself as a finished product," Clément, *Lives and Legends*, pp. 117–120, 176–78. She is commenting on what is perhaps the central Lacanian text for the issues raised here, "The Subversion of the Subject and the Dialectic of Desire in the Freudian Unconscious," *Ecrits, A Selection*, trans. Alan Sheridan (New York: Norton, 1977), pp. 292–325.

voicing that only comes into consciousness for us *or* the Wife after it has happened. No more than we was she expecting it; no more than we could she have predicted it. "But—Lord Crist!" is the Wife's "*C'était donc ça!*" which Jameson translates perfectly into modern Californian: "Wow!" ("Pleasure," 1).

What is registered here post hoc (or *après Ça*)[15] is the invasion of the "rational" narrative order of the text by something else that seizes on some pretext in the narrative and displaces the conscious, communicative, narrating ego. Yeats's "How can we know the dancer from the dance?" is not a dancer's question. Such a moment of bliss is a moment of ecstasy in the etymological sense, a standing out or away from awareness, a loss of the self. Such ecstatic moments are quite common in the *Canterbury Tales;* they occur whenever a speaker registers (usually after the fact, as above) *the effect of getting caught up in the tale, lost in the telling:* "But now, sire, lat me se, what I shal seyn. / A ha! By God, I have my tale ageyn" (III, 585–86). *Jouissance* is what runs counter to predictable, one might say institutionalized, pleasure, like eating a meal or otherwise meeting a need or satisfying a demand. It forces its way into the present—in something as small, perhaps, as an apparently gratuitous shift of tense—and displaces meaning and reference, logic and sequence. This is one reason Barthes insists on calling it perverse: it is counterrational, counterinstitutional. The masculine law of pleasure is that you must take it in its proper, lawful place, the place of genital heterosexuality in marriage. For the Wife of Bath this kind of pleasure is caught in the iron mesh of male domination as the *bele chose* that can be commodified because it can be located, identified, given a consistent value. "Lord Crist!—whan that it remembreth me" records the traces of a pleasure that will not hold still to be sold. It may well occur at the site where the law prescribes its presence, and the Wife says that sometimes for her it has—but not because the law called it forth. Even in the now of telling, it manifests itself as part of an *other* order beyond the phallus, the memory of a dancing that is itself part of the dance of her *jouissance* across the text of her telling. As it happens, the following is about the cinema, but suppose it were about that cinema of the mind, memory:

15. *Ça* is the French translation of *das Es*, the term of Freud's conventionally given to English readers in Latin as the id.

It suffices that the cinema capture the sound of speech *close up* (this is, in fact, the generalized definition of the "grain" of writing) and make us hear in their materiality, their sensuality, the breath, the gutturals, the fleshiness of the lips, a whole presence of the human muzzle (that the voice, that writing, be as fresh, supple, lubricated, delicately granular and vibrant as an animal's muzzle), to succeed in shifting the signified a great distance and in throwing, so to speak, the anonymous body of the actor into my ear: it granulates, it crackles, it caresses, it grates, it cuts, it comes: that is bliss.

(Barthes, *Pleasure of the Text,* 67)

And so is this:

> Fro thennes forth the Jues han conspired
> This innocent out of this world to chace.
> An homycide therto han they hyred,
> That in an aleye had a privee place;
> And as the child gan forby for to pace,
> This cursed Jew hym hente, and heelde hym faste,
> And kitte his throte, and in a pit hym caste.
>
> I seye that in a wardrobe they hym threwe
> Where as thise Jewes purgen hire entraille.
> O cursed folk of Herodes al newe,
> What may youre yvel entente yow availle?
> Mordre wol out, certeyn, it wol nat faille,
> And namely ther th'onour of God shal sprede;
> The blood out crieth on youre cursed dede.
>
> O martir, sowded to virginitee,
> Now maystow syngen, folwynge evere in oon
> The white Lamb celestial—quod she—
> Of which the grete evaungelist, Seint John,
> In Pathmos wroot, which seith that they that goon
> Biforn this Lamb and synge a song al newe,
> That nevere, flesshly, wommen they ne knewe.
>
> This poure wydwe awaiteth al that nyght
> After hir litel child . . .
>
> (*Prioress's Tale,* VII, 565–87)

The first thing that functions as a signifier of the coming of bliss here is the way the voice breaks with the narrative. We can hear whatever is happening *kick in* over the stanza break as the speaker goes back again to what she has just told: "*I seye that in a wardrobe* they hym threwe." This is immediately followed by a set of apostrophes, a figure that is inherently counternarrative and creates imaginary others to whom the speaker's passion addresses itself. Even more striking is the astonishing leap, again mediated by a stanza break, from the hatred, mire, and blood of the second stanza to the vision of the "white Lamb celestial" in the third. The speaker's voice literally overpowers the story in jarring shifts of tone and mood that seem to take hold of the tale and the speaker and ravish them away.

Perhaps the most remarkable thing about the passage is the sense of fragmentation it conveys by the sharp breaks in style and subject from stanza to stanza and the interruptions of the telling. Such features connect what is happening here with Barthes's point that *jouissance* is an affair of gaps and edges:

> Is not the most erotic portion of the body *where the garment gapes?* In perversion (which is the realm of textual pleasure) there are no "eroge-nous zones" (a foolish expression, besides); it is intermittence, as psy-choanalysis has so rightly stated, which is erotic: the intermittence of skin flashing between two articles of clothing (trousers and sweater), between two edges (the open-necked shirt, the glove and the sleeve); it is this flash itself which seduces, or rather: the staging of an appearance-as-disappearance.
>
> (Barthes, *Pleasure of the Text,* 9–10)

Of course this argument needs to be turned around. Barthes is talking about the experience of reading and the way *jouissance* fastens on gaps in the text, but he is also clear that as an experience this manifestation is a matter of individual, if unconscious, history and preference—no text will do it for everyone.[16] But if the gap and the edge do function as he says, then their presence in a text can be used to signify the unshared bliss of another, to create a kind of *jouissance* effect. I must insist again that I am neither psychoanalyzing nor deconstructing Chaucer's text; I am trying to describe what it represents. In the case of the Prioress, for example, it is the sudden apostrophes that *make a space* for her bliss, like holes in the text, and tell us where the garment, the weave of the text she is telling, gapes for her.

The Prioress is sometimes convicted of sentimentality, usually with respect to her portrait in the *General Prologue*—her feelings for her lapdogs, her sympathy with mice, and so forth—but also sometimes

---

16. See the particularly illuminating section of *The Pleasure of the Text,* 62–63. Barthes is playing with Lacan's notion of *béance;* see, for example, Lacan, "Subversion of the Subject."

over her tale as well.[17] If sentimentality means excessive indulgence in emotion, the expenditure of a disproportionate amount of emotional energy on an inappropriate object, then it is another word for *jouissance,* one that gets at the uncomfortable *impropriety* of bliss, especially for those who witness it without experiencing it. The Prioress's excess has always had an unsettling effect on readers, starting with the poet-narrator, whose extraordinary break in impersonation, the "quod she" in the above passage, serves notice, among other things, that he wants to dissociate himself from what is being said. But the multiple breaks in decorum that occur here are not entirely contained by a relatively dismissive characterization like sentimentality. As the poet's own break suggests, the gap threatens to spread. Since bliss is something that escapes the ordering of knowledge and the law, it can be a *threat* to the idea of society itself. In terms of the institutional structure and its mystification, *jouissance* is what zeroes in on the chinks—the gaps—in the armor of society and threatens to show it up for the rattling, jerry-built construction it is. When an innocent tale in praise of innocence suddenly becomes the site of something other, the focus of disturbing, excessive pleasures, the result is the establishment of a fault line that may lead to larger disturbances. The Prioress's investment of darker, aggressive forces in her tale, the ruthlessness of her pleasure in hating others, even if they are for the moment imaginary, is unsettling in the passage and has been unsettling in her tale, as the recurrent controversy over its anti-Semitism testifies.

Perhaps most unsettling of all is how uncaring the Prioress herself is. She takes her pleasure as it comes to her, and her imagination betrays its readiness to use the law as a pretext for its own enjoyments. Her pleasure in her tale, because it is private, is subversive without being competitive, though it does seem to express resentment at male domination, as the other tales told by women also seem to do.[18] The Prioress's *jouissance* makes what it wants and what it can of the given institutional structure without care and without responsibility. If she is perforce situated beyond the phallus, on the other side of knowledge,

17. See, for example, Donaldson, *Chaucer's Poetry,* 1044–46, 1096–98.
18. *"Jouissance,"* says Lacan somewhere, "comes easily to the slave, and it will leave the work in bondage." I would not want to say that the Prioress is unaware of the effect she creates. There is something calculated in her outrageousness that reads as doing what she likes not only in spite of but also *because of* the effect it has on others.

then her answer to the question, What is woman's desire? cannot be something knowable, reducible to a concept that would make it predictable. It can only be an experience, the experience of whatever turns her on. ✓

JOUISSANCE AND THE "MASCULINE" IMAGINATION: THE NUN'S PRIEST AND OTHERS

What makes *jouissance* "feminine" or "masculine" has nothing to do, except contingently, with the physical sex of the subject who experiences it, nor does the simple fact of ecstasy, the breakthrough of unconscious energy into language and experience. Rather, it is a matter of how such an experience is handled, and especially how it is related to the institutional structure—the tale and the society—it interrupts. It is not really the manifestation of libido that is at stake but the social construction of it, what options there are for dealing with it once it appears. This social construction is what seems to be gendered in Chaucer and what appears to have consequences for the construction and maintenance of gender. The "masculine" imagination tends to disapprove of *jouissance* and be made uncomfortable by it because of the stake it has in the stability of institutions and meaning. It feels the need to limit or disavow the outbreak of instinctual energy, erotic or aggressive, as the reporting (male) poet does with his "quod she" in the *Prioress's Tale*. Whatever we see the traces of in those moments when the Pardoner either forgets the sequence of his tale ("Thise riotoures thre of whiche I telle" [VI, 661]); or withdraws libidinal investment from it (as in his loss of interest in the narrative at its conclusion); it does not seem to make him happy. There is rather a sense of giddiness, a sort of edgy dancing over the void, in the sudden shifts—of tense, for instance—and the ironic reversals of the sermon section of the tale,[19]

---

19. Kierkegaard begins by treating the possibility of this kind of dissolution as funny, within the framework of naive consciousness, which he calls immediacy:

> When [immediate persons] are in despair, there is nothing they desire more than to have been someone else or to become someone else. . . . [It] is difficult to keep from smiling over one who despairs in this way, who, humanly speaking and despite being in despair, is so very innocent. As a rule, one who despairs in this way is very comical. Imagine a self (and next to God there is nothing as eternal as a self), and then imagine that it suddenly occurs to a self that it might become someone other—than itself. And yet one in despair this way, whose sole desire is

as there is in the sudden outbreak of free-floating paranoid aggression that deranges pronoun reference in this passage from the *Reeve's Tale:*

> And by the throte-bolle he caughte Alayn,
> And he hente hym despitously agayn,
> And on the nose he smoot hym with his fest.
> Doun ran the blody streem upon his brest;
> And in the floor, with nose and mouth tobroke,
> They walwe as doon two pigges in a poke.
>
> (I, 4273–78)[20]

A moment like this, when the Reeve seems to turn as much animus against his hero Alayn as against his opponent Symkyn the Miller, points in its own way to the kind of self-destructive dissolution of the ego and the distinctions it maintains between itself and others that the Pardoner also displays.

Similarly, in the *Nun's Priest's Tale* there is a great deal of play with genres, levels of style, and modes of discourse, sanctioned in part by

---

this most lunatic of lunatic metamorphoses, is infatuated with the illusion that this change can be accomplished as easily as one changes clothes. The man of immediacy does not know himself, he quite literally identifies himself only by the clothes he wears, he identifies having a self by externalities (here again the infinitely comical). There is hardly a more ludicrous mistake, for a self is indeed infinitely distinct from an externality.

(*Sickness unto Death*, 53)

Kierkegaard's somewhat nagging insistence that this condition must be funny combines with the similarity of the man of immediacy to Nietzsche's old women in a way that helps bring out the tone of masculine disenchantment here. Suppose this comical misapprehension about the impermanence of the self as only the shifting play of its surfaces were actually the truth about it:

Every existence that is within the qualification spirit, even if only on its own responsibility and at its own risk, has an essential interior consistency and a consistency in something higher, at least in an idea. Such a person has great fear of any inconsistency, because he has an immense apprehension of what the result can be, that he could be torn out of the totality in which he has his life. The slightest inconsistency is an enormous loss, for, after all, he loses consistency. In that very moment, the spell is perhaps broken, the mysterious power that bound all his capacities in harmony is diminished, the coiled spring is slackened; everything perhaps becomes a chaos in which the capacities in mutiny battle one another and plunge the self into suffering, a chaos in which there is no agreement within itself, no momentum, no *impetus*.

(*Sickness unto Death*, 107)

See the discussion of *corps morcelé* below, pp. 277–80.
20. On this passage see Sklute, *Virtue of Necessity*, 116.

the carnivalesque license that is provisionally granted to beast fables
and Menippean satire.[21] The tale notoriously both creates and violates
a lot of edges and boundaries, more so than any other tale, with the
possible exception of *Melibee*.[22] In the process it allows its narrator a
lot of erotic fantasy (for example, Chaunteclere's harem) and a lot of
aggressive freedom as well, as in this passage, which is also a direct
expression of the pleasure of the text:

> Lo, in the lyf of Seint Kenelm I rede,
> That was Kenulphus sone, the noble kyng
> Of Mercenrike, how Kenelm mette a thyng.
> A lite er he was mordred, on a day,
> His mordre in his avysioun he say.
> His norice hym expowned every deel
> His sweven, and bad hym for to kepe hym weel
> For traisoun; but he nas but seven yeer oold,
> And therefore litel tale hath he toold
> Of any dreem, so hooly was his herte.
> *By God! I hadde levere than my sherte*
> *That ye hadde rad his legend, as have I.*
>
>   (VII, 3110–21, emphasis
>   added)

The pleasure taken in making fun of the Prioress and her little clergeon
(a theme already touched on at 3050–57) is blended here with the sheer
bliss in the lines themselves at the wondrous, fortuitous coincidence of
texts, *ç'était donc ça!* This looks like what Barthes might call delicious
knowledge. Yet such moments of *jouissance* are matched by glints of
nihilistic terror—"But casuelly the shippes botme rente" (3101), or the
apocalyptic subtext of the fox chase (3389, 3394–96, 3401)—that are
not present in the Wife of Bath's performance, nor yet those of the two
nuns. Donaldson's suggestion that the theme of the tale is the institutional function of rhetoric as a defense against an inscrutable reality
(*Chaucer's Poetry*, 1106) is in line with the sorts of anxieties that beset the "masculine" imagination, the intimations of meaninglessness,

21. From this perspective it is possible that the Cook's fragment is the one instance
of what I have called "feminine" imagining that is unequivocally assigned to a male
speaker in the *Canterbury Tales*.

22. The best account of *Melibee*, with particular reference to *jouissance* and the
function of the text in the Canterbury framework, is Kempton, "Chaucer's Tale of
Melibee."

helplessness, and lack of control out of which all that talk and all those authorities are generated.

Moreover, what the tale does with these moments of slippage, whether pleasurable, vertiginous, or both, seems very unlike the Wife of Bath's shifting of roles at the end of her tale to protect and defend the pleasures she has unrepentantly taken in the course of it. The Nun's Priest comes to suspect, with reason, that he will have to pay for his pleasures, and this suspicion leads him first to try to dissociate himself from them:

> But for I noot to whom it myght displese,
> If I conseil of wommen wolde blame,
> Passe over, for I seyde it in my game.
> Rede auctours, where they trete of swich mateere,
> And what they seyn of wommen ye may heere.
> *Thise been the cokkes wordes, and nat myne;*
> I kan noon harm of no womman divyne.
>   (3260–66, emphasis
>   added)

This transparent attempt to deal with the perils of having disclosed his *privetee* too openly may or may not convince the Prioress, but it does not appear to reassure the Nun's Priest, who might be said, unlike the Wife of Bath and his employer, to be unsure of what he can get away with. He therefore tries to socialize his losses by making his own problem the theme of the tale: how to deal with the fox, the creature that shows up when you take your pleasures heedlessly and sing without reflecting. The image of Chaunteclere's father, the very old Adam of roosters, standing on tiptoe and crowing at the top of his voice with his eyes closed is not a bad representation of the narcissistic self-absorption of the id, as the fox is of its aggressive hungers, and both are images of the drives that roost and raven in the tale's narrator.

Without pursuing an extremely complex analysis further, I can point to this self-conscious and practically motivated self-allegorization as an instance of the operations of the "masculine" imagination insofar as the Nun's Priest chooses or is compelled to treat his private pleasure as a public issue, something for which he must apologize and do penance and from which he must draw a moral—in fact several morals. What is "masculine" about the Nun's Priest's *jouissance* is what he does with it afterward: his concern, however forced or even insincere, with its public implications and consequences, and the need to contain and channel it into controlling institutional forms. Private pleasure, the eros and aggression that are anterior to the law and speak surreptitiously from behind it, are what has to be repressed to acknowledge the law's power and keep it empowered. The same is true of woman, and it is no accident that biological femininity and *jouissance* are often linked in this society—to say nothing of others. The carnality the Wife of Bath has to deal with is a "nature" that men have projected onto women to avoid facing it in themselves,[23] and uneasily, sometimes unconsciously but always practically, they know it: The woman tempted me, and I did eat, is not an excuse God finds convincing. "Femininity" is therefore precisely what has to be repressed to keep disenchantment from breaking out and to keep society, including the fraud of gender itself, from being revealed as the rickety construction that, for all its terrible power, it is. Even women are supposed to repress it and become sons of Eve.

What is funniest and most poignant about this requirement is that no one, man or woman, is able to do it even if they want to. There are no masculine or feminine subjects in the *Canterbury Tales;* there are only "masculine" and "feminine" positions with which subjects have to deal and in relation to which they have to place themselves. The *Knight's Tale* is perhaps the most thoroughgoing and complex enactment of the "masculine" imagination in the poem, as the Wife's is of the "feminine," and like hers his tale embodies an intricate deployment of feminine and masculine identifications. The Knight has to deal with his own bisexuality and his own *jouissance,* and I will come to both of these in due course. I will begin, however, with what may appear to be a different sort of engagement of the subject with an institution. In French *genre* refers to both literary forms and grammatical or sexual gender. *La loi du genre* actually translates better into Middle English than into modern English, as "the lawe of kynde," the law of natures and sorts of poems and persons. As we shall see, the *Knight's Tale* is centrally concerned with the connections between these usages. It traces an itinerary that runs at last to a vision of the natures of men and women but begins with a consideration of kinds of poems: epic and romance.

23. This point, banal enough by now, is particularly well made by Joan M. Ferrante, writing at a time when it was less banal, in *Woman as Image in Medieval Literature.*

3

THE INSTITUTION OF THE SUBJECT
A Reading of the *Knight's Tale*

9

The Knight's Critique of Genre I
Ambivalence and Generic Style

Everyone is acquainted with movements in art—two examples: Mannerist painting of the late sixteenth and early seventeenth centuries, Art Nouveau in painting, architecture, furniture and objects—which do more than simply "have a style." Artists like Parmigianino, Pontormo, Rosso, Bronzino, like Gaudi, Guimard, Beardsley and Tiffany, in some obvious way cultivate style. They seem to be preoccupied with stylistic questions, and indeed to place the accent less on what they are saying than on the manner of saying it.

To deal with art of this type . . . a term like "stylization" . . . is needed. "Stylization" is what is present in a work of art precisely when an artist does propose the by-no-means inevitable distinction between manner and matter, theme and form. When that happens, when style and subject are so distinguished, that is, played off against each other, one can legitimately speak of subjects being treated (or mistreated) in a certain style.

. . . "Stylization" in a work of art, as distinct from style, reflects an ambivalence (affection contradicted by contempt, obsession contradicted by irony) toward the subject matter. This ambivalence is handled by maintaining, through the rhetorical overlay that is stylization, a special distance from the subject.

Susan Sontag, "On Style"

EPIC

It seems likely that the issue of impersonation has given readers more trouble in the *Knight's Tale* than in the tales of the Pardoner and the Wife of Bath at least in part because, unlike those two pilgrims, the Knight has no declared interest in self-presentation. At the end of the *General Prologue* he agrees in a bare three lines to tell the first tale (I, 853–55) and commences at once on the narrative: "Whilom, as olde stories tellen us, / Ther was a duc . . ." (859–60). Since his announced aim is only to tell a story, and he is not his own subject as the Wife and Pardoner are theirs, it is not surprising that his voice is relatively recessive and self-effacing, directing us more toward the narrative than the narrator, even when, as he does at the end of Part I, he steps back

to address the audience directly: "Yow loveres axe I now this questioun: / Who hath the worse, Arcite or Palamoun?" (1347–48). Even
those critics who have been willing to consider the role of the Knight
in the *Knight's Tale* have tended to follow its narrator's lead and
minimize his agency, his active working on and with the story. They
are inclined to categorize the traces of him they find not as conscious
self-presentations but as self-revelations, frequently of the unconscious
or self-betraying kind. We have heard—when the issue of the story's
narrator has been raised at all—of a naive and idealistic Knight who
does not see how his own story questions his beliefs, a romantic Knight
caught by reality but aspiring to the ideal, a Knight in bad faith whose
successes have led him to dodge the darker implications of his world.
I do not know of an interpretation that consistently gives the Knight
credit for understanding and facing his own tale, for being fully capable of seeing in it what we see.[1]

Yet a voice-oriented reading of the tale brings out a narrator who is
the consistent agent of the full range of the poem's effects: its humor
and pathos as well as its splendor; its horror and grim realism as well
as its shining idealism; its insistence on chaos, madness, and the brute
misery of the human condition as well as its praise of order and the
noble life. Such a reading restores to the Knight two areas of concern
that are ordinarily seen primarily as background, as matters of conscious concern, if at all, to Chaucer as maker of the poem rather than
to the Knight as teller of the tale, and in so doing restores to him his
disenchantment as well. The two areas I have in mind are the relation
of the tale to the historical state of knighthood in the fourteenth
century and the relation of the tale to its literary sources. In the first
instance, I will be concerned to show that the tale functions as both a

1. Let me at once single out Neuse, "The Knight," as an honorable, if ultimately only
partial, exception to this generalization. Neuse's article remains for me the best single
discussion of the tale and the nearest precursor of my own approach to it. For examples
(by no means exhaustive) of the versions of the Knight listed in the text, see the
following: (1) Naive and idealistic: Howard, *Idea,* who, despite his penetrating remarks
on what he calls the obsolescence of knightly ideals in the fourteenth century (94–97,
113), does not allow the Knight himself access to the ironic vision that reveals it (esp.
227–37); Salter, "Introduction," in *Chaucer: The Knight's Tale and the Clerk's Tale,*
7–36; Spearing, "Introduction," in *Selected Tales from Chaucer: The Knight's Tale,*
48–50; Thurston, *Artistic Ambivalence,* esp. 68. (2) Realistic but aspiring: Foster,
"Humor in the *Knight's Tale.*" (3) Bad faith or worse: Ebner, "Chaucer's Precarious
Knight"; Helterman, "Dehumanizing Metamorphoses"; T. Jones, *Chaucer's Knight,*
passim.

representation of and a *response to* the well-attested decline of chivalry in the period: the mercenary greed, the constant treachery and switching of sides, the brutal and unnecessary violence visited on the defenseless, and the continual subordination of chivalric ideals to political necessities that fill the pages of Froissart and Terry Jones, to search no further afield. Whatever may be said against Jones, he can tell us what the Knight has seen because he provides a set of glosses on what is more obliquely, but no less insistently, represented in the tale itself. If we can see these things, and if, despite William Brandt, Froissart could see them, it should come as no surprise that the Knight sees them too and that, again like the Wife and the Pardoner, he has attitudes toward the social conditions that constitute his estate.[2] Like Froissart, the Knight is aware that if chivalry is to be sustained as a viable ideal, it must come to terms as best it can with those human weaknesses of the strong that make them so dangerous and with the demands of practical politics. Ultimately I will argue that the tale itself is such an act of coming to terms with historical and social reality, an instance of the doing of knighthood. Both the Knight's maintenance of chivalry and his disenchanted criticism of it *are* the story he tells.

In fact, the track of the Knight's historical disenchantment with chivalry as an institution is most clearly registered, at least at first, in his dissatisfaction with its most cherished fantasies, which are also his own. From the beginning he places the tale in relation to its "sources" in the larger sense of the generic discourses of epic and romance that

---

2. In the case of Froissart this is not the place to make the argument. The reader is directed, however, to the tale of the ill-fated Franco-Burgundian and Hungarian expedition against the sultan Bajazet that occupies much of the latter portion of Book IV of the *Chronicles*, especially to the extraordinary chapter 89 of that book and above all to the Count de Nevers's report of the Turks' opinion of the schism in chapter 91: "The sultan thought our faith erroneous, and corrupted by those that ought to have kept its purity; and the Turks laughed and made their jokes at it. . . . I believe they are perfectly well acquainted . . . with our schisms in the church, and how the Christians are at variance with one another, respecting the two popes of France and Italy; and the Saracens are wonderfully surprised how the kings of the different countries suffer it" (654). Such outspoken assessments are not rare in Book IV. Brandt's *Shape of Medieval History* has been an influential exponent of the historical structuralist position that "most aristocratic writers [of chronicles] assume aristocratic stances even while they write about them; they do not notice things that do not cohere within those stances" (81). Though he specifically exempts the socially marginal Froissart from the extreme form of this class-conditioned perception, he does not recognize the actual critical and analytical thrust of the *Chronicles*. I do not wish at this point to enter into the controversy over Terry Jones's book. For a sensible recent contribution, see Brown and Branch, Review of Terry Jones, *Chaucer's Knight*.

supply much of its ideological justification in mystified forms. It is important to see that the details of the tale operate in the context of these larger discursive fields, that they are "stylized" in Sontag's sense of the word. Here we can turn immediately to the text, which provides a clear, if complex, characterization of the speaker's attitude toward his sources at its outset:

> Whilom, as olde stories tellen us,
> Ther was a duc that highte Theseus;
> Of Atthenes he was lord and governour,
> And in his tyme swich a conquerour
> That gretter was ther noon under the sonne.
> Ful many a riche contree hadde he wonne;
> What with his wysdom and his chivalrie,
> He conquered al the regne of Femenye,
> That whilom was ycleped Scithia,
> And weddede the queene Ypolita,
> And broghte hire hoom with hym in his contree
> With muchel glorie and greet solempnytee,
> And eek hir yonge suster Emelye.
> And thus with victorie and with melodye
> Lete I this noble duc to Atthenes ryde,
> And al his hoost in armes hym bisyde.
>   And certes, if it nere to long to heere,
> I wolde have toold yow fully the manere
> How wonnen was the regne of Femenye
> By Theseus and by his chivalrye;
> And of the grete bataille for the nones
> Bitwixen Atthenes and Amazones;
> And how asseged was Ypolita,
> The faire, hardy queene of Scithia;
> And of the feste that was at hir weddynge,
> And of the tempest at hir hoom-comynge;
> But al that thyng I moot as now forbere.
> I have, God woot, a large feeld to ere,
> And wayke been the oxen in my plough.
> The remenant of the tale is long ynough.
> I wol nat letten eek noon of this route;
> Lat every felawe telle his tale aboute,
> And lat se now who shal the soper wynne;
> And there I lefte, I wol ayeyn bigynne.
>   (859–892)

This opening passage enacts a motion, which the tale itself will recapitulate, from the there and then ("whilom") of fable, the ideal and heroic past, to the colloquial immediacy of here and now on the pilgrimage. The Knight is isolating his particular tale from the vast storehouse of "olde stories" in which it is embedded, bringing it forward for his present audience. His initial act thus calls attention to itself as a *selection* from sources and in particular an act of compression in the fiction that is analogous to Chaucer's act of selecting, editing, and compressing Boccaccio and Statius (the latter is a source the Knight acknowledges himself [2294]) outside the fiction.[3]

This selective operation on what we can identify in a broad sense as a prior text[4] identifies the Knight's telling as an act of rereading the generic discourse of chivalry something like the Wife of Bath's recounting of her autobiography and even more like the Pardoner's handling of his exemplum. Of course any retelling of a story the teller does not make up is like this, but what makes the more active editorial image apposite in the *Canterbury Tales* generally and in the *Knight's Tale* in particular is the way the text features a set of *attitudes toward the source as such*. At the simplest level the Knight is aware, and says so, that the story in its original form (something like "The Deeds of Theseus," perhaps) is not suitable to the present occasion: at the very least it is too long. But the text also registers the attraction that storied world has for him, and nowhere more than when he begins to disengage himself from it. The number of things he announces that he will not tell us (growing more and more concrete and detailed up to the tempest, when he breaks off) and the way the voice lingers over the repeated rhymes, *femenye/chivalrye, Ypolita/Scithia*, all betray a reluctance to let go of what "I wolde have toold yow," the clear and noble representation of his own tradition enshrined in the old books. This attraction is in tension with, and finally controlled by, the Knight's awareness of the need to discipline his imagination, to accede to the

<hr />

3. Compare the discussion of Janekyn's book and the sources of the *Wife of Bath's Prologue* above, chapter 5. There is a convenient summary of Chaucer's use of the *Teseida* in *Riverside Chaucer*, 827, and a helpful account of the general tenor of his changes in Pearsall, *Canterbury Tales*, 117–21.

4. "The Knight's learning comes not, as a clerk's learning would have, from books, but from a body of lore some of which was preserved in books but most of which was probably passed on orally. It is useful when we think of medieval oral traditions to suppose that there were separate traditions for separate groups—a 'folklore' of the people, a 'knightlore' of the aristocracy, a 'clerklore' among churchmen." Howard, *Idea*, 228. It is worth remembering, however, how often the Knight refers to his sources as "olde bookes" and the like. It seems clear that at least in the case of this story the speaker thinks of it as a predominantly literary thing, though generic rather than specific.

claims (perhaps the impatience) of others, and to make something of his story that recognizes the demands of the situation in which he speaks. The motion from past to present and literature to life is also a motion from nostalgia to social responsibility. But the speech is structured in such a way as to bring out the effort as well as the control, the sense that there is something to be controlled. It is important to keep this double attitude or ambivalence firmly in view since it is one of the great stylistic facts of the poem and ultimately a key to its meaning.

The *Knight's Tale* is a romance grafted onto an epic, the story of the loves of the young Theban knights Palamon and Arcite for the Amazon Emelye, sister-in-law of Theseus, in the aftermath of Theseus's conquest of Amazonia, "the regne of femenye," and in the wake of his equally epic destruction of Thebes itself. The poem presents itself as a continuation of the last book of the *Thebaid* of Statius. This structural fact, which has been variously noted by critics,[5] is itself the index of a particular way of proceeding on the part of the narrator: he tells a story (a love story) that is easiest to identify as a romance, but he begins with a set of epic themes in an epic world, and here already the ambivalence that concerns me is manifest.

In the foreground of the narration of the conquest of Thebes that opens the story proper is the heroic image of Theseus, "In al his wele and in his mooste pride" (895), hastening off to right the wrongs of the Theban women before he has even brought his bride home to Athens and slaying the villain Creon (the apparent source of the evil) "manly as a knyght / In pleyn bataille" (987–88). This heroic image is fostered by the often-noted stylization of this world, a kind of epic formality of language and clarified largeness of gesture whereby distressed ladies faint ceremonially before speaking their formal complaints of Fortune's false wheel.[6] The generic intent of this stylization, its epic *vouloir dire,* is to abstract and idealize the action so as to celebrate the

5. The most useful discussion of the relations of the tale to epic remains Haller, "Epic Tradition." There are good brief treatments of the issue as well in Cooper, *Structure of the Canterbury Tales,* 91–93, and Pearsall, *Canterbury Tales,* 117–21. Important new ground is broken, especially with regard to the different treatments of Statius, Boccaccio, and Chaucer in relation to one another, in Hanning, " 'Noble Designs and Chaos.' "
6. The best discussion of this kind of epic style, including the staccato parataxis typical of the opening of the *Knight's Tale,* is Auerbach, *Mimesis.* The first five chapters are relevant, but see especially the account of Tacitus and late classical historiography, 29–35, and chapter 5, "Roland Against Ganelon," 83–107. Compare Brandt's account of

clarity and decisiveness of the heroic individual and his deeds, untrammeled by more realistic considerations. Indeed the text concentrates so firmly on Theseus and his might that the image of the hero tends to overpower the larger forces in whose name he putatively acts. The Argive women may be waiting in the temple of Clementia for redress of grievances they ascribe to Fortune, but it is Theseus they have been awaiting for two weeks (928–29), and it is to him as the "Lord, to whom Fortune hath yiven / Victorie" (915–16) that they appeal—not just anyone's clemency will do. When the ladies have dramatized their low position on Fortune's wheel with a symbolic (and simultaneous) fall (948–511), it is Theseus alone who raises them:

> Whan he saugh hem so pitous and so maat,
> That whilom weren of so greet estaat;
> And in his armes he hem alle up hente,
> And hem conforteth in ful good entente.
>
> (955–58)

Realistic description (*all* of them?) is subordinated to the symbolism of the single sweeping gesture of lifting up as an image for the redress of what the second line construes as a sad case, the *casus feminarum illustrium*. The language presents Theseus as dominating and controlling the motion of the wheel, as if he had replaced Fortune. Similarly, when the hero rides to Thebes:

> The rede statue of Mars, with spere and targe,
> So shyneth in his white baner large
> That alle the feeldes glyteren up and doun;
> And by his baner born is his penoun
> Of gold ful riche, in which ther was ybete
> The Mynotaur, which that he wan in Crete.
> Thus rit this duc, thus rit this conquerour . . .
>
> (975–81)

That banner does not announce "Mars is coming" but "*Theseus* is coming." The image of the god is part of the splendor of the hero's display, almost like the trophy of his earlier deeds, the Minotaur, that

---

what he calls the aristocratic style in medieval chronicles, *Shape of Medieval History*, 81–105. In both cases first-rate structural and stylistic description is to a degree vitiated by failures of interpretation.

accompanies it: the hero is more real than the god. The Knight's concentration on Theseus and his glory thus stresses the primacy of the duke's heroic will. He is initially presented not so much as the embodiment of larger forces of order that much criticism has seen in him later in the tale but rather as an independent generator of action, the lord of Fortune and more effective than the gods, who makes order in the interest of his own heroic reputation: he swears "Upon the tiraunt Creon him to wreke / That al the peple of Grece sholde speke / How Creon was of Theseus yserved" (961–63).

Though the general attitude in the tale toward the deeds of Theseus seems clearly positive, those deeds also have darker implications. The conspicuously brusque epic style of the description has its traditional effect of concentrating attention on the celebration of the hero, but it also sometimes works to bring the darker implications forward in a way that smokes the edges of the bright image of the hero's glory. Thus the description of Theseus's first sight of the mourning women:

> "What folk ben ye, that at myn homcomynge
> Perturben so my feste with criynge?"
> Quod Theseus. "Have ye so greet envye
> Of myn honour, that thus compleyne and crye?
> Or who hath yow mysboden or offended?
> And telleth me if it may been amended,
> And why that ye been clothed thus in blak."
> (905–11)

Awareness of potential envious enemies comes first here, almost as a reflex. It is followed by awareness of an alternative—the presence of a wrong, instantly conceived by Theseus as "to be righted—by me"; only then, apparently, does the visual detail of the black garments register. It is as if Theseus's actual visual perception were preprogrammed to give priority to the details of sensory data most relevant to his heroic being.[7] This is the first instance in the poem of an attention to the processes of visual perception that will issue later in an extended treatment of the masculine gaze. For the moment, however, it is enough to note how the presentation catches the element of heroic self-regard in epic seeing, the jealous and contentious care for one's own reputation that are characteristic of this ethos. Similarly, if the

7. See Van, "Theseus and the 'Right Way,' " 86–87.

single combat with Creon presents the good side of the heroic capability for violence, the effects of that violence on Thebes—"And rente adoun bothe wall and sparre and rafter" (990)—seem less easily justified.[8]

The Knight completes his narration of Theseus's noble deed with a brief account of the burning of the desecrated Argive corpses, leaving the sacrilege atoned and the "noble conquerour" resting in possession of "al the contree as hym leste" (1004). He follows immediately, however, with a more realistic image of the "pilours" ransacking and stripping in "the taas of bodyes dede" (1005). This more disenchanted description lets something harsher, and closer to the concrete experience of war, invade the stylized world of the tale. It sounds a theme that will later be embodied in the Temple of Mars and Arcite's broken body and does so in a style that departs noticeably from the rhetorical level of what precedes it. Not that this sort of treatment of defeated armies is unusual or even necessarily reprehensible in Chaucer's time; it is neither, as M. J. Keen's discussion of sieges in *The Laws of War in the Later Middle Ages* (119–33) makes clear.[9] Rather, it is a question first of *literary* decorum. This concentration on details of war that are at once violent and mundane sorts a little uncomfortably with the less concrete and more elevated image of combat that precedes it, and it introduces a specific and "modern" note that contrasts with the relatively timeless epic world. The passage qualifies, and perhaps questions slightly, the smoothness of the celebratory epic surface in a way that can be brought back to Theseus as well. Its echo of the Argive widow's account of what Creon did—"Hath alle the bodyes on an heep ydrawe" (944)—makes it easier for us to reflect that in disposing of one heap of corpses, Theseus has created another.

Such touches suggest that the Knight is not entirely uncritical of the epic ideal as he finds it embodied in his "olde stories." There is something disturbing about the purity of Theseus's epic self-assertion, even

---

8. Questions about this act of Theseus have often been raised in the literature: by Van, "Theseus and the 'Right Way' "; by Webb, the first modern assassin of the duke's character, "Reinterpretation of Chaucer's Theseus," 290–91, with citations of fourteenth-century protests against pillaging; by Underwood, "First of *The Canterbury Tales*," in Owen, *Discussions of the Canterbury Tales*, 39; and by James Smith, "Chaucer, Boethius," who blames the Knight for Theseus's vacillating character.

9. But see the documents cited in Webb, "Reinterpretation of Chaucer's Theseus," passim.

in a good cause, because it seems too heedless of consequences, especially social and political ones, and the style of the description tends to bring this out. If the heroic individual is given the powers of Fortune and the gods, he is also identified as the source of the bad effects of those powers as well as the good. The role of style in promoting this effect is especially clear in the passage that concludes the first, epic phase of the tale and introduces the protagonists of what is to follow:

> Nat fully quyke, ne fully dede they were,
> But by hir cote-armures and by hir gere
> The heraudes knewe hem best in special
> As they that weren of the blood roial
> Of Thebes, and of sustren two yborn.
> Out of the taas the pilours han hem torn,
> And han hem caried softe unto the tente
> Of Theseus; and he ful soone hem sente
> To Atthenes, to dwellen in prisoun
> Perpetuelly—he nolde no raunsoun.
> And whan this worthy duc hath thus ydon,
> He took his hoost, and hoom he rit anon
> With laurer crowned as a conquerour;
> And ther he lyveth in joye and in honour
> Terme of his lyf; what nedeth wordes mo?
> And in a tour, in angwissh and in wo,
> This Palamon and his felawe Arcite
> For everemoore, ther may no gold hem quite.
>   (1015–32)

Though not much is made immediately of what Theseus has done to Thebes, the lineage of Palamon and Arcite keeps their public and political identity marginally alive in the passage and supplies a tacit reason for Theseus's actions. But although it is likely that he imprisons the Theban princes because they are members of a family that might otherwise cause him trouble, the fact that we are not told why he does it deflects attention from Theseus's concern for order or even realpolitik and stresses once again the arbitrariness of his power and his individual will.[10] The last lines, with their hieratic, wheel-of-Fortune contrast of the magnificence of the conqueror and the wretchedness of

10. Kolve has written well on the initial harshness of the image of Theseus, *Imagery of Narrative*, 98–102.

the vanquished, contribute to this effect by presenting the situation as if it were concluded and without further consequences, "perpetuelly," "for evermoore." As we shall see, Palamon and Arcite's political identity continues to dog the tale to its end, though they themselves do all they can to suppress and evade it. But even on first reading we cannot but be aware that the story has barely begun, and this recognition enforces a generic awareness of literary probabilities: conventional expectations about a story of this sort include the expectation that complications will soon follow, as of course they do. The Knight's voicing here, therefore, represents not his own assessment of the situation but the rhetorical miming of an epic style that subordinates questions of the consequences of heroic action to the memorializing of the hero's *res gestae*.

This sort of controlled but continual exaggeration of the hieratic stiffness of an antique, epic style, which I have been tracing throughout the opening of the poem, bespeaks the presence of a narrator for whom it is the embodiment of an antique, inadequate vision, one that will ultimately need to be brought up to date so as to render the heroic individual more responsive, and responsible, to the requirements of order and the noble life. This is the last time in the poem that we will see Theseus so abstractly and absolutely. From now on he will constantly be dealing with the consequences of this briefly frozen moment, exposed to increasingly realistic and modern pressures that will finally transform him, bringing him forward from the idealized past into the Knight's real world.

ROMANCE

The image of Palamon and Arcite torn from the heap of Theban bodies is presented in such a way as to suggest a new birth, and something of that effect is immediately reinforced by a shift in generic style from epic to romance, from heroic combat and the cries of the vanquished to the flowering of springtime and lovers' groans. Political issues appear to fade away, and war becomes something undertaken, if at all, in the service of love. Among the things that register this shift are a new concentration on nature (including human nature, in line with the interest of romance in the seasonal rhythms of generation) and on psychological experience:

> This passeth yeer by yeer and day by day,
> Till it fil ones, in a morwe of May,
> That Emelye, that fairer was to sene
> Than is the lylie upon his stalke grene,
> And fressher than the May with floures newe—
> For with the rose colour stroof hire hewe,
> I noot which was the fyner of hem two—
> Er it were day, as was hir wone to do,
> She was arisen and al redy dight,
> For May wole have no slogardie anyght.
> The sesoun priketh every gentil herte,
> And maketh it out of his slep to sterte,
> And seith "Arys, and do thyn observaunce."
> This maked Emelye have remembraunce
> To doon honour to May, and for to ryse.
> Yclothed was she fressh, for to devyse:
> Hire yelow heer was broyded in a tresse
> Bihynde hir bak, a yerde long, I gesse.
> And in the gardyn, at the sonne upriste,
> She walketh up and doun, and as hire liste
> She gadereth floures, party white and rede,
> To make a subtil gerland for hire hede;
> And as an aungel hevenysshly she soong.
>
> (1033–55)

This description, a set piece unlike anything in the poem that precedes it, concentrates on natural, seasonal energy and its general effects, though it is scarcely a realistic description of nature. The description has a leisurely, aestheticizing quality and manifests its willingness to take time, not over the deeds of the hero, but over what Auerbach calls "graceful vignettes of established custom, one might say of a ritual which shows us courtly society in its setting of highly developed conventionality."[11] The lady's individuality is of little importance to the forces being described here—so little, in fact, that she is assimilated to the season, made its embodiment and one of its effects, like the lily and the rose.[12] Indeed, as it proceeds, the description increasingly sublimates and chastens the erotic restlessness it conveys at its beginning. By the end of the passage artifice has taken over: the lady's hair moves

11. *Mimesis*, 114. The quotation, describing Chrétien's *Yvain*, is taken from chapter 6, "The Knight Sets Forth," 107–24, which presents a description of romance style as fertile and suggestive as the preceding discussion of epic (see above, note 5).

12. The blending of girl and season is noted by Spearing, *Knight's Tale*, 40.

into a braid, and the flowers into a garland; the pricking of the seasonal urge is contained in a courtly garden and a May song, and the lady herself is etherealized away from her wakeful stirrings into an angel. The passage is an instance of the way art, the cultural art that makes poetic *reverdies* as well as gardens, strives to tame the forces of sexuality, just as human making strives to contain other forces of disorder in great dungeon towers like the one "evene joynant to the gardyn wal" (1060).[13]

But as with the epic earlier, the containment of unruly forces in this romance world is incomplete, for the same power at work in Emelye as she "romed up and doun" in the garden (1069) is also stirring in Palamon, who "Was risen and romed in a chambre an heigh" (1065) and now "Goth in the chambre romynge to and fro" (1971).[14] The verbal echoing hints at the seasonal component in Palamon's "wo," the erotic energies looking for an outlet, and the description of his falling in love at first sight confirms it:

> And so bifel, by aventure or cas,
> That thurgh a wyndow, thikke of many a barre
> Of iren greet and square as any sparre,
> He cast his eye upon Emelya,
> And therwithal he bleynte and cride, "A!"
> As though he stongen were unto the herte.
>
> (1074–79)

The fortuitousness implied by "aventure or cas" is qualified by the stress given to Palamon's aggressively active vision ("cast his eye") and the weighty obstacles it overcomes on its way to the lady.

Though Palamon's looking is portrayed as active, the prince himself experiences its effects passively as something he undergoes. This passivity suggests that the active character of his desire is not conscious and that he does not know he is looking for an object even before he finds it. It is clear from the presentation that there is more projecting

13. The images of prison and garden in the tale, and their connectedness, have been analyzed by Kolve, *Imagery of Narrative*, 85–157, and by Green, *World Views and Human Power*.
14. The complex verbal play on "romynge," which extends well beyond this passage, has been noted and analyzed by Kolve, *Imagery of Narrative*, 89–91, though he reads it, rather more romantically than I do, as an affirmation of the cousins' will to freedom.

than perceiving going on here: this second account of a male look in
the poem is linked to the *reverdie* that precedes it—is in fact a kind of
extension of it—because both glances, the narrator's and Palamon's,
gaze at a woman but see a goddess:

> "I noot wher she be womman or goddesse,
> But Venus is it soothly, as I gesse."
> And therwithal on knees doun he fil,
> And seyde, "Venus, if it be thy wil
> Yow in this gardyn thus to transfigure
> Bifore me, sorweful, wrecched creature,
> Out of this prisoun help that we may scapen.
> And if so be my destynee be shapen
> By eterne word to dyen in prisoun,
> Of oure lynage have som compassioun,
> That is so lowe ybroght by tirannye."
>
> (1101–11)

Here we catch Palamon in the act of shifting, like the tale itself, from
epic to romance. By constituting Emelye as Venus, Palamon makes it
possible to ask her for things no real lady could be expected to supply,
and the things he asks for testify to his primary concerns: his own fate
and that of Thebes. It might be said that Palamon displaces his previous epic situation into his loving, in the sense that he conceives love as
an answer to, or replacement for, his political problems. The poem
thus moves from Theseus's heroic gaze to Palamon's romantic one, but
in such a way as to suggest that the two styles of looking are connected
behind their surface differences. As we soon discover, he plans to do
for romantic reasons—to gain Emelye—what he might previously
have done anyway for political-heroic ones: raise an army and attack
Theseus (1281–90, 1482–86).

The same displacement, whereby old situations continue in force
under cover of new ones, is equally apparent in Arcite. He construes
Palamon's cry on seeing Emelye as a response to their imprisonment—
a natural enough mistake, but one that also reveals what is most on
Arcite's mind, especially since he proceeds to give a lecture on it:

> "Why cridestow? Who hath thee doon offence?
> For Goddes love, taak al in pacience
> Oure prisoun, for it may noon oother be.
> Fortune hath yeven us this adversitee.

Som wikke aspect or disposicioun
Of Saturne, by som constellacioun,
Hath yeven us this, although we hadde it sworn;
So stood the hevene whan that we were born.
We moste endure it; this is the short and pleyn."
(1083–91)

Arcite seems unusually concerned not only to establish the fated, unalterable character of their situation but also to blame it on forces of destiny and powers above, about which little can be done. When his turn to fall in love comes a few lines later, like his cousin he immediately conceives the lady as an object of worship, but he does so in keeping with the passivity in the face of the gods and the stars displayed earlier. If Palamon asks too much of the lady, Arcite seems to ask too little: "And but I have hir mercy and hir grace, / That I may seen hire atte leeste weye, / I nam but deed; ther nis namoore to seye" (1120–22).

What is really striking about the wrangling that follows their vision of Emelye is how quickly the two knights move away from any concern with the lady herself. She becomes a kind of stipulation, a conventional unattainable object, and Palamon and Arcite concentrate on their relationship to one another. Each of the cousins conceives of himself as a victim, driven and fated to both imprisonment and love, but what this victimization seems to mean is that they feel free, paradoxically, to use their loving as an excuse to engage one another more competitively and with less regard for ordinary conventions of civility than they otherwise would. The adverbs that characterize their speeches, "despitously" (Palamon, 1124) and "ful proudly" (Arcite, 1152) catch the contentious quality of the discussion and its greater concern with individual ethos and self-justification than with Emelye: "And now *thow* woldest falsly been aboute / To love *my* lady, whom *I* love and serve" (1142–43, emphasis added).

To compare these events to their counterparts in the *Teseida*, where Palemone and Arcita stay close and sympathize with one another's hopeless passion for the same lady, is to realize how *un*courtly the situation here remains and how little of a civilizing effect the romance situation exerts on the cousins. The despair at their public situations that lurks behind their initial speeches finds its way as well into their dealings with one another after the vision of Emelye, in the form of a thoroughly dark assessment of human relations and human possibility. Though it is certainly true that there are contingencies at work that the cousins can do little about, nothing requires that they abandon control of those aspects of the situation they do command. Arcite's espousal of the old clerks' saw "who shal yeve a lovere any lawe" (1164) need not produce the wholesale breakdown of human ties implied by his image of dogs wrangling over a bone (1177–80) nor his despairing conclusion, "And therfore at the kynges court, my brother, / Ech man for hymself, ther is noon oother" (1181–82). It may be in line with Arcite's passivity, his sense that love overrides all conventional distinctions, for him to say that a man must love despite himself "Al be she mayde, or wydwe, or elles wyf" (1171), but the statement too easily ignores differences that most people, even lovers, manage to sustain.[15]

Thus, throughout the romance reopening of the tale the tendency of romance to abstract from the real world a celebratory image of idealized courtly social behavior as "an absolute aesthetic configuration" is never quite achieved.[16] There is a continual sense that incompletely tamed motives, from the erotic impulses associated with, and directed at, Emelye to the aggressive ones that arise between Palamon and Arcite, are at work just beneath the surface: the romance style of the tale gives us a sublimation that does not fully conceal what it and the characters attempt to sublimate.

But these observations are not only mine. As with the epic situations earlier, here the speaker not only uses romance situations and language: he also takes positions with regard to them and to the characters who are involved in or employ them. The Knight's handling of the following episode, in which Perothous secures Arcite's release, suggests that he is alert to the questionable aspects of the scene he has just recounted between Palamon and Arcite. The Knight makes something of the juxtaposition by making the relationship between Theseus and his friend a tacit comment on what has gone before:

> A worthy duc that highte Perotheus,
> That felawe was unto duc Theseus
> Syn thilke day that they were children lite,
> Was come to Atthenes his felawe to visite,

15. See Smith, "Chaucer, Boethius," 4–12, and Robinson, *Chaucer and the English Tradition*, 123.
16. Once again I follow Auerbach, *Mimesis*, 120.

And for to pleye as he was wont to do;
For in this world he loved no man so,
And he loved hym als tendrely agayn.
So wel they lovede, as olde bookes sayn,
That whan that oon was deed, soothly to telle,
His felawe went and soughte hym doun in helle—
But of that storie list me nat to write.
Duc Perotheus loved wel Arcite,
And hadde hym knowe at Thebes yeer by yere,
And finally at requeste and prayere
Of Perotheus, withouten any raunsoun,
Duc Theseus hym leet out of prisoun
Frely to goon wher that hym liste over al,
In swich a gyse as I you tellen shal.

                                        (1191–1208)

The Knight's brief digression, highlighted all the more when he recognizes it as such and breaks it off, holds up the achieved and sustained ideal of brotherhood in the "olde bookes" and measures his disapproval of Palamon and Arcite against it. He conspicuously takes a moment out from the story to remind himself and us that not all sworn brothers are like the Theban cousins before returning to the plot.[17]

A cluster of attitudes toward romance conventions that is fully as complex as those taken toward epic ones (and rather more fully developed) emerges again in the speaker's handling of the twin formal complaints of Palamon and Arcite that close Part I of the tale. The complexities are consistently registered as shifts of voice:

How greet a sorwe suffreth now Arcite!
The deeth he feeleth thurgh his herte smyte;
He wepeth, wayleth, crieth pitously;
To sleen hymself he waiteth prively.
He seyde, "Allas that day that I was born!
Now is my prisoun worse than biforn;
Now is me shape eternally to dwelle
Noght in purgatorie, but in helle.
Allas, that evere knew I Perotheus!

---

17. This function of the passage has been noticed by Cooper, *Structure of the Canterbury Tales*, 94. She points out that "the Classical legend of Pirothous is different; it is Chaucer who specifically turns it into an example of friendship stronger than death," but she does not ascribe it to the narrating Knight. See Hoffman, "Ovid and Chaucer's Myth of Theseus and Pirothoüs," 252–57.

> For elles hadde I dwelled with Theseus,
> Yfetered in his prisoun everemo.
> Thanne hadde I been in blisse and nat in wo.
> Oonly the sighte of hire whom that I serve,
> Though that I nevere hir grace may deserve,
> Wolde han suffised right ynough for me.
> O deere cosyn Palamon," quod he,
> "Thyn is the victorie of this aventure.
> Ful blisfully in prison maistow dure—
> In prison? Certes nay, but in paradys!
> Wel hath Fortune yturned thee the dys,
> That hast the sighte of hire, and I th'absence.
> For possible is, syn thou hast hire presence,
> And art a kynght, a worthy and an able,
> That by som cas, syn Fortune is chaungeable,
> Thow maist to thy desir somtyme atteyne.
> But I, that am exiled and bareyne
> Of alle grace, and in so greet dispeir
> That ther nys erthe, water, fir, ne eir,
> Ne creature that of hem maked is,
> That may me helpe or doon confort in this,
> Wel oughte I sterve in wanhope and distresse.
> Farwel my lif, my lust, and my gladnesse!
>   (1219–50)

The Knight's enjoyment in developing the elegant paradoxes and hyperboles of this complaint is patent; he likes working up the rhetoric, miming it, and giving himself to it—so much so that he then turns around and does it again with Palamon. One effect of the often-noted careful balancing of speeches between the two knights in the first part of the tale is that we can be treated to (and the Knight can produce) twice as much of this nonsense as we might otherwise get. The Knight is well aware that it is nonsense. The image of Arcite lying in ambush for himself (1222) pushes his woe in the direction of parody, as does the too-close look at Palamon a little later:

>   the grete tour
> Resouneth of his youlyng and clamour.
> The pure fettres on his shynes grete
> Weren of his bittre, salte teeres wete.
>   (1277–80)

Palamon's yowling and the fact that he has great shins are matters too closely observed, too physical, to sustain the decorum of courtly grief.

But it is precisely because the Knight does not take these performances too seriously that he can enjoy them as performances.

About halfway through Arcite's complaint, however, something curious happens:

> Wel oughte I sterve in wanhope and distresse.
> Farwel my lif, my lust, and my gladnesse!
>   Allas, why pleynen folk so in commune
> On purveiaunce of God, or of Fortune,
> That yeveth hem ful ofte in many a gyse
> Wel bettre than they kan hemself devyse?
> Som man desireth for to han richesse,
> That cause is of his mordre or greet siknesse;
> And som man wolde out of his prisoun fayn,
> That in his hous is of his meynee slayn.
> Infinite harmes been in this mateere.
> We witen nat what thing we preyen heere;
> We faren as he that dronke is as a mous.
> A dronke man woot wel he hath an hous,
> But he noot which the righte wey is thider,
> And to a dronke man the wey is slider.
> And certes, in this world so faren we;
> We seken faste after felicitee,
> But we goon wrong ful often, trewely.
> Thus may we seyen alle, and namely I,
> That wende and hadde a greet opinioun
> That if I myghte escapen from prisoun,
> Thanne hadde I been in joye and perfit heele,
> Ther now I am exiled fro my wele.
> Syn that I may nat seen you, Emelye,
> I nam but deed; ther nys no remedye.
>
> (1249–74)

It is a little difficult, on first reading, to decide who is speaking here. Arcite's "Farwel my lyf" (1250) has a ring of finality sufficient to give the sense of a new beginning to the more general reflections that follow. Since those reflections themselves appear to comment critically on the practice of complaining about Fortune that Arcite has just been indulging in, it is tempting to construe them as the narrator's comment on Arcite's speech rather than as a continuation of it.[18] This effect is

---

18. The effect was not lost on the scribes of Ellesmere and Hengwrt, both of whom insert before line 1251 the paragraph sigil that does duty in their manuscripts for quotation marks indicating a change of speaker.

strengthened by the generality of the passage, the way it carefully avoids the first-person singular and any direct reference to Arcite's specific situation except as one general example ("And som man wolde out of his prisoun fayn") out of a number that illustrate not only the uncertainty of the human condition but also its wretchedness. The examples—a desire for riches that causes murder or simply eventuates in "greet siknesse," the released prisoner slain by his treacherous servants, the oddly concrete yet obscurely allegorical drunkard taken from Boethius—generate a rather dark image of the world at large in terms remote from frustration in love. Only when Arcite comes back to his own situation, at "Thus may we seyen alle, and namely I," can the speech be securely located as his. There is a momentary effect of disjunction in the text here whereby its voicing seems to slip, to become dislocated momentarily, and then to be reascribed to Arcite.

Something similar happens again in Palamon's complaint. There are no withheld pronouns here to create confusion about who is speaking; the speech is clearly ascribed to Palamon: "Thanne seyde he,'O crueel goddess' " (1303). The peculiarity is rather that there are sections of the speech that seem both strongly felt and oddly arbitrary or irrelevant in Palamon's circumstances. We do not see how he got here from the pangs of love and jealousy:

> What governance is in this prescience,
> That giltelees tormenteth innocence?
> And yet encresseth this al my penaunce,
> That man is bounden to his observaunce,
> For Goddes sake, to letten of his wille,
> Ther as a beest may al his lust fulfille.
> And whan a beest is deed he hath no peyne;
> But man after his deeth moot wepe and pleyne,
> Though in this world he have care and wo.
> Withouten doute it may stonden so.
> The answere of this lete I to dyvynys,
> But wel I woot that in this world greet pyne ys.
>
> (1313–24)

Once again the trouble is not that no sense can be made of these reflections as coming from Palamon. But it is a little surprising to find him suddenly so philosophical—and to judge from the bathos of the concluding lines, in which he gives up the problem as beyond his powers, Palamon is a little surprised too, or at any rate he is out of his depth.

The effect in both of these complaints is of a certain dark, Boethian seriousness entering the tale suddenly and a little awkwardly. Both speeches allude to the *Consolation* and are to that degree anachronistic, belonging more to the world of the narrator than that of the characters. In this and other ways the text contains the traces of the speaker *behind* the characters, making them more philosophical and imparting his concerns and language as it were around them or over their heads, so that the speeches are double-voiced, functioning one way "in character" and another as intimations of the Knight's interests. The Knight is surely mocking Palamon's lovesick jealousy with such things as his outrageous homographic pun "So woodly that he lyk was to biholde / The boxtree" (1301–2). He lets the two complaints play off against one another and the situation so as to bring out the projections and passivity of the Thebans. He does not, however, seem entirely unsympathetic to Palamon and Arcite's intimation of a profound and uncaring senselessness at the heart of things; it is an intimation he seems to share and one he here goes out of his way to bring into the tale. It is as if he were looking for a means to express these concerns and finding it difficult to do so. The extent to which Palamon and Arcite are confounded by these serious matters, unable to deal with them or even to express them without confusing their own feelings with whatever laws—if any—may govern the universe, is an indication of the extent to which the tale itself as presently constituted is unfit to express such concerns with the seriousness the Knight feels they deserve. His restlessness with this situation produces the oddities of impersonation and voicing just analyzed, the effect of certain issues *intruding* on a context that does not contain them comfortably.

A voice-oriented reading of Part I, then, produces a record of the speaker's transactions with his preexistent story, the ways he finds both to pass the story on and to convey his feelings about it. As it unfolds, his telling embodies the range of those feelings: he is attracted to and enjoys not only the events of the tale but also the conventional styles in which they are packaged, and he shows this enjoyment by producing polished versions of epic and romance topoi, heroic battles, courtly landscapes, and lovers' complaints. At the same time the Knight maintains a certain distance from the tale and the conventions of its telling; he is amused by their pretentiousness and is not above parodying them. Finally, he is disturbed by certain aspects of the same idealism that attracts him and the same irresponsibility that amuses him. He takes some of the issues the story raises more seriously than the tale itself, in its present form, appears to do.

It is characteristic of the Knight's way of conducting the tale in its opening stages that his questioning and qualifying of the story proceeds by indirection, that is, by tacit juxtaposition of plot elements and contradictory speeches. He repeats the tale pretty much as it comes to him from the old books, and the attitudes he displays toward the story tend to express themselves situationally or structurally, by implication and at the edges of the action. One reason for this indirection is no doubt that, as I have suggested before, the Knight is attracted to the. language, attitudes, and conventions of his sources even when he also finds them silly or disturbing. In any case the fact that all of these attitudes find expression relatively indirectly is an index of the problem: the Knight has not yet managed to make the tale speak *for* him; his own voice speaks from the sidelines or in the ironic twist of a phrase, or conspicuously and somewhat uncomfortably appropriates the speeches of the characters. The relation between speaker and characters remains primarily that of teller here, tale there.

The Knight's Critique of Genre II
From Representation to Revision

THE KNIGHT: DISENCHANTMENT AND AGENCY

When at the end of Part I of the *Knight's Tale* the Knight returns explicitly to the occasion of the telling here and now on the pilgrimage, he makes a gesture of socialization whose perfunctory incompleteness confirms his disengagement. The *demande* at the end of the *Franklin's Tale*, "Which was the mooste fre, as thynketh yow?" (V, 1622), is a genuine request, an attempt to give what the Franklin has made of his story fulfillment in the world of the pilgrims and make his tale a genuinely social act.[1] By contrast, the Knight's *demande*, "Who hath the worse, Arcite or Palamoun?" (I, 1348), primarily conveys his judgment of the inconsequentiality of the story thus far for us here and now. It is fit only for this sort of trivial courtly game, a judgment the Knight enforces by refusing to stop to play it: "Now demeth as yow liste, ye that kan, / For I wol telle forth as I bigan" (1353–54). In context the gesture seems like a passing nod to the audience, a recognition of their presence and a reaffirmation of the teller's responsibility to do more than amuse or enchant himself with the courtly games of ancient nobility, which by now make him a little impatient. In line with this impulse, from the very beginning of Part II of the tale the Knight asserts his presence more actively and explicitly and adopts a more overtly skeptical and critical attitude toward the world of the story and the self-dramatizations of the characters. This attitude comes out, for example, in such things as the conventional description of the lovelorn Arcite back in Thebes, hollow-eyed and pale, pining alone (1355–71), a description capped by the blunt statement:

---

1. See Berger, "F-Fragment," 155–56; for the *demande* in the *Knight's Tale*, see Payne, *Chaucer and Menippean Satire*, 210, and Fichte, *Chaucer's "Art Poetical,"* 85.

> And in his geere for all the world he ferde
> Nat oonly lik the loveris maladye
> Of Hereos, but rather lyk manye,
> Engendred of humour malencolik
> Biforen, in his celle fantastik.
>
> (1372-76)

Arcite's behavior suggested not merely lovesickness but actual clinical insanity or mania. A similar effect is obtained by the later description of Arcite musing in the grove:

> Into a studie he fil sodeynly,
> As doon thise loveres in hir queynte geres,
> Now in the crope, now doun in the breres,
> Now up, now doun, as boket in a welle.
>
> (1530-33)

The Knight's willingness to generalize ("thise loveres") and his over-homely colloquialism make plain his lack of identification with the state of mind of a romantic lover. Clearly he is more willing to speak out about such matters in Part II than he was in Part I.

One result of this willingness is the foregrounding of the Knight himself as an agent, whose activity as a storyteller comes to occupy a more central position in the telling. Indeed, as the tale proceeds he goes out of his way to call attention to his telling by making the seams of the story awkwardly conspicuous, as, for example, in his presentation of the meeting of Palamon and Arcite in the grove. The presence of the escaped Palamon hiding in the bushes deflects attention from the lyric intensity of Arcite's soliloquy reviewing the irony of his fate (1542-71) because it stresses the way some of the things he says are there to satisfy the needs of exposition: "But ther as I was wont to highte Arcite, / Now highte I Philostrate, noght worth a myte" (1557-58) is something Palamon needs to know for the action to proceed. A few lines later Arcite concludes his meditations with appropriate despair by falling into a trance "a longe tyme" (1573). Palamon, feeling a cold sword slide through his heart at his cousin's revelations, "As he were wood, with face deed and pale" (1578), starts up out of the bushes to deliver an impassioned denunciation. We, alas, wondering what happened to the awkward pause that must have occurred while Palamon waited for Arcite to wake up, may notice how conspicuously the narrator is sacrificing narrative consistency to local effect. His manner of proceeding brings out his presence and agency in the story, the extent to which he is rigging it for his own purposes as he proceeds.[2]

It is in this light, I think, that we must view the various allusions to Fortune, destiny, and the hidden order governing human life in this part of the tale. Far from functioning as serious attempts to identify a larger pattern of meaning in the events of the story, these reflections are placed so as to call attention to the improbable tissue of coincidences, the bits of lucky timing and the fortuitous meetings, that make up the plot.[3] The Knight goes out of his way to remind us "Yet somtyme it shal fallen on a day / That falleth nat eft withinne a thousand yeer" (1668–69)—that is, to remind us just how unlikely it is that not only Palamon and Arcite but also Theseus should end up in the same grove at the same time. Passages like "The destinee, ministre general" (1663ff, discussed above in the Introduction, pp. 4–5) or "feeld hath eyen and the wode hath eres" (1522), precisely because they are overblown in their contexts and invoke too grandiose a set of causes for the minor events they are supposed to cause, make us more aware that the story is being rigged by its narrator to arrange the events of the plot to suit his own ends and, indeed, to comment on the tale as it comes to him from the old books.

The point is not that the Knight is telling his story ineptly. Rather, he is deliberately exaggerating certain of its features to bring out more clearly the buried assumptions about human action that are prepackaged in the style as well as the events of old heroic tales. This purpose is one reason he is so interested in conventions and conventional language, in epic styles of warring and romance styles of loving: he knows that conventional style, like any style, is itself a form of action in the world with its own particular implications. If the skeptical humor of his comments suggests that he is not enchanted by courtly

---

2. See Blake, "Order and the Noble Life," 17–18.

3. "The Knight's narrow selection from the *Teseida* of times, places and characteristics of the players in the drama deepens the story's already inherent improbability and throws into relief a series of momentary events which, because they are not related in logical and obvious ways, invariably produce conflicts of perception. In general, the Knight's emphasis on disconnected moments and tableaux instead of on sequence and motivation has the effect of focusing our attention on the curious dichotomies under whose auspices life and action take place." Payne, *Chaucer and Menippean Satire*, 235. See her discussion of "The destinee, ministre general," 236–37.

conventions, in the sense that he is not taken in by them, and is on the whole disinclined to credit a romantic view of knightly loving, the consistent bearing of his interventions makes the further point that he is also disenchanted in the more technical sense that we have already examined in the Pardoner and the Wife of Bath: what the characters and the old books see as the product of transcendent forces the Knight identifies as humanly originated.

This disenchanted perspective is in fact present in Part I, though in the relatively tacit form characteristic of that section of the poem. As a contrast to the Theban cousins' general and constant tendency to ascribe their condition to all sorts of cosmic powers—to Arcite's "So stood the hevene whan that we were born" (1090) or to Palamon's "But I moot been in prisoun thurgh Saturne, / And eek thurgh Juno, jalous and eek wood" (1328–29)—the Perothous episode, for example, calls attention to a more proximate and practical level of causality in the story. Most immediately, Palamon and Arcite are not in prison because of Fortune or the gods but because of Theseus.[4] It is he who put them there, and it is he who releases Arcite without ransom, not because of fate but because of his old friend (and Arcite's) Perothous. A similar effect is provided by juxtaposing the circumstantial account of the "forward, pleynly for t'endite" (1209) that Theseus lays down for Arcite's exile (1210–18) with Arcite's long-winded courtly woe at receiving his freedom, in which he speaks of Fortune, providence, the elements, and the uncertainty of the human condition without once mentioning Theseus's part in his misfortune. When Palamon, bewailing his own continuing imprisonment, remarks that now Arcite will be able to go back to Thebes, raise an army, and win Emelye (1285–94), the fact that this course of action never occurs to Arcite stresses his continuing passivity, the unquestioning way he accepts whatever life hands him and treats it as fate. His comment "Now is my prisoun worse than biforn" (1224) points up the extent to which his manacles are mind-forged and his prison more a state of mind than a set of real circumstances since he continues to inhabit it once he is out. Even in Part I of the tale the Knight's presentation continually suggests a set of

---

4. As A. J. Minnis succinctly puts it, "Although Theseus has sentenced Arcite and Palamon to life-imprisonment, they tend to blame their plight on fortune and the stars and not on their captor." *Chaucer and Pagan Antiquity*, 122. Chauncey Wood has a trenchant analysis of the cousins' misuses of astrology, *Chaucer and the Country of the Stars*, 45–47.

causes of the action—"natural" or sexual forces, political expediencies or social relations—to which Palamon and Arcite apparently remain unresponsive and which in fact their projective, cosmically obsessed style of consciousness actively prevents them from seeing. In Part II, however, these causes are brought forward and displayed more prominently in what amounts to a representation of practical consciousness in action and a fuller representation of the institutional character of genre.

PALAMON AND ARCITE:
EPIC AND ROMANCE AS PRACTICE

Let us return to Arcite's lonely vigil in Thebes. After his misery has lasted "a yeer or two," a period the Knight dismisses a bit impatiently with "What sholde I al day of his wo endite?" (1380), Arcite has a vision in a dream:

> Hym thoughte how that the wynged god Mercurie
> Biforn hym stood and bad hym to be murie.
> His slepy yerde in hond he bar uprighte;
> An hat he werede upon his heris brighte.
> Arrayed was this god, as he took keep,
> As he was whan that Argus took his sleep;
> And seyde hym thus: "To Atthenes shaltou wende,
> Ther is thee shapen of thy wo an ende."
> And with that word Arcite wook and sterte.
>
> (1385–93)

The presentation here allows the suspicion that this vision is less a Macrobian *oraculum* than a product of Arcite's condition.[5] We have already been told that he is disordered in his "celle fantastik," the part of his brain that is responsible for producing images, and "Hym thoughte" keeps the question open. But more important is the comic brusqueness of the god's appearance and message because of the way it is played off against a more detailed account of the consequences. Though Arcite begins by deciding heroically to see Emelye and die (1394–98), he quickly recognizes the new advantages of his changed appearance:

---

5. The point is noted by Lumiansky, *Of Sondry Folk*, 44.

And with that word he caughte a greet mirour,
And saugh that chaunged was al his colour,
And saugh his visage al in another kynde.
And right anon it ran hym in his mynde,
That, sith his face was so disfigured
Of maladye the which he hadde endured,
He myghte wel, if that he bar hym lowe,
Lyve in Atthenes evermoore unknowe,
And seen his lady wel ny day by day.
And right anon he chaunged his array,
And cladde hym as a povre laborer,
And al allone, save oonly a squier
That knew his privetee and al his cas,
Which was disgised povrely as he was,
To Atthenes is he goon the nexte way.

(1399–1413)

The theatricality and self-consciousness of Arcite's gesture (there is
no mirror, large or small, in Boccaccio) is heightened by the immediacy
and detail of his mental calculations, which focus on the *practical*
possibilities of his appearance, and this practicality is extended to the
rest of the episode. Arcite returns to Athens romantically all alone—
save for a squire carefully disguised to match his master. Arcite offers
himself romantically "to drugge and drawe" (1416) for his ladylove,
and this action is only reasonable since, as the Knight unromantically
explains a few lines later, "he was yong and myghty for the nones, /
And therto he was long and big of bones" (1423–24). It appears that
Arcite's plan to serve in romantic humbleness has not taken sufficient
account of his innate "gentilesse," a quality that is at once apparent to
everyone (1417–21, 1431–41), and results in his rapid advancement in
Theseus's service. But even this storybook rise is presented with a less-
than-romantic attention to the financial considerations that help make
it possible. Theseus, impressed with the young man, puts him into
more "worshipful servyse" (1435) so that Arcite can exercise his "vertu"
and gives him "gold to mayntene his degree" (1441). Moreover:

And eek men broghte hym out of his contree,
From yeer to yeer, ful pryvely his rente;
But honestly and slyly he it spente,
That no man wondred how that he it hadde.

(1442–45)

Throughout the episode both the supernatural instigation of the events and their idealized romantic quality are subordinated to the decisive and well-planned character of the enterprise and undermined by the Knight's insistence on how well everyone knows how to "go on" in their mastery of the practical human actions and necessities on which the alarums and excursions of the romance image are grounded.

The Knight presents Palamon's escape from Theseus's prison similarly. First the hero's plight is summarized with grisly relish:

> In derknesse and horrible and strong prisoun
> This seven yeer hath seten Palamoun
> Forpyned, what for wo and for distresse.
> Who feeleth double soor and hevynesse
> But Palamon, that love distreyneth so
> That wood out of his wit he goth for wo?
> And ek therto he is a prisoner
> Perpetully, noght oonly for a yer.
>   (1451–58)

Palamon is in jail perpetually, that is, within nine lines he will be out:

> It fel that in the seventhe yer, of May
> The thridde nyght (as olde bookes seyn,
> That al this storie tellen moore pleyn),
> Were it by aventure or destynee—
> As, whan a thyng is shapen, it shal be—
> That soone after the mydnyght Palamoun,
> By helpyng of a freend, brak his prisoun.
>   (1462–68)

The ascription of that most useless of facts in a story of this kind, a precise date, to the old books does indeed bring them forward for a moment in all the irrelevance and diffuseness the Knight is trying to reduce to order. Such features of their style as the cavalier dispensing of vast amounts of time and the lip service paid to notions like "aventure or destinee" are quickly overwhelmed by matters of more immediate concern and by more proximate causes: the "helpyng of a freend," the detailed recipe for the narcotic that gets the jailer out of the way (1470–74), and Palamon's practical plans to raise an army when he gets back to Thebes. Once again the text focuses on what the heroes do for themselves and how they go about doing it.

It is, I think, sufficiently clear in the examples just examined that neither the characters nor the "original" version of the story from which the narrating Knight is working quite share his disenchanted perspective. That perspective is conveyed by his extrafictional comments and by his *disposition* of narrative and stylistic elements that in themselves do not reflect the emphasis on human agency that this telling generates, which suggests that part of his aim is a reflexive critique of those elements themselves. That is, his active handling of the tale is increasingly directed toward exposing how conventional chivalry as an institution and conventional romance as a form encourage the mystification of human agency. He counters this mystification, to which the cousins are prey, by identifying his own agency and the demands of the practical world at work beneath the surface of style and events. He brings out a "real" situation which Palamon, Arcite, *and the old books* mistake for the operation of Fortune, destiny, and the gods—for the way things are.

For the Knight, the most important matters elided or glossed over by his sources are the workings of eros and politics in human life. It is significant that he insists on joining the two together when, for the first time in the tale, he steps back to reflect in his own voice on its meaning:

> O Cupide, out of alle charitee!
> O regne, that wolt no felawe have with thee!
> Ful sooth is seyd that love ne lordshipe
> Wol noght, his thankes, have no felaweshipe.
> Wel fynden that Arcite and Palamoun.
>
> (1623–27)

It is precisely their confusion of the relations between love, lordship, and "felaweshipe" or society that most consistently draws the Knight's fire on Palamon and Arcite, as in the Perothous episode, and that he seems most at pains to bring out. He keeps us aware of these elements operating behind and controlling our view of the action and especially our view of the Theban cousins.

The most important political element in the poem is the Theban question, despite the fact that the story appears on the surface largely to disregard it. In fact Thebes is constantly present. In Boccaccio when Theseus takes the city, in Book II of the *Teseida,* he razes it to the ground and scatters its people at the instigation of the Argive women, so that when Arcite is released from Athens, he has no city to return to;

Book IV then details his wanderings over Greece. That the city is not destroyed in the *Knight's Tale* makes it easier for the narrator to keep "Thebes with his olde walles wyde" (1880, cf. 1331) hovering in the background of the story in a more sinister way and makes its exclusion from the foreground more conspicuous. The allusive relation of this story to the *Thebaid* has a similar function. As Haller points out ("Epic Tradition," 44ff), the story keeps bringing up kinstrife as a Theban tradition, here transposed from lordship to love: Palamon and Arcite are blood kin and sworn brothers whose relationship deteriorates in ways that recall Eteocles and Polynices, and the love-and-lordship passage, which articulates these themes, occurs at a moment when the cousins are about to repeat a version of the final single combat of the brothers.[6] As Haller also suggests (71), Palamon and Arcite, being innocent of the meaning of Theban history or unable to learn from it, seem doomed to repeat it.

But it is not accurate to say that the Theban cousins are entirely unaware of the political dimension of their situation. Palamon's plan to bring an army back to Athens, for instance, which is twice enunciated though never carried out, is one of the ways the issue is kept before us, and it is bound to suggest that he has some awareness of political possibilities: he may well suspect that Thebes is only waiting for a leader like him.[7] In fact, for men obsessed with love, both of the heroes think about Thebes a good deal from their first sight of Emelye on. Palamon looks to the lady, as Venus, for the relief of "oure lynage" (1560) the first time he addresses her, and Arcite is still brooding about the fate of the city more than seven years later when he goes to pay homage to May in the grove. Both men keep the presence of Thebes alive in the story, though not, apparently, at the center of their attention, which is directed to Emelye. Arcite's soliloquy in the grove, framed as a lover's lament, provides one of the best and most suggestive examples of the effect:

6. See also McCall, *Chaucer Among the Gods*, 90–91.
7. Indeed, it is not clear to me that Arcite is entirely unaware of the bearing of Theban history on his situation. I find his remark, "And therfore *at the kynges court*, my brother, / Ech man for hymself, ther is noon oother" (1181–82, emphasis added), suggestive, as also his example of the released prisoner "That in his hous is of his meynee slayn" (1258), if only as examples of how his sensibility may have been formed by the Theban experience.

"Allas," quod he, "that day that I was bore!
How longe, Juno, thurgh thy crueltee,
Woltow werreyen Thebes the citee?
Allas, ybroght is to confusioun
The blood roial of Cadme and Amphioun—
Of Cadmus, which that was the firste man
That Thebes bulte, or first the toun bigan,
And of the citee first was crouned kyng.
Of his lynage am I and his ofspryng
By verray ligne, as of the stok roial,
And now I am so caytyf and so thral,
That he that is my mortal enemy,
I serve hym as his squier povrely.
And yet dooth Juno me wel moore shame,
For I dar noght biknowe myn owene name;
But ther as I was wont to highte Arcite,
Now highte I Philostrate, noght worth a myte.
Allas, thou felle Mars! Allas, Juno!
Thus hath youre ire oure lynage al fordo,
Save oonly me and wrecched Palamoun,
That Theseus martireth in prisoun.
And over al this, to sleen me outrely
Love hath his firy dart so brennyngly
Ystiked thurgh my trewe, careful herte
That shapen was my deeth erst than my sherte.
Ye sleen me with youre eyen, Emelye!
Ye been the cause wherfore that I dye.
Of al the remenant of myn oother care
Ne sette I nat the montance of a tare,
So that I koude doon aught to youre plesaunce."

(1542-71)

It is clear enough that Arcite has not forgotten the plight of Thebes
in pursuing Emelye. It seems instead to be constantly on his mind,
something he feels the need to unburden himself of when he is alone,
and in fact fully two-thirds of the speech is given over to it. The issue
of hopeless love arises only in the last nine lines, so that when Arcite
declares that his lovesickness sets his "oother care" at naught, we are
inclined to doubt him. Juno and Mars are blamed most strongly at
those points in the speech where if the gods were not against him,
Arcite might well feel that his city and his lineage would require him to
take some action against the very Theseus he now serves as a love-
struck squire. Arcite's pseudonym, Philostrate, says something about
his motives in choosing it because it explicitly proposes (to Theseus,

among others) a role for him at court as love-struck, which confines him to a conventional form of loving and excludes political or heroic possibilities. The soliloquy suggests that this role has its burdens in terms of what it excludes. These are matters that, from a heroic point of view, Arcite cannot afford to consider too closely because of his position as servant to his mortal enemy. We see that he is blaming the gods where he might more plausibly blame Theseus, but we also see why.[8]

In the light of all this badly displaced political concern, it looks as if Arcite, having named his rival and cousin together with the enemy he serves, switches abruptly to the overmastering pains of love as a means of *escape* from what would otherwise be a paralyzing consciousness of the contradictions that beset him and of the possibility that he might have to do something to resolve them himself. It is better, he seems to think, to concentrate on Emelye's eyes than to challenge Theseus. The speech is a paradigm of the conspicuous displacement of epic and political concerns into love and chivalry first noted with respect to Palamon's gaze at Emelye and typical of the first part of the poem in general. Those concerns are half concealed in such a way that they remain active, present-as-excluded to haunt the characters and the tale. Epic is not simply transposed by Chaucer or even the Knight so that, as Haller puts it, love "takes the place of the usual political center of the epic" ("Epic Tradition," 68). Rather, we see that the Theban princes are portrayed as making this transposition themselves. They try to confine themselves to lovers' roles and defend themselves against unwelcome or insupportable practical and political responsibility by disclaiming it in favor of gods, fates, and the power of love. These characters are in *mauvaise foi* in the technical, Sartrean sense: they are actively concealing from themselves their complicity in their situations, a procedure Harry Berger, Jr., calls practical unconsciousness:

> Let's assume with Giddens that 'every social actor knows a great deal about the conditions of reproduction of the society of which he or she is a member,' and can draw upon 'tacit stocks of knowledge . . . in the

8. I might note in passing that Arcite's account of Thebes and its fate moves at once from Cadmus and Amphion, the founders of the city, to himself, omitting the entire history of the royal line from Oedipus through Eteocles and Polynices to Creon. It thus skips over the relatively recent history of human choices and conflicts for which human responsibility might have to be assigned, in favor of a more flattened, fated image. The history most relevant to Arcite's current situation is conspicuous by its absence.

constitution of social activity': this is practical consciousness. Practical unconsciousness is then the tacit knowledge of techniques for occluding, ignoring, forgetting, whatever knowledge one has that interferes with belief in one's commitment to a discourse. The successful reduction of agents to conduits [for institutional structures] presupposes the discursive ability to find and apply the arguments by which they can convince themselves and, if necessary, deceive themselves. To give Kant's dictum a Sartrean skew, when it is necessary to curtail knowledge in order to make room for bad faith, practical unconsciousness is put to work.[9]

What begins in the description of Emelye's garden as a gesture of the Knight's in shifting from one kind of literary world to another has, by this point in the poem, been identified more clearly as a psychic process of characters who adopt and internalize available conventions of behavior as a response to the difficulties of their situations. The Knight makes an issue of what it means to tell an epic story in romance terms by presenting us with characters who try to live their lives in terms of generic deflections of this sort.

We are now in a position to begin to account more fully for the Knight's uses of genre in the tale and for the attitudes those uses embody. The Knight would almost certainly agree with Northrop Frye that romance is a form of fantasy, "the search of the libido or desiring self for a fulfillment that will deliver it from the anxieties of reality, but will still contain that reality" (*Anatomy of Criticism*, 110), but he also agrees—in practice—with Fredric Jameson that "genres are essentially literary *institutions*, or social contracts . . . , whose function is to specify the proper use of a particular cultural artifact" (*Political Unconscious*, 106) and that such uses are themselves inherently ideological.[10] The Knight's disenchantment extends to his treatment of the traditional genres of epic and romance: he sees that what others, including Palamon and Arcite, have taken for objective structures of experience is in reality a set of human constructions or institutions that

---

9. Berger, "What Did the King Know?" 831.

10. "Genre is essentially a socio-symbolic message, or in other terms, . . . form is immanently and intrinsically an ideology in its own right" (*Political Unconscious*, 141). Jameson's chapter on genre and romance, "Magical Narratives: On the Dialectical Use of Genre Criticism," 103–50, which is in part a critical commentary on the sentence just quoted from Frye, is of great theoretical interest. Its discussion of romance, however, is of little use for Chaucer, in large part because of Jameson's concentration on what might be called post-precapitalist formations to the neglect, among other things, of medieval romance.

attempt to answer to human wishes and human fears. In the case of romance his portrayal of such things as Arcite's soliloquy shows his understanding of the practical psychological uses of courtly conventions, but his more general handling of generic styles demonstrates an awareness as well of the larger ideological interests and social agencies genres carry. This complex psychological and social awareness emerges most clearly in the early stages of the poem from the Knight's tracing of institutional relations and his presentation of the *interplay* between epic and romance elements.

When early in Part II Arcite goes to the grove to bewail his unhappy fate, the narration is full of studied verbal and situational echoes of the garden/prison scene in Part I. He rides "to doon his observaunce to May" (1500) on a courser "startlynge as the fir" (1502), which image evokes the pricking of the season in Arcite by a kind of synecdoche. When he arrives, he sings a song in praise of "faire, fresshe May," makes a garland as Emelye did (1507–12), and "rometh up and doun" as before. His soliloquy on the fate of Thebes and the malice of the gods is close in theme and spirit to his first speech in the prison, and when Palamon accosts him, the argument that develops between the two is essentially the same as it was at first, a point Palamon himself recognizes with his "As I ful ofte have told thee heerbiforn" (1584). The Knight goes to some trouble to evoke a sense of a scene replayed, which here has the effect of emphasizing how little difference the seven intervening years have made. Palamon and Arcite are still at the mercy of erotic forces they do not understand, still held prisoner by their own projective evasions of responsibility for their situations, still defensively repeating the same conventional postures.

But the evocation of similarity functions here as a ground for the presentation of differences so that the new elements play back on the opening of the tale. Just as the Wife of Bath reinterprets earlier moments of her prologue by later ones, so the Knight revises the first part of his story retrospectively by supplying a new version of it that fills in what was previously left out. In the case of the duel in the grove the new material centers on the issue of male competition and its relation to institutions. As the two cousins prepare for their combat, the Knight focuses on the oddity of knightly ritual conducted privately and solemnly in the wilderness. His description moves jarringly from the slightly absurd stiffness of the formalities between the two knights to the animal ferocity of their combat:

> Ther nas no good day, ne no saluyng,
> But streight, withouten word or rehersyng,
> Everich of hem heelp for to armen oother
> As freendly as he were his owene brother;
> And after that, with sharpe speres stronge
> They foynen ech at oother wonder longe.
> Thou myghtest wene that this Palamon
> In his fyghting were a wood leon,
> And as a crueel tigre was Arcite;
> As wilde bores gonne they to smyte,
> That frothen whit as foom for ire wood.
> Up to the ancle foghte they in hir blood.
> And in this wise I lete hem fightyng dwelle,
> And forth I wole of Theseus yow telle.
>
> (1649–62)

Theseus's observation that the two "fighten heere / Withouten juge or oother officere, / As it were in a lystes roially" (1711–13) catches some of the effect and again points up its peculiarity.

The Knight does not, however, view the combat simply as absurd. The animal imagery brings out as well a sense that the fight is not just a game and that powerful natural forces are in play and serious consequences at stake; the latter point is heightened by the intrusive simile on the "hunters in the regne of Trace" (1638):

> That stondeth at the gappe with a spere,
> Whan hunted is the leon or the bere,
> And hereth hym come russhyng in the greves,
> And breketh bothe bowes and the leves,
> And thynketh, "Heere cometh my mortal enemy!
> Withoute faille, he moot be deed, or I."
>
> (1639–44)

Only Robert Hanning has taken note of this extraordinary passage, which is, as he points out, unique to the Knight and Chaucer.[11] He is right to call it Hemingwayesque; to my knowledge it is matched as a portrayal of the specifically psychological disturbances of the chivalric experience only by Froissart's eerie account of the Counts of Foix in Book III of the *Chronicles*. Here the voice of the narrator identifies in the present tense with the anxiety of the hunters and imagines it more

---

11. Hanning, " 'Noble Designs and Chaos,' " 536–37.

vividly than the actual combat between Palamon and Arcite with its conventional blood-up-to-the-ankles. The Knight's intervention allows some of the real terror of fighting to invade the more distant and literary scene.

But precisely because of this heightened intensity and realism there is something admirable about Palamon and Arcite's attempt to contain their violence in chivalric formality. Though the Knight may feel that these forms are misplaced and misapplied here, they nonetheless do much to keep animal ferocity in check and prevent the fight from being merely that struggle of dogs over a bone that Arcite had predicted, and they lend the proceedings a certain measure of dignity. There is something right about the two knights' instincts for control, if not about their enactment of them, and this sense is a clue to the *value* the Knight sees in romance forms and ideals.[12] The duel in the grove is a moment when the undercurrent of aggression that has marked relations between Palamon and Arcite almost from the beginning of the tale threatens to explode into overt violence, and as such it supplies a gloss on the earlier scenes—on just such things as Arcite's dog-and-bone image, for example—of competitive wrangling between them. This sort of individualistic and violent contentiousness is of course more openly displayed in epic, which could be thought of as the ideology of this strife and striving at the roots of manhood and society, an ideology that glorifies as heroic character what is here more bluntly seen as a battle of beasts. From this perspective there is real value in romance when considered as the ideology of a chivalry that favors and sustains values like courtesy, loyalty, service, justice, and community over the strife of each against all that the unmitigated heroic ideal threatens to become. Seen in this light, the duel in the grove helps us read the initial move from epic to romance in the poem as the assertion of a more refined and more socialized drive to order, though one that is in the case of the Theban cousins mostly unconscious, and helps explain the positive side of the Knight's ambivalence toward courtly conventions.

The negative side of that ambivalence arises from the Knight's awareness that romance can too easily lose touch with the fundamental heroic contentiousness and self-assertion that it tries to sublimate and can too easily encourage the belief that what has been covered up

12. The passage is well discussed by Kolve, *Imagery of Narrative*, 112.

has thereby ceased to exist. This self-deceiving tendency in romance sensibility makes the Knight as suspicious of it as he is attracted to it and leads to the procedures whereby he continually questions his romance by continually calling attention to the displaced epic motives that underlie its chivalrous postures. In the case of Palamon and Arcite the trouble is that even given their freedom, the most they seem to be able to do—the most, so to speak, that they are presently fit for—is to reproduce these postures in a way that masks, without genuinely mitigating, the erotic and aggressive motives and the practical and political concerns they merely displace.

Though the Knight, by situating these romance conventions in the world of his more hardheaded and colloquial sensibility, can show that this is so, he does not find in Palamon and Arcite the capability to change things or the opportunity to bring his interests into the story more directly so as to give them more concrete embodiment and play. This situation has partly to do with the *condensation* of epic thus far in the story, with absolute power and heroic efficacy located exclusively in the figure of Theseus at the beginning of the tale and repressed elsewhere. One consequence of the flight of Palamon and Arcite from the epic and political implications of their situation is that they are strikingly subservient to Theseus throughout the story in the ways they think as much as in their actions. They are constantly accusing one another of being traitor to Theseus, and Palamon even accuses himself once: "I am thilke woful Palamoun / That hath thy prisoun broken wikkedly" (1734–35). The sterility of their conventional postures derives in part from the fact that they have little opportunity for more effective action, though the Knight also shows that they internalize and embrace their helplessness, however unconsciously. This helplessness is in large part, of course, a function of the plot. The totality of Theseus's achievement at the beginning of the poem, leaving him with moral superiority, military victory, and all the women, has ultimately something totalitarian about it. It creates an imbalance of power that blocks political compromise and resolution as well as natural generation and continuity. Theseus is so completely the primal father that I sometimes wonder at the paucity of psychoanalytic commentary on the tale, though in the Knight's world the tendency of competitive, heroic *ellen* to absorb all the available *lof* to itself, leaving those unable to compete unmanned if not precisely emasculated, seems more apt.

Theseus really is something like Beowulf, at least at the beginning of the tale.[13]

At any rate, given the circumstances, there will have to be a redistribution of power. The hovering threat of Thebes will have to be recognized so that it can be dealt with, and sexuality and generation will have to find more direct and available channels of expression if the forces of eros and society—these are, after all, the classic themes of romance, love, and war—are to achieve adequate representation in the world of the tale. Since power over these forces is presently, if unrealistically, locked up in Theseus, and since no one else in the tale seems capable of gaining access to them, the only way to socialize his arbitrary power will be for him to give some of it up.

THESEUS: IMPERSONATION AS REVISION

The Knight's account of Theseus's hunting suggests that the duke also feels the prick of the season in his way, that he too is subject to its forces:

> This mene I now by myghty Theseus,
> That for to hunten is so desirus,
> And namely at the grete herte in May,
> That in his bed ther daweth hym no day
> That he nys clad, and redy for to ryde
> With hunte and horn and houndes hym bisyde.
>
> (1673–78)

In Theseus's case it is the aggressive or epic inflection of seasonal energy that is particularly stressed, in keeping with his heroic nature. Theseus's choice of prey gives the Knight the opportunity for verbal play with the notion of the "grete herte" (the latter word is repeated four times in fifteen lines),[14] bringing out that for Theseus, to serve Diana after Mars (1682) is to sublimate his fundamental urge for mastery from war to hunting. We know, though Theseus does not, that Palamon and Arcite are in the grove "In which ther was an hert, as men hym tolde" (1689), and they are great hearts, men dangerous as wild beasts (as we are again reminded when they are described as fighting

13. See Berger and Leicester, "Social Structure as Doom."
14. The pun is noted by Van, "Second Meanings," 71–72.

260 The Institution of the Subject

"breme, as it were bores two" at 1699) and proper objects for Theseus's "vertu." It is thus no surprise that he throws himself between
them and demands to know what they are doing.

As in the case of Arcite's journey to the grove, the description of the
scene connects it with an earlier one, this time with the opening scene
of the poem.[15] Theseus is riding, as before, "With his Ypolita, the faire
queene, / And Emelye, clothed al in grene" (1685–86). When he comes
upon the dueling princes, "Under the sonne he looketh, and anon / He
was war of Arcite and Palamon" (1697–98), which echoes "He was
war, as he caste his eye aside" (896) in the earlier episode. Once again
he acts immediately and decisively, and once again his assertion of
control is harsh and direct, a judgment delivered without pause or
second thought:

> This is a short conclusioun.
> Youre owene mouth, by youre confessioun,
> Hath dampned yow, and I wol it recorde;
> It nedeth noght to pyne yow with the corde.
> Ye shal be deed, by myghty Mars the rede!
>
> (1743–47)

The point of these parallels emerges in what follows the closest of
them, the reaction of the weeping women who throw themselves at
Theseus's feet, crying "Have mercy, Lord, upon us wommen alle!"
(1757), a direct echo of "Have on us wrecched wommen som mercy"
(950), spoken by the Argive widow from a similar position. The Knight
asserts his control of the story here and calls attention to this scene as
a replay of the first to focus attention on what changes and on the light
the changes cast retrospectively on the opening of the poem. It is clear
that Theseus shows himself in a new light as he masters his ire, exercises his empathy with the lovers ("I woot it by myself ful yore agon, /
For in my tyme a servant was I oon" [1813–14]), and applies new
methods to a new situation. It is also clear that there is more empathy
(from Theseus) and sympathy (from the women) available in this scene
than previously. People are less hieratically separated from one another, better able to appreciate the feelings and problems of others,
and more inclined to compromise and make exceptions. A fairly common observation of readers is that Theseus changes and even im-

15. The echoes are noted by Cooper, *Structure of the Canterbury Tales,* 95.

proves.[16] The effect of the change is that Theseus begins to give expression to precisely those concerns whose exclusion up to now has stalled the tale, and *this brings him closer to the Knight.*

The clearest evidence of this phenomenon is Theseus's speech on love:

> The god of love, a benedicite!
> How myghty and how greet a lord is he!
> Ayeyns his myght ther gayneth none obstacles.
> He may be cleped a god for his myracles,
> For he kan maken, at his owene gyse,
> Of everich herte as that hym list divyse.
> Lo heere this Arcite and this Palamoun,
> That quitly weren out of my prisoun,
> And myghte han lyved in Thebes roially,
> And witen I am hir mortal enemy,
> And that hir deth lith in my myght also,
> And yet hath love, maugree hir eyen two,
> Broght hem hyder bothe for to dye.
> Now looketh, is nat that an heigh folye?
> Who may been a fool but if he love?
> Bihoold, for Goddes sake that sit above,
> Se how they blede! Be they noght wel arrayed?
> Thus hath hir lord, the god of love, ypayed
> Hir wages and hir fees for hir servyse!
> And yet they wenen for to been ful wyse
> That serven love, for aught that may bifalle.
> But this is yet the beste game of alle,
> That she for whom they han this jolitee
> Kan hem therfore as muche thank as me.
> She woot namoore of al this hoote fare,
> By God, than woot a cokkow or an hare!
>   (1785–1810)

This speech echoes and develops the Knight's own speech beginning "O Cupide, out of alle charitee!" (1623ff), reproducing the tone of its ironic praise of love and giving voice for the first time in the world of the characters to an assessment of Palamon and Arcite's behavior that reflects the Knight's own feelings about it. Theseus's criticism of courtly loving singles out the themes of love and lordship and the lack

16. See, for example, Huppé, *Reading of the Canterbury Tales*, 66–67; Haller, "Epic Tradition," 82; Fifield, "The *Knight's Tale*," 101–2; Van, "Theseus and the 'Right Way,' " passim.

of social payoff, of a link between service and reward, which the Knight earlier commented on. Conventional loving of Palamon and Arcite's sort creates a situation in which an outside observer, judging from a feudal perspective, has to say that love is a bad lord.

What *happens* in the poem after the women plead for mercy is that Theseus becomes a spokesman for the Knight and brings his concerns into the story directly and explicitly almost for the first time.[17] He is used to reflect more accurately the tacit elements of the world of the tale that the Knight has been trying to bring out. To begin with, though Theseus does experience a feeling of "pitee" based on his ability to understand Palamon and Arcite, it is not the only reason he does what he does. When the Knight says that Theseus "spak thise same wordes *al on highte*" (1784, emphasis added), he reflects an awareness of the difference between thoughts spoken "softe" to oneself and a public speech, and the speech itself is among other things a political action. If Palamon and Arcite seem inattentive to the question of Thebes (and we may reflect that it has been lucky for Theseus that this is so), the duke himself is not. His characterization of the situation shows his awareness of political possibilities that have not been realized in the tale thus far but whose continuing threat he recognizes *in the act of forestalling it:*

> Lo heere this Arcite and this Palamoun,
> That quitly weren out of my prisoun,
> And myghte han lived in Thebes roially,
> And witen I am hir mortal enemy,
> And that hir deth lith in my myghte also.
>   (1791–95)

> And ye shul bothe anon unto me swere
> That nevere mo ye shal my contree dere,
> Ne make werre upon me nyght ne day,
> But been my freendes in all that ye may.
>   (1821–24)

---

17. There is a parallel here with the partial taking over of the voices of Palamon and Arcite at the end of Part I. We can actually watch the process taking place in the lines that lead up to the "god of love" speech. As Theseus's ire is mastered by his reason, his reflections are presented first in indirect discourse, "As thus: he thoghte wel that every man / Wol helpe hymself in love, if that he kan" (1767–68), where certain details sound like things the Knight agrees with and amplifies or explains to us: "And eek his herte hadde compassioun / Of wommen, *for they wepen evere in oon*" (1770–71, emphasis

No doubt Theseus sympathizes with the Thebans' love-stricken condition, but he also sees that that condition and his possession of Emelye give him a tactical advantage in a game the princes do not seem to know they are playing. Theseus is the first character in the tale to recognize and attempt to deal cogently with the lurking political dangers that have hitherto been displaced and that are all the more dangerous for that reason. He makes a project of a more viable relation between love and lordship, a state marriage that will cement a treaty, and in doing so reveals his implicit awareness of the inadequacy of his earlier handling of the Theban problem. The danger of conquest is that it breeds a hidden enemy, the smiler with the knife. The terrible father and the conquering epic hero are more powerful in myth than in life, where they may too easily become targets by the very splendor of their isolation. Theseus's actions here do not spring solely from an unsituated rage for order or a general respect for institutional forms. They are firmly motivated as well by a set of practical concerns that reflect the pressures of the political world.

This is not to say, however, that Theseus becomes any less forceful or dominating in his general style—only that he is being masterful about different things. The language in which he proposes the tournament is remarkable for its assertive tone:

> And forthy I yow putte in this degree,
> That ech of yow shal have his destynee
> As hym is shape, and herkneth in what wyse;
> Lo heere youre ende of that I shal devyse.
> My wyl is this, for plat conclusion.
>
> (1841–45)

> Thanne shal I yeve Emelya to wyve
> To whom that Fortune yeveth so fair a grace.
> The lystes shal I maken in this place.
>
> (1860–62)

This assertiveness too is a reflection of the Knight's sensibility and an index of his active impersonation. In taking explicit responsibility for evoking and channeling destiny and controlling the effects of For-

---

added). As the description proceeds, it moves into directly quoted interior monologue, "And softe unto hymself he seyde, 'Fy' " (1773), and finally into the public discourse that reflects the Knight's own earlier comment.

tune—for giving these extrahuman forces human meaning—Theseus becomes the spokesman for the Knight's demystifying assertion of human agency and the representative of a more realistic and active attitude toward the exercise of human power. Theseus becomes for the Knight a way of situating within the tale his own skeptical attitude toward the passivity that notions like Fortune and destiny can too easily encourage.

Beyond even this purpose, the Knight adopts the role of Theseus as a technique for instituting wholesale revisions in the world of the tale itself. As Theseus takes the situation in hand within the story, so does the Knight outside it. They both take responsibility for the making of meaning, and in fact Theseus is the instrument the Knight uses to do so: the duke's building of the lists and the temples of the gods in Part III is the occasion for the Knight's insertion in the tale of everything it has hitherto excluded or repressed. The opening of the third part of the tale, in keeping with the Knight's emerging emphasis on human agency, concentrates on the hero's activity "the dispence / Of Theseus, that gooth so bisily / To maken up the lystes roially" (1882–84). Theseus designed the lists, paid the workmen (1900), and caused the temples in the walls to be made (1903–5). All this "Hath Theseus doon wroght in noble wyse" (1913). The Knight's concern is to make clear the human origin of the lists and temples, to keep them from looking natural or inevitable as if they had fallen from the sky. This concern, rather than the philistinism that has sometimes been imputed to him, informs the Knight's interest in "dispense." His colloquial, even homely, emphasis on the "mete and wages" (1900) given the workmen and on the fact that the temple of Mars "coste largely of gold a fother" (1908, cf. 2087–92) is demystifying, aimed at keeping the realm of concrete human needs and skills—geometry, carving, "ars-metrike"—before us.

This perspective is enforced and sustained by the Knight's own manner of telling, both in the description of the temples and in Part III as a whole. One of the most notable stylistic features of this section of the poem is its relative stasis and lack of plot, its subordination of narrative and dialogue to description and set speeches. It patently takes time out from the story, interrupting it to concentrate on decorative detail. The effect of this technique is to draw attention away from the story as a succession of events and place it more on scenic factors, on the panorama of the world of the tale rather than its motion. At the same time, however, the technique as the Knight deploys it also calls attention to his own activity as describer since he is conspicuously the one taking so much time out: "But yet hadde I foryeten to devyse / The noble kervyng . . ." (1914–15). The main movement of the tale in Part III, then, is in the motion of the narrator's voice and consciousness through the description: Part III is more clearly an event of speaking than a succession of external actions. As in the *Wife of Bath's Prologue*, Part III of the *Knight's Tale* shifts attention from *histoire* to *récit*, from the plot of the story to the plot of the storytelling (see above, chapter 3). In this telling the Knight displays his own *choices* as to what to describe and how to describe it: "Why sholde I noght as wel eek telle yow al / The portreiture that was upon the wal?" (1967–68). We are thus directed to the *interaction* of the voice with the scene described, to the point where individual voicing in the present of describing comes to override the visual "objectivity," the pastness, and the traditional iconographic meanings of the "matere."[18] The Knight's analysis of the human use of institutions such as temples and gods is a product of his own active use of those same institutions. Whatever Theseus may have meant by the lists is subordinated to what the Knight makes them mean.

As we shall see, what the Knight makes the lists mean is an image of the forces he sees at work behind and beneath the surface of the tale, which have hitherto been occluded, and of his own ambivalence toward those forces. He focuses from the beginning on the symbolic possibilities of the lists. He stresses "That swich a noble theatre as it was / I dar wel seyen in this world ther nas" (1885–86) and that "swich a place / Was noon in erthe, as in so litel space" (1895–96). "Theatre" and "so litel space" direct us to the metonymic or microcosmic functions of the scene, whereas the hyperbolic uniqueness of the lists suggests their potentially exemplary qualities. It is as if the whole society of the poem, represented, significantly, by its technologists or "crafty men," comes together under Theseus's direction to build a symbolic image of its own most central concerns.[19] The Knight's perspective stresses symbolization itself as a specifically human constructive activity undertaken in response to specific human needs and fears.

18. For accounts of the iconographic traditions of the temples, see McCall, *Chaucer Among the Gods*, 1–17 (chap. 1) and 68–73 (discussion of the *Knight's Tale*); Twycross, *Medieval Anadyomene*; Kolve, *Imagery of Narrative*, 113–122.

19. Compare Page DuBois's clear and elegant summary of the functions of *ekphrasis* in epic, *History, Rhetorical Description and the Epic*, 1–8.

It seems to me no accident that the temples of the gods, as the Knight presents them, are largely images of the *enemies* of culture, images made by culture itself in an effort to contain and control those enemies. That is, the temples are not so much objective representations of divine or natural forces as they are institutions—structures made, consciously or nonconsciously, by human art, human desire, and human terror.

Regarding Knighthood

A Practical Critique of the "Masculine" Gaze

What has perhaps prevented this description from being properly appreciated is the fact that the allegory does not move and so may not seem to be real allegory. The heart of allegory is that the characters engage in action, for only by what they do can we get the story. . . . Here the figures merely stand, and the reader has to supply the action in his imagination. He must, from his own experience, bring Foolhardyness to life—and the poem gains great vividness when he does—send Messagerye on her errands, and imagine the effect of "Beaute withouten any atyr." If he does so he gets, not a novel, but a realistic Anatomy of Sexual Attraction, which is anything but cold and dull.

Dorothy Bethurum, "The Center of the *Parlement of Foules*"

Il faut se dire, bêtement, que si on ne peut assimiler—entre eux d'abord—les aphorismes sur la femme et le reste, c'est aussi que Nietzsche n'y voyait pas très clair ni d'un seul clin d'oeil, en un instant, et que tel aveuglement régulier, rythmé, avec lequel on n'en finira jamais, a lieu dans le texte. Nietzsche y est un peu perdu. Il y a de la perte, cela peut s'affirmer, dès qu'il y a hymen. Dans la toile du texte, Nietzsche est un peu perdu, comme une araignée inégale à ce que s'est produit à travers elle, je dis bien comme une araignée ou comme plusieurs araignées, celle de Nietzsche, celle de Mallarmé, celles de Freud et d'Abraham. Il était, il redoutait telle femme châtrée. Il était, il redoutait telle femme castratrice. Il était, il aimait telle femme affirmatrice. Tout cela à la fois, simultanément ou successivement, selon les lieux de son corps et les positions de son histoire. Il avait affaire en lui, à tant de femmes.

Jacques Derrida, *Spurs: Nietzsche's Styles*

DESIRE UNMASKED: THE TEMPLE OF VENUS

The opening of the description of the temple of Venus immediately raises an issue that will become central to the meaning and function of the three temples in the poem, the issue of the relation of visualization to description, of seeing to language: "First in the temple of Venus maystow se / Wroght on the wal, ful pitous to biholde, / The broken slepes" (I, 1918–20).[1] The address to the audience in the present tense,

---

1. Kolve has noted some of the problems, *Imagery of Narrative*, 121–22.

as if the temple were still there and available for our actual inspection, stresses its objectivity, its independence of language and the occasion of describing. "Maystow se" thus functions as a pointer to the generalized, perennial quality of the temple and its contents, which is to say its traditional character, and the form of the description, for the most part composed of relatively unanalyzed lists of conventional figures, tends to confirm this quality. We might think of such a posture as inviting imaginative visualization, as asking us to construe *ekphrasis* as an account of how the object appears; and to a degree, especially toward the end of the description in the account of the statue of the goddess, the passage does appeal to sight. Paradoxically, however, most of the description is not visually oriented. Instead we are given interpretation presented as if it were vision, allegorical and historical-exemplary figures—Narcissus, Solomon, Hercules, "Pleasaunce and Hope, Desir, Foolhardynesse" (1925)—who tell us what the temple means rather than what it looks like. The effect is thus somewhat reminiscent of Theseus's first sight of the Argive widows or Palamon's first sight of Emelye in that it embodies the culture-laden character of what passes for perception, the way a conventional interpretation or reading of eros is already inscribed and naturalized in the visual artifact. At this level if there is anything that unifies the description as a "visual" presentation, it is what Sartrean phenomenologists, and Lacanian psychoanalysts after them, call *le regard*, the gaze or look of the Other, which refers to the co-optation of the visual field by the social construction of desire and its imposition on the subject.[2] The nonconscious cultural strategy that lies behind the ascription of this disjunctive, listlike series of juxtaposed elements to the visual field is the

2. The fullest treatment of "the look" is Sartre's in *Being and Nothingness*, 340–400. Sartre gives a clear, brief account in "Faces, Preceded by Official Portraits," 157–63. Lacan's discussion is in Seminar XI (1964), reprinted as "Of the Gaze as *Objet Petit a.*" Lacan assumes familiarity with Sartre (though since Sartre does not believe in the unconscious, Lacan is also critical) and the extensions of Sartre in Merleau-Ponty, *Phenomenology of Perception* and *The Visible and the Invisible*, and is, for this American reader at least, virtually incomprehensible without them. As in the case of castration and the phallus, the most useful accounts of the look have come out of the feminist appropriation of Lacan, particularly in the area of film theory. See Mulvey, "Visual Pleasure and Narrative Cinema," reprinted in Bill Nichols, ed., *Movies and Methods*, 2:303–315, along with the bibliography supplied by Nichols on the development of the discussion. I would like to thank Yvonne Rainer for introducing me to this whole discussion and for the skeptical eye she has kept on my attempts to come to terms with it. Her own treatment of these themes, among others, is her film *The Man Who Envied Women* (1986), which is required viewing for anyone who is trying to think about them.

exploitation of the way sight is structured so as to foster *méconnaissance*, the belief of, among others, the infant in Lacan's mirror stage, that because something *looks* like a single object it is in fact a unified whole that belongs in its apparent togetherness.[3] The image of the temple, and especially the statue of the goddess, thus purports to present in the mode of "ther maystou se," of simple thereness, the *content of desire*—or at least of male desire. At this level, I take it, the paintings on the wall of the temple represent the vicissitudes of love, and the statue represents its goal, a supposedly timeless image of woman as a beautiful object that draws desire toward it and presents itself as desire's fulfillment.

There is, however, another level at which the description may be taken, a perspective that rereads the cultural text of the temple more textually and, in particular, more contextually. This perspective is that of the narrating Knight, whose deployment of details shapes and qualifies the general presentation, in part by contextualizing the temple in terms of the previous narrative of the tale, and gives the description a critical and negative tone. Though the opening of the passage (1918–35) is superficially balanced in terms of both good and bad aspects of loving—Plesaunce and Hope as well as Bauderie and Force—it begins with a catalogue of the courtly lover's pains and never drifts far from them:

> The broken slepes, and the sikes colde,
> The sacred teeris, and the waymentynge,
> The firy strokes of the desirynge
> That loves servantz in this lyf enduren.
>
> (1920–23)

Of the flat allegorical personifications barely listed in this opening passage, only one, the last, is actually given a description and an iconography, and this makes her stand out: "Jalousye, / That wered of yelewe gooldes a gerland, / And a cokkow sittynge on hir hand" (1928–30). Jealousy's garland carries us back to the knights' first sight of Emelye in her garden (1054) and to Arcite in the grove (1507), both occasions of jealous wrangling between the cousins.[4] Palamon and

---

3. Lacan, "Mirror Stage." See the helpful discussion by Clément, *Lives and Legends of Jacques Lacan*, 84–92.

4. Cooper, *Structure of the Canterbury Tales*, 95, has noted the connection between the two scenes, though not the tie to the Temple of Venus.

Arcite are the kind of lovers whose experience we see generalized on the wall of the temple, and the presentation here reduces that style of loving to a mask for the fundamental jealousy that informs it, the contentious and competitive struggle for the object of desire conceived as a possession, not a person. This struggle, masked in this way, is, we may recall, the consistent mode of Palamon and Arcite's love, which is presented primarily as worship of, and rivalry for, a lady who remains abstract and idealized, no realer to them than to us. It is the rivalry that absorbs them. Jealousy herself functions as a kind of symbolic compression and clarification of the object of desire in the male world of the tale; she sums up "the circumstaunces / Of love, which that I rekned and rekne shal" (1932–33) as a female figure who mocks the dream of possession with the symbol of cuckoldry she holds in her hand, pointing to the male fear and distrust of female independence that underlies the idealization.

In fact, the whole of the temple of Venus is unmasked and rendered conspicuous as a mystified version of love by the Knight's handling; his textual dynamism consistently undercuts the static and ideal image the temple was built by culture to present. Prospectively the *form* of the description is, as I suggested above, relatively disjunctive, listlike, a series of juxtaposed sections. Taken as the presentation of an independent object in the world, this form reflects the way the pleasures and pains of love seem to its "servants" to be enjoyed and endured passively, as if they were external phenomena imposed on lovers piecemeal and arbitrarily from without rather than obeying the inner logic of the will that constitutes them. The temple thus embodies and conceals—in Diane Manning's word, enshrines[5]—the projection and passivity earlier exemplified in Palamon and Arcite. Within this form, however, a contextual reading constructs a rhizomatic network of connections between both the parts of the description itself and the previous action of the tale, and these connections outline the structure of jealousy and rivalry that, as the Knight sees it, is the truth of chivalric eros.

Thus, the account of the "mount of Citheroun" (1936–54) is formally distinct from what precedes it, another scene on the wall, and may seem at first reading to be a jumble of unrelated traditional elements drawn from the *Roman de la Rose* and a variety of other

5. Manning, "Temple of Venus."

classical and Christian sources. It is, however, no accident that the Knight begins this phase of the description with "al the gardyn" (1939), a place that is traditionally guarded by *Oiseuse,* the carefree *otium* held to be necessary for the enjoyment of love's *deduit,* and a place that has been presented in these terms earlier in the poem as Emelye's proper scene. This is the ideal on which Palamon and Arcite have fixed their desire, to the exclusion, as we have seen, of other political and social necessities. In the temple of Venus the effects of desire spread out from the garden into history and society just as they have done in the tale, despite—or because of—the Thebans' failure to attend to them:

> Nat was foryeten the porter, Ydelnesse,
> Ne Narcisus the faire of yore agon,
> Ne yet the folye of kyng Salomon,
> Ne yet the grete strengthe of Ercules—
> Th' enchauntementz of Medea and Circes—
> Ne of Turnus, with the hardy fiers corage,
> The riche Cresus, kaytyf in servage.
>
> (1940–46)

The pressure of the description here is unremittingly negative, stressing the various ways love unmans the masculine, the heroic, the guardians of public life, while turning women into "masculine" avengers who destroy their families and change men into beasts. Male suspicion of Venus and women as the destruction of society is close to the surface in this description, and the whole issue of love and lordship lurks in it only slightly displaced. The Knight's summary of this phase of the tableau catches what is important for him about it:

> Thus may ye seen that wysdom ne richesse,
> Beautee ne sleighte, strengthe ne hardynesse,
> Ne may with Venus holde champartie,
> For as hir list the world than may she gye.
> Lo, alle thise folk so caught were in hir las,
> Til they for wo ful ofte seyde "allas!"
> Suffiseth heere ensamples oon or two,
> And though I koude rekene a thousand mo.
>
> (1947–54)

Once again he brings out the essentially martial, masculine terms in which such an image of eros is conceived: "champartie," etymologically is a drawn battle or field of combat (cf. "love ne lordshipe,"

1625ff), where the struggle is for mastery—the strong survive, and the weak go down. Love is a matter of *winning,* and both the summary listing of the exempla (we are not encouraged by the presentation to reflect deeply on the stories behind the names) and the dismissive final couplet stress the totalizing character of this vision. The narrating Knight seems to be saying, All love stories boil down to this; I will not bore you with further instances.

The Knight's presentation thus produces a critique of the image of woman as goddess and of the self-deception inherent in the idyll (at once ideal, idol, and idle) of love as *deduit,* escape from strife:

> The statue of Venus, glorious for to se,
> Was naked, fletynge in the large see,
> And fro the navele doun al covered was
> With wawes grene, and brighte as any glas.
> A citole in hir right hand hadde she,
> And on hir heed, ful semely for to se,
> A rose gerland, fressh and wel smellynge;
> Above hir heed hir dowves flikerynge.
> Biforn hire stood hir sone Cupido;
> Upon his shuldres wynges hadde he two,
> And blynd he was, as it is often seene;
> A bowe he bar and arwes brighte and kene.
> (1955–66)

The most important image in this portrait is the garland, not because it is unusual or visually compelling but because of its contextualization in the tale: it is the one detail that connects the statue to other parts of the temple, that is, to the figure of Jealousy. This latter figure flickers just behind and beneath the surface glamor of the statue "fressh and wel smellynge." Her marigolds are the other side of Venus's roses, as the cuckoo's song is of the sound of the "citole." Jealousy is included but displaced as the essential meaning of the image of male desire to which the entire temple reduces. The slightly prurient veiling of the naked goddess from the navel down stresses how posed she is, with her doves and roses, to attract male attention and pursuit, and at the same time hints at how many other important aspects of eros and the feminine this image conceals, as Solomon, Turnus, and the others found to their cost. It is less Cupid's traditional blindness, the arbitrariness of desire as the "masculine" psyche conceives or fantasizes it, that the portrait chooses to emphasize than the "arwes bright and keene" that conclude it—a martial image and one that picks up the sense conveyed elsewhere in the description of armed threat concealed behind sensuous sweetness. The Knight's portrayal of Venus reveals how selective, how self-deceiving, and ultimately how anxiously distrustful the "masculine" gaze at the female body, and by extension the desire to possess that body, can be.

DARK IMAGINING: THE TEMPLE OF MARS
AND THE LOOK AS AGGRESSION

In the description of the Temple of Venus it is a little difficult to tell where the Knight stands in relation to it. Though he seems clearly to identify the aggressive motives that are displaced by the conventional fantasy of *deduit,* it is also the case that his disenchanted reading of desire seems to spill over onto its object. The temple of Venus presents not desire as such but *woman* as the enemy, and this presentation is an index of the extent to which the disenchanted reading here remains a simple contrary or mirror of what it purports to criticize. The presentation of the temple simply reverses valences by identifying what is taken for the promise of peace as in fact the cause of strife. This position is, in its misogyny, as traditional and conventional as the more benign idealizing one, a fact that may help to explain why the temple of Venus remains the most opaque and the most literary of the three temples. The extent to which its sources and sensibility are products of the old books, relatively untransformed by the agency of the speaker, is pointed up by contrast with the other temples, especially the temple of Mars, where, without having to speculate on the boyhood of Chaucer's Knight, it is still possible to speak of the emergence of something in the tale that is closer to its narrator's experience.

The Knight's handling of the temple of Venus has at least the advantage of bringing out the predominance of aggressive motives in the pursuit of desire. The temple of Mars focuses on these motives, and on the violent masculinity that the first temple tries to repress, in a much more open way. It lends itself much more richly than the temple of Venus to a contextual reading that revises (in fact literally re-sees) earlier moments in the tale so as to bring out what was earlier concealed by the misleading glorifications of epic and romance convention or the rationalizations and self-deceptions of the characters. Theseus's temple of Mars is a sort of temple *en abîme:* it has another temple of Mars painted on the wall inside it.[6] This second temple is presented as if it were somehow also Theseus's temple: a careful reading establishes that when the northern light shines through the door (1987), the description must shift from the painting on the wall to the "real" building, but the uninterrupted flow of the voice obscures the change. In part this apparent confusion allows the Knight to imagine the temple in its proper and appropriate *symbolic* landscape as a transformation of previous symbolic places in the tale. The first such scene in the temple is a vision of the garden and the prison reinterpreted as the desolation of nature:

> First on the wal was peynted a forest,
> In which ther dwelleth neither man ne best,
> With knotty, knarry, bareyne trees olde,
> Of stubbes sharpe and hidouse to biholde,
> In which ther ran a rumbel in a swough,
> As though a storm sholde bresten every bough.
> And dounward from an hille, under a bente,
> Ther stood the temple of Mars armypotente,
> Wroght al of burned steel, of which the entree
> Was long and streit, and gastly for to see.
> And therout came a rage and swich a veze
> That it made al the gate for to rese.
> The northren lyght in at the dores shoon,
> For wyndowe on the wal ne was ther noon,
> Thurgh which men myghten any light discerne.
> The dore was al of adamant eterne,
> Yclenched overthwart and endelong
> With iren tough; and for to make it strong,
> Every pyler, the temple to sustene,
> Was tonne-greet, of iren brighte and shene.
>
> (1975–94)

This blasted forest is the third picture of a natural landscape in the poem. It is preceded by and linked with the garden and the grove (on which the temple stands) in a progression that moves from generation to destruction and from feminine to masculine. The original garden, as we have seen, is a version of the garden of *deduit.* It is a fantasy of order and control that attempts, like its original in the *Roman de la*

6. See Skeat, *Oxford Chaucer,* 5:78–79.

Rose, to sublimate sexual and aggressive energies into the forms of courtship and "courtoisie," the idealization of woman and the exclusion of male power. The description of the grove in Part II already qualifies this image by letting some of the wildness and aggression suppressed in the garden back into nature, largely through its images of animal ferocity and the hunt, and by supplying a scene for more aggressive male competition. The forest in the temple shows generative nature overcome by the "armypotente" violence of Mars and reduced to a wasteland hostile to life "in which ther dwelleth neither man ne best." This is the proper setting for the temple of Mars, which, as William Frost noticed, is like a dungeon.[7] It is in fact specifically reminiscent of Palamon and Arcite's prison "evene joynant to the gardyn wal" (1060) in Part I. Palamon and Arcite, as servants of Venus, believe that the garden controls the prison and that their fate beams in on them from the goddess beyond their bars. The temple of Mars revises this image and registers more accurately the direction of power: the wind of violence that devastates the wood comes from inside the gate of the temple, which is itself shaken by the force it strives to contain. That wind might be taken as a gloss on Palamon's original gaze, forcing its way "thurgh a wyndow, thikke of many a barre / Of iren greet and square as any sparre" to Emelye. The potential for conflict implicit in that gaze has by now broken its prison and taken over the tale. Theseus must strive to recontain it in the very lists within which the temple of Mars now stands.

The Knight's second recapitulation of an earlier scene, Theseus's conquest of Thebes, with the ruined town and "taas" of corpses, is similarly placed in a context that declares the character of battle more openly:

> The careyne in the busk, with throte ycorve;
> A thousand slayn, and nat of qualm ystorve;
> The tiraunt, with the pray by force yraft;
> The toun destroyed, ther was no thyng laft.
>
> (2013–16)

These lines specifically recall the opening of the tale, but they are also part of the larger scene of destruction on the temple wall and therefore

---

7. Frost, "Interpretation of Chaucer's *Knight's Tale*," 111.

function retrospectively to fill in the hints supplied by the "pilours" earlier, giving us the conquest of Thebes as the Knight knows it really was. The temple of Mars, he implies, is what the battlefield looks like, at Thebes and always: "Ther is no newe gyse that it nas old" (2125), as he later remarks. Further, he provides here the clearest direct characterization in the poem of what it is like to be Theseus and of the implications and consequences of heroic preeminence: "Saugh I Conquest, sittynge in greet honour, / With the sharpe swerd over his heed / Hangynge by a soutil twynes threed" (2028–30). The whole of the temple of Mars testifies to the Knight's awareness of the human potential for terrible, mad violence—"woodnesse," criminal insanity, "laughynge in his rage"—and to his determination to reveal it behind the chivalric veils it usually wears. Aggression is for him something deeply rooted in the psyche and the race—perhaps more deeply than eros itself since the temple of Venus suggests that love is only an excuse for strife or leads inevitably to it. The stability of nature and society hangs, like the life of Conquest, by a wire.

We have yet to deal, however, with the strangest feature of the telling, the speaker's shift from "ther maystow se," used in the temple of Venus to "ther saugh I," reiterated five times in thirty-three lines in the description of the temple of Mars. In the first place, this phrase associates the appearance of the temple and its details with the speaker's personal experience, as if he had seen them and were now describing from memory. Though this association may perhaps be appropriate to the more concrete, contextualized style of the account, it sorts oddly with the fiction of ancient Athens and the patently literary character of the description. Even odder is the fact that the distancing effect ordinarily imparted by the past tense is continually countered by the vividness of visualization that dominates the description. The painted scene on the walls of the temple comes alive as a landscape full not only of motion but also of sound, the shaking of doors and the rumbling of winds. As opposed to the static catalogues of allegorical names in the temple of Venus, the figures on the wall of the temple of Mars are seen, and seen in color: "The crueel Ire, reed as any gleede; / The pykepurs, and eke the pale Drede" (1997–98). They take on particular and individual life—or death: "The sleere of hymself yet saugh I ther— / His herte-blood hath bathed al his heer / The nayl ydryven in the shode anyght" (2005–7); or most vivid of all, "Yet saugh I brent the shippes hoppesteres" (2017), where the precision and originality of the image—burning ships bobbing on the water like dancing girls—stresses the individuality of the remembering speaker over the general or exemplary character of the scene. Thus the refrain "ther saugh I," "yet saugh I," acts to remind us not only that the speaker has seen these things—"The colde deeth, with mouth gapyng upright" (2008), "Woodnesse, laughynge in his rage" (2011)—but that *he is seeing them again now as he speaks.*

Consider the couplet "Ther saugh I first the derke ymaginyng / Of Felonye, and al the compassyng" (1995–96). "Ymaginyng" here acts as a pivot between two meanings. In the first instance it means image making, or painting: Felony is one of the pictures on the wall. "Al the compassynge," however, changes the meaning of "ymaginying" to planning, something Felony does before he proceeds to carry out his designs—and something much harder to put in a picture. Such effects keep us aware that what we have before us in the Knight's language is not really a description of a scene but his own "derke ymaginyng" drawn in part, as "saugh I" suggests, from his own memory and experience. The temple of Mars seems to function for the speaker as a pretext to remember and reexperience scenes of battle in somewhat the way that the duel between Palamon and Arcite conjures up the encounter of hunter and boar, whose location in "the regne of Trace" (1638) associates it, not accidentally, with the present "grisly place" (1971). The temple is a focus for this imagining and the affect that goes with it, a place where images of violence and the energy attached to them enact themselves and leave their traces.

In keeping with this sense of an uncanny, negative *jouissance* speaking in the place of the narrating subject at these moments, the logic that connects the Thracian hunter with the temples of Venus and Mars is psychoanalytic and can be glossed in Lacanian terms. The account of aggression that Lacan gives in "Aggressivity in Psychoanalysis" traces it to the complex of drives and feelings that are differentiated in the subject in and around the mirror stage: (1) The infant experiences itself primordially as a *corps morcelé*, a mass of conflicting drives and disjointed parts not clearly differentiated, if at all, from events and objects in the outside world, the mother and her parts (such as the breast) being the central and original instance. (2) At the time of the mirror stage the child forms a project: to become as whole and single in feeling and reality as its reflection, or specular image, appears to be. Note that this specular integrity is attributed by the child to others and that in fact for the mirror stage to occur the child need only make the connection between its own body and those it sees around it—a real mirror is not necessary: " 'I'm a man' . . . at most can mean no more than 'I'm like he whom I recognize to be a man, and so recognize myself as being such.' In the last resort, [such] formulas are to be understood in reference to the truth of 'I is an other'" ("Aggressivity in Psychoanalysis," 23). (3) The very fact of positing the illusory specular unity, however, makes the subject *aware of itself as fragmented,* as alienated from its fantasy image of itself, and therefore as subjected to desire. What is crucial in the present context is that this fragmentation and self-alienation is accompanied by aggressive feelings insofar as the tension between the subject's ideal image of himself and his experience of himself (my use of the masculine subject pronoun here is deliberate, though I am not sure Lacan's is) "structures the subject as a rival with himself" ("Aggressivity in Psychoanalysis," 22). (4) This fundamental and aggression-producing split is castration, though it does not initially settle on the marks of gender as its content, and as such it structures all subsequent social relations on the model of *invidia,* which Lacan, in a move that helps to connect what is going on here to the Pardoner, takes from Augustine:

> St. Augustine foreshadowed psychoanalysis when he expressed [aggressivity] in the following exemplary image: '*Vidi ego et expertus sum zelantem parvulum: nondum loquebatur et intuebatur pallidus amaro aspectu conlactaneum suum*' (I have seen with my own eyes and known very well an infant in the grip of jealousy: he could not yet speak, and already he observed his foster-brother, pale and with an envenomed stare). Thus, with the *infans* (pre-verbal) stage of early childhood, the situation of spectacular absorption is permanently tied: the child observed, the emotional reaction (pale), and this reactivation of images of primordial frustration (with an envenomed stare) that are the psychical and somatic co-ordinates of original aggressivity.
>
> ("Aggressivity in Psychoanalysis," 20)

What Lacan adds to Augustine's bitter look is that the experience of looking itself seems literally to tear the looker to pieces, to enforce his awareness of himself as fragmented, in contrast to what he supposes is the state of his foster brother. As Lacan points out, *invidia* comes from *videre,* a fact that allows him to connect the fundamental meaning of envy with the look:

> In order to understand what *invidia* is in its function as gaze [*regard*] it must not be confused with jealousy. What the small child, or whoever, *envies* is not at all necessarily what he might want. . . . Who can say that the child who looks at his younger brother still needs to be at the breast? Everyone knows that envy is usually aroused by the possession of goods which would be of no use to the person who is envious of them, and about the true nature of which he does not have the least idea.[8]

In other words, the child envies the wholeness he misses in himself and mistakenly, specularly, ascribes to the Other. The function of the "goods" in the situation is as a fantasy object that is supposed to give the other his wholeness and might supply the subject's lack if he had it instead; jealousy is the *méconnaissance* of *invidia*. It is thus "the subject's internal conflictual tension . . . which determines the awakening of his desire for the object of the other's desire: here the primordial coming together (*concours*) is precipitated into aggressive competitiveness (*concurrence*)" ("Aggressivity in Psychoanalysis," 19). The object itself is fundamentally a function in a structure of desire rather than an actual thing, and therefore it is referred to—whatever it may happen to be in a given instance—as the *objet petit a,* where *a* stands for small-a *autre* as opposed to the generalized Other:

> Such is true envy—the envy that makes the subject pale before the image of a completeness closed upon itself before the idea that the *petit a,* the separated *a* from which he is hanging, may be for another the possession that gives satisfaction, *Befriedigung.*
>
> (Lacan, "What Is a Picture," 116)

If we assume, as Lacan does, that one of the ways culture and history enter into this process is by constituting such objects, a set of institutional constructs offered as generic fulfillments of desire, so to speak, then it becomes apparent how the progression from the temple of Venus (the culturally instituted object of desire as focus of Jealousy/ *invidia*) to the temple of Mars reverses or undoes the itinerary from *corps morcelé* to *objet petit a* that Lacan posits as the development of

---

8. Lacan, "What Is a Picture," 116. See Mitchell's discussion of the distinction between need and desire in Mitchell and Rose, *Feminine Sexuality,* 5–6. I have given a more oedipal version of this dynamic in chapter 7, pp. 181–82.

the child.[9] Given the fragmented, paratactic quality of the juxtaposed visual images and the vivid, violent content of what is seen in the description of the temple of Mars, we might speak here of a *style morcelé*, on the model of the Lacanian *corps morcelé* or fragmented body that is said to appear in dreams and fantasies "when the movement of the analysis encounters a certain level of aggressive disintegration in the individual"—that is, a regression to an image of the self as it feels itself to be in the moment when it undertakes the project of self-integration in the mirror stage. There is, at any rate, something both fantasmic and regressive about what threatens to break out of the temple of Mars. If the temple provides a necessary corrective to more benign and mystified views of the role of force in human life, it may also be felt that there is something hyperbolic and overdone about so concentratedly black a view of universal destruction precisely because of the subjective intensity with which it is experienced and portrayed. Especially toward the end of the description this black view seems to run away with the Knight:

> Yet saugh I brent the shippes hoppesteres;
> The hunte strangled with the wilde beres;
> The sowe freten the child right in the cradel;
> The cook yscalded, for al his longe ladel.
> Noght was foryeten by the infortune of Marte.
> The cartere overryden with his carte—
> Under the wheel ful lowe he lay adoun.

> (2017–23)

As the Knight's description of the horrors of war builds to this climax, his visualization of horrors seems to become more compelling to him than the clear connection of those horrors to war, and his concern with the infortune of Mars is deflected into an account of

---

9. The role of institutional constructs in mediating this process by supplying it with particular content is suggested in a passage of Lacan's that has an eerie relevance to the arena, the lists, and the temples in the *Knight's Tale*. Since I do not believe in archetypes, I am not sure what to make of the concurrence of imagery, except perhaps as testimony to the durability of certain institutional forms of subjectivity:

> The formation of the *I* is symbolized in dreams by a fortress, or a stadium—its inner arena and enclosure, surrounded by marshes and rubbish-tips, dividing it into two opposed fields of contest where the subject flounders in quest of the lofty, remote inner castle whose form (sometimes juxtaposed in the same scenario) symbolizes the id in a quite startling way.

> ("Mirror Stage," 5)

infortune (or inFortune) generally, as the ambiguous line about the carter under the wheel hints. The temple of Mars encourages the Knight to a vision even darker than that of aggression. He loads it not merely with the effects of human violence but with everything that can go violently wrong with human life, those things for which men are responsible and those they do not control. Again we could speak of a regressive state in which the distinction between self and other, one's own body and the world, is temporarily lost. This tendency points to a temptation the Knight feels to a kind of apocalyptic despair at the violent ruin human life is exposed to, a temptation to allow his "derke ymaginying" to take over the temple and the world. The apocalyptic impulse to load all human misfortune into the here and now of the imagined scene can be seen in the examples of the deaths of Caesar, Nero, and Antony, "al be that thilke tyme they were unborn" (2033), and the despair can be felt in "Suffiseth oon ensample in stories olde; / I may nat rekene hem alle though I wolde" (2039–40). As opposed to the dismissive tone of the similar lines in the description of the temple of Venus (1953–54), this statement catches the speaker's continuing sense of the overwhelming, perennial presence of destruction and death: Any examples I can give, he seems to say, only scratch the surface; these things are everywhere and always happening.

There are, however, counterforces at work in the passage toward a cooler and more analytical view of the phenomena described, and these are in active tension with the dark imagining. The list continues: "Ther were also, of Martes divisioun, / The barbour, and the bocher, and the smyth, / That forgeth sharpe swerdes on his styth" (2024–26). Though these figures can be integrated with what precedes them, the fact that editors since Tyrwhitt have felt the need to explain both the presence of the artisans and the misfortunes that Robinson calls "scarcely of epic dignity" (in Chaucer, *Works,* 2d ed., 677), suggests that there is something peculiar going on in the passage. The craftsmen are no doubt to be explained as instances of professions appropriate to Martian temperaments "according as they shall be well or evill disposed," as Thomas Wright puts it (quoted in Skeat, *Oxford Chaucer,* 85), but this abstract astrological perspective is not one the previous account of the temple has prepared us for,[10] especially since these

10. A possible exception is "sovereyn mansioun" (1974), but it is recessive in context prospectively: the meaning "astrological house" only emerges in retrospect from the end of the portrait.

trades evoke a more positive set of sublimations of the urge to mastery
than the rest of the temple offers. We are dealing no doubt with what
Wright called "the confusion . . . of the god of war with the planet to
which his name was given, and the influence of which was supposed to
produce all the disasters here mentioned" (ibid.). The point, however,
is that this "confusion" is conspicuous. Not only are incompatible
versions of Mars present side by side, indicating that at this point in his
speaking the Knight is offering different notions in conflict with one
another, but the Knight himself notices it as well. As the first editor to
gloss the peculiarities of the description of the temple, the Knight
points out that the presence of Caesar and the others is anachronistic:
"Al be that thilke tyme they were unborn, / Yet was hir deth depeynted
ther-biforn / By manasynge of Mars, right by figure" (2033–35). Having noted the difficulty, he proceeds to do something about it. "By
figure" is ambiguous here; it may mean that the actual figures of the
Roman heroes are painted on the wall, or that their deaths are represented only in some symbolic prefiguration. If the passage begins by
seeming to prefer the first explanation ("Depeynted was the slaughtre
of Julius" [2031]), it ends by opting for the second, figural one: "So was
it shewed in that portreiture, / As is depeynted in the sterres above /
Who shal be slayn or elles deed for love" (2036–38). The Knight
corrects himself, rationalizing the description as he works through it.
The mention of "the sterres above" gives a habitation more abstract
and remote from the anthropomorphic projection of an antique god to
those threatening extrahuman forces and locates them beyond and
above what can be seen or painted.

What seems to *happen* in the latter portion of the description of the
temple of Mars is that the Knight is briefly caught up in the regressive
tendency I have outlined. His own imaginative visualization of the
scene as the locus of all human ills begins to allow the god of war to
encroach on territory that more properly belongs to Saturn. The effects
of war, aggression, and destruction are what the Knight knows best of
the features of human existence the temples embody.[11] It is precisely
his intimate knowledge of, and respect for, these effects that can tempt
him to let them run away with the poem and take over the world. As

11. As I hope I have shown, this observation owes nothing to speculation on the
Knight's fifteen "mortal batailles" or the like; it is based in specific features of the text in
this particular passage.

he becomes aware of this tendency, he checks it, in himself and in the description, and begins to discriminate more carefully between those aspects of Mars that are associated with the psyche—human aggression—and those that are allied, however obscurely, with some form of external necessity. This distinction generates the stretch between Mars as god of war and Mars as planet that the portrait of the temple encompasses.

As a result of this process, the description of the statue of Mars that ends the account of the temple is tensed between images of the god and what he symbolizes that remain not entirely compatible—not so much contradictory as simply different from one another, drawn from different universes of explanation:

> The statue of Mars upon a carte stood
> Armed, and looked grym as he were wood;
> And over his heed ther shynen two figures
> Of sterres, that been cleped in scriptures,
> That oon Puella, that oother Rubeus—
> This god of armes was arrayed thus.
> A wolf ther stood biforn hym at his feet
> With eyen rede, and of a man he eet;
> With soutil pencel was depeynted this storie
> In redoutynge of Mars and of his glorie.
>
> (2041–50)

The figure of Mars himself is scarcely described here. Though the first two lines gesture toward offering the appearance of an object in space, they derive greater resonance from their verbal reference back to earlier features of the temple, "Woodness," and the unfortunate carter. Moreover, these two references are attached to different fields of association. The first, the cart, revives the context of Mars as Fortune, external necessity, whereas the second brings back the image of the laughing killer. The rest of the portrait splits between these two perspectives. Puella and Rubeus, considered as constellations and figures of geomancy, make what is meant by Mars more abstract and distant, a matter of planetary influences and other remote forces requiring interpretation. The wolf, by contrast, is an image of the bestial ferocity of the aggressive impulse as it is manifested in the psyche and in human relations, the animal hunger to devour others that is at the root of what we might call Mars in men. These two versions of Mars come from different realms and coexist in the portrait without forming a synthesis. The account is divided between two fields that bracket the statue itself, the stars above and the wolf below, and this division might be taken as an index of the extent to which the notion of Mars as a single, visualizable individual with a personality gives way in the Knight's telling to a more abstract and allegorical idea of relatively impersonal and unvisualizable forces internal and external. The experience of subjectivity, the fragmentation of self that the Knight seems to skirt in his narration, eventuates here in the presentation of Mars as a split subject.

The final couplet of the description calls attention to the "storie" we have seen and heard as the product of human art. It puts the images back on the walls and so brings us back to Theseus's temple and a set of motives for its making—"in redoutyng of Mars and of his glorie"— that are at least ambiguously related to (and much simpler than) the Knight's own complex motives as these have shown themselves working in the body of the telling. The end of the portrait thus completes a movement of distancing and control; the overcoming of the outlaw affects the experience of describing let loose. Yet that experience has also left its mark precisely in our sense of the difference between Theseus's temple back in Athens and the old books, on the one hand, and what the Knight has made of the temple in the virtual now of describing, on the other. If, like those old artisans and scribes, he has built something to contain and control Mars, his representation seems more alert to the complexity and danger of what is depicted and to the extent to which the things called Mars may be summoned but not contained by making images of them. The Knight's presentation of the temple of Mars seems to call attention to the continuing mystery of what Spenser, who learned a great deal from these temples, would later call "powers . . . more than we men can fayne" (*Epithalamion*, 413–14)[12] and to the way human classifications of the things that drive and destroy human life fail to explain them completely. As we shall see further, the Knight seems to ascribe much of this inadequacy to his pagan sources—Theseus's epic, classical culture—and this ascription suggests that in the act of making the traditional materials of the

___

12. The Spenserian triple pun *fain/feign/fane,* to desire, make up, and enshrine, active here and elsewhere in his poetry, is a nice gloss on Chaucer's temples as well.

temple answer to and express his own contemporary experience, he has also become more aware of the limitations of the tradition, of the irreducible difference between Theseus's temple as an actual artifact situated at a particular historical moment and the symbolic meaning his own imagination has been using it to develop. Perhaps this awareness explains why the issues of anachronism and the pastness of the past become more active in the tale from this point on.

There is one final detail of the description of the statue that remains to be considered. The names Puella and Rubeus, "the girl" and "the (male) ruddy one", have the odd effect of placing both Venus and Mars as gendered figures, feminine and masculine, *over* the statue of Mars in a dominant position. I do not think this effect is an error whereby "Chaucer (or someone else) seems to have confused . . . Puer with Puella" (Skeat, *Oxford Chaucer*, 83), that is, to have confused a geomantic figure associated with Mars with one associated with Venus, because this line picks up and reinforces the equally anomalous "Who shal be slayn or elles deed for love" (2038) that occurs shortly before. In the context of the description of all three temples such details seem to me to point to yet another limitation of the temple of Mars. The temple of Venus, as we saw, represents a cultural *méconnaissance* of the sources of aggression as woman, a blaming of the object for the desire directed at it. As such, it proposes a misleading image of feminine dominance that the temple of Mars corrects by evoking an image of aggressive violence that is as resolutely male as the other was female—so much so, in fact, as to exclude real sexual relations (and the trouble gender is) entirely. There are no women at all in the temple of Mars—except Puella.[13] Her presence, along with that of Rubeus, is indicated by a verb, *shynen,* whose present tense is at odds with the past tenses of the rest of the description of the statue, and this discrepancy suggests an impulse in the speaker to exempt this pair from the closure, the pushing back into the past, that otherwise dominates the telling. As the temple of Diana will show, the situation of women and the fact of gender difference are not eliminated by the masculine dominance asserted in the temple of Mars, and the two shining figures

13. Mars's involvement with Venus, leading to his entrapment by Vulcan, mentioned by Statius in his account of the temple of Mars (*Thebaid* 7.61–63), is suppressed here and only reappears in Arcite's prayer at 2383–90.

above the god's statue keep that problematic difference in place and in play even here.

VENUS REVISED: THE TEMPLE OF DIANA
AND THE KNIGHT'S BISEXUALITY

From the beginning of the description of the temple of Diana the Knight shows a certain inclination to haste, even impatience: "Now to the temple of Dyane the chaste, / As shortly as I kan, I wol me haste, / To telle yow al the descripsioun" (2051–53). This inclination may be due in part to a sense of his audience, of whom he is otherwise solicitous in such things as supplying glosses for potentially confusing classical names (2062–64), and the description is the shortest of the three. But if so, it seems to me important to note this greater awareness of the audience and its feelings for what it says about the movement and development of the speaker's consciousness through the description of the temples as a whole. Because the account of the temple of Mars is dominated by intense visual imagining, it projects a speaker who is, until near the end, caught up in the immediacy of his own describing and therefore relatively unaware of his listeners. The reemergence of audience awareness in the portraying of the temple of Diana is thus an index of a more self-conscious and critical attitude toward the description itself and of a speaker who is less self-involved and more concerned for others. The movement from the temple of Mars to that of Diana recapitulates the opening of the poem (see above, pp. 224–26) in its enactment of an emergent concern with the *use* of what is narrated, and this more active assertion of the speaker's control over the significance of what he tells is confirmed by other features of the temple of Diana as well.[14] The Knight builds this temple and designs its goddess with an eye to not only the traditional image of Diana but also the other two temples in Theseus's arena, especially that of Venus, of which this temple is a critical revision. He makes this goddess something new, particularly with regard to the image of the feminine in the tale.

14. No such place occurs in any of the sources of the tale, and certain of the figures in it, of whom the most interesting is Callisto, have been transferred from Boccaccio's temple of Venus. Clearly Chaucer had his own, critical, ideas about the proper placing and significance of what he found—or did not find—in his sources, and, as I argue in the text, so does the Knight.

Unlike in the other two temples, there is no landscape in the temple of Diana specific to the goddess. This absence is appropriate since the traditional idea of Diana with which the description begins is of a woman who has opted out of the socialized spaces of garden and fortress to pursue her own *daungerous* independence as virgin and huntress. The exemplary figures painted on the walls all move within the ambiance of this fairly narrowly conceived conventional figure, "Dyane the chaste" (2051), and her world "Of huntyng and of shame-fast chastitee" (2055). I take it that the image of Diana as virgin hunt-ress is as much a culturally enforced masculine fantasy as is that of Ve-nus earlier. Diana's power is fuelled by male guilt and fear: guilt at what the masculine world does to women, and fear of how they may feel about it. The three main figures on the wall, Callisto, Daphne, and Acteon, outline the structure of this set of feelings. Callisto is the most complexly beset by conflicting demands on her sexuality. First victim-ized by the male—she is raped by Jove—she attempts to hide her ensuing pregnancy from Diana so as to remain with the virgin band. When her condition is discovered, the goddess casts her out to the vengeance of Juno, who transforms her into a bear, to be hunted by her own son. Just as he is unwittingly about to kill her, the two are stellified by Jove.[15] Daphne might be taken as a response to Callisto's victimization or perhaps better as a masculine projection of how women may feel about male sexuality if Callisto is an instance of its consequences. She is the maiden without defenses fleeing the aggres-sively pursuing male, and her transformation renders her flight perma-nent. Her escape from unwelcome male desire is metamorphosis, the forced renunciation of her humanity—she is "yturned til a tree" (2062), a fate more welcome to her than submission.[16] Acteon's story is a reflex of Daphne's and embodies male suspicions of how women might well want to reciprocate, if they could, for being made into prey. The goddess is a woman who takes on the skills, weapons, and inde-pendence of the male and turns him, like Acteon, into the hunted "For vengeaunce that he saugh Diane al naked" (2066). Of course this

15. Ovid tells the story of Callisto in *Met.* 2.409–530. The tales of Daphne and Acteon are at 1.453–567 and 3.138–252 respectively.
16. Daphne is a proto-Diana figure even before Apollo chances on her. Hating the wedding torch as if it were a thing of evil, she asks her father Peneus to let her roam the woods always: " 'da mihi perpetua, genitor carissime,' dixit / 'virginitate frui!' " (*Met.* 2.486–87).

reactive, vengeful rejection of the male look, like Daphne's flight, entails choosing to give up sexuality, maintaining purity and independence at the cost of social existence and the generative possibilities of feminine nature and leaving the men to tear each other apart for nothing, like Actaeon's or Arcite's dogs (1177–78). But the Knight's presentation stresses rather the more active disadvantages for women of an image of chastity that is constructed by male fears and fantasies of female refusal. His portrayal of Callisto, in particular, leaves the actions of Jove and Juno in the background and concentrates on the anger of Diana as the principal cause of Callisto's fate, stressing how the goddess participates in the victimization of an aspect of her own "feminine" nature:

> Ther saugh I how woful Calistopee,
> Whan that Diane agreved was with here,
> Was turned from a womman til a bere,
> And after was she maad the loode-sterre.
> Thus was it peynted; I kan sey yow no ferre.
> Hir sone is eek a sterre, as men may see.
>
> (2056–61)

The question of the Knight's attitude toward these myths is raised, though not settled, by his treatment of them. He does not simply list the names without comment as he does in the temple of Venus; he *fusses* over these stories, giving us a slightly teasing selection of details as he visualizes the fate of Actaeon. Yet the ultimate effect of the presentation is one of disengagement. Though the phrase "ther saugh I" is more frequent in this description than in the temple of Mars, it has a different effect. The assertion of personal experience seems checked by the distancing effect of the past tense, coupled as it is with a series of comments to the audience that makes the Knight less the imaginer of these stories than a commentator on their depiction by the temple artists. "Thus was it peynted; I kan sey yow no ferre" is slightly critical and impatient, as if to say, Don't ask me what it means—that's how they did it. Stellification seems less a technique for identifying the cosmic forces behind human situations, as the stars were in the temple of Mars, and more a peculiar pagan notion. The Knight's gloss on Daphne's name, "I mene nat the goddesse Diane, / But Penneus dogh-ter, which that highte Dane" (2063–64), similarly recognizes the re-cherché, overliterary quality of these antique stories for a modern audience that may not share either his knowledge or his interest. This is the old books' version of chastity, and the Knight is critical of it as both bookish and outmoded. The effect is summed up in "Ther saugh I many another wonder storie,/The which me list nat drawen to memorie" (2073–74). The Knight sees some interest in these old tales but not enough to make them worth lingering over. "Dyane the chaste," though she perhaps makes him a little uneasy, does not really engage his imagination.

The reason, I think, is that this version of female independence is not only a reactive and masculine image, too completely a response in kind to the temple of Venus (Diana is, for one thing, too powerful, in much the way Venus is, to be an accurate representation of the real condition of women), but also too benign and above all too partial as a representation of what the Knight knows about woman's fate. As Lori Nelson points out, the traditional Diana represents "an impulse to retreat from the potentially painful world of social relations to the less complicated realm of nature and hunting"; as such, she awakens the Knight's "distaste for any flight from experience, masculine or feminine."[17] This aversion leads him to move fairly quickly and perfunctorily through the world of chastity narrowly defined, indicating its archaic and limited character as he goes, in order to concentrate on a more realistic and problematic image of the feminine situation in the statue of Diana:

> This goddesse on an hert ful hye seet,
> With smale houndes al about hir feet,
> And undernethe hir feet she hadde a moone—
> Wexynge it was and sholde wanye soone.
> In gaude grene hir statue clothed was,
> With bowe in honde, and arwes in a cas.
> Hir eyen caste she ful lowe adoun
> Ther Pluto hath his derke regioun.
> A womman travaillynge was hire biforn;
> But for hir child so longe was unborn,
> Ful pitously Lucyna gan she calle
> And seyde, "Help, for thou mayst best of alle!"
> Wel koude he peynten lifly that it wroghte;
> With many a floryn he the hewes boghte.
>
>   (2075–88)

17. Nelson, "Temples in the *Knight's Tale*."

The traditional image of Diana with her accoutrements of the chase remains in place here, but it is revised and complicated by the details that allude to her other natures and functions. This is the triune goddess of "thre formes" that Emelye will later address. Luna's waxing and waning moon, on which the statue stands, evokes the natural, cyclic rhythms of fertility and connects her with the processes of generation. With her downcast eyes fixed "Ther Pluto hath his derke regioun," the goddess regards the dark or Hecate phase of her own identity as Proserpina, the bringer of spring and new life in the natural round of seasons. Finally, the travailing worshipper calls on her as Lucina, the goddess of generation's fruition, childbirth. As the temple presents it, chastity is only a phase in the development of feminine nature, one that must give way to other phases if that nature is to be fulfilled in the continuation of the race. (I pass over for the moment the consideration that it might seek other fulfillments as well or instead.) The description here confronts the initial image of Diana with the aspects of her own sexual being as a woman that, as virgin huntress, she is trying to avoid or suppress.

This vision is not, or not merely, an instance of smug patriarchal functionalism on the Knight's part. The forces introduced here are large-scale determinants of the feminine condition, obscurely linked to the rhythms and powers of the body, the seasons, and the heavens as well as to the masculine-dominated institutional structures that appropriate them. These forces are larger than individuals and, in a certain sense, independent of individuals. They are facts about herself that a woman has to contend with in her biological and social existence, and the Knight's appreciation of these facts and the problems they engender engages his sympathy. The suppliant woman in labor is a more sharply imagined and clarified version of Callisto, suffering the *burdens* of her femininity. This image of the brute misery of the human condition is as compelling as any in the temple of Mars, and it is rendered more poignant by the fact that the suppliant's cry goes unanswered.

I do not mean to imply that the Knight is some sort of feminist or supporter of the rights of women—quite the contrary—but he does see the burden and the victimization that gender categories and myths place on women, and the evocation of that burden and victimization is a considerable part of his critique of the stock images that perpetuate the status quo. The poor, bare, forked animal that is the last we see of the temple of Diana is, ironically, a grim triumph of the Knight's demystifying enterprise of stripping away the veils of institutional and individual projection that male-dominated society uses to conceal from individuals the truth of their condition. The Knight's portrayal of the temple of Diana is a way of criticizing the masculine reductions of the temple of Venus by bringing forward everything that is concealed beneath the artificial nature of her glassy green waves—the organs of generation and the processes associated with them that desire and the illusion of possession participate in without controlling. We have come a long way from the initial image of Emelye imprisoned in her garden.

The anonymous sufferer at the end of this process also helps to explain how the temples came into being in the first place. That is, the woman crying out in her pain to an unhearing personification of her own being and situation is an image and embodiment of the desperate human *need* for gods. She is the only worshipper in the three temples, but she gives us something against which to measure them all because as suffering human being, if not as woman qua woman, she supplies what has been missing in them, an image of their creator. As the poem presents them, divinities like Venus, Mars, and Diana are generated to put something with a name and a nature that can be appealed to in the place of the mysterious forces of eros, aggression, and necessity that seem to take their own way without heed of human plans or human pain. The Knight understands this need and sympathizes with it, but it is part of his insight, embodied in the laboring woman and the other victims in the temples, that these defenses defend least when they are needed most. If the gods are thought of as the causes of what happens in human life, they distract attention from the real forces, especially those within human beings themselves, that they fail to control. His revision of the gods aims consistently at cutting through the merely local and historical, remaking them into images of what he takes to be a perennial human situation and returning what has been projected on the heavens to men and women.

But what of the fact that this victim *is* a woman?

I have been at some pains to show that the progression of the three temples as a whole, from male art to female necessity, is an enactment of the Knight's impulse to elicit and confront the psychic and institutional realities that he senses concealed behind the cultural representations of tradition and the old books. As I have also tried to demonstrate, especially in my discussion of the temple of Mars, this demystifying enterprise is a matter not just of criticizing representations external to the speaker but also of encountering the impulses, images, fantasies, and feelings that *the narration itself* produces in— and as—the describing subject as part of the act of telling. In the Knight's account of the three temples, as in the Wife of Bath's account of her life or the Prioress's account of the death of the little clerk, one of the things that emerges is a portrayal of the encounter of the subject with *unanticipated affect* attached to what is narrated, registered in this tale as the shifting relations of "ymagining" between seeing and saying. The patterning of that encounter appears to be a progression from a description conducted in the mode of practical consciousness to an outbreak of repressed material into consciousness,[18] followed by the control or containment of the outbreak in a mode much closer to discursive consciousness—or at any rate more self-conscious. Thus, to summarize, the account of the temple of Venus registers a critical attitude toward what is being described, but one that in many ways accepts unreflectively the responsibility of woman for male desire that the traditional image tacitly proposes, therefore perpetuating the male look that constitutes Venus. The description of the temple of Mars counters this projective tendency by evoking the masculine aggression that the temple of Venus displaces; but in doing so, it touches off a complex of excitations and anxieties in the speaker that seem momentarily to move beyond his control, as if, for whatever reasons, there were something deeply disturbing about so direct a confrontation with male violence. The description of the temple of Diana then returns to a more distanced and controlled mode of description as well as to the image of woman, this time in a way that restores to her her proper and private pain: it identifies what belongs to woman as defined by what she suffers, not what she "does." This revision is in line with other images of women previously in the tale, the Argive widows at its be-

18. Just to be clear: neither the Knight nor Chaucer needs a theory of the unconscious to be aware of its effects, that is, of the unanticipated affect that accompanies certain thoughts. All that is necessary is an experience like that of speaking the encounter of the boar hunter at 1638–46, a passage that comes to seem more and more central to the fundamental experiences the tale is concerned with.

ginning and the court women who plead for mercy for Palamon and Arcite in the grove, insofar as both these groups are put in the position of having to respond to what men have done in their contending and having to speak for the private and familial emotions such contention largely excludes or ignores. The nameless suppliant in the temple of Diana is a representation of this position at its most private and helpless, the point where more general, feminine forced dependencies are inscribed in the female body.

A parallel between Theseus's encounter with the women in the grove (1742–84) and the Knight's movement from the temple of Mars to that of Diana will help to clarify the latter. In both cases a male actor is disengaged from the epic perspective of violent action through sympathetic engagement with a point of view the tale specifically posits as feminine. As the court ladies' intervention, "Have mercy, Lord, upon us wommen alle!" (1757), induces a reflective attitude in Theseus, the temple of Diana, whose suffering acolyte is an embodiment of that cry, seems deeply implicated in the Knight's ability to take a distance on the temples of Venus and Mars—to have, like Theseus, second thoughts. If this parallel is accurate, it suggests how the image of woman in the temple of Diana functions as a *feminine identification* for the Knight, an image of the gendered other that helps him to channel and control the disturbing affects generated by the temple of Mars. From this point of view the whole of the description of the temples in its unfolding can be taken as an expression of the Knight's bisexuality, the interplay of his masculine and feminine identifications across the text. It should be clear by now that this move is not a question of isolating some "feminine" essence that is somehow revealing itself or magically getting expressed in the subject; rather, it is a question of what the subject *assigns* to the "feminine," *how he himself constructs gender*. What is interesting about the Knight's construction of gender is that it rejects the traditional images of woman associated with courtship, the public expression of erotic desire, and courtly or romance convention, as masculine projections in favor of an image that associates the feminine with institutional and biological victimization and with private experience. The internalized character of this image as an identification is expressed as sympathy: the Knight has little sympathy with the image of woman as Venus, and little more for "Dyane of chastitee," but he has a lot with the women behind the goddesses, as we shall see even more clearly when we come to Emelye's prayer. Though it seems improbable that these sympathies, identifications, and interactions are discursively planned, it makes as little sense to speak of them as unconscious. Rather, it is a matter of practical consciousness and practical choices, of knowing, if I may put it so, how to use a woman, knowing what she is good for.

I 2

The Unhousing of the Gods
Character, Habitus, *and Necessity in Part III*

Although the description of the temples in Part III provides a wedge for the entry of many of the Knight's central concerns into the *Knight's Tale*, the images of the gods are not wholly satisfactory for him as representations of those concerns, in part because those images are too concentrated and visual. The temples and statues, precisely because they are able to symbolize psychological and social forces compendiously, lend themselves too easily to the counterallegorical kind of visualization or imagining seen most strongly at work in the description of the temple of Mars. Even the account of the temple of Diana, with its more intellectual listing of aspects of the goddess that need to be decoded and its relative impatience with the traditional iconography of the virgin huntress, is still too compacted and scenic—indeed, too brief—to render the agency of psyche and society in human life with the particularity they exhibit in concrete conditions. These "defects" of the temples emerge most clearly in retrospect when seen in the context of the drift of Part III as a whole, which moves from the initially formidable temples of the gods to the individually realized prayers of newly differentiated and more complex characters. This move from ekphrasis to dramatization, visual to verbal, has the effect, among other things, of reducing the gods to antiquated comic appendages of the human situation by the end of Part III.[1]

The account of the assembly of the warriors of Palamon and Arcite, centered on the portraits of Lygurge and Emetrius, forms an intermediate state between the temples and the prayers. In it certain aspects of the temples, particularly that of Mars, are brought down to earth. We may note in passing the effect on the atmosphere and feel of the story that the Knight's introduction of his own experience into the tale via

---

1. The whole tale is characterized by this general movement; it is worth remembering that it ends with a long, complex speech.

the temple of Mars allows. He seems to find it much easier to put himself into the scene and imagine the preparations for the tournament as if it were to happen now:

> For if ther fille tomorwe swich a cas,
> Ye knowen wel that every lusty knyght
> That loveth paramours and hath his myght,
> Were it in Engelond or elleswhere,
> They wolde, hir thankes, wilnen to be there—
> To fighte for a lady, benedicitee!
> It were a lusty sighte for to see.
>
> (I, 2110–16)

The Knight's listing of the armor and weapons of the combatants (2119–27), his "Ther maistow seen" at 2128, and the extended *occupatio* that lingers over "The mynstralcye, the service at the feeste" and other particulars of a full and distinctively modern chivalric world while pretending to dismiss them (2197–2206) testify to the concrete and contemporary reality with which his imagination invests the scene and to the attraction it holds for him.[2] Within this context the descriptions of the two kings undoubtedly function to increase, with metonymic compactness, the richness and splendor of the world of the noble life, as Charles Muscatine saw:

Here the imagery is . . . conventional, framed in the flat to express the magnificence that befits nobility. I have noted that after all the description of these two kings they hardly figure in the narrative. The inference, however, is not that the portraits are a waste and an excrescence, "merely decorative," but that they perform a function that is not directly related to the action and is independent of the question of character. They contribute first to the poem's general texture, to the element of richness in the fabric of the noble life. More specifically, Chaucer solves the problem of describing the rival companies by describing their leaders; not Palamon and Arcite but their supporting kings. Their varicolored magnificence, like Theseus' banner, makes the whole field glitter up and down—black, white, yellow, red, green and gold. Their personal attributes—the trumpet voice of Emetrius, the great brawn of Lygurge, their looks, like lion and griffin—give both a martial quality that we are to attribute to the whole company.

(Chaucer and the French Tradition, 182)

2. Robinson, following Cook, notes that the passage is full of "medieval realism." See Chaucer, *Works,* 2d ed., 678, note to I, 2095 ff.

All true. Yet Muscatine's protostructuralist tendency to apply his perceptions too broadly, a tendency that limits his fundamental and pioneering study, leads him to neglect the bearing of the passage in context and give its more specific connections with what precedes it and its function at this particular point in the tale less weight than they deserve.

For one thing, the placing of these set pieces immediately after the temple descriptions allows the portraits of the two kings to resonate with the temples, especially that of Mars. Lygurge and Emetrius are something like the statues in the temples: they are described with the same technique of formal, static portraiture, and each is in a commanding position with fierce animals at his feet, reminiscent of Mars's wolf and perhaps Diana's hounds. The looks Muscatine mentions are something like that of Mars, "grym as he were wood" (2042). In addition, Emetrius is specifically described as "ridyng lyk the god of armes, Mars" (2159), and his sanguine humor and voice "as a trompe thonderynge" (2174) connect him to his planet and his profession. Although I am not convinced by Walter Clyde Curry's argument that Lygurge and Emetrius represent Martian and Saturnalian man, respectively, any more than I am by those scholars who have tried to find allusions to specific historical figures in the portraits, I can see what inspired both enterprises.[3] The descriptions are portentous; they convey the feeling that they allude to and contain more than they specify. The description of Emetrius in particular has a specificity that creates a "reference effect"—we want to know the why of details like his "citryn" eyes, his golden ringlets, his humor, and his freckles—that invites equally iconographic or historical explanation without settling clearly on either.

The point would seem to be that these are real men who also embody and carry with them forces allied with those presented in the temples. Lygurge and Emetrius are semiallegorical in that they are a way of moving threats and powers like those of Mars off the temple walls and into characters, giving them a specific locus in the action of the tale. These are men *like* gods insofar as they dispose of and (barely) control destructive forces that they may unleash at any time.[4] This

3. Curry, *Medieval Sciences*, 130–37. The most thorough attempt at historical allegory remains Cook, *Historical Background*.
4. I cannot, therefore, agree with Elizabeth Salter that "when we are told that 'The grete Emetrius, the kyng of Inde . . . cam rydyng lyk the god of armes, Mars' (2156–

resemblance is clearest in the workings of the pervasive animal imagery in the portraits. The two kings' "pets" function symbolically, as Muscatine also sees, to give us information about the men themselves—they are masters of the beasts they have tamed and muzzled and are akin to them. But this symbolic dimension gains added resonance as part of a larger chain of animal images stretching back at least to the grove and consistently focused on the animal ferocity that always lurks beneath chivalric display. Given this context, what stands out about these descriptions is how little the violence is concealed, how barely it is controlled, how close it is to the surface. Emetrius's griffin nature glares out plainly in his feral, glowing eyes from beneath the barbaric splendor of the wreath of gold "arm-greet" that crowns him. The effect in both portraits of a rich magnificence that only just covers the potential savagery beneath is summed up for me in the cloak Emetrius wears in lieu of "cote-armore": "With nayles yelewe and brighte as any gold, / He hadde a beres skyn, col-blak for old" (2141– 42). Emetrius takes on the power of the bear totemically (one imagines that he killed it himself), and that power, like the bear's claws, is only thinly gilded with the rich fabric of the noble life. His alaunts do not go "with mosel faste ybounde" (2151) for trivial reasons.

Emetrius is superficially more civilized, less barbaric of physique and ornament, and somewhat more individualized than his companion. Yet the continuity of his portrait with that of Lygurge is sustained by the lion look, the trumpet voice, the tame eagle, and one final detail that is perhaps more disturbing in its implications than anything else in the passage. Muscatine's observation that Lygurge and Emetrius function metonymically for the assembled chivalry, that we are to attribute their martial quality to the whole company, is brilliantly right but not

---

2159), we are clearly meant to recall only one aspect of the martial god: misery, cruelty, death are obscured by magnificence" (Knight's Tale and the Clerk's Tale, 28). Salter does not specify who "means" us to forget the temple of Mars and under what conditions. As readers we are of course free to remind ourselves by going back to the more disturbing passage (and there are some worse ones yet to come). If the reference is, as seems likely, to the speaker of the poem, the question of intention is undecidable in the passage itself since what Salter takes as a cover-up could as easily be seen as a giveaway. I have chosen the latter option on the basis of the transitional character of the passage between the temples and the prayers, though I am willing to admit that the undecidability of the passage taken by itself can also easily be seen as a function of an ambivalent attitude on the part of the speaker. To take the Knight seriously as a speaker is to see that he is *both* disturbed and stirred by the manifestations of Mars.

pursued far enough. He seems not quite to see how specifically the language of the end of Emetrius's portrait points the metonymy:

> An hundred lordes hadde he with hym there,
> Al armed, save hir heddes, in al hir gere,
> Ful richely in alle maner thynges.
> For trusteth wel that dukes, erles, kynges
> Were gadered in this noble compaignye,
> For love and for encrees of chivalrye.
> *Aboute this kyng ther ran on every part*
> *Ful many a tame leon and leopart.*
> (2179–86, emphasis added)

The displacement of the last of Emetrius's symbolic animals to a position following the description of his knights has the effect of assimilating them to one another. The knights are figuratively (and not so figuratively) the predators, as Lygurge's hundred are muzzled hounds "as grete as any steer, / To hunten at the leoun or the deer" (2149–50). By the logic of metonymy the violence concentrated in the two kings is properly to be distributed to the companies they lead. What began as a painted symbolic landscape on the wall of the temple of Mars—the landscape of violence—is now an active potential presence in the story waiting to be unmuzzled. Though Lygurge and Emetrius may not figure much in the narrative directly and by name after all this description, they do so figure in the tournament, and the force their description here carries into the poem is a large determinant of the atmosphere of that battle and its edgy aftermath. The expansion of the metonymy and the potential effects of an encounter between *two hundred* such men are what Theseus must anticipate and try to control.

As I have already suggested, the prayers of Palamon, Arcite, and Emelye, taken together, complete what might be called the undoing or deconstruction of the gods, whereby they are replaced, in a special and complex sense, by the characters. I will begin the explication of this process by examining the complementary prayers of Palamon and Arcite, which are often noted, plausibly enough, as one place in the tale that offers a relatively unequivocal means of differentiating between the two protagonists because Palamon prays to Venus for Emelye whereas his cousin asks Mars for victory. For reasons that will emerge I do not find it easy to take a straightforward stand on the question of whether the two heroes are significantly different from one another;[5] but I think it is fair to say, to begin with Palamon, that this is the most individualized view of him the poem gives us,[6] though the effect arises not so much from what he requests as from the way he requests it. There is perhaps something attractive and touching about his humility and his admission of helplessness before Venus, "I am so confus that I kan noght seye / But 'Mercy, lady bright' " (2230–31), as well as his renunciation of renown, vainglory, and "pris of armes" (2241). Yet Palamon's eye is still firmly on the main chance; he will forgo victory if he can be assured of its fruits, to "have fully possessioun / Of Emelye, and dye in thy servyse" (2242–43). Nor can we say, for all his disregard of arms and his sense that love is something that takes place in an enclave cut off from other concerns,[7] that Palamon transcends the fundamental masculine sense of love as a zero-sum competition embodied in the temple of Venus. Give me my love, he says:

> And if ye wol nat so, my lady sweete,
> Thanne preye I thee, tomorwe with a spere
> That Arcita me thurgh the herte bere.
> Thanne rekke I noght, whan I have lost my lyf,
> Though that Arcita wynne hire to his wyf.
> This is th'effect and ende of my preyere:
> Yif me my love, thow blisful lady deere.
>
> (2254–60)

Palamon's "I don't care" is a way of saying he cares so much that he would rather die than see Arcite win Emelye, and the fact that this sentiment concludes his prayer suggests how fully he remains involved in the idea of eros as a competition.[8] Possession is a key notion here, "So that I have my lady in myne armes" (2247), and what differentiates Palamon from Arcite is primarily his conception of what it means to possess the object of desire.

5. The most trenchant proponent of the view that they are *not* significantly different has been Donaldson in *Chaucer's Poetry* and again in *The Swan at the Well*. Lumiansky's full discussion, *Of Sondry Folk*, 39–49, is reasonably representative of the other side.

6. The same is perhaps not true of Arcite's prayer since his dying speech has also to be considered.

7. See the above discussion of love as *deduit* in the temple of Venus, 270–72.

8. Compare Palamon's speech to Theseus in Part II, "But sle me first, for seinte charitee! / But sle my felawe eek as wel as me; / Or sle hym first" (1721–23).

In his prayer Palamon thinks of Venus in terms that the courtly tradition usually assigns to the beloved lady. He calls the goddess "lady myn," "lady bright," "my lady sweete," and "thow blisful lady deere" and asks her for mercy and pity from his position of helpless subservience. Further, he announces his intention to continue his courtly service to Venus until death, even (or especially) after he has gained his desire, and this intention produces an odd declaration:

> As wisly as I shal for everemoore,
> Emforth my myght, thy trewe servant be,
> *And holden werre alway with chastitee.*
> That make I myn avow, so ye me helpe!
> (2234–37, emphasis added)

What can he mean? Though I do not suppose that Palamon consciously intends the slightly libertine or otherwise indecorous implications of his statement, there is a problem lurking in his language precisely in the context of "possessioun," of actual marriage to Emelye.[9] At the very least the statement brings out how little Palamon is concerned with Emelye as a person, and our view of her in the following prayer at her most human and embattled cannot but heighten this

---

9. Something of what Palamon has in mind may be indicated by a passage from the *Teseida* that is not represented in the *Knight's Tale*. At the very end of the poem, after Emelia and Palemone are married, Boccaccio reports:

> Vero, è che per le offerte, che n'andaro
> Poi la mattina a'templi, s'argomenta
> Che Vener, anzi che'l di fosse chiaro,
> Sette volte raccesa e tante spenta
> Fosse nel fonte umoroso.
>   (12.77)

It is true that because of the offerings sent to the temple in the morning, it was thought that Venus, before the day turned bright, had been seven times enkindled and as many times extinguished in the fountain of love.
>   (*Book of Theseus*, trans. McCoy, 327,
>   apparently reading "amoroso" for
>   "umoroso")

If this passage does explain Palamon's meaning here, it hardly eases the problem of decorum: does he suppose his prayer is what Venus, his "blisful lady deere," wants to hear? Does he suppose it is what Emelye wants? One can see the advantages for a male lover of general projections of "feminine" character like Venus and Diana, as components of the institution of woman in society, when it comes to forcing erotic attention on an unwilling woman since they allow him to make assumptions about her nature that need not take her preferences fully seriously. It is more comfortable to have goddesses struggle over these things than persons.

302   The Institution of the Subject

impression. This lack of concern makes it harder to maintain, as critics sometimes do, that Palamon deserves to win Emelye for reasons of poetic justice because he wants her for herself.

· It seems more accurate to say that what Palamon wants is both to possess Emelye and to sustain the image of woman as courtly goddess that he has associated with Venus from his first sight of the lady. He envisions success in his enterprise as a continuation of love service, of worship:

> Youre vertu is so greet in hevene above
> That if yow list, I shal wel have my love.
> Thy temple wol I worshipe everemo,
> And on thyn auter, where I ride or go,
> I wol doon sacrifice and fires beete.
>
> (2249–53)

Palamon emerges in this prayer as an example of the sort of psyche that built the temple of Venus and structured its own nonconscious assumptions into the idea of the goddess, the institutions of courtship and marriage, and the succeeding generations of men who internalized that institutional framework as a "natural" way of organizing and understanding their own drives. Though Palamon is not aware of it, his strategy for dealing with desire is to sublimate it into worship, which is among other things a way of safeguarding the purity of the desire in the mode of courtly suffering, and keeping the difficulties of relationship with a real woman at a safe distance. Such a Venus is an ideal no real lady could fulfill or would want to fulfill, though she may be constrained to it. The venerian construction of woman is aware of this difficulty without attending to it, and the dichotomy in the speech between goddess and possession as well as the hint of the double standard in "holden werre alwey with chastitee" may not bode well for Emelye.[10] Whether this uneasy possibility is so or not, Palamon stands

---

10. I wonder similarly about the implications of Palamon's invocation of Venus "For thilke love thow haddest to Adoon" (2224). According to Ovid (*Met.* 9.519–52), Venus loves Adonis fearfully, in the conviction (accurate, as it turns out) that if he is allowed to engage in virile pursuits she will lose him. It appears that Palamon expects Venus to be moved by his humility but also that he expects her (and women) to try to restrain him in the exercise of masculine "vertu." There is a slight tinge of *mauvaise foi* in Palamon's prayer because of the sexual and martial restlessness that stirs in it beneath the professions of humility and service. Does it matter in this poem that Adonis was a boar hunter? Might it have been in Thrace?

forth here as a genuinely venerian personality, not in the sense of one dominated by a planet, a balance of humors, or a goddess but as an example of the use of the *habitus* or way of holding oneself toward the world that is embedded in practical consciousness. "Venus" is a set of preformed attitudes that are available for the character to deploy in expressing himself and articulating what he feels and wants to say without having to reinvent the whole of sexual relations and the structuring of desire for himself. More clearly and more complexly than previously in the poem, Palamon's goddess is the image of his own condition, his desires and tensions, drawn from the cultural stock and written on the sky.

The same is true of Arcite with respect to Mars. The interest in Arcite's prayer, as in Palamon's, lies in his characterization of his god as a key to his own personality. As with the travailing woman in the temple of Diana, listening to a devotee at prayer rather than looking at an image makes it easier to ask what such a god is for, what needs and desires in the worshiper the god answers to. His own prayer reveals Arcite as a martian personality whose *habitus* produces a different but allied set of habits of response from those of Palamon to the fundamental contingencies of desire and otherness. His stance is a kind of mirror image or Blakean contrary of Palamon's, indicating that there is a common system of assumptions behind them. Arcite's basic image of desire is as an *offense,* a word he continually returns to: "I am yong and unkonnynge, as thow woost, / And, as I trowe, with love offended moost / That evere was any lyves creature" (2393–95).[11] The offense is constituted by the threat desire poses to the self-sufficiency and independence of heroic will—in Lacanian terms, to the illusory, hoped-for specular unity of the self. Arcite sees Mars as such a successful will from the beginning of the prayer—"And hast in every regne and every lond / Of armes al the brydel in thyn hond, / And hem fortunest as thee lyst devyse" (2375–77)—and he reminds the god of an experience of desire that tells much about Arcite's own sense of it:

> Thanne preye I thee to rewe upon my pyne.
> For thilke peyne, and thilke hoote fir

11. He uses it, in fact, just *before* he sees Emelye for the first time in Part I, when he inquires of the stricken Palamon, "Why cridestow? Who hath thee doon offence?" (1083).

> In which thow whilom brendest for desir,
> Whan that thow usedest the beautee
> Of faire, yonge, fresshe Venus free,
> And haddest hire in armes at thy wille—
>
> (2382–87)

Not only is desire a torment and a burning fire, a kind of attack (the image is repeated at 2503–4); its object is something to be *used,* subjected to one's will almost like a prisoner of war, as the flicker of a pun on "armes" in the last line suggests.

Arcite does not confine himself to the satisfaction of desire; he reminds the god also of its consequences:

> Although thee ones on a tyme mysfille,
> Whan Vulcanus hadde caught thee in his las,
> And foond thee liggynge by his wyf, allas!—
> For thilke sorwe that was in thyn herte,
> Have routhe as wel upon my peynes smerte.
>
> (2388–92)

The example seems an odd one, at least in the sense that one might suppose Mars would prefer not to be reminded of this experience, but Arcite urges it on the god to gain his sympathy and remind him of what it feels like to be at the mercy of desire. The assumption is that the feeling is so peremptory and lawless that it may be expected as a matter of course to break through the constraints of ordinary social arrangements—I am reminded of Arcite's earlier "A man moot nedes love, maugree his heed. / . . . / Al be she mayde, or wydwe, or elles wyf" (1169–71). The attempt to satisfy desire is therefore exposed to the constant threat of vengeful retaliation, or at least humiliation, and one must suppose that these threats (those of Theseus) weigh on Arcite as he speaks.

The whole passage is so classically oedipal that I am almost embarrassed to point it out; but there is more, and worse, to come. The idea that women have the power to arouse uncontrollable desire independently of what men may will is common to both venerian and martian consciousness, to both Palamon and Arcite. In the former case it leads to the deification of female power and the attempt to sublimate desire into worship. In the latter case, however, the idea leads to the definition of woman, reduced to the desire she causes, as an enemy—the dying Arcite will call Emelye "my sweete foo" (2780). The venerian decision to worship a woman from afar is in part a response to the fear of Diana, that is, the fear that the woman may refuse closer contact. This fundamental fear and distrust of feminine independence, the inability to believe that a woman might want him for himself, comes out more explicitly and rather more disquietingly in the martian attitude:

> For she that dooth me al this wo endure
> Ne reccheth nevere wher I synke or fleete.
> And wel I woot, er she me mercy heete,
> I moot with strengthe wynne hire in the place.
>
> (2396–99)

Though Arcite is "only" talking here about winning the tournament, the last line quoted is sufficiently vague in reference that, coupled with the active and hostile role assigned to the lady ("*dooth* me al this wo endure") and the earlier image of Mars using the beauty of Venus, it allows us to wonder to what extent the idea of doing battle *for* Emelye is separated in Arcite's mind from doing battle *with* her for her favors. The rather raw image of relations between the sexes in the prayer as a whole allows the specter of rape to flicker behind the language of war here. I have already disparaged Palamon's concern for Emelye; I am not sure it is entirely a defense of Arcite to point out that his prayer for "victorye" may not in fact neglect the lady—it may include a request for victory over her.

I do not mean to imply that Arcite intends to rape Emelye, or even that, consciously or unconsciously, he wants to. What is involved in tracing out the rhizomatic connections of the language at work in these speeches is seeing how they register a set of quasi-institutionalized psychosocial structures and contradictions that invade and unsettle the most innocent and "personal" experiences. On the one hand, what speaks here is the general dynamic of the lack—the dynamic of *invidia* and the *objet petit a,* which moves from the temples into more complex and diffuse representation in the characters. It is worth remembering that in this dynamic possession of "The" woman is evidence of control over the offense of the lack, castration: she is what makes the denial of castration possible by "proving" that her possessor has the phallus she lacks. Insofar as this control is what they are really fighting over whether they know it or not, Palamon and Arcite may be said to instantiate the general dynamic. By this point in the poem, however, this sort of observation is of fairly limited range. Psychoanalytic theory (as opposed, one expects and hopes, to psychoanalytic practice) provides a general framework within which certain aspects of human behavior can be understood, but it does tend merely to reproduce itself—and thereby invite the criticism that it makes every story the same story—at the level of individual and, historically, social differentiation. As I have tried to suggest, the prayers of Palamon and Arcite articulate the *differing* inflections of their *uncertainty*, their inability to resolve, for instance, the institutionalized contradictions between eros and aggression that make any act of love an act of war as well, and vice versa.[12] Any analysand will attest that there comes a point, as here, when the way the primary structures of desire are inflected and deployed is of more consequence than the fact of their simple presence, and that deployment is a social as well as a personal matter.[13]

Arcite's prayer makes particularly clear the specifically psychic functions of Mars as an idea and an institution. Arcite subordinates himself to the god as an ego ideal, an image of what he would most like to be. His final vow is illuminating in this regard:

> And eek to this avow I wol me bynde:
> My beerd, myn heer, that hongeth long adoun,
> That nevere yet ne felte offensioun
> Of rasour nor of shere, I wol thee yive,
> And ben thy trewe servant whil I lyve.
> Now, lord, have routhe upon my sorwes soore;
> Yif me [victorie]; I aske the namoore.
>
> (2414–20)

The recurrence of "offensioun" here points once again to the importance of the absolute integrity of the heroic individual. As in folk magic, where hair retains part of its owner's life, to refrain from cutting one's hair is to preserve the integrity and independence of one's body as an emblem of the inviolability of one's heroic being. To cut it is conceived as an offense because it involves submitting to a diminishment of wholeness and power, becoming *morcelé*, losing pieces of oneself. Arcite does not feel strong enough or confident enough to assert such absolute self-sufficiency for himself; he is diminished by

---

12. For an excellent detailed analysis of extreme forms of this situation, see Theweleit, *Male Fantasies*, vol. 1, *Women, Floods, Bodies, History*.

13. See Bourdieu, *Outline of a Theory of Practice*, 78–79, and the theoretical remarks of Chodorow, *Reproduction of Mothering*, 49–50, and her argument throughout.

desire and beset by the uncertainties of the coming battle. But he can conceive a being who is that powerful, a being already institutionally in place as a cultural ideal, and he submits to it to make its power his own. He offers to offend himself in honor of Mars to forestall being offended in more consequential ways by others. Like Palamon, Arcite comes into focus in his prayer as a relatively specialized type, a specific form of consciousness that has been differentiated and defined by the progress of the tale out of the more general heroic-chivalric context of the early phases of the story. The Knight comes to use Palamon and Arcite to outline the fundamental components of chivalric romance— in the broadest terms love and war—in a way that both separates those components from one another and defines them more precisely, at the same time remaining aware of how they form an interdependent system. The basic masculine situation the tale develops is one in which, for example, simultaneous fear and desire of women and feelings of aggression and worship toward them are taken by the characters as constants, as what they all have to deal with. Within this basic situation there are various structures of practical consciousness or institutional routes that may be said to organize the fundamental contradictions (while perpetuating them) so that practical choices are possible for individuals within the system, and it is the range of these choices— the human uses of divinities—that the Knight's own practice in Part III reveals.

Because the process is a differentiating and developing one, it is not particularly helpful to try to read Palamon and Arcite in any detail in these martian and venerian terms back from the prayers as consistent and differentiable character structures in the earlier parts of the poem. The two cousins develop toward these positions from a more undifferentiated set of similar dispositions and tensions, and from one point of view their choices of gods must be seen precisely as choices they come to make, though not necessarily consciously, from the available stock that culture supplies for meeting the situation in which they find themselves.[14] From another, and ultimately more relevant, point of view by

14. This is one reason it is difficult to take a straightforward position on the issue of the difference or lack of it between the two knights. That question has various answers at various times; but even when they are relatively well-differentiated, as here, they are still presented as the same in important ways: they are masculine as opposed to feminine (as the tale develops that opposition), naive as opposed to disenchanted, and so on. In

this stage in the tale Mars and Venus, especially as they are character-ized in the prayers of Palamon and Arcite, are *habitus*, clusters of practices developed by the Knight as a way of differentiating and describing elements in the story that his sources in their unrevised form do not supply. This development is a function of his practical prefer-ence for concrete experience as the context in which he can let what he knows—practically—about love and war come out in the particular life of individuals. The general, the "structural," whether in the form of the pagan pantheon, Boethian philosophy, or the codes of chivalry, only takes on meaning for him as it is encountered in practice, and that is why he is always more interested in how conventions are used than in what they claim to be in themselves. The tale is, among other things, an unfolding record of his own encounter with his own tradition as embodied in the noble old story, and his consistent tendency is to make that story reflect and respond to his own experience. By this point in the tale the characters are patently doing the same thing: they respond to the problems they face by giving emphasis and credit to what they can use in their own traditions and culture; they make individualizing, practical *choices* that commit them not only to particular courses of action but also to particular personalities. They are thus instances of how personality itself—the subject—is institutionally constructed, not as an unconscious *expression* of institutional structure and power, but as the result of the active *use* of them.

Because the characters do become more like the narrator as the tale proceeds, they become realer to him: he takes them more seriously, their dilemmas take on more existential bite, and he sympathizes with them more. This change is nowhere more evident than with Emelye, both because, in contrast to Palamon and Arcite, her individuality is developed so much more fully than it was at the beginning of the tale and because she is so much more constrained in her choices and in what she can hope for from her goddess. The Knight brings out her

---

one sense the question as formulated is pitched at the wrong level. Palamon and Arcite are not persons with consistent personalities throughout the story; they are characters in a story with affinities to other stories of the same kind (generic types) whose sameness or difference is a function of the interaction of those generic characteristics with the practi-cal needs of this telling by this narrator. The real bearing of the question, in any event, is on the issue of *ethical* difference as it affects their deserts in the outcome of the tale, and that is an issue better left to later.

humanity more completely than that of either Palamon or Arcite perhaps because he himself is more ambivalent about what her situation entails. Though he is critical of the two cousins for their mystification of women and uses Theseus to say so directly, he is himself tempted by some of the attitudes he disparages. His ambivalence comes out most clearly in his description of the rites of Diana, which engage him more than those of Venus or Mars. He begins with the famous line that associates Emelye with natural cycles and subordinates her to them, as she was when she appeared as Venus in the garden: "Up roos the sonne, and up roos Emelye" (2273). The lines that follow record a curious struggle in the speaker's voice, a complex wavering of attention. His description of the rites has at first a certain summary tone reminiscent of the dispatch with which he handles Palamon's sacrifice to Venus a few lines earlier, "Al telle I noght as now his observaunces" (2264). He points to the archaic quality of Diana's ceremony as if to dismiss it: "The hornes fulle of meeth, *as was the gyse*— / Ther lakked noght to doon hir sacrifice" (2279–80, emphasis added). As his narration proceeds, however, the Knight lingers self-consciously over the rites:

> Smokynge the temple, ful of clothes faire,
> This Emelye, with herte debonaire,
> Hir body wessh with water of a welle.
> But hou she dide hir ryte I dar nat telle,
> But it be any thing in general;
> And yet it were a game to heeren al.
> To hym that meneth wel it were no charge;
> But it is good a man been at his large.
> Hir brighte heer was kembd, untressed al;
> A coroune of a grene ook cerial
> Upon hir heed was set ful fair and meete.
> Two fyres on the auter gan she beete,
> And dide hir thynges, as men may biholde
> In Stace of Thebes and thise bookes olde.
>
> (2281–94)

The Knight seems to place himself momentarily and a little voyeuristically in Actaeon's position, peeping at Diana bathing as if about to reveal the secrets of the goddess and provoke her wrath. Taking a lesson from Actaeon he pulls back, yet his continued fascination is evident: I dare not tell; it would be fun to tell; it is better not to; well,

I'll tell just a little. The Knight's imagination seems drawn to participate in the male look that constitutes woman as a creature of sexual mystery and threat and thereby deprives her of individuality and independence. To see Emelye as the embodiment of feminine *daunger*, as Diana, is to lock her up again in the institutional constraints and mystifications that the Knight associates with the old books. It is amusing that his final dismissal of this perspective keeps his ambivalence in play by providing what amounts to a footnote telling us where to go if we really want to know the secret he dares not reveal, but his relegation of the rites to "Stace of Thebes and thise bookes olde" nonetheless represents an act of self-control.[15] As in the description of the temple of Mars and elsewhere, we see the Knight working through and mastering his own attraction to a point of view he ultimately considers inappropriate and misleading.

The image of woman projected by the temple of Diana counters the worshipful empowering of the feminine enshrined in the image of Venus by providing an example of female suffering and helplessness. As I have suggested, this image is connected to other instances of the dependence of women in the tale, such as the Theban widows and the ladies of Theseus's court. It seems likely that these versions of woman do not altogether escape the masculine constructions of chivalric consciousness insofar as they partake of the stereotype that makes true knighthood a matter of the defense of helpless women. The Knight seems to share the feelings of Theseus along these lines, in the relatively benign form expressed when the latter allows the court women to persuade him not to kill Palamon and Arcite but to let them tourney for the hand of Emelye instead: "And eek his herte hadde compassioun / Of wommen, for they wepen evere in oon" (1770–71). Like Theseus, the Knight in the early parts of the tale feels protective of women, but he also patronizes them: he is willing to lump them together as "they" in ways that stress their generic lack of virile *fortitudo*. This sense of superior, protective distance allows the Knight to be as critical as he is of the more worshipful and fearful image of woman as goddess, whether Venus or Diana, that dominates the ro-

15. The fact that, as Kittredge pointed out, the reader will not find a description of the rites in Statius, who of course has no temple of Diana, simply enforces the sense that the reference is to a genre—books of that sort—rather than a specific source, the literary as opposed to the actual.

mance sensibilities of Palamon and Arcite. If he can be tempted by those stereotypes, as his momentary hesitation over the rites of Diana suggests, he can also draw on his sense of the helplessness of women as a counter. As I have also suggested, the role of the suffering worshiper in the temple of Diana, in recalling the Knight from the disturbances generated by his imagining of Mars, shows that this image can also function as a way of mitigating and controlling the ferocity of masculine aggression. From this point of view Diana's votary need not be thought of as anything much more individualized than a reminder of "what we are fighting for," in the idealized and desexualized version that has served knights in shining armor from the Sir Galahad of the Arthurian vulgate cycle to the more hard-bitten and ironic but no less protective Philip Marlowes and Travis McGees of our own day, with whom the Knight at times has some affinity.

Emelye as she manifests herself in her prayer, however, is something else again, for if she is not Diana, she is not Callisto either: as the Knight presents her here, she is the most complex character in Part III. Emelye knows she will probably have to be married despite her preferences, and this knowledge puts her in a position where it is difficult for her to identify completely and confidently with the aggressive *daunger* of Diana. Like the Knight, and like Callisto, she fears the goddess's harsh response to what may happen to her: "As keepe me fro thy vengeaunce and thyn ire, / That Attheon aboughte cruelly" (2302–3). The potential similarities of her situation to those of Callisto and the nameless worshiper in the temple of Diana give added resonance to her desire to remain chaste. Emelye is painfully aware not only of the independent pleasures she is about to lose but also of the new burdens she will have to take up:

> I am, thow woost, yet of thy compaignye,
> A mayde, and love huntynge and venerye,
> And for to walken in the wodes wilde,
> *And noght to ben a wyf and be with childe.*
> Noght wol I knowe compaignye of man.
> (2307–11, emphasis added)

Confronted with the masculine world and her entry into it, Emelye is not aggressive in her rejection—unlike Diana, she can ill afford to be. Rather, she prays to be effaced from it:

> And Palamon, that hath swich love to me,
> And eek Arcite, that loveth me so soore,
> This grace I preye thee withoute moore,
> As sende love and pees bitwixe hem two,
> And fro me turne awey hir hertes so
> That al hire hoote love and hir desir,
> And al hir bisy torment, and hir fir
> Be queynt, or turned in another place.
>
> (2314–21)

Emelye's fantasy here is one of escape from the impersonality of her own sexuality, from the fact that a woman attracts masculine desire and has effects in the male world whether she wants to or not. Her wish is *not to appear,* to be effaced from the male look as if she had not been and had not produced the effects she never wanted or even knew about until too late. Once again, as with Palamon and Arcite, we are given an image of the concrete human needs and tensions out of which the gods are created, larger and simpler than life because untrammeled by the pressures that lead their worshipers to project them; but in Emelye's case Diana does not supply an institutional model and support, as Venus and Mars do for Palamon and Arcite. Emelye must somehow come to terms with a situation in which she, as the nominal cause and center of all the trouble, has little to say about its outcome. She has to hedge all her bets:

> And if so be thou wolt nat do me grace,
> Or if my destynee be shapen so
> That I shal nedes have oon of hem two,
> As sende me hym that moost desireth me.
>
> (2322–25)

Emelye is trying to find such possibilities as she can for personal fulfillment in circumstances that offer her no good choices, and because of her dilemma the troubled woman stands out—she is far more real and compelling than the goddess to whom she appeals. As with the worshiper in the temple of Diana, the poignancy of Emelye's condition is heightened because the goddess, who is in reality no more than a flattened and mythologized version of the place of woman in the system that disposes of her, cannot grant her prayer. The mumbo jumbo of sputtering fires and bloody firebrands that accompanies Diana's refusal to help forms a compact and enigmatic prefiguration of a sorrow greater than Emelye can anticipate, the funeral pyre of Arcite that she will have to light near the end of the poem. It is as well an echo of the pyre lit at the behest of the Argive women at the poem's beginning; hence, in its participation in a larger structure of images, it reads as a figure of the fate of woman in a world where men kill one another competing for women who have not asked them to.

In place and in context, however, Diana's manifestations are no more than epic and narrative machinery that heightens by its flatness the humanity of the baffled and fearful woman whose last words in the poem, "What amounteth this, allas" (2362), leave her suspended and alienated as Palamon and Arcite are not. The Knight evokes in Emelye a character whose situation, in what might be called her forced disenchantment, is in some ways closest to his own. Venus and Diana are, the poem suggests, aspects of the institution of woman as the society of the tale constructs it. Precisely because neither of these institutional identities fits her while both constrain her, Emelye appears not as a woman defined and absorbed by mythic archetypes or "feminine nature" but as a person caught between competing role definitions and trying to find a place of her own and a set of practices she can use. As such, she is a figure of the Knight's understanding of the problems generated for a woman by her *difference from the institutions* that are supposed to define her, an index of his own disenchanted distance from the conventions that shape his tale and his world and of his self-consciousness about that distance. What is most extraordinary of all about Emelye is the Knight's ability to imagine her, to put himself in the place of the other and try to think what it must be like for a woman to live in the world that men have made. She is testimony to the uses of impersonation.

One of the points I have been concerned to make in dealing with the presentation of the divine machinery in Part III of the *Knight's Tale* is fairly well represented already in the critical literature and is economically expressed by Richard Neuse:

> In the first place, therefore, the gods stand for things as they are, *moira*. The artists who have adorned the temple walls see no chasm between earthly reality and the divinities that rule over it. Second, the divine presences sum up certain ways of life to which men dedicate themselves.

In another sense, they have a *psychological* function: the god a person serves is his ruling passion. The gods are men's wills or appetites writ large.

("The Knight," 303)

A number of other commentators have also noted that the gods are "merely extensions of the human personalities,"[16] but Neuse's formulation remains the most suggestive for me because it outlines compactly the three levels of causality that are discriminated in the Knight's presentation of the gods: in reverse order, individual psychology, institutions or the social construction of reality, and necessity, Neuse's *moira*. Widespread as these insights are, they have not had as much effect as they deserve on the interpretation of the tale—largely, I would argue, because they have not been connected with the issue of voicing or seen in terms of something the Knight *does* to the story, and does progressively. The order in which Neuse presents the three levels of meaning is in fact the order in which they are developed in the tale. It moves from a world in which whatever happens is presented in mystified form as external to the agents, as "the way things are," through a presentation of the institutional constructs that structure experience, to a world in which psychological vectors and human actions are paramount. If the Knight hesitates in the temple of Mars between the causal claims of psychology and external necessity, by the time he reaches the end of Part III he has chosen the former. Issues first raised and imported into the tale in the temples have, by the time the Knight gets to the prayers, found their way into the psychology of the characters, who emerge not only as complex individuals but also as venerian, dianan, and martian personalities, versions of those institutional aspects of the human psyche that produced the pagan gods. The *direction* of the Knight's interpretation of his "matere" is consistent; it allows us to assign priorities among the symbolic elements Neuse and others have isolated and say something definite about the relation of the gods in the poem to its characters. That the gods are merely extensions of the humans is something the poem uncovers. Far from being a means of importing into the story a level of true and objective

16. Fletcher, "Role of Destiny," 48. See also Whittock, *Reading of the Canterbury Tales*, 66; Schmidt, "Tragedy of Arcite"; Kean, *Making of English Poetry*, 2:5; and Gaylord, "Role of Saturn," 179.

order external to humanity that is operative in the universe and only hidden from imperfect human knowledge—what we might call the Lady Philosophy reading of the poem—the gods are, or become, human creations, ways men and women try to make an order they cannot find outside them.

This is not to say, however, that the Knight entirely neglects the aspect of what I have called necessity in his presentation of the gods. That aspect, though kept relatively recessive, is also kept running in the poem, largely through astrological allusion. I have already discussed some of the ways the Knight shows his awareness, in the temples, of forces either entirely extrahuman, like "infortune," or within humans but not directly amenable to human will, forces like aggression or the biological rhythms of generation that may be dealt with in various personal and institutional ways but cannot be eschewed. In his account of the prayers of the three protagonists the Knight, while focusing on psychological and social factors, maintains this perspective in his framing of the scene. He reports that Palamon went to the temple of Venus "In hir houre" (2217); that Emelye made her sacrifice "The thridde houre inequal" (2271) after Palamon, that is, two hours later; and that Arcite made his "The nexte houre of Mars folwynge this" (2367), that is, three hours after Emelye. As several commentators have demonstrated, the tale aspires to scientific exactitude in matters of dates, hours, and astrological houses.[17] This interest is sufficiently strong that the conflict of scientific timekeeping with the more "poetic" methods of the old books is occasionally noted by the Knight, as when he includes his own skeptical aside along with the information that Palamon rose with the lark, "Although it nere nat day by houres two, / Yet song the larke" (2211–12). The effect of these references to the planets that govern the hours of the day is to keep before us the medieval (modern for the Knight) revision of the pagan deities into the planets and therefore keep the pressure of larger cosmic forces at least marginally in play.

Yet it is misleading, I think, to maintain with Curry that "Chaucer" simply discarded the ancient mythological machinery, substituting

17. Skeat, in *Oxford Chaucer*, 5:86, notes to I, 2217 and 2271; North, "Kalenderes Enlumyned Ben They," 151–52; and Robinson, in *Riverside Chaucer*, 837, notes to I, 2217 and 2271.

Boethian destiny and the planetary influences of medieval astrology.[18] The Knight has a use for the older view of the gods as personalities as well as the newer one that takes them as impersonal influences, and therefore he gives us both side by side. I have already analyzed this effect in the description of the statue of Mars (see above, pp. 281—84); it is continued by the planetary allusions that frame the prayers and highlighted by the speech of Saturn that concludes Part III. The point of this procedure, in line with the analytical and differentiating thrust of the Knight's imagination in this part of the poem, is that it registers his sense of the distinction between the psychological and social components of the situation in the story (and in human life generally) and those that come from somewhere beyond, the distinction between human and nonhuman agency. By the end of Part III this distinction, previously concealed or confused by the mystifications of chivalric convention and the characters, has emerged more clearly in the dual treatment of the gods. On the one hand, they have, so to speak, descended into the characters and taken on their fullest life precisely as human personalities. The Knight knows and shows that a great deal of what is taken in literary tradition, chivalric consciousness, and ordinary life as the product of powers above is in fact humanly produced, and the gods are his major vehicle for registering this insight. On the other hand, as planets the gods *also* and independently become a way of calling attention to powers that, if they are not precisely above, are at any rate beyond. They evoke the role of the entirely other in human life. I might point out here that this discrimination says little about the *nature* of necessity and in particular that it should not be taken to imply a benign Boethian or Dantean cosmos ruled by the sight above or a First Mover dispensing order in a fair chain of love. Though these are issues better left to a consideration of the last part of the poem, we have abundant evidence already of the Knight's dark imagining, his suspicion that whatever is running the cosmos does not concern itself with human needs.

Thus, by the end of Part III the Knight has reduced the gods to their origins, and one result of this process is that the antique and literary machinery of personifications is left rather stranded between the forces whose contradictions that machinery originally functioned to reconcile, forces the Knight has used the machinery itself to reevoke and

18. Curry, *Chaucer and the Medieval Sciences*, 119ff.

separate. This means, among other things, that the machinery comes increasingly to be seen as only machinery, and archaic and outmoded machinery at that. The latter half of Part III is full of touches that recognize and dismiss what is out of date in the story, from the unfamiliar and highfalutin titles like "Cytherea"—"I mene Venus, honurable and digne" (2216)—to "alle the rytes of his payen wyse" (2370) that we do not get to see Arcite perform. The fiction of the power of the gods is maintained throughout the narration of the prayers themselves in the portentous series of omens and answers that follow each prayer. Though these contain a number of comic touches, like the darkly muttered "Victorie!" of Mars, that suggest that the Knight does not take them seriously, the gods are generally allowed to speak with authority: "Among the goddes hye it is affermed, / And by eterne word writen and confermed, / Thou shalt ben wedded unto oon of tho" (2349–51). Working against such assertions of the unalterability of divine purposes and the "eterne word" is a gradual buildup of mythological allusions to the affairs and quarrels of the gods: to Daphne, Actaeon, and Adonis; to Venus, Mars, and Vulcan. By the time Arcite reminds Mars of his adulterous affair with Venus and their humiliating capture by her husband, the characters may be said to be actively, though apparently unwittingly, embarrassing the gods by calling attention to their all-too-human inability to control their own passions and destinies.

This perspective, what we notice that the characters do not, is confirmed when we get backstage:

> And right anon swich strif ther is bigonne,
> For thilke grauntyng, in the hevene above,
> Bitwixe Venus, the goddesse of love,
> And Mars, the stierne god armypotente,
> That Juppiter was bisy it to stente,
> Til that the pale Saturnus the colde,
> That knew so manye of aventures olde,
> Foond in his olde experience an art
> That he ful soone hath plesed every part.
> As sooth is seyd, elde hath greet avantage;
> In elde is bothe wysdom and usage;
> Men may the olde atrenne, and noght atrede.
> Saturne anon, to stynten strif and drede,
> Al be it that it is agayn his kynde,
> Of al this stryf he gan remedie fynde.
>
> (2438–52)

As Joseph Westlund noted, there is more disorder among the gods than there is among the humans, who at least have tried to establish an impartial institutional method for deciding the conflict.[19] It appears that Venus and Mars have promised victory to their respective worshipers without bothering to consult one another or anyone else and that Diana does not tell Emelye who will win her because the goddess does not yet know. This confusion is a measure of how the Knight's presentation of the gods has developed from the formidable figures of the temples. Whereas there it was possible to see them as dominating and influencing human beings so as to make them what they are, here it is clear that the positions have been reversed: the actions and responses of the gods are dictated by what happens on earth, and Olympian society is a reflection of its earthly original—chaotic, political, and in need of guidance and authority.

Olympian society is also subject to various forms of manipulation, special interests, and backroom dealings, as the presentation of Saturn and his "remedie" reveals. The tone of the Knight's introduction is noticeably ironic, and the promise that Saturn will allay the strife "Al be it that it is agayn his kynde" is not reassuring. Though we do not yet discover what the solution is, Saturn gives a fair idea of where his sympathies lie, more on the side of his kin than with any abstract idea of justice. He addresses Venus as "My deere doghter" (2453) and tells her to dry her tears and not to worry about nasty old Mars:

> Though Mars shal helpe his knyght, yet nathelees
> Bitwixe yow ther moot be som tyme pees,
> Al be ye noght of o compleccioun,
> That causeth al day swich divisioun.
> I am thyn aiel, redy at thy wille;
> Weep now namoore; I wol thy lust fulfille.
>
> (2473-78)

This is really the only place in the tale where the Knight gives direct expression to a sense of the way things work in the world that is more dominant in the Man of Law, though it can be felt in the tacit political implications of such things as Theseus's original imprisonment of Palamon and Arcite, in the suggestion of an old-boy network operating to bring about the release of Arcite from "perpetual" imprisonment at the behest of Perothous, and, as we shall see, in a number of the events

19. Westlund, "Impetus for Pilgrimage," 530.

of Part IV.[20] This characterization of Saturn as behind-the-scenes operator evokes a fully disenchanted view of social and political life (it surely belongs in Terry Jones) as constituted simply by the interplay of conflicting wills: by deals, power struggles, and shifting collocations of individual and group interests. The experience that gives Saturn's eld its "greet avantage" scarcely seems like a garnering of higher truths; it seems to represent instead an understanding of the fundamental competitiveness of life in the world of this tale that makes diplomacy the continuation of war by other means.

Saturn is particularly grotesque here because of his grim self-characterization, sharply and rather jarringly juxtaposed to his words of grandfatherly comfort. His speech to Venus presents his double aspect as personification and planet so baldly as to render conspicuous the comic incompatibility of the two perspectives:

> "My deere doghter Venus," quod Saturne,
> "My cours, that hath so wyde for to turne,
> Hath moore power than woot any man.
> Myn is the drenchyng in the see so wan;
> Myn is the prisoun in the derke cote;
> Myn is the stranglyng and hangyng by the throte,
> The murmure and the cherles rebellyng,
> The groynyng, and the pryvee empoysonyng;
> I do vengeance and pleyn correccioun,
> Whil I dwelle in the signe of the leoun.
> Myn is the ruyne of the hye halles,
> The fallynge of the toures and of the walles
> Upon the mynour or the carpenter.
> I slow Sampsoun, shakynge the piler;
> And myne be the maladyes colde,
> The derke tresons, and the castes olde;
> My lookyng is the fader of pestilence.
> Now weep namoore; I shal doon diligence
> That Palamon, that is thyn owene knyght,
> Shal have his lady, as thou hast him hight."

> (2453-72)

Saturn presents himself as the lord of disasters that appear to occur independently of any consistent principle or cause. He operates sometimes in the interests of justice, sometimes in the interests of disorder

---

20. This view is perhaps also involved in certain aspects of Palamon and Arcite's Theban past; see above, chapter 10, nn. 7 and 8.

and rebellion; sometimes his effects are humanly mediated and motivated, sometimes (and here particularly I feel the traces of the Knight's dark imagining) they occur without reference to human concerns: the walls fall indifferently on the (military) miner and the carpenter, on those who are trying to build them up and those who want to bring them down. It is thus generally accurate to say that Saturn is a way of locating and giving a name to the Knight's intimations of chaos and dark meaninglessness as well as an image of mischance less schematic and simplified than Fortune and her wheel.[21]

But the presentation of Saturn as a whole diminishes the impact and seriousness of this perspective at this point in the poem. The sinister implications of his activity are chastened, turned off by their ascription to a comic and melodramatically boastful old man plotting to please his granddaughter. This effect seems to me entirely in keeping with the Knight's use of the gods in Part III of the poem. He has used them to introduce what he sees as a set of perennial facts about the human situation. But the more successfully the gods do this, the more they call attention to their own limitations in their own time and their difference from what they have been used to convey. As we have seen, the pagan deities are used in the poem to evoke large-scale forces, psychic, social, and destinal, that cannot finally be fully anthropomorphized and located in a god or goddess. One might venture the generalization, for which I am indebted to Harry Berger, Jr., that for the Knight the reality of evil is felt in inverse proportion to the extent to which the evil is personified. This rule is particularly true of the kind of evil that the figure of Saturn alludes to. The forces in the psyche represented by Venus, Mars, and Diana are amenable to human control by some such process as the Knight has applied to them. If they are understood for what they are, not projected into the external world, there is some hope that people may be able to contain and direct them either through experienced self-knowledge and self-control, like Theseus in the grove, or through relatively rational institutions such as the tournament aspires to be.[22] This is the burden of the first half of Part IV, up to the

---

21. It is interesting that the characterization of mischance is thus shifted from a feminine figure to a masculine one. Whatever else this shift means, it is consonant with the general tendency in much of the tale to revise or replace traditional antifeminist images and identify the sources of violence and mishap with masculinity.

22. Though this seems to me to be an accurate statement of the assumptions that operate behind the working of the poem, it also seems important to note that there is

death of Arcite. The end of Part IV, and of the poem, concentrates on the human resources available for dealing with contingencies men did not make and cannot predict. In the Knight's view it is inappropriate to treat such forces as if they had a single directing source and will behind them because, as we shall see, such a view encourages the abrogation of human responsibility for the sustaining of human value and human meaning and pulls toward passivity and despair. As the Knight's presentation of Saturn suggests, a god is not a good way of talking about this kind of threat, which is better examined as it is actually encountered in human life in particular situations. The gods have served their purpose, and it is time to return to narrative:

> Now wol I stynten of the goddes above,
> Of Mars, and of Venus, goddesse of love,
> And telle yow as pleynly as I kan
> The grete effect, for which that I bygan.
>
> (2479–82)

---

something missing in the view of the world it implies. It is characteristic of the deep structure of the Knight's imagination to prefer a vision of life as *essentially* a matter of the confrontation of fate by heroic individuality. There is a certain equivocation or wavering in his portrayal of institutions between seeing them as *constitutive* of such confrontation itself and seeing them as necessary but supplementary epiphenomena of it, which successful heroism can master and transcend. I will return to this issue at the end of this reading of the *Knight's Tale*.

13

Choosing Manhood
The "Masculine" Imagination and the
Institution of the Subject

The success of Part III of the *Knight's Tale* as a way of infusing the story with its narrator's own sensibility and experience—of making the past present and the romantic realistic—is measured in part by the vividness with which the Knight imagines and describes the scene of the tournament and its action in Part IV. Perhaps the most striking instance of this immediacy is "But herkneth me, and stynteth noyse a lite" (2674), a moment when the shouts of the Athenian crowd at Arcite's victory and the world of the pilgrimage where the Knight is telling the tale seem to merge most completely—though with the proviso that the world of the tale is the more real one for him since we do not imagine the pilgrims joining the shouting. The immediacy and fulness of the world of the tournament are the most notable things about it as Part IV opens. The present tense—"Ther maystow seen devisynge of harneys" (2496)—is used to describe a dense, technical list of arms, ornaments, and activities whose modernity in the Knight's world is well attested by commentators.[1] Everywhere we look there are throngs of people, armorers and commoners as well as lords, "Heere thre, ther ten, holdynge hir questioun, / Dyvynynge of thise Thebane knyghtes two" (2514-15) in a way that will not be unfamiliar to modern enthusiasts of athletic events: "Somme seyde he looked grymme, and he wolde fighte; / 'He hathe a sparth of twenty pound of wighte' " (2519-20).

This sense of the presence and familiarity of the scene to the speaker is, as I have suggested, the outcome of the process of telling the tale, the result of a good deal of practical labor on his part in dealing with a

---

1. See Robinson's notes, in Chaucer, *Works*, 2d ed., 680, especially to lines 2491ff.

story that begins by seeming rather remote, literary, and unreal to him.[2] What the Knight has done with the gods in the course of Part III is a paradigm of what he has done with the tale as a whole: his procedure throughout has been to revise it, that is, give it new meanings and a new life in the present while at the same time definitively outmoding and discarding its old meanings. This procedure is perhaps clearest with the gods, both because they are so much the focus of attention in the center of the poem and because there is little temptation to suppose that the narrator gives them any credence except as opportunities for revision and symbolization. The resources of classical myth, the temples and the gods, have been the Knight's vehicle for bringing the tale up to date in the sense that he has used them to introduce greater depth and complexity in line with his own experience into the world of the story; but they can only exercise this function when they cease to mean what he understands them to have meant for classical culture and become the symbols he has made of them. Even more than the statue of Mars, the figure of Saturn is a subject split between a set of disenchanted human motives and manipulations on the one hand and a set of inscrutable external forces on the other. The one thing he is not is a god, an autonomous, centered self directing events according to his own will and power. The treatment of the tournament participates in this modernizing movement in a way that makes particularly evident that it *is* modernizing. The Knight's sense of history, like the Wife of Bath's sense of her past, takes its direction backward from the now of speaking and experience: the image of the past is a function of the needs of the present, to the point where what is seen as archaic is essentially what is seen as not of use and not illuminating, like pagan rites.

2. Like most other aspects of the tale, its attitude toward history and the idea of the historical is not susceptible of a single unchanging characterization such as might note that Theseus is a medieval ruler in a classical setting and conclude that the tale therefore shares in a general medieval insensitivity to anachronism and even, perhaps, a deficient notion of history. The relation of present to past is one of the problems the poem itself addresses and is therefore caught up in the *process* of the tale—it changes as the story develops. A much more sophisticated awareness of the complexity of "medieval" attitudes (the word *medieval* itself carries a theory-laden prejudgment: the middle of what?) to the pagan past has developed in Chaucer criticism of the 1980s, as exemplified in work like A. J. Minnis's *Chaucer and Pagan Antiquity* (though relatively traditional in its theoretical assumptions) or, better still, in works whose approach is more firmly centered on the historicizing agency of Chaucer's text, such as John Fyler's *Chaucer and Ovid* and Winthrop Wetherbee's *Chaucer and the Poets*.

The Knight's practice suggests, however, that among the needs of the present, for him, are the sense of authority and tradition that are invested in the idea of the past as a storehouse of exemplary chivalry and noble deeds; the one place in the tale that explicitly takes account of the problem of anachronism is, so to speak, a defense of the past. In Part III the Knight completes his list of the weapons borne by the warriors in Palamon's party—breastplate, "gypoun," Prussian shield, and the rest—with the remark "Ther is no newe gyse that it nas old" (2125). Framed by all that modern weaponry, the line feels like a response to a potential accusation of anachronism (I take it the Knight himself feels the description is a bit too contemporary). It seems clear that he wants to say that the past has influenced the present and have it appear so in his tale despite the pressure of his own constructive activity; but, interestingly, he answers the charge in effect with an assertion of the perennial character of the modern. The Knight's sense that the essential things about human life were in Theseus's time as they are now demands that the times of the old books be reconstructed from the point of view of the now, and that is how he has proceeded. When that procedure becomes too evident, he moves to reassert the authority and independence of the past as an origin, but without discursively formulating them, *so as to be able to say that things have always been, in their essentials, as they are now.* What ties the present and the past together for the Knight and gives the past its relevance is the "human nature" that emerges (that is, is constructed) as the common element in the two, in particular the chivalric-heroic masculine nature he ascribes in different versions to all the male characters in the tale. It is to the operations of this perennial character in a predominantly modern institutional setting that the first section of Part IV addresses itself.

Theseus is awakened by the bustle of the noble life, "mynstralcie and noyse that was maked" (2524), in this atmosphere of realistic immediacy and introduces his modification of the original plan of the tournament, changing it from an affair of "mortal bataille" to one of capture to avoid destruction of noble blood. It is worth noting the differences between this and earlier expressions of "the myghty dukes wille." Theseus is trying to impose his will not just on a pair of helpless captives but also on a society whose complexity is evident in the richness with which it is manifested here. As a result, he is presented—

and takes care to present himself—as far less absolute and arbitrary in his actions and decisions than he was at the beginning of the tale or even in the grove. Theseus's "vertu" shows itself here in the efficacy of his social engineering, the magnificence but also the care with which he controls and orchestrates the complex flow of events. When he becomes aware of the hubbub outside his palace, he does not respond at once, as he did before, but holds his chamber (2525) until the disorder has been organized, "Til that the Thebane knyghtes, bothe yliche / Honured, were into the paleys fet" (2526–27). Instead of speaking his will in his own voice, Theseus disposes himself symbolically above the assembled host "Arrayed right as he were a god in trone" (2529) and has his design proclaimed by a herald, who also takes on the responsibility for crowd control (2533–36). The herald's announcement of the rules of the contest is a good example of the continuous and unremitting attention to detail that characterizes the organization of the tournament:

> No man therfore, up peyne of los of lyf,
> No maner shot, ne polax, ne short knyf
> Into the lystes sende or thider brynge;
> Ne short swerd, for to stoke with poynt bitynge,
> No man ne drawe, ne bere it by his syde.
> Ne no man shal unto his felawe ryde
> But o cours with a sharpe ygrounde spere;
> Foyne, if hym list, on foote, hymself to were.
>
> (2543–50)

This announcement is, of course, more than just documentary realism. The new form of the tournament represents an attempt to forestall ultimate confrontation between Palamon and Arcite and their followers, an attempt to institutionalize mercy. The detailed enumeration of just which weapons and styles of combat are allowed and which are not, and the *need* for such precise rules, suggest the difficulty of the task. Given the fundamental contentiousness of chivalric consciousness, it is hard to enforce mercy because it is not a quality that comes naturally to the devotees of Mars, especially in the heat of battle. Theseus's aim is to allow the natural aggression of the combatants play, but as far as possible only *in* play: "God spede you! Gooth forth, and ley on faste! / With long swerd and with mace fighteth youre fille" (2558–59). Only through careful control of the conditions of mock combat can men such as the Lygurge and Emetrius of Part III be kept from destroying one another.

Similarly, in his account of the procession from the palace to the lists the Knight celebrates the ordered magnificence of the display, with particular appreciation for the way the procession maintains both hierarchy among the spectators and balance between the two sides, even to the exact timing of their entry into the lists:

> Whan set was Theseus ful riche and hye,
> Ypolita the queene, and Emelye,
> And othere ladys in degrees aboute.
> Unto the seetes preesseth al the route.
> And westward, thurgh the gates under Marte,
> Arcite, and eek the hondred of his parte,
> With baner reed is entred right anon;
> And in that selve moment Palamon
> Is under Venus, estward in the place,
> With baner whyt and hardy chiere and face.
> In al the world, to seken up and doun,
> So evene, withouten variacioun,
> Ther nere swiche compaignyes tweye.
>
> (2577–89)

Gone is the fortuitousness and improbability of the meeting in the grove precisely because the task of ensuring that the right people meet one another under the right circumstances is no longer entirely dependent on Fortune or destiny. What we are really asked to admire here are Theseus's powers of organization as he provides a framework for the resolution of the conflict between Palamon and Arcite that is more plausible, more magnificent, and more meaningful than what the sight above was apparently able to manage in Part II.

It need not lessen our appreciation of Theseus's achievement that some dark imagining shades its edges. The Knight notes and approves the hierarchy and explicit order of these preparations, but he also notes that they have a practical, as well as an aesthetic or symbolic, function—they make it easier to establish that the fight is fair:

> For ther was noon so wys that koude seye
> That any hadde of oother avauntage
> Of worthynesse, ne of estaat, ne age,
> So evene were they chosen, for to gesse.
> And in two renges faire they hem dresse.

Whan that hir names rad were everichon,
That in hir nombre gyle were ther noon,
Tho were the gates shet.

(2590–97)

The potential presence of guile is introduced not to question the pretensions of the tournament, as might have been the case earlier in the
tale, but to show that Theseus's planning has anticipated and fore-
stalled it. The duke's ordering of the event is as attentive to the lawless-
ness of guile and force as it is to more humane values of mercy and
right. The success of the tournament as an institution, as a triumph of
human making, is measured by its ability to respond to human needs
and desires while containing and withstanding human failings.

The Knight's own rhythm of narration in this part of the tale oscillates between a free-ranging spontaneity of observation (often accompanied by a tone of excitement and a feeling of participation in the
events described) and an attention to the ordering of the scene that has
the effect both of enabling the spontaneity and containing it, keeping
it in check. It seems that it is precisely because he and Theseus have
organized the tournament so carefully that the Knight can give himself
so fully to the combat when it comes. The fighting is described with
remarkable vividness in the present tense in an almost cinematic style:
the eye leaps disjointedly from scene to scene; the voice speaks in
end-stopped lines of one image a line, unlike the measured and formal
deployment of substantial blocks of narrative characteristic of the
earlier parts of the tale:

> Ther shyveren shaftes upon sheeldes thikke;
> He feeleth thurgh the herte-spoon the prikke.
> Up spryngen speres twenty foot on highte;
> Out goon the swerdes as the silver brighte;
> . . . .
> He thurgh the thikkeste of the throng gan threste;
> Ther stomblen steedes stronge and doun gooth al,
> He rolleth under foot as dooth a bal.
>
> (2605–8; 2612–14)

These lines seem to reflect the Knight's experience not so much of war
as of tourneying as a sport and record his recreative participation
in the scene as he imagines it. This effect is strengthened for me
by the way many of the lines allude to the specifically English vernacu-

lar tradition of alliterative heroic verse,[3] as if the Knight were taking time out from his more classically oriented epic and its latinate-romance style for a more homely, unpretentious, and innocent kind of entertainment.

I have not made much use of the terminology of *jouissance* in reference to the *Knight's Tale* so far, though it is fully relevant for a number of reasons. In the first place, I have felt the need to be careful about the associations of erotic pleasure the word carries, even though the technical Lacanian use of it does not always include them in any direct sense. The care seems necessary because the most important "lawless affects" whose agency is represented in the tale have more to do with aggression than with sexuality. The Knight, though certainly not untouched by heterosexual erotic feeling (as his various accounts of looking at women, whether mediated by the Thebans or conducted himself, attest), does not seem as affected either positively or negatively by it as by manifestations of violence, competition, and masculine striving. It is certainly clear that there are moments when the Knight gets caught up in his telling in a way that indicates the workings of unconscious energy. Such moments as the description of the Thracian boar hunters and the temple of Mars betray the operation of the Barthesian formula for *jouissance*, "*I know that these are only words, but all the same . . .*" (*Pleasure of the Text*, 48), but they do not seem to have much to do with pleasure in the ordinary sense.

One reason for this lack of pleasure is no doubt the Knight's respect for the personal and social dangers that the exercise of aggression entails and his horror at the effects of violence. His negative view of aggression is both a cause and an effect of his sense of social responsibility, his care for and about the institutions that promote justice, peace, honor, and the other ornaments of the noble life his tale celebrates. It is not hard to see how this set of concerns fits in with those of the "masculine" imagination as I have characterized it previously. That imagination is, as I have said, made uneasy by manifestations of *jouissance*, whether erotic or aggressive, because of its general commitment to the law and the going institutional structure, and the Knight's subjectivity seems to manifest a fairly self-conscious form of

3. Noted by Salter, Introduction to *The Knight's Tale*, 16–17.

this commitment. Thus, though it is obvious that the nodal moments of the tale are occasions of strong disturbance and ambivalence, it is mostly the negative side of the ambivalence and the effort of control that is dominant in them. The Knight's description of the tournament is one of the few places in the tale where he allows himself to take relatively unproblematic pleasure in strife and gives himself over to the exercise of his own delight in armed competition and the excitement of fighting. To see him do so is perhaps to realize more clearly that these feelings are always present in him and that it is his fear of the violence in himself as much as in others that drives his ambivalence and his strong sense of the need for control. In fact, the pleasure associated with aggression is usually displaced for the Knight into pleasure felt at the trappings, the institutional constructions and values that surround and channel aggression and thereby give it play. Though I have stressed the Knight's ironic and skeptical attitude toward the mystified forms of chivalric ideals generally expressed by Palamon and Arcite, in part because this ironic dimension of the tale has been somewhat undervalued in other readings, there can be no doubt about the fact of his love for these ideals themselves. He is fully aware of the homosocial bonding[4] that comradeship in arms generates—surely he wishes that Palamon and Arcite were more like Theseus and Perothous—and of the value of institutions like the tournament as a way of bringing men together. It is impossible to miss the comradeship he himself feels and his enthusiasm:

4. I take the term from Sedgwick, *Between Men*. As she points out, it allows us to acknowledge the component of desire in male-male relationships without having to say that they are somehow "really" homosexual. Her notion of homosocial desire creates a space "for making generalizations about, and marking historical differences in, the *structure* of men's relations with other men" (1–2). The famous passage that is always quoted with respect to medieval chivalry in this regard is from Jean de Beuil's *Le Jouvencel*.

What a joyous thing is war, for many fine deeds are heard and seen in its course. . . . You love your comrade so much in war. When you see that your quarrel is just and your blood is fighting well, tears rise to your eyes. A great sweet feeling of loyalty and pity fills your heart on seeing your friend so valiantly exposing his body to execute and accomplish the command of our Creator. And then you prepare to go and live and die with him, and for love not to abandon him. And out of that there arises such delectation, that he who has not tasted it is not fit to say what a delight is. Do you think that a man who does that fears death?

(In Vale, *War and Chivalry*, 30)

> For if ther fille tomorwe swich a cas,
> Ye knowen wel that every lusty knyght
> That loveth paramours and hath his myght,
> Were it in Engelond or elleswhere,
> They wolde, hir thankes, wilnen to be there—
> To fighte for a lady, benedicitee!
> It were a lusty sighte for to see.
>
> (2110–16)

In the tournament description, as I have suggested, it is the care taken to specify the limits of the combat in advance that allows the speaker to relax and give himself to the scene as fully as he does.

As the description proceeds, however, the Knight begins to draw back from his immediate enjoyment of the proceedings and focus again on their implications and potential consequences. The rhythm of the "masculine" imagination, with its need to contain *jouissance* and fill the gaps in the social body that its emergence threatens to reveal, reasserts itself. He singles out the principal contestants, Palamon and Arcite, and the imagery he applies to them points up that this is more than a rough game and reminds us of what is being simultaneously let loose and contained here. Arcite pursues Palamon, as cruel on the hunt as "tygre in the vale of Galgopheye, / Whan that hir whelp is stole whan it is lite" (2626–27), and Palamon desires to slay his cousin like a "fel leon" of Belmarye "That hunted is, or for his hunger wood" (2630–31). By now such animal images function not only as reminders of the fight in the grove but also resonate with what has been added to them of savagery and danger in the temple of Mars and the descriptions of Lygurge and Emetrius. The Knight seems to carry the description up to the point where the original scene in the grove is about to play itself out, and then to pull up short:

> The jelous strokes on hir helmes byte;
> Out renneth blood on bothe hir sydes rede.[5]
>   Som tyme an ende ther is of every dede.
> For er the sonne unto the reste wente,
> The stronge kyng Emetreus gan hente
> This Palamon, as he faught with Arcite,
> And made his swerd depe in his flessh to byte,
> And by the force of twenty is he take

5. Compare II, 1655–60.

Unyolden, and ydrawen to the stake.
And in the rescus of this Palamoun
The stronge kyng Lygurge is born adoun,
And kyng Emetreus, for al his strengthe,
Is born out of his sadel a swerdes lengthe,
So hitte him Palamoun er he were take.
But al for noght; he was broght to the stake.
His hardy herte myghte him helpe naught:
He moste abyde, whan that he was caught,
By force and eek by composicioun.

(2634–51)

This replay of the earlier scene serves to remind us of the differences between the two scenes and the superiority of the tournament to the earlier duel as a way of handling the issues at stake in the strife between the Theban princes. Even if one of the cousins had succeeded in killing his rival in the grove, he would not have been significantly nearer to winning the lady since neither Theseus nor Emelye was aware of the situation. Here, however, Theseus can declare that "Arcite of Thebes shal have Emelie, / That by his fortune hath hire faire ywonne" (2658–59). Destruction of noble blood, the probable outcome of the fight in the grove, has been avoided by the efforts of the struggling knights who diffuse and defuse the animal violence of Palamon and Arcite within the orderly framework of the rules devised for the tournament by Theseus. The need for violent competition has been both satisfied and controlled "By force and eek by composicioun," a line that analyzes the components of Theseus's apparently successful institutional solution. In addition, it seems likely that the Theban question, with all its potential for further destruction of noble blood, is well on its way to being settled, at least for Athens, by the alliance of a prince of the Theban royal house with the sister-in-law of the Athenian duke. Theseus has been able to wrest a complex and satisfying human meaning from the blind forces of human conflict and chance encounter with which the tale began. He has controlled fortune by making a space in which all the possible dangerous chances have apparently been allotted safe meanings, and this fact gives point to his announcement of Arcite's victory as well as to the joy of the spectators: "Anon ther is a noyse of peple bigonne / For joye of this, so loude and heighe withalle / It semed that the lystes sholde falle" (2660–62).

But the last line of the passage describing this triumphant celebration is uneasily reminiscent of the temple of Mars, where the wind of violence shakes the very edifice built to contain and celebrate it (1975–94). It is as if something inherent in the tournament itself threatens the stability it is trying to achieve. The reasons for this uneasiness are not far to seek, and they have relatively little to do with the fortuitous disaster that is about to befall Arcite—that fall is a different problem and poses a different sort of threat to order. It should be remembered that in socializing the strife between Palamon and Arcite, Theseus has given up to others a large part of his original life-and-death power over the cousins. He has let that power out of his own hands for what the poem shows to be good reasons, but there remains something ambitious and risky about his having done so. The elaborate edifice of temples, tournaments, and philosophical speculation that the tale erects on the quarrel is a bit gratuitous—Theseus and the Knight clearly intend to do more than settle the affair of Palamon and Arcite in the quickest and simplest manner. The risks this ambition takes arise from the necessity of allowing others to have a hand in determining the solution, especially given the character of those others. The feral and competitive urge to mastery of the heroic character is for the Knight its fundamental nature, a psychological bedrock to which the tale returns again and again, and such a character is not easily dissuaded from bloody arguments, bloody occasions, and the judgment of blood. The animal imagery applied to Palamon and Arcite in the tournament and the fact that the symbolically weighted Lygurge and Emetrius are singled out by name as being borne down in the struggle to subdue Palamon and separate the cousins testify to the power of the impulse to destroy a rival in the Thebans, a power measured in part by the force needed to deflect it. It is true that Palamon and Arcite have stronger motives for killing than the other participants in the tournament, but it is also true that as long as they both remain alive, *someone* might feel that the outcome is not really and finally decisive.[6]

Such a disappointed partisan of Palamon turns up immediately in the person of Venus, whose reaction qualifies and undercuts the sup-

6. These considerations seem to me to qualify Aers's criticism of Theseus's modification of the rules of the tournament to spare the shedding of noble blood:

This modification cannot be taken as a rejection of his former life, since he determines to continue with the tournament he has planned and the decision to settle the question of whom Emily should marry by sheer violence—rather than

posedly universal joy of the cheering people by reminding us of the presence of unresolved tensions in the outcome of the tournament and the potential presence in the audience of those who want their wills and may be moved to take further steps to get them:

> What kan now faire Venus doon above?
> What seith she now? What dooth this queene of love,
> But wepeth so, for wantynge of hir wille,
> Til that hir teeres in the lystes fille?
> She seyde, "I am ashamed, doutelees."
> Saturnus seyde, "Doghter, hoold thy pees!
> Mars hath his wille, his kynght hath al his boone,
> And, by myn heed, thow shalt been esed soone."
> (2663-70)

I do not think there can be any question here of taking the gods seriously as gods. In keeping with the overall tendency of the poem and the achievement of Part III, they come before us in all-too-human form as representatives of what the feelings of a segment of the real human audience of the tournament may be. Venus is concerned for her honor, as knights are, not about the place of love in a cosmic scheme. Once again the perspective taken on the gods is double since the comic detail of Venus's tears falling in the lists presumably means that it has begun to rain—no doubt the result of a planetary conjunction that a better-informed scholar than I might dig out of the astrological information the poem supplies—and that the ground is becoming dangerously slippery. But this event belongs to a very different order of causes—which is why the line is jarring—one difficult to reconcile comfortably with the psychological and partisan involvement of Venus and Saturn as spectators and plotters.

In fact, the *cause* of Arcite's fall is rather perfunctorily handled here and is subordinated to a consideration of its effects. We are told that he takes off his helm "for to shewe his face" (2677) and rides around the

---

by consulting the oracles, drawing lots, detailed inquiry into the knights, or by letting Emily do what she wants and reject them both, preventing the violence altogether.

(*Creative Imagination*, 180)

Given the violent world of the tale, which Aers himself describes admirably, the ineffectuality of any of these alternatives seems patent, calculated to increase strife rather than allay it.

arena "Lokynge upward upon this Emelye" (2679), which inspired in Neuse the curiously moralistic reflection that Arcite should have looked where he was going ("The Knight," 309). The point is surely how natural and harmless these actions are, and yet how disproportionately deadly they can be in the wrong circumstances. The "furie infernal" (2684) who "causes" Arcite's horse to shy is a mere device, conspicuously a *furia ex machina* from the old books[7] and the last appearance of the discredited divine machinery in the poem: the gods do not contribute as speakers and doers to the poem's resolution. What engages the Knight is the physical and emotional horror of what Arcite undergoes: the harshly realistic description of the damage inflicted by his own saddle-bow, his color "As blak . . . as any cole or crowe, / So was the blood yronnen in his face" (2692–93), the sudden transformation of his armor from a protection to a burden and a danger that must be cut off him (2696), and the final chilling detail that "he was yet in memorie and alyve, / And alwey criyinge after Emelye" (2698–99).

The Knight's harsh imagining of Arcite trapped in his suddenly and ruinously broken body, fully conscious and still desiring the lady he has just won and lost, is so intense and compelling that the sudden shift of perspective and tone in the lines that immediately follow is genuinely and deliberately shocking: "Duc Theseus, with al his compaignye, / Is comen hoom to Atthens his citee, / With alle blisse and greet solempnitee" (2700–2702). No less surprising is the way the Knight leaves Arcite and his plight in suspension for fully forty lines to complete his account of Theseus's feasting of the other contestants and their final departure from Athens. The voice shifts its attention from a private misery to a public celebration in a way that puts a strain on the speaker and on us—as well as on the participants. The celebration is of course haunted by what has happened to Arcite, especially in the early part of the account of it where we see the participants trying to

---

7. This fury is interesting. Her meaning is at least double. As a patent pagan invention and a piece of conspicuous plot machinery she is an index of the *absurdity* of what happens in the grim existentialist sense, a kind of tag for the senselessness of the occurrence, and her association with Saturn strengthens this aspect of her meaning. At the same time furies are traditionally spirits of blood revenge, allied with the lust of the kin to exact blood recompense for any slight or defeat. In this aspect the fury keeps alive the atmosphere of unsettled heroic contention in its more primitive forms that Venus also suggests and that continues to haunt the tournament in what follows. And of course she is a woman, whatever that means.

persuade themselves that Arcite will be healed (2705–6). But as he continues, the speaker concentrates more and more on the other knights voicing their relief that no one else is irreparably injured and trying to remedy their own hurts "for they wolde hir lymes have" (2714).

What is being asserted here is the necessity, and the difficulty, of attending to the ordering of public life in the face of individual misfortune. The difficulty is measured by the strain in the ordering of the narrative and the shock of the shift from Arcite's cries to bliss and "revel al the longe nyght" (2717). The necessity appears in the account of the purposes of Theseus's feasting:

> For which this noble duc, as he wel kan,
> Conforteth and honoureth every man,
> And made revel al the longe nyght
> Unto the straunge lordes, as was right.
> Ne ther was holden no disconfitynge
> But as a justes or a tourneiynge;
> For soothly ther was no disconfiture.
> For fallyng nys nat but an aventure,
> Ne to be lad by force unto the stake
> Unyolden, and with twenty knyghtes take,
> O persone allone, withouten mo,
> And haryed forth by arme, foot, and too,
> And eke his steede dryven forth with staves
> With footmen, bothe yemen and eek knaves—
> It nas arretted hym no vileynye;
> Ther may no man clepen it cowardye.
> For which anon duc Theseus leet crye,
> To stynten alle rancour and envye,
> The gree as wel of o syde as of oother,
> And eyther syde ylik as ootheres brother;
> And yaf hem yiftes after hir degree,
> And fully heeld a feeste dayes three,
> And conveyed the kynges worthily
> Out of his toun a journee largely.
> And hoom wente every man the righte way.
> Ther was namoore but "Fare wel, have good day!"
>
> (2715–40)

This passage gives the clearest expression in the poem thus far to the *precariousness* of what the tournament has achieved because the voice is so obviously haunted by the opposite of what it is trying to assert:

that the tournament is over and all has gone smoothly. The voicing of the passage is peculiar in that at "For fallyng nys nat but an aventure" it begins to shift from simple description to conspicuous, rhetorical assertion. The speaker seems to be trying to convince someone of a set of dubious propositions by piling up too much evidence. Since one of the dubious propositions is that Palamon's defeat was an "aventure," a chance occurrence of the same class as Arcite's fall, one can see how it might cause trouble whoever offers it. The problem is not, as it will be later, that the senselessness of Arcite's "aventure" renders human effort and achievement meaningless but that it is to be feared that the issues of winning and losing, the connection between victory and heroic worth, will not go away. Palamon lost and he did not die, and the specter of what a friendly tournament might turn into if someone were disposed to assert, despite all the evidence to the contrary, that his defeat is evidence of "vileynye" or "cowardye" is close to the surface. This danger is especially pressing because such an imputation could easily spill over from Palamon onto his unsuccessful defenders, who consequently must not be allowed to suppose that their failure is anything more than an "aventure."

Theseus's dismissal of the two hundred knights is the culmination of the theme I have been tracing, the fragility of human institutions—of society—in the face of specifically human resistance to sociability and order—to civilization. Throughout Part IV the Knight's description registers Theseus's constant vigilance to anticipate, contain, and assuage the contentious violence of heroic honor, the Mars in men. Once again Theseus forestalls occasions of "rancour and envye" by his powers of persuasion and by staging demonstrations of the equal honor of both sides: ceremonies of gift giving and feasting that proclaim "the gree as wel of o syde as of oother." There is something of a sigh of relief in the "Fare wel, have good day" that concludes his ceremonial conveyance of "the kynges"—Lygurge and Emetrius—a full day's ride out of town.

This final act of balancing the two sides might also be seen as the culmination of the balancing and equalizing of Palamon and Arcite that is so notable a feature of the poem from its beginning and over which so much critical ink has been spilled. As the question is usually posed and debated, the issue is whether, on the one hand, Palamon and Arcite are virtually indistinguishable and of equal merit so that the problem of their relative deserts is not relevant to the tale or, on the other hand, one of them is morally superior and does or does not deserve what he gets. My own position on this question is that they are separate but equal, that is, that they are or become identifiably different personalities or dispositions within the larger economy of chivalric-heroic consciousness but that this differentiation has no *ethical* significance for the outcome of the tale. So much should be clear already from my analysis of their prayers in Part III, and I will add here, in anticipation of matters to come, that I think the whole question of ethical superiority or inferiority is a misleading approach to the tale because the Knight does not believe in poetic justice. What interests me more at the moment, however, is that like other things in the poem, the question of the equality of Palamon and Arcite becomes in Part IV an active issue Theseus must address. Whatever the truth of their merits and deserts, Theseus has an interest in making them look as equal as possible to ensure that the tournament will appear to be a fair contest and himself "[a] trewe juge, and no partie" (2657). His efforts to achieve this appearance are evident in the way he organizes the procession to the lists and the order of the tournament, and the Knight abets him in his own descriptions of the taking of Palamon (2641–51, 2723–30).

By contrast, but for the same reasons, once the tournament is over, Theseus also has an interest in being able to say that some decisive difference between the two cousins has been established. One might think that demonstrating a difference could be left to the contestants themselves, but in the passage I have been considering it emerges that the outcome cannot be allowed to reflect ethically on the characters of the two princes or their followers for reasons having to do with social stability. That is why Theseus proclaims that Arcite has won Emelye "by his fortune" when it is obvious that the efforts of his knights must have had something to do with it and that the decision is actually reached, as the Knight says, "By force and eek by composicioun." The Knight's cajoling and uneasy tone in urging the same position in the description of the aftermath of the tournament reflects his own appreciation of the importance of adopting it and at the same time his awareness of its flimsiness. As with the later First Mover speech, the poem has anticipated its critics by setting up a situation—and making an issue of it—in which it is simultaneously necessary to differentiate between Palamon and Arcite and to keep them equal. But the poem also shows, as the critics generally do not, that there are no good—that is, objective—answers to the question and that its resolution, since it cannot be "solved," depends on directing attention to whichever of the contradictory aspects of the situation it is tactically desirable to stress at a given moment. We are thus directed not to the *interpretation*—the "actual" difference or equality between the knights—but to the *interpreter*, to the Knight and Theseus. We focus on the extent to which it is only the latter's vigilance, quickness, and resourcefulness, the sense of when and how to employ authority or diplomacy, that keeps the institutional framework and the social order that depends on it intact.

The Knight's account of the tournament is based on and develops his demystifying description and analysis of the lists earlier in the poem. His awareness of the importance of human agency in constituting and preserving the framework of society, most fully developed in Part III, carries over into Part IV in his revised view of the heroism of Theseus and the pressures with which it must deal. Precisely because justice and the institutions whereby it is dispensed are not supported and guaranteed by some external and objective cosmic order, Theseus must work hard to give his tournament the look of order and authority. Justice, like other human institutions, is for the Knight a human meaning, an *agreement* among men that is easily broken. Hence Theseus must continually stage and dramatize his impartiality so as to avoid the imputation of having a partisan interest in the outcome of the contest and thus becoming part of the struggle to establish a meaning rather than the arbiter of that struggle. He must array himself as a god enthroned because he has no real god behind him to guarantee his authority. The Knight makes this clear by the attention he pays to Theseus's facework, in particular his attention to what the labor of ordering costs the duke. The cost is measured not so much in the failure of Theseus's plan to settle the quarrel between Palamon and Arcite—though that is obviously a factor—as in the weight of responsibility for managing every detail of the conduct of the tournament and its aftermath, the flexibility, foresight, and imperturbability he must continually maintain whether he wants to or not. Like the Knight, Theseus may well want to attend to Arcite, but his public responsibilities dictate that he forgo his private grief until it is safe to indulge it.

This is obviously a different Theseus from the authoritarian, if benevolent, despot of the first half of the poem, and in fact a more heroic one. Because so much more is demanded of him than the straightforward Creon bashing of Part I, and because he has to exercise

self-control as well as the control of others in the interests of an order
he must put before his own will, Theseus is a more serious and responsible figure and a more realistic and impressive image of the chivalric
ideal. His actions in the first section of Part IV provide an example of
what human responsibility for human order entails and of an achievement, limited as it is, that is more valuable to the Knight than conquest.
The threats to human order that men themselves pose, and that therefore with sufficient skill and self-discipline men should be able to
control, Theseus has controlled. What such a hero can do against
contingencies no man can anticipate remains to be seen.

When at last the Knight does return to Arcite, his concentration on
the facts of dying is merciless:

> Swelleth the brest of Arcite, and the soore
> Encreesseth at his herte moore and moore.
> The clothered blood, for any lechecraft,
> Corrupteth, and is in his bouk ylaft,
> That neither veyne-blood, ne ventusynge,
> Ne drynke of herbes may ben his helpynge.
> The vertu expulsif, or animal,
> Fro thilke vertu cleped natural
> Ne may the venym voyden ne expelle.
> The pipes of his longes gonne to swelle,
> And every lacerte in his brest adoun
> Is shent with venym and corrupcioun.
> Him gayneth neither, for to gete his lif,
> Vomyt upward, ne dounward laxatif.
> Al is tobrosten thilke regioun;
> Nature hath now no dominacioun.
> And certeinly, ther Nature wol nat wirche,
> Far wel phisik! go ber the man to chirche!
> This al and som, that Arcita moot dye.
>
> (2743-61)

The technical and scientific language of anatomy and medicine con-
tributes something to the unsentimental tone of the description, but
insofar as such language might imply the consolations offered by a
scientific understanding of terrible natural facts, it is overcome as
surely as medicine itself by the failure of Arcite's *vis naturalis*. The
ugliness of what is happening to Arcite's body keeps punching through
the Latin terms, as when we are made to see just what is meant
physically by "vertu expulsif": "Vomyt upward ne dounward laxa-
tif." The colloquial English words that lace the description—"bouk,"

"shente"—and the almost flippant dismissal that concludes it contribute to the effect. There is something deliberately cold, "realistic," and held back here, something of the clinical detachment of Homer, whose works Chaucer presumably did not know. This kind of description is not a heroic convention in any tradition available to the poem. If the temple of Mars is any indication, it is something the Knight has seen: the reality of fatal injury stripped of chivalric glamorizing, stripped almost of any *meaning* beyond the process itself, the insignificant horror of a senseless accident.

The Knight withholds the imputation of significance from the facts of Arcite's dying in part to give that privilege to Arcite himself and let his hero *be* a hero under the most demanding circumstances. Arcite is allowed to feel and state the futility of his life in words that have always resonated for readers throughout the poem, and rightly so:

> Naught may the woful spirit in myn herte
> Declare o point of alle my sorwes smerte
> To yow, my lady, that I love moost,
> But I biquethe the servyce of my goost
> To yow aboven every creature,
> Syn that my lyf may no lenger dure.
> Allas, the wo! Allas, the peynes stronge,
> That I for yow have suffred, and so longe!
> Allas, the deeth! Allas, myn Emelye!
> Allas, departynge of oure compaignye!
> Allas, myn hertes queene! Allas, my wyf,
> Myn hertes lady, endere of my lyf!
> What is this world? What asketh men to have?
> Now with his love, now in his colde grave
> Allone, withouten any compaignye.
> Fare wel, my sweete foo, myn Emelye!
>   (2765–80)

The language of this speech is highly conventional, both as a philosophical complaint and as a love lament. It is reminiscent of the long Boethian complaints of Palamon and Arcite in Part I as well as of their more courtly set pieces scattered through the poem. Here of course such language is earned in a way it has not been previously, transformed and deepened by the context of its utterance. Baffled by a sorrow and bitterness he cannot speak, Arcite falls back on the conventions that have served his aspirations, his folly, and his self-deceptions. Both the continuing idealism and the pathetic emptiness of his situation resound in "I biquethe the servyce of my goost," a service the lady has even less chance of knowing and rewarding than she did "the peynes stronge, / That I for yow have suffred, and so longe!" Arcite's situation also, however, gives new point and bite to conventional courtly ways of characterizing women. With "endere of my lyf" and "my sweete foo" Arcite comes closer, in the circumstances, to blaming Emelye for his desire and its outcome than he has at any other time. On that score at least we cannot feel that he has learned much more about the world than the grim experiential truth behind the language he used so unthinkingly before, that human beings are "Allone, withouten any compaignye" and that there is nothing outside them that is constrained to answer to human aspirations and achievement.[8]

But within the masculine ethic of the poem if nothing else will give meaning to a man's life, he can still, with the cooperation of other men and women—the human community—try to confer it himself. It is Arcite's heroism as the poem defines it that, radically limited as he is and in the face of the nothingness to which he goes, he chooses to try to make his death mean more than absurdity and despair. Drawing back from his bitterness, he gets ahold of himself for the rest of his brief life:

> And softe taak me in youre armes tweye,
> For love of God, and herkneth what I seye.
>   I have heer with my cosyn Palamon
> Had strif and rancour many a day agon
> For love of yow, and for my jalousye.
> And Juppiter so wys my soule gye,
> To speken of a servaunt proprely,
> With alle circumstaunces trewely—
> That is to seyen, trouthe, honour, kynghthede,
> Wysdom, humblesse, estaat, and heigh kynrede,
> Fredom, and al that longeth to that art—
> So Juppiter have of my soule part,
> As in this world right now ne knowe I non
> So worthy to ben loved as Palamon,
> That serveth yow, and wol doon al his lyf.
> And if that evere ye shul ben a wyf,
> Foryet nat Palamon, the gentil man.

> (2781–97)

8. Salter, Introduction to *The Knight's Tale*, has an illuminating discussion of Arcite's death, 28–31.

Again little has changed in Arcite's fundamental understanding of the world. Emelye especially remains, as she has been throughout the poem, an *objet petit a*. She is still primarily a pretext for relations between Palamon and Arcite, the unconsulted medium first of their competition and now of their reconciliation, and the Knight is, as I shall argue shortly, not unaware of this. But it is nonetheless true that nothing becomes Arcite's life like his leaving of it. Constrained as he is, even naive as he is,[9] Arcite gives up his claim to Emelye and his enmity with Palamon in the name of those values, "trouthe, honour, knyghthede" and the rest, that he asserts and affirms as more important than his quarrel and his death. By doing so, he gives his death meaning in terms of those values. Like Theseus, though more openly and more dramatically, Arcite sacrifices his desires, his projects, and even his death to the maintenance of a larger human community. He takes human responsibility for a human meaning by trying to affirm a continuity that will last beyond him.

That this perspective—one might as well call it existentialist since that is its closest modern equivalent[10]—is the compelling one for the Knight, certainly more compelling at this point than some cosmic order or divine reward for human virtue, is firmly established by his account of Arcite's passing:

> His spirit chaunged hous and wente ther,
> As I cam nevere, I kan nat tellen wher.
> Therfore I stynte; I nam no divinistre;
> Of soules fynde I nat in this registre,
> *Ne me ne list thilke opinions to telle*
> *Of hem, though that they writen wher they dwelle.*
> Arcite is coold, ther Mars his soule gye!
> Now wol I speken forth of Emelye.
> (2809–16, emphasis added)[11]

9. He is naive, for example, about Jupiter. As Salter points out, "It has not been possible for Arcite to learn the full lesson of divine malice" (Introduction to *The Knight's Tale*, 29).

10. It seems probable that Arcite himself is not a classic existentialist hero because it seems probable that he believes in the transcendent value of his act. The probabilities shift when one considers him from the point of view of the tale as a whole and its narrator, as I go on to suggest in the text.

11. In *Chaucer and Menippean Satire* F. Anne Payne notes this passage as an instance of the Knight's "faintly macabre Menippean humor" (252), part of a set of attitudes she characterizes more fully at 244–45.

This is the Knight's most important, because most direct, statement in the tale of the priorities I have tried to show him maintaining throughout it. He is resolute in cutting off all consideration of consolatory possibilities in higher realms. He knows quite well what philosophers and preachers have to say about these matters, but that is not where his interests lie. What is important about the passage is that it keeps us *here*, in the human world, where higher purposes, if any, remain inscrutable, no transcendent justice that makes human sense appears plainly, and the human survivors have to pick up the pieces. The Knight makes it clear that this is his own choice: he would not wish, he says, to tell of the fate of departed souls if it were in his sources, which he says it is not, though we know it is. If "Chaucer" does not follow Boccaccio—and Arcite's spirit—because he chose to use the rest of the passage from the *Teseide* on which this passage is based in that terrible moment when Troilus looks down to laugh at all *our* woe (*Troilus and Criseyde* 5.1814–27), the Knight insists that all such flights above the human situation are not his concern. Our woe and what we do about it without help from beyond *is* his concern. Here we are in the human world, and here we will remain to the end of the tale: the First Mover is something Theseus tells us about, not something we see. It is within this deliberately chosen framework of human actions and meanings that the Knight places his poignant image of Arcite's heroism, which, like Theseus's, is the more heroic for being enacted against such limited and limiting possibilities, for being something harder to do than win a tournament.

Of course, Arcite is lucky. He gets to make his single magnificent gesture and pass on, dying young and with his reputation intact, as Theseus notes in a curious passage in the First Mover speech (3047–56). The extreme exigency of his situation makes possible the *purity* of his chivalric idealism because he does not have to live on to deal with its consequences. Something of the naiveté of his response is measured by the fact that Emelye's marriage to Palamon is not within her choice, as he seems to expect it should be (2796–97), and does not take place until other, political considerations make it expedient. For the Knight, the doing of chivalry is ultimately something that does not and cannot rest in single gestures, and the real task for a maker and sustainer of order lies not in dying, however gloriously and generously, but in going on. But this attitude does not mean that the more "mature" and responsible perspective is easy for the Knight to maintain or that he is not moved by Arcite's tragedy and triumph—he is moved, perhaps too much. Palamon and Arcite function throughout the tale, and nowhere more than in its conclusion, as representatives or impersonations of the Knight's own enchantment with, and attraction to, a pure and mystified version of the chivalric ideal and its conventions. They are the innocent core of the more tough-minded and realistic attitude that comes to be embodied in Theseus. As I have shown, the Knight is genuinely ambivalent about this pure ideal: he loves and admires it as much as he appreciates its danger and its folly. The extent and depth of the Knight's identification with Arcite and what he represents is evident not only in his moving account of the young man's death but also in the way he frames it and reacts to it and in the effort he makes to control his own tendency to despair over it.

This latter tendency comes out most clearly in the speech of Egeus, which the Knight appropriates conspicuously as his own. The speech comes at the end of a passage (2817–36) that describes the grief of the survivors, particularly the weeping of women, which the Knight treats summarily and a little impatiently: "What helpeth it to tarien forth the day / To tellen how [Emelye] weep bothe eve and morwe?" (2820–21). The effect is that of a voice pushing aside inappropriate and useless responses to an occurrence that cannot be helped and must be dealt with more adequately and sternly than by womanish tears—there is something here of the tough, unsentimental tone used to describe Arcite's injuries. The initial effect of the end of this passage is perhaps that the more adequate way is to be found in Egeus:

> No man myghte gladen Theseus,
> Savynge his olde fader Egeus,
> That knew this worldes transmutacioun,
> As he hadde seyn it chaunge bothe up and doun,
> Joye after wo, and wo after gladnesse,
> And shewed hym ensamples and liknesse.
>
> (2837–42)

These lines promise a more distanced, philosophical, and consoling perspective, based on wide experience of "This worldes transmutacioun," that will put Arcite's death in place and in proportion. But the part of Egeus's speech the Knight gives us is shorn of its "ensamples" and of the "muchel moore" Theseus's father said to the people "that they sholde hem reconforte" (2850–52). In the form we have it in, it is notoriously problematic,[12] and it is difficult to see what gladdened Theseus:

> "Right as ther dyed nevere man," quod he,
> "That he ne lyvede in erthe in som degree,
> Right so ther lyvede never man," he seyde,
> "In al this world, that som tyme he ne deyde.
> This world nys but a thurghfare ful of wo,
> And we been pilgrymes, passynge to and fro.
> Deeth is an ende of every worldly soore."
>
> (2843–49)

The Knight purports to edit Egeus's speech down to what he takes as its essential message, and that message is one of despair.[13] The world and human life are a thoroughfare full of woe bounded only by the implacable recurrence of death, a perspective enforced by the tautological form of Egeus's aphorism and the speech as a whole. The image of human life as a pilgrimage loses its potential consoling power because the goal that would make good the labor of the journey becomes simply death itself, and in context the last line is close to counsel to suicide. What in its original form, as Egeus delivered it, might have been something more like the First Mover speech is handled by the Knight so as to bring out both the endless labor and the essential absurdity of human life and effort. If Egeus occupies the position of Saturn in a system of structural parallels between the gods and the characters that some criticism has seen in the tale,[14] he does so in the revisionary mode of parts III and IV. That is, he is an instance of a saturnian mind, one that views and constitutes the world in this despairing way. As such, he is also a part of the Knight, a locus of the narrator's darkest imagining and a spokesman for the vision of an indifferent, casually malignant universe that presses on the tale from

12. See, for example, Salter, Introduction to *The Knight's Tale*, 30, and Neuse, "The Knight," 304.

13. In terms of the source, the speech of Egeus is a new addition: in Boccaccio (*Teseide* 9.9–12) what he says is briefly paraphrased, and the point is made that he cannot comfort Theseus and that no one pays him any heed. Thus in the *Knight's Tale* Egeus is given more weight as a character but in support of a more pessimistic vision.

14. For example, Muscatine, *Chaucer and the French Tradition*, 178ff; Neuse, "The Knight," 304 (with schematic diagram); and Kean, *Making of English Poetry*, 2:5. The notion has become a commonplace.

its beginning. This is what lurks behind the speeches of Palamon and Arcite in Part I and behind the anomalous features of the temples and the gods in Part III. This is what has finally found voice in the tale as a human statement—no grinning Saturn, merely an old man telling what he has seen—about the meaning of Arcite's death and the meaninglessness of human life.

Arcite and Egeus together outline a central tension in the consciousness of the Knight and form one set of poles within and between which his ambivalence moves. This is the characteristic ambivalence of what I have called the "masculine" imagination. Arcite (along with Palamon) gives a voice to the human hunger for transcendence, for permanent and stable meaning and value on which ideals and heroism can be based. Throughout the poem the Theban cousins embody this hunger in the mode of naive belief. As we have seen, the Knight's criticism of them consistently fastens on their projections of order, stability, and meaning onto gods and destinies. The Knight is disenchanted, in the neutral, Weberian sense, as the princes are not. His disenchantment is what allows him to see that the things Palamon and Arcite believe to be objective and independent entities—honor and "trouthe" as well as Venus and Mars—are in fact human institutions. Part of his distrust of such institutions is based on the way they encourage men and women to believe in them as metaphysical facts and thereby distract attention from human responsibility for keeping order in the self and in society.

But the Knight is not the Manciple, nor yet is he the Pardoner. He does not simply debunk the institutions he distrusts; he revises them, and that means, among other things, that he *keeps them alive* in the positive sense of active and intentional preservation. One reason for this conservative impulse that runs in tandem with the critical one is the Knight's respect for the forces of disorder in the psyche and the world that human institutions manage to organize and contain. The need for such forms becomes all the more urgent when they are seen as the only things standing between society and the violence of its members. But as the Knight sees it, the efficacy and stability of institutions like chivalry largely *depends* on their nonconscious, internalized, and mystified character, their apparent givenness, because eros, aggression, and necessity are for him incorrigible: he does not believe most people are strong enough or self-controlled enough to do without external stays against their own darker natures and against nothingness. What they feel they owe to chivalry keeps Palamon and Arcite from turning into animals in the grove, keeps the participants in the tournament from letting it become any more like the landscape of the temple of Mars than it does, and allows Arcite the heroism of his death. The presentation of Egeus suggests that the group of those who cannot do without the illusion of transcendence at times includes the Knight himself.

Egeus's speech is one of the moments in the tale—the descriptions of the temple of Mars and of Arcite's funeral pyre are two others—when the Knight comes closest to the Pardoner in feeling the pull of the despairing form of "masculine" disenchantment, the conviction that the loss of transcendence makes the world and life in it worthless, and like the Pardoner, the Knight puts this despair in the voice of an old man.[15] One reason Arcite can die as he does is that he does not know what Egeus knows, what he might have learned "In age, if that ye so longe abyde" (VI, 747). To keep going, the Knight needs those aspects of himself, the Palamon and Arcite in him, that are stirred and moved by "trouthe, honour, knyghthede, / Wysdom, humblesse, estaat, and heigh kynrede, / Fredom, and al that longeth to that art," just as he needs the more experienced and skeptical perspective of which Egeus is both a representative and a distortion. The Knight's generally more balanced and competent relation to his world is dependent in part on his ability to move comfortably between these aspects of himself, as compared to the Pardoner's self-destructive ambivalence toward the three rioters and the Old Man. The task facing the Knight at the end of the tale is the same as the task facing Theseus: one might even put it that his task is to be Theseus, that is, to find and sustain a balance between a too-innocent and mystified faith in the efficacy of human constructions and a despairing denial of all human value—between Palamon and Egeus.

Such, at least in outline, is the structure and deployment of the "masculine" imagination in the Knight and his tale and the relation of that imagination to the psychological and institutional pressures it keeps alive and has to deal with. There is still to be considered, how-

15. The association of old men with this general perspective is obviously common in Chaucer. Pandarus is an example of it in some of his moods (*Troilus and Criseyde* 2.393–99), and the Reeve makes himself into a walking embodiment of it.

ever, the question of the "feminine" identifications I have previously traced, the bisexuality whose expression is most fully bound up in the Knight's attitudes toward Emelye. Let me begin with a problem in the castigation (as editors call it), the making chaste, of that unruly and lawless feminine body, the text.[16] The relation of one couplet in the description of Arcite's triumphal ride around the arena, printed by Robinson as lines 2681–82, is problematic in multiple ways. It does not appear in the two "best" manuscripts, Ellesmere and Hengwrt, though it is in Corpus and other copies of the tale. Almost all modern editions print it, apparently in tacit agreement with Robinson that the lines "seem to be by Chaucer, though he may have intended to cancel them" (in Chaucer, *Works*, 2d ed., 681). I do not pretend to know what the real reasons for this textual situation are, but I can see why a question about the appropriateness of the couplet might arise since it brings a peculiar and rather sour tone into the account of Arcite's triumph. The hero looks up at Emelye, "And she agayn hym cast a freendlich ye /(*For wommen, as to speken in comune, / Thei folwen alle the favour of Fortune*)" (2680–82, emphasis added). I think the couplet is genuine, though I can also see why Chaucer (or a scribe) might, to phrase it tendentiously, have been ambivalent about having it in the tale. I think it is genuine because it reintroduces into the tale a kind of disparagement of women that was already present in the description of Theseus's pity "Of wommen, for they wepen evere in oon" (1771) and that returns more densely in the description of the grief at Arcite's death:

> What helpeth it to tarien forth the day
> To tellen how she [Emelye] weep bothe eve and morwe?
> For in swich cas wommen have swich sorwe,
> Whan that hir housbondes ben from hem ago,
> That for the moore part they sorwen so,
> Or elles fallen in swich maladye
> That at the laste certeinly they dye.
> . . . .
> "Why woldestow be deed," thise wommen crye,
> "And haddest gold ynough, and Emelye?"
> (2820–26; 2835–36)

16. I am grateful to Stephanie Jed of the University of California, San Diego, for pointing out the use of the term in editing and its etymology, in a lecture on the Latin text on Lucretia of the Italian humanist Colluccio Salutati delivered at the University of

The textually problematic couplet seems, obscurely, to be *blaming* Emelye for favoring Arcite and Fortune; the other two passages point to the weakness and lack of self-control of women's grief and to a kind of moral and philosophical crassness in their understanding of tragedies like this one. What they all have in common, perhaps, is the implication that women are not capable of a properly stoic fortitude in the face of the vagaries of Fortune, a properly masculine and heroic indifference to the course of external events. In all three instances, however, I also notice a tendency to move away from Emelye as an individual as quickly as possible and treat her as merely an instance of generic feminine characteristics that amounts, conspicuously, to a refusal to let her speak her feelings in her own voice.

Indeed, to begin to speculate on what Emelye's feelings might actually be in these two instances, given what we saw of her and heard her say in Part III, is to begin to understand the problem. Her friendly look at Arcite (which is in all texts of the tale) may represent a way of trying to come to terms with a difficult situation in which, for example, Emelye must begin to think of how to live with a man whom she will now have to marry and who may or may not be the one of the cousins who "moost desireth" her. If the problematic couplet is allowed to remain, it actually makes it more likely that we will notice Emelye's behavior and wonder about it because it singles her out in the scene in the very act of trying to reduce her to an instance of typical femininity. Similarly, though women may all weep both eve and morrow or pine away when their husbands are gone from them, Emelye was not, as far as we know, actually married to Arcite when he died.[17] We do know that she did not want to be an occasion of strife, but we also know that she did not want to be married.[18] Can her grief, which is surely real, be entirely unmixed with relief?

California, Santa Cruz, in 1985. Carolyn Dinshaw of the University of California, Berkeley, is completing a book on Chaucer that documents the pervasiveness of the image of the text as a female body in the Middle Ages.

17. Though Theseus does call Emelye Arcite's "wyf " in the First Mover speech, the *Knight's Tale* does not reproduce the deathbed marriage that takes place in the *Teseide*.

18. Chaucer's changes from Boccaccio keep this issue much more alive in the *Knight's Tale* than it is in the *Teseide*, where Emelia is much more involved with eros, much more flirtatious and self-conscious from the beginning, and hence much more likely to be willing to love.

What the Knight seems to be trying to do in these passages is to convert Emelye into a feminine stereotype to avoid considering her personal situation too closely.[19] What works against this conversion and makes the stereotyping feel uncomfortable is our memory (and his) of how intensely and sympathetically he imagined Emelye and her circumstances in Part III. I think the Knight himself feels uncomfortable and communicates his discomfort in the somewhat rushed and forced character of his speaking and its exaggerated machismo. At some level he knows he is doing her an injustice by suppressing her voice. Since that voice is also one of his, we are again dealing with a character who is also part of the Knight. As elsewhere in the *Canterbury Tales*, the feminine here represents the claims of private experience over against public necessities. The Knight clearly understands the commodity status of women in chivalric society, and he has shown himself able to imagine sympathetically what that status costs women in general and Emelye in particular. She is thus a carrier for him of the intimation that those costs are too high and that the entire chivalric institutional structure may not be worth what it demands of individuals. But in Part IV what is at stake is the preservation and maintenance of public order, for which it is necessary that a fiction of Emelye's private identification with her public role be created and sustained. In the interests of that fiction Emelye's private feelings will have to be sacrificed, as will the Knight's sympathy with her. This is not a simple, unconsidered male chauvinism but a complex and considered one, a choice of priorities. The structures of social order in the Knight's world are also the structures of male domination, and when order, itself sufficiently fragile as he sees it, is threatened, its preservation is more important than the private feelings of women or the Knight himself. For him, injustice is inherent in the nature of the world and of society, and the question is always one of choosing which injustices must be redressed and which will simply have to be lived with.

The choices the Knight finally makes in the tale constitute the feminine according to the general institutional and psychological pat-

19. Similarly, in the description of Arcite's funeral Emelye is made primarily a functionary in the ritual, an agent of custom "as was the gyse" (2941). The Knight says he will not discuss "how she swowned whan men made the fyr, / Ne what she spak, ne what was hir desir" (2943–44). This passing over of Emelye is again conspicuous and again a little nervous.

tern I have analyzed in Part II of this book as something that has to be repressed in the individual and suppressed in society to preserve the chivalric world and its institutions. The instance of the *Knight's Tale* is particularly useful in understanding this process because it so plainly demonstrates that the pattern is the result of practical *choices* on the part of individuals who both make use of institutions and actively keep them in existence as a result of that use.[20] The Knight's gender identity is not something he makes up all by himself but something he chooses and *keeps on choosing* in the face of other possibilities, roles, and identifications. The consequences of that choice are as fully social as they are personal, involving the adoption of a set of procedures and attitudes for dealing with others as well as for conceiving and conducting the self. It is this duality that I have tried to express in the title of this part, "The Institution of the Subject," hoping to catch by it the way the subject in Chaucer is understood and presented both as something transpersonal, socially constructed, and institutional and as something that has to be continually instituted, kept in existence by its own activity.

20. This double activity is what Giddens terms the duality of structure: "Structure as the medium and outcome of the conduct it recursively organizes; the structural properties of social systems do not exist outside of action but are chronically implicated in its production and reproduction" (*Constitution of Society*, 374). See also *Central Problems*, 77–81.

14

Doing Knighthood

Heroic Disenchantment and the Subject of Chivalry

The language of the Sophoclean heroes surprises us by its Apollonian determinacy and lucidity. It seems to us that we can fathom their innermost being, and we are somewhat surprised that we have such a short way to go. However, once we abstract from the character of the hero as it rises to the surface and becomes visible (a character at bottom no more than a luminous shape projected onto a dark wall, that is to say, *appearance* through and through) and instead penetrate into the myth which is projected in these luminous reflections, we suddenly come up against a phenomenon which is the exact opposite of a familiar optical one. After an energetic attempt to focus on the sun, we have, by way of remedy almost, dark spots before our eyes when we turn away. Conversely, the luminous images of the Sophoclean heroes—those Apollonian masks—are the necessary productions of a deep look into the horror of nature; luminous spots, as it were, designed to cure an eye hurt by the ghastly night.

Nietzsche, *The Birth of Tragedy*

We borel men been shrympes.

Harry Bailly, in *The Monk's Prologue*,
(VII, 1955)

The Knight's description of Arcite's funeral is at first an image of noble and measured grief, fittingly expressed in forms of dignity and splendor. Theseus decides on the place to hold the ceremony in accord with its appropriateness to the young knight's career:

> That in that selve grove, swoote and grene,
> Ther as he hadde his amorouse desires,
> His compleynte, and for love his hoote fires,
> He wolde make a fyr in which the office
> Funeral he myghte al accomplice.
>
> (2860–64)

The duke has Arcite laid on a bier spread with cloth-of-gold and arrayed "of the same suyte" (2873), crowned with laurel and sur-

rounded by his weapons. The dead hero is carried in a formal procession down streets draped in black, with nothing omitted that will
make the service "The moore noble and riche in his degree" (2888).
Throughout this section the Knight's voice concentrates on visual
detail and the sequence of actions performed. There are no disruptions
of tone or decorum, and no particular need arises to reflect on where
the story is coming from: we are simply being told how Theseus went
about the stages of the "sepulture" of Arcite.

About halfway through the description, however, a sharp break
occurs—the extraordinary subverted *occupatio* in which the Knight
tells in detail for forty-seven lines what he does *not* intend to describe:

> But how the fyr was maked upon highte,
> Ne eek the names that the trees highte,
> As ook, firre, birch, aspe, alder, holm, popler,
> Wylugh, elm, plane, assh, box, chasteyn, lynde, laurer,
> Mapul, thorn, bech, hasel, ew, whippletree—
> How they weren feld shal nat be toold for me;
> Ne hou the goddes ronnen up and doun,
> Disherited of hire habitacioun,
> In which they woneden in reste and pees,
> Nymphes, fawnes and amadrides.
>
> (2919–28)

One function *occupatio* always has in the tale is to call attention to the
Knight as editor, the speaker over against the "matere," picking and
choosing from the old books: it reminds us that the Knight is neither
simply seeing nor simply making up what he narrates but *citing* it, a
complex relation that partakes of both. *Occupatio* brings the speaker
before us and breaks the transparency of the narration. This particular
instance presents the speaker to us as a man in conflict not only with
his source but with himself, obsessively continuing to describe something he also seems to feel he should not be spending so much time on.
What is the nature of this conflict?

The lines just quoted are conspicuously literary, just the sort of list
that is found in old poems—in Vergil, Ovid, Statius, Joseph of Exeter,
Guillaume de Lorris, Boccaccio, and Chaucer, for example.[1] The
speaker presents himself as someone who is conscious of what he is
telling as *like a poem*—a classical, mythological, patently fictional

---

1. See my discussion of a similar list in the *Parlement of Foules*, "Harmony of
Chaucer's *Parlement*," 21–22.

poem at that. Insofar as we become aware of him making this comment, we also become aware of him being less convinced by the action and seeing it as something unreal, bookish, and distant from his own experience outside of poetry. Part of the effect of the long *occupatio,* which continually leads us with its "ne . . . , ne . . ." structure to expect imminent closure and a new topic, is to create a tone of impatience with the details being listed, as if they were not worth attending to.

This impatience is indicative of more than just skepticism about the account of events the Knight finds in the old story; it is primarily a comment on the events themselves, that is, on the funeral ceremony as a way of coming to terms with the implications of Arcite's death. What becomes unreal to the Knight in the course of the description is the claim of all this ceremony to console, to express and then dispel grief so that all can be as it was before. As the *occupatio* proceeds, it becomes the focus of an Egeus-like despair in which all human attempts to ameliorate or conceal the intimations of meaninglessness bound up in Arcite's fate are seen as fakery and delusion, mere literary self-deception.

This effect is centered in the pyre itself, and especially in the fire, which is as strong a symbol for the Knight here as it is for the Wife of Bath, though with a different inflection. Where she comes to identify fire with psychic and sexual energy of the sort that can be drawn on to break down the barriers set up by repressive institutions, the Knight seems to use it as a focus for the worst fears of the "masculine" imagination and associates it with the kind of violence, whether human aggression or hostile necessity, that destroys order and meaning. There is something ambitious, symbolic, and larger than life about the pyre itself from the time it is first mentioned, when we are told that it "with his grene top the hevene raughte" (2915). The subsequent description of its making and consuming keeps this dimension alive and increases it. Though the list of trees is a literary commonplace, its length serves to justify the depopulation of the grove, which, at first confined to mythy woodland deities, ends in a manner both more realistic and more sinister:

> Ne hou the beestes and the briddes alle
> Fledden for fere, whan the wode was falle;
> Ne how the ground agast was of the light,
> That was nat wont to seen the sonne bright.
>   (2929–32)

There is a momentary atmosphere of something genuinely ghastly here that echoes the landscape of the temple of Mars with its broken trees, "In which ther dwelleth neither man ne best" (1976). The hyperbolic destruction of the grove has interesting and disturbing implications for the symbolic topography of the poem. At the end of Part II Theseus says, "The lystes shal I maken in this place" (1862), a detail not found in Boccaccio, where the arena predates the quarrel between Palamon and Arcite. Chaucer's alteration thus makes the lists more of an ad hoc institution created for a specific occasion and thus stresses more pointedly the power and energy of human making. But in the description of the funeral the Knight makes the destruction of the grove sound so total that we may wonder whether the lists that Theseus built on its site go up in flames too.[2] Certainly it seems appropriate to his mood here that he should leave the possibility hanging: more than wood is being burned in his mind.

The image of desolation uncovered in these lines is quickly—too quickly—covered again in those that follow. The Knight's description of the building of the pyre has an insistent, repetitious, and somewhat strained quality that derives from the movement of the voice. In the story the Greeks are merely covering the pyre, but in the telling the Knight makes it sound like someone is covering up:

> Ne how the fyr was couched first with stree,
> And thanne with drye stikkes cloven a thre,
> And thanne with grene wode and spicerye,
> And thanne with clooth of gold and with perrye,
> And gerlandes, hangynge with ful many a flour;
> The mirre, th'encens, with al so greet odour.
>
> (2933–38)

The Knight's telling embodies a feeling of discomfort, a rush to decorate the ruined grove out of existence and return to a more dignified and consoling image. But that image is once again too golden, flowery, and unconvincing. When the fire is lit, it threatens to devour the works of man, as the building of the pyre has already devoured the gods and nature:

---

2. Kolve, *Imagery of Narrative*, 130–31, has noted the spatial anomaly and gives a good account of its general symbolic bearing, though without either ascribing it to the Knight or explaining why it occurs where and when it does.

> Ne what jeweles men in the fyre caste,
> Whan that the fyr was greet and brente faste;
> Ne how somme caste hir sheeld, and soome hire spere,
> And of hire vestimentz, whiche that they were,
> And coppes fulle of wyn, and milk, and blood,
> Into the fyr, that brente as it were wood.

(2945–50)

The funeral of Arcite does not *work* for the Knight. Though he experiences a temptation to be beguiled by its noble furnishings, he also finds them hollow. The long *occupatio* records his alternating attraction to, and contempt for, them, a process that feeds itself like the flames as it escalates throughout the description. The more extravagant the gesture made to honor Arcite, the emptier, thinner, and more fictional it looks and the more the need for a still grander gesture: the more the fire is fed, the more insanely it rages.

The description of the funeral makes it absolutely clear that the dark and bright images of chivalry and its institutions are related parts of a consistent system. Both are rooted in the same rage for order, the same desire that meaning be something objectively determined, stable, and permanent—here, that Arcite's personal and symbolic value can be established and properly celebrated. The perception that such a project must fail, that no ceremony can make up for the loss of Arcite and what he represents, leads to the perception of the rites as thin, fictional, and unconvincing and to the contempt for them that surfaces in the passage. But this contempt is itself a version of "masculine" disenchantment because it is a despairing form of the hunger for meaning. It is a form like the Pardoner's in that it constrains things that may have more diverse, independent, partial, and historical meanings into the single meaning of meaninglessness, while remaining nostalgic for what has been lost and ready to try to deceive itself into finding it again. Since the Knight in effect appropriates the funeral from the old books and makes it into an instance of the process just described, we can also see here again that he shares the tendencies he identifies in others and *undergoes* them. His attraction to a mystified world feeds his satirical cynicism, which in turn increases the attraction. His dark imaginings are reflexes of his bright ones, and vice versa.

Yet perhaps there is a way in which the funeral does work. If it does not convince the Knight of the real efficacy of symbolic gestures, it does seem finally to remind him of the need for a kind of self-control the Pardoner is unable to achieve. There is in principle no end or limit to the hunger for finality that informs the description of the funeral and creates its increasingly wide oscillation between images of nobility and images of destruction. What needs to be changed is not the ceremony itself, by tinkering with its detail and symbolism, but the attitude taken toward it. Arcite's funeral is, after all, not the total embodiment of heroic worth it aspires to be any more than Arcite himself was; nor is his death in fact the destruction of nature and society, even symbolically. That is too much to demand of a single event and too much to load on one man's life. Arcite's death and burning do represent an instance of both the impressiveness and the fragility of human making and doing, but not one that can or should be expected to resolve the tension. Like any mourner, the Knight has to accept that the meaning a man's life and death will bear is partial, provisional, and temporary and must ultimately be left unresolved.[3]

Something like such an attitude seems finally to come for the Knight out of the experience of working through once again in the description of the funeral his attraction to, and need for, final and consoling meanings. Toward the end of the description he begins to push the scene away from him to distance and place it:

> And how that lad was homward Emelye;
> Ne how Arcite is brent to asshen colde;
> Ne how that lyche-wake was yholde
> Al thilke nyght; ne how the Grekes pleye
> The wake-pleyes; ne kepe I nat to seye
> Who wrastleth best naked with oille enoynt,
> Ne who that baar hym best, in no disjoynt.
> I wol nat tellen eek how that they goon
> Hoom til Atthenes, whan the pley is doon;
> But shortly to the point thanne wol I wende
> And maken of my longe tale an ende.
>
> (2956–66)

As this passage proceeds, the *occupatio* begins to function as a real exclusion of matter given at length in the old books as the Knight disengages from the description and from the Greeks with their an-

---

3. See Crampton, *Condition of Creatures*, 91.

tique rites.[4] His final vision of the proceedings seems to identify not just the funeral games but the whole ceremony—and his description of it—as a form of "pley." This word gets at the staged, theatrical quality of the performance as well as its lack of seriousness. It identifies what has just occurred as a kind of recreation, a pause from more serious responsibilities, for which the Knight's reference to "my longe tale" seems to apologize. Identifying the funeral description as play locates it as something less consequential and heavily symbolic, from which the Knight now turns back to "the point" (2965) and to his duties to his audience.

The sense of someone collecting himself, turning away from a merely personal concern and toward concern for others, then picking up the threads of the tale again, carries over into what follows:

> By processe and by lengthe of certeyn yeres,
> Al stynted is the moornynge and the teres
> Of Grekes, by oon general assent.
> Thanne semed me ther was a parlement
> At Atthenes, upon certein pointz and caas;
> Among the whiche pointz yspoken was,
> To have with certein contrees alliaunce,
> And have fully of Thebans obeisaunce.
> For which this noble Theseus anon
> Leet senden after gentil Palamon,
> Unwist of hym what was the cause and why,
> But in his blake clothes, sorwefully
> He cam at his comandement in hye.
> Tho sente Theseus for Emelye.
>
> (2967–80)

"Lengthe of certeyn yeres" distances Arcite's death and the funeral, pushing them back into the past and away from the speaker. "Thanne semed me" is curious—it hovers between trying to remember what was in the source and making an interpretation of something in the source that may not have been so clearly a "parlement" as what is presented here—the Knight's habitual attempt to imagine what the occasion must really have been like. The past tense is even odder because it seems to refer to an impression formed on some previous

---

4. The sense of antiquity, of outmoded customs and pagan deities—nymphs, fauns, hamadryads, and the like—is of course part of what registers the effect of unreality throughout the passage. Here it seems to function as a way of letting go of the scene, putting it back in the past where it belongs.

occasion of hearing or reading the tale, not to this telling, and therefore constitutes the story as something independent of the speaker's feelings about it. The effect is of someone talking half to himself—"Now let me see . . ."—gathering himself in preparation for what is to come and returning from his own dark imaginings to the objectivity of the events of the tale, like Theseus's moment of silence and sigh before beginning the final speech. The next lines place the whole affair of Palamon, Arcite, and Emelye in a sharply reduced and practical context, only one among a number of affairs of state of varying importance to be settled in the press of other business, and not so urgent that it needed to be settled earlier. This political context is extremely important for what follows, not only because it does cut the story down to size, so to speak, but also because it reminds us of the unsettled Theban question as a vital strand in the tale that remains unknotted. Theseus is now going to attend to a project he has been working on in one way or another for ten years, a problem that needs to be addressed yet again after the failure of the tournament and the death of Arcite. This setting of the scene is also important because it makes the political motivation of the First Mover speech explicit and unequivocal.[5] It matters to the Knight that we see the speech as an attempt to answer the set of specific, practical circumstances it is situated in, not just a general philosophical reflection taking Arcite's death as an example about the meaning of life. The temptation to that sort of general reflection and hungry symbolizing is what the Knight has contained and controlled in himself and the story in the course of his telling of the funeral; the First Mover speech may supply a guide to the meaning of the story, but it will be of a different sort.

Since the studies by William Frost and Charles Muscatine that initiated modern criticism of the *Knight's Tale* a critical consensus has developed that the First Mover speech is problematic.[6] Elizabeth Salter's trenchant and well-documented contention that the difficulty with the speech "does not lie in reconciling the death of Arcite with a divinely ordered plan, but in reconciling the noble statement of this plan with the ugly manifestation of divine motives and activities which

---

5. See Aers, *Creative Imagination*, 188, who notes that this emphasis is not present in Boccaccio.

6. Frost, "Interpretation of Chaucer's *Knight's Tale*" (1949); Muscatine, "Form, Texture, and Meaning" (1950); idem, *Chaucer and the French Tradition* (1957), 175–90.

Chaucer has allowed his poem to give" (Introduction to *The Knight's Tale*, 31) has been sufficiently, and deservedly, influential that even those critics who wish to affirm that the speech is a serious statement of a doctrine that informs the tale as a whole feel that they have to address the apparent discrepancy. As with the tale, criticism of the speech tends to divide between happy-enders, who assert that the conclusion of the story redeems the world it presents, and disbelievers, who assert that it does not—between what might be called a Palamonian view of the tale and an Egean one.

The former group of critics usually attends to the more-or-less abstract message or argument of the speech, its *vouloir dire* rather than its diction, and looks for ways to make good the action of the tale in the doctrine. They respond to that aspect of the speech and the tale that Neuse has sensitively characterized as the "invitation to judge this world [of the tale] by a standard that lies outside it and within the world of the pilgrims at whose head the Knight appears" ("The Knight," 312). These critics are by no means unaware of the feeling of discrepancy demonstrated by Salter between the speech's presentation of healing doctrine and the earlier events of the story, but they do assume that the apparent discrepancy was originally made good by a lost historical context of belief that conditioned the expectations and understanding of the audience and filled in the gap that a historically uninformed modern reading encounters. In this view the critic need not distinguish the voices of God, medieval culture, Chaucer, the Knight, and Theseus because, as Geoffrey puts it in another context, "hir sentence is al oon" (VII, 952).

It would be more reassuring if the same were true of the critics themselves, especially if they could agree on the justification of the doctrine that solves and saves the poem. Where earlier readers in this tradition, like Frost, were content to explicate the Boethian Neoplatonism for which there is at least some warrant in the language of the speech, commentators since Salter have divided over whether, for example, medieval belief in the sanctity of kingship (it is true because the just ruler Theseus says it is) or in the symbolic and spiritual significance of marriage (it is all right because they get married in the end) justifies the ways of gods to men.[7] The "solution" of the poem

---

7. The significance of Theseus as a type of the just ruler is stressed by Robertson, *Preface to Chaucer*, 260–63. The importance of the traditional symbolic meaning of

thus comes to reside in systematic constructs that are not, strictly speaking, in the poem itself, however likely it may be that they affected medieval habits of reading.

The multiplication of critical voices is in some ways even more apparent among critics who feel that the internal context of the poem—the fact of the discrepancy—overrides the historical and ideological force of external contexts (and probably did so, at least for some readers, in the fourteenth century). Such readers are perforce committed to some form of ironic reading of the tale since what they have to explain is why, if the speech does not fulfill the function it seems plainly designed to have of explaining the unhappy events of the story, it is in the tale at all. I am obviously more in agreement with this school than with the other, and I have silently appropriated many of their insights in what follows; but what really interests me about this criticism is the tone of Egean disenchantment that frequently creeps into it. These critics often seem upset at the subversion of attractive ideals implied by the inadequacy of the speech and end by *blaming* it—either on a Theseus whom we are to differentiate from "Chaucer" and perhaps the Knight or on a failure of "Chaucer's" art, a confusion the poet himself was unable to resolve. Thus we have Neuse's characterization of the speech as "the tyrant's plea, 'To maken vertue of necessitee' " and Theseus's watchword as "politics as usual" ("The Knight," 305); Aers's Marxist outrage at the "opportunistic eclecticism" with which Theseus masks his class interests in the speech, a set of values that "were not Chaucer's although they do represent major tendencies in western civilization" (*Creative Imagination*, 192); and Terry Jones's misanthropic and Monty Python–like enthusiasm for the way his "Chaucer" uses the speech and the tale to unmask the institution of chivalry in the fourteenth century for the corrupt and contemptible mess it really was (*Chaucer's Knight*). We have also Salter herself (why are so many critics of this persuasion English?) trying to

---

marriage is most fully developed by Kean, *Making of English Poetry*, 2:1–59; see also Ruggiers, "Some Philosophical Aspects," and Burlin, *Chaucerian Fiction*, 105–111. Ian Robinson, generally admirably skeptical in a tough-minded Salterian mode about the tale, is inexplicably drawn by the value of heroic reputation, the idea that it makes a crucial difference that Arcite's name will live in fame, *Chaucer and the English Tradition*, 139–40. Other proponents of the happy-ending view of the tale whose work I have found useful include Halverson, "Aspects of Order," who weaves the most complex web of interconnected orders, and Cameron, "The Heroine in the *Knight's Tale*."

exonerate her "Chaucer" by praising his sympathy with "a situation in which innocent creatures confront the wilful use of absolute power," despite the fact that the sympathy "disturb[s] the overall balance of his work" (Introduction to *The Knight's Tale*, 36). Finally, there is Alfred David's presentation of a Chaucer victimized by the conflict between his "nostalgic wish for an order that might have been once upon a time" and the "reflexes of [his] native skepticism" (*Strumpet Muse*, 88), who saved the flawed work this conflict produced by assigning it to—or blaming it on—the Knight after it had been written.[8] In an ironic reading of the speech and the tale we have to settle for the conclusion that either the poet or the world is in some way unpleasantly awry, and the critics make plain their distaste for this conclusion.

I shall return to the matter of disenchantment shortly, but the prior question seems to be one I have been asking all along: who *is* talking here, and to what effect? The critical disagreement over the speech seems like a setup for the application of Leicester's razor (see above, pp. 5–6) since what both groups of critics neglect is the speech's *voicing*, especially the way that voicing anticipates and enacts the very problem that concerns them. Like so many other Canterbury pilgrims—such as the Wife of Bath and the Pardoner—the Knight is a critic of his own tale, commenting on and questioning the traditional styles and values of a story he did not make up himself in the very act of passing it on, that is, of telling it. He is also the first critic to notice the discrepancy between the ideal order Theseus's speech proposes and the reality of the world of the tale. He shows that he has noticed by making the problem a problem *in the speech itself* and by making the tension that divides critics the central tension of the passage, a fact about it rather than a judgment of it.

On the one hand, it is clear that the speaker of the speech would like to maintain the larger principle of order that the first school of critics fastens on, which is no doubt what encourages them to do it. This speaker is arguing for the benign influence of the First Mover as transmitted through the fair chain of love: he wants to say that the universe has a hidden order and that Arcite did not die in vain. We

8. With his usual acumen David correctly identifies the *terms* of the conflict but locates it outside the poem itself in "Chaucer" 's career. The argument of his book is that the poet moves from moral certainty to disenchantment as he ages. Suppose it could be shown that Chaucer's earliest works (supposing we knew which they were) were as disenchanted as his later ones?

might imagine this *vouloir dire* as the speaker's advance plan for the speech. At the same time, however, the way the speaker deploys his argument, voicing his program in the practice of actual delivery, points to his own awareness of the difficulties that preoccupy the second set of critics. These difficulties keep undermining the argument and the speaker's belief in it, bringing out his own disenchantment and even his despair at the specter of a world without discernable human meaning. The consistent movement of the speech as a whole and of each of its parts is from positive general statements to negative particular examples that bring out the subtext of "derke ymagynynge," and it is this movement and its repetitions that I want to concentrate on here.

Theseus's speech begins with a forthright statement of the perfection and order of the divine plan as it is constituted in the mind of the First Mover and carried out according to his will:

> The Firste Moevere of the cause above,
> Whan he first made the faire cheyne of love,
> Greet was th'effect, and heigh was his entente.
> Wel wiste he why, and what thereof he mente;
> For with that faire cheyne of love he bond
> The fyr, the eyr, the water, and the lond
> In certeyn boundes, that they may nat flee.
>
> (2987–93)

The trouble with this account is that it locates a perfection in realms above that all too obviously does not obtain here on earth, and when the speaker turns to "this wrecched world adoun," he immediately betrays his consciousness of the fact:

> "That same Prince and that Moevere," quod he,
> "Hath stablissed in this wrecched world adoun
> Certeyne dayes and duracioun
> To all that is engendred in this place,
> Over the whiche day they may nat pace,
> Al mowe they yet tho dayes wel abregge.
> Ther nedeth noght noon auctoritee t'allegge,
> For it is preeved by experience,
> But that me list declaren my sentence."
>
> (2994–3002)

The wretchedness of the world is far more compelling to the speaker than its order, even more so because of the contrast with the beauty and serenity of the cause above, and that wretchedness appears to distract him from his message. It is perhaps an assurance of the ultimate orderliness of things that they cannot outlast their established duration, but the reflection that they may abridge it at the very least calls unwelcome attention to the ability of men to disrupt the divine plan by violence and at worst evokes suicidal feelings akin to Egeus's "Deeth is an ende of every wordly soore" (2849)—feelings that might arise from the contemplation of a world so wretched that one cannot bear to wait out one's allotted span. "Al mowe they yet tho dayes wel abregge" feels like a slip that lets out something unintended, and the following lines on authority, experience, and the speaker's desire to declare his sentence enforce this effect. The man who a few lines earlier appeared to be confidently enunciating doctrine is now explaining himself instead, and the slightly lame aside indicates his awareness that something has gone wrong and his attempt to cover it up. This lameness is especially evident because what he insists is obvious—that the Mover has established the durations of things—is not so in fact, and this recognition makes him seem overinsistent and unconvinced of his own assertion. The initial image of the relations between the First Mover and the world makes the former too perfect, the latter too wretched, and each too cut off from the other for either the speaker's comfort or the audience's consolation.

This failure leads the speaker to a new start, an attempt to recharacterize the relations between the one and the many in more careful, logical, and scientific language:

> Thanne may men by this ordre wel discerne
> That thilke Moevere stable is and eterne.
> Wel may men knowe, but it be a fool,
> That every part dirryveth from his hool,
> For nature hath nat taken his bigynnyng
> Of no partie or cantel of a thyng,
> But of a thyng that parfit is and stable,
> Descendyng so til it be corrumpable.
> And therfore, of his wise purveiaunce,
> He hath so wel biset his ordinaunce
> That speces of thynges and progressiouns
> Shullen enduren by successiouns,
> And nat eterne, withouten any lye.
> This maystow understonde and seen at ye.
> (3003–16)

This new account of the Neoplatonic ladder or great chain of being has the desired effect of establishing a connection between the terrestrial and supramundane spheres. It uses the logical principle of the derivation of the part from the whole to argue the hierarchical deployment of being in the universe and thus manages to include the limited existence of earthly things, the parts and cantles, in a larger order that is founded on something more perfect than its members.

But as soon as the argument descends from the overall perfection of the system to specific cases, trouble arises again:

> Loo the ook, that hath so longe a norisshynge
> From tyme that it first bigynneth to sprynge,
> And hath so long a lif, as we may see,
> Yet at the laste wasted is the tree.
> Considereth eek how that the harde stoon
> Under oure feet, on which we trede and goon,
> Yet wasteth it as it lyth by the weye.
> The brode ryver somtyme wexeth dreye;
> The grete tounes se we wane and wende.
> Thanne may ye se that all this thyng hath ende.
>
> (3017–26)

The problem here is that as the speaker describes them, the cantles become too concrete, too obtrusive, and too laden with value to occupy their subordinate place in the argument and in the whole comfortably. The speech began with the assertion that the limited duration of earthly things was obvious and did not need to be demonstrated. That being so, we would expect the argument to turn fairly quickly to a demonstration of the value earthly things do have and the contribution they make to the larger order despite their transitory life. Instead the speaker continues to make and remake the point that everything passes, creating a growing sense not of order but of waste and desolation, the landscape of the temple of Mars. The mighty oak, the solid stone, and the great town that men use wood and rock to build are all caught up in the speaker's vision of the entropic drift of the world, and especially of human values, toward decay and meaninglessness. When the speech turns to human affairs, this saturnian subtext is even more in evidence:

> Of man and womman seen we wel also
> That nedes, in oon of thise termes two—
> This is to seyn, in youthe or elles age—

> He moot be deed, the kyng as shal a page;
> Som in his bed, som in the depe see,
> Som in the large feeld, as men may see;
> Ther helpeth noght; al goth that ilke weye.
> Thanne may I seyn that al this thyng moot deye.
>
> (3027–34)

Besides the obvious tendency of the voice to continue to linger over the varieties of universal demise, "He moot be deed, the kyng as shal a page" denies the efficacy of the hierarchical principle that is supposed to guarantee order in the universe at large, at least to human society. The human realm is once again cut off, as it was at the beginning of the speech and as it has been throughout the tale, from the realm of orderly process the speech is trying to assert. The attempt to trace the descent of order by degrees is continually subverted by a more powerful counterimpulse to level everything in a common fate.[9]

The next section of the speech returns from the many back to the one, anthropomorphizing the one more fully than before as Jupiter, a being less abstract, with motives and feelings perhaps more like ours. This return appears to be an attempt to give an image of the Mover as actively involved in human affairs and reassert the benevolent concern the speech has so far failed to demonstrate:

> What maketh this but Juppiter, the kyng,
> That is prince and cause of alle thyng,
> Convertynge al unto his propre welle
> From which it is dirryved, sooth to telle?
> And heer-agayns no creature on lyve,
> Of no degree, availleth for to stryve.
>
> (3035–40)

Paradoxically, the very desire to assert benevolence in Jupiter and return to a context of order and divine care for earthly things makes the bitter subtext stand out even more strongly. "What maketh this but Juppiter, the kyng" is too closely juxtaposed to "Thanne may I seyn that al this thyng moot deye" and its accompanying desolate vision to function effectively as an assertion of benign control. It is too easy to read it as an accusation, especially when we realize that the "propre

9. Spearing, *Knight's Tale*, 77, has noted the connection of this passage to the speech of Egeus.

welle" to which Jupiter converts all can only, logically and syntacti-cally, be death. Over and over, what emerges behind the reassuring image of Jupiter and the philosophical vocabulary of the argument is the dark imagining of a world too much like the one the speech is supposedly combating and of gods more like the ones we see in the tale: distant, inscrutable, capricious, cruel—our murderers.

In terms of formal organization the next section of the speech, dealing with the more specific human situation of dying young, contin-ues the logical plan of the argument: to move from the general asser-tion of cosmic order to a demonstration of its effects in particular instances and ultimately in the case before us. In terms of the *deploy-ment* of the argument, however, this passage marks another new start, like line 3003 earlier. It denotes a shift of attention from the relative passivity of men as elements in the divine order, and the despair that view engenders, toward a more active stance, recommending that we not only accept but also affirm the actions of a higher will, necessity:

> Thanne is it wysdom, as it thynketh me,
> To maken vertu of necessitee,
> And take it weel that we may nat eschue,
> And namely that to us alle is due.
> And whoso gruccheth ought, he dooth folye,
> And rebel is to hym that al may gye.
> And certeinly a man hath moost honour
> To dyen in his excellence and flour,
> Whan he is siker of his goode name;
> Thanne hath he doon his freend, ne hym, no shame.
> And gladder oghte his freend been of his deeth,
> Whan with honour up yolden is his breeth,
> Than whan his name apalled is for age,
> For al forgeten is his vasselage.
> Thanne is it best, as for a worthy fame,
> To dyen whan that he is best of name.
>
> (3041–56)

The speech here attempts to exemplify the attitude it enjoins and make a virtue of necessity. The speaker offers what must be an interpretation of Arcite's death, though he does not yet use the young knight's name, pointing out ways in which that death can be seen to be for the best. His speech here is not just a logical demonstration that it is better to die young with one's fame unblemished, though that is its form, but also an active *urging* that the hearers understand Arcite's death in this way. This purpose is clearest in "gladder oghte his freend been of his deeth" because it is so obviously directed to Palamon, a gesture that evokes the specific context in which the speech is being delivered more explicitly than has been the case so far. This gesture reminds us in a general way that the speaker has an agenda (not necessarily a hidden one) and a practical interest in seeing that certain people adopt the view he is suggesting.

But if the speaker wants others to put this virtuous construction on the particular necessity of Arcite's death, it quickly becomes apparent that he has trouble doing so himself. For the third time in the course of the speech the attempt to assert a benevolent order ruling human affairs evokes in the speaker himself a heightened awareness of everything in the situation that suggests the opposite:

> The contrarie of al this is wilfulnesse.
> Why grucchen we, why have we hevynesse,
> That good Arcite, of chivalrie flour,
> Departed is with duetee and honour
> Out of this foule prisoun of this lyf?
> Why grucchen heere his cosyn and his wyf
> Of his welfare, that loved hem so weel?
> Kan he hem thank? Nay, God woot, never a deel,
> That both his soule and eek hemself offende,
> And yet they mowe hir lustes nat amende.
>   (3057–66)

The resurgence of the Egean attitude is most clearly signaled by "this foule prisoun of this lyf," coming hard upon the attempt to say that it is for the best that Arcite died as he did. Once again we hear the dark side of that assertion, the feeling that the world as it is is something Arcite is well out of. In addition, the tone of complaint ("grucchyng") at the decrees of the First Mover remains stubbornly present in the speech in the repetitions of the word itself. That the speaker has to urge his audience so insistently not to grumble suggests that he does not expect them to be persuaded and that he is not persuaded himself. He even admits that Arcite would not be persuaded if he were still alive. To assert that Arcite's cousin "loved him so weel" is itself touchy and can easily remind us of the strife we are being urged to put behind us. But to add that Palamon and Emelye "both his soule and eek himself offende" is to bring back everything that Arcite lost by dying young in his excellence and flower because it is not clear that the speaker's *vouloir dire*, "They offend him by continuing to grieve and by not making themselves happy, as he would have wished," can easily escape the counterintimation, "They will offend him and his memory by their marrying, doing what he died trying to prevent." The phrase *make a virtue of necessity* usually implies standing up to difficult circumstances and taking them as an opportunity to display one's virtues. What the speaker's aside about Arcite brings out here is the extent to which he realizes that his praise and dismissal of the dead hero is a cosmetic papering over of Arcite's fate, an attempt after the fact to make necessity look like virtue.

There is no comfort in this speech for its speaker. The more he tries to assert the order and meaning of life, the more he has to struggle with his own conviction that it has no intrinsic order or meaning. Instead of comfort there is responsibility, the pressing need for human agents to supply the deficiencies of the gods and try to confer order where it is lacking. Notice how active the "I" is here:

> What may I conclude of this longe serye,
> But after wo I rede us to be merye
> And thanken Juppiter of al his grace?
> And er that we departen from this place
> I rede that we make of sorwes two
> O parfit joye, lastynge everemo.
> And looketh now, wher moost sorwe is herinne,
> Ther wol we first amenden and bigynne.
>
> (3067–74)

The most important single fact about the speech is that it continually labors, line by line and paragraph by paragraph, to put a positive and socially productive interpretation on the situation it addresses. It does so in the teeth of not only the difficulties of the objective situation but also the doubts of the speaker himself. The speech demonstrates yet again that if the last enemy is *le néant*, the first enemy and the most potent obstacle to overcoming the not-we is the self, with the dream of perfect order and the nightmare of despairing nothingness that it generates out of its own subjectivity. The first kind of order the speech demonstrates is the inner ordering of self-control, ceaselessly sustained against the twin temptations of the dream and the nightmare.

The second kind of order the First Mover speech strives for is the maintenance and furthering of human meaning, including the idea of order itself. By the end of the speech it is clear that it is the speaker who sustains the First Mover rather than the other way around. It is apparent that for this speaker, in the human world as encountered and experienced there is no First Mover, no sight above, no externally given order in human affairs. But this lack only means that it is all the more important for human beings themselves—or at least men—to make and sustain order, and in this context the speech urges that we *behave as if* there were a First Mover and thereby try to bring about the order He symbolizes. The speech is an ongoing attempt to sustain the fabric of society and its institutions in the face of those threats, internal and external, to which it is subject. This effort extends to the preservation of the institutionalized ideal of order itself, embodied in Jupiter or the First Mover, as a model for men to emulate and a means to urge them to it. The speaker *rehabilitates* and keeps available an idea that has social value so as to put it to social use.

I have been careful in my reading of the First Mover speech to refer to the speaker rather than choosing between Theseus and the Knight because there are significant ways in which here, if ever, they are the same. It seems obvious that the Knight intends the First Mover speech as the tale's "message," his own attempt, for the benefit of his listeners, to come to terms with the philosophical and existential issues the tale raises. In addition, there is the equally obvious engagement of his voice and mind in the making of it, the here-and-now mental and emotional struggle the speech embodies. This identification of the Knight's voice with that of Theseus completes a long process begun at least as early as the scene in the grove. It is one of the triumphs of the tale because it is an index of how what Theseus does for the First Mover is a version of what the Knight does for Theseus, for the tale, and for chivalry itself. By the end of the tale Theseus is a more limited but also more realistic and serviceable agent of order than he was at its beginning. He must accept a situation in which he has less power and more responsibility for the power he does have and in which he has had to plan and improvise around setbacks and unforeseen eventualities, making use of whatever he can cobble together from the practical resources his situation and his culture provide. The First Mover in his speech is a conspicuously frail and patchy human construction whose principal value is that it can be used as part—and only part—of an attempt to bring about a little more political stability than there was before in the chancy and contentious world of competing heroic wills. "What may

I conclude of this longe serye" points not only to the length and difficulty of the speech itself but also beyond it to the rest of the story, to the continuing effort of conquest and battle as well as of politics and persuasion, thinking and speaking, that has been necessary to bring about some limited improvement in the order of human life. The speech is both an instance and a reminder of that long and ceaseless process, an embodiment not of order itself but of the labor of ordering.

If we look at Theseus in this way it becomes apparent that his efforts in the story are doubled by the Knight's protracted effort of thought and speech in the telling, the "longe serye" and long seriousness that is the tale itself, to produce precisely this image of Theseus and his world. What the prime mover is for Theseus, Theseus is, as the hero of the tale and the man who makes it all come out right, for the Knight. If the order Theseus espouses is to be convincing, it must not be too easily achieved and the Knight must keep the hero of his tale, like the First Mover, from becoming too remote and unreal, too consoling or not consoling enough. The Knight brings Theseus to the point where the two of them speak together out of a realistic and embattled human situation to express a major Chaucerian theme from the Knight's particular perspective: that though society is dependent on institutions, institutions are equally and crucially dependent on people to keep them alive and functioning effectively.[10] What the Knight does to Theseus, and to the story, is force the mystified and treacherously overconsoling heroic images in the old books—in the chivalric tradition as it has been handed down to him—into confrontation with the real political and social conditions under which, the Knight knows, order and the noble life are carried on. He thereby makes those golden images *responsible* to and for the iron world in which they exist; he strives to make them useful both as warnings against overconfidence and encouragements to responsible aspiration.

The Knight belongs to a tradition of civilizers, and he is committed to that activity. But he is sharply aware that among the greatest dangers to civilization are the forms of civility themselves if they lull its guardians into ignoring their responsibility for maintaining them. That is why he is so hard on the story, especially in its early parts. He is also convinced, however, that these forms are, despite their frailty, all that stands between human beings and the chaos of, on the one hand, their

10. See the remarks on structuration, chapter 13, note 20.

own inner drives and, on the other, an objectively meaningless world. Hence he ultimately *preserves* institutions, such as the gods, the tournament, and the funeral, by revising them. The most important of these institutions is the story itself, as an emblem of chivalry properly understood and an embodiment of order and the noble life. I remarked in the introduction that it did no harm to accept the proposition put forward by the Canterbury frame that the *Knight's Tale* is the tale the Knight tells, so long as we recognize that such a proposition implies nothing in advance about the knight who tells it. Now, as we approach the end of an analysis of that voice of the text, we can see how the fact that the speaker is a knight adds a certain urgency to the probing examination of what knighthood is. The speaker of the *Knight's Tale* does in fact identify himself with his estate, whose ideals are set forth in the Knight's portrait in the *General Prologue*. But one thing he knows about that estate is that it is not a preexisting entity but an institution and an *activity*. As such it needs to be explored, clarified, and above all enacted. The tale is not only an image of knighthood and the noble life but also an exemplary instance, consciously and deliberately presented, of the *doing* of knighthood. The telling itself is one version of what a knight does. It is, once again, a version of the institution of the subject, the active identification, in the mode of practical consciousness, of self and estate that constructs and maintains them as the subjectivity and the subject of chivalry.

If the knighthood enacted is a diminished thing, a matter of one slightly shaky political alliance that is more practical politics than splendor and is achieved only at considerable cost, that diminution is no doubt due in part to the often-cited belatedness, obsolescence, and decline of chivalry and its ideals in the fourteenth century. Indeed, as I suggested before, these conditions may well have produced not only in Chaucer but also in the Knight himself the disenchantment that enables the critique. But I think that is not how the Knight sees it. As I have shown, he conceives of the forces and dangers he evokes in the tale as both incorrigible and perennial, having constantly to be dealt with in every time and place, in Theseus's Athens as now. Yet he also sees (indeed experiences) that to concentrate too fixedly and exclusively on the perennial and incorrigible recurrence of human violence and senseless external necessity encourages a kind of despairing nihilism to which his existentialist humanism is as much prey as it is unalterably opposed. The real salvation of chivalry, if there is one, is its commitment to the practical—to the particular, the immediate, what needs to be done to make and preserve order here and now in a marriage, an alliance, or the telling of a story. Limited successes are the best that can be hoped for and may well require the best a man has to give.

For this reason the end of the tale continues to focus on the labor of ordering. Theseus may hold up the First Mover as a model for human society to emulate, but he knows that he cannot count on Jupiter's help or even on Jupiter's persuasiveness. He has to keep working on the situation to ensure its outcome:

> "Suster," quod he, "this is my fulle assent,
> With al th'avys heere of my parlement,
> That gentil Palamon, youre owene knyght,
> That serveth yow with wille, herte, and myght,
> And ever hath doon syn ye first hym knewe,
> That ye shul of youre grace upon him rewe,
> And taken hym for housbonde and for lord.
> Lene me youre hond, for this is oure accord.
> Lat se now of youre wommanly pitee.
> He is a kynges brother sone, pardee;
> And though he were a povre bacheler,
> Syn he hath served yow so many a yeer,
> And had for yow so greet adversitee,
> It moste been considered, leeveth me;
> For gentil mercy oghte to passen right."
>   Thanne seyde he thus to Palamon the knight:
> "I trowe ther nedeth litel sermonynge
> To make yow assente to this thyng.
> Com neer, and taak youre lady by the hond."
>   Bitwixen hem was maad anon the bond
> That highte matrimoigne or mariage,
> By al the conseil and the baronage.
>
>   (3075–96)

The speed and suddenness of the announcement after the slow puzzling through of the First Mover speech and the dispatch with which the ensuing state marriage is carried out make this speech something of a political tour de force, in which Palamon, whom we are specifically informed does not know why he has been summoned to Athens (2297), is hustled into making a decision and contracting an alliance he might otherwise want to consider more carefully. It is not clear, however, that Emelye is unaware of Theseus's plans. She presumably had some information about the original decision of the Athenian parliament to "have fully of Thebans obeisaunce"; and though Theseus's "Lene me youre hond, for this is oure accord" virtually forces her compliance in this public situation, it can also be read as a reminder to her of something she has agreed to beforehand. Whether or not she knows, however, it is apparent that Theseus works actively here to bring about her assent. His tone to Emelye hovers between coercion and persuasion, between trying to talk her into womanly feelings of pity and mercy and reminding her of her responsibilities to the state; "He is a kynges brother sone, pardee" could be construed as both. Our last view of Theseus in the poem is of a man still alert to the disruptive potential of others, still anticipating and forestalling trouble. That he does so particularly with Emelye shows that he (and the Knight) remain aware that this solution to the situation has cost not only the life of Arcite but also the independence, and perhaps the happiness, of Emelye. The tensions of psychological ambivalence and institutional contradiction that have characterized the tale throughout remain alive, though suppressed, at its close. The need to keep attending to persuasion shows as well that the solution is sufficiently fragile that it needs to be shepherded along right up to the last moment: there is no guarantee that the marriage will work, either as a personal relationship or as a political alliance—and the two forms of success may well be connected.

Such things are only hints and undertones in the situation at the end of the poem, but their continuing possibility helps shape the concluding lines:

> And thus with alle blisse and melodye
> Hath Palamon ywedded Emelye.
> And God, that al this wyde world hath wroght,
> Sende hym his love that hath it deere aboght;
> For now is Palamon in alle wele,
> Lyvynge in blisse, in richesse, and in heele,
> And Emelye hym loveth so tendrely,
> And he hire serveth so gentilly,
> That nevere was ther no word hem bitwene
> Of jalousie or any oother teene.
> Thus endeth Palamon and Emelye;
> And God save al this faire compaignye! Amen.
> (3097–3108)

The third and fourth lines of this passage are sufficiently free in syntax to admit being read either as "God send the man who has paid dearly for it his love" or "God send Palamon the love of him who paid dearly for it," that is, the love of Christ. Even if the second reading is admitted, as an intimation of a yearning for some more complete fulfillment for the characters in Christian terms than the story has been able to provide them, the Knight's voicing of this hope remains conditional, relatively unfocused, and certainly not a possibility developed anywhere else in the tale: it remains a brief prayer. The impression the passage gives is of a rapid and perfunctory closing down of the story. It is a version of "They lived happily ever after," in which the Knight has little interest, and the contrast between this conventional flatness and our final view of Theseus suggests that the conclusion is not intended to provide any real closure for the poem. We are not really asked to believe that even these two characters (the statement is limited to them) never had any trouble again. Rather, we are asked to note that this story is over and that there is no need to tell more of it. Life and the labor of order go on as stories do not, and once the point has been made and the example given, the end of the story is no longer a conclusion; it is merely where the teller chooses to stop.

The closure of the *Knight's Tale* is, as Aers has pointed out, merely conventional, which is to say social.[11] The tension the ending does not resolve is passed on beyond the boundaries of the tale itself, first of all to the disagreement between the assessment of the "gentils" and that of the Miller that the *Miller's Prologue* records. The *Canterbury Tales* is full of instances of what might be called conventional or social closure, in which the audience agrees, often tacitly, to act as if a resolution has taken place when in fact it has not. The end of the *Pardoner's Tale* is an obvious instance of this phenomenon, as is, in a different way, the end of the *Wife of Bath's Tale*, where such things as the social implications of the Wife's performance are deflected by the quarrel between the Friar and the Summoner and deferred to the Clerk's and Merchant's tales.

In the *Knight's Tale*, interestingly, the tension of its lack of closure has been passed on to subsequent readers, who have often seemed less to comprehend the tension than to be inscribed in it, to recapitulate

11. See Aers, *Creative Imagination*, 194.

and undergo it. That is, the kinds of closure for the tale that the critical tradition has generally supplied have already been anticipated and criticized by the tale itself. My division of the critics into yea sayers and nay sayers, idealistic dreamers and despairing Egean misanthropes, is no doubt something of an exaggeration, and I will address this issue shortly. But it seems to me that there is enough truth to that division to make the problem and the reasons for it worth exploring. If an *écrivain* is a Writer in the exalted Romantic sense, and if Barthes has identified one who uses writing instrumentally, as in the making of a laundry list, as an *écrivant*,[12] critics of the *Knight's Tale* often seem to find themselves unwittingly in the position of what might be called *écrivisses*, or p(r)awns of the text, writing from a place predetermined and always already undermined by it.

This situation seems to me to be evidence that the Knight is right about the inescapability of the hunger for closure and stable meaning in human makeup. The critics betray the same need for ethical solutions, the same sense that there ought to be some genuine connection between what men do and what happens to them, as the characters—and the same disenchanted discomfort at the possibility of meaninglessness. The desire of critics to provide a level of closure for the tale, if only to demonstrate that its "deficiencies" are somehow made good at another level by such things as the actual benevolence of a Christian providence unknown to pagan Theseus, is also allied to the nearly universal tendency to ignore the primacy of human agency in the tale, including the slighting of the Knight as narrator. It is a voice-oriented reading that uncovers how a tale famous for its portrayal of man as a plaything of forces beyond his control is in fact fascinated by specifically human power. The critics often seem as reluctant as the characters to acknowledge the role of human agents, and especially the Knight himself, in the constitution of the story and the world. But the Knight, though he experiences that same incorrigible hunger for closure and final meaning and the same ambivalence about the status of human action, is committed to trying to *resist* these tendencies. He strives instead to keep the open character of the world in view and put up with the discomfort such a stance entails, to remain clear-eyed in the face of human weakness and the threats of necessity, and not to be fooled or despair.

12. Barthes, "Écrivains et écrivants."

Having so ringingly reduced my colleagues to a subordinate position in relation to the Knight (and of course myself), I find my own ambivalence reasserting itself in reflections like, Aren't they right after all? Doesn't the tale actively encourage responses like theirs? Isn't it something of a mousetrap that goes out of its way to disguise its real meaning and mislead its audience? Such questions point again, I think, to some genuine issues about the tale. The problem might be put as follows: the Knight's revisionary enterprise in the tale involves both the critique or deconstruction of chivalric institutions, insofar as these claim to have ontological status independent of human making, and at the same time the rehabilitation and maintenance of these institutions as structures useful and necessary for the preservation of order. As I have said, the Knight is not the Manciple or the Pardoner; he does not simply expose his society and its structures but also strives to preserve them. He does not propose institutional *alternatives* to gods, tournaments, or chivalry, the traditional cultural furnishings of his world. Though I do not necessarily condemn the Knight for not being revolutionary, I do notice that this conservatism has the effect of leaving in place a set of institutions whose structure encourages remystification, perhaps the most notable example being the First Mover. The Knight's reasons for this procedure are fully presented in the tale and parallel to a degree what I have called his "masculine" and "feminine" identifications: on the one hand the conviction that the truth about human life is too hard for most people to bear (a set of feelings that often get identified as womanish) and on the other hand the experienced awareness of the male heroic potential for terrible violence that chivalric institutions must continually strive to contain. That the Knight shares the impulses he fears adds a certain weight and seriousness to his view of the world. If there is something elitist in these convictions, and there is, they are at least based on an experienced assessment of human weakness, the Knight's own as well as others', and to say of the tale that it favors established institutions and public values over individual freedom and private fulfillment should also be to recognize that the tale and its speaker are the first to be ambivalent about these issues and the costs of the choices that create them.

But we need not accept the Knight's world, however solidly it is portrayed or deeply it is felt, as *the* world—the Miller, for one, does not—and a more distanced view of the tale's assumptions allows certain characteristics of the Knight's imagination as a social agent to emerge. If the tale does not have two speakers, as theories of unimpersonated artistry suggest, it does project two audiences: those who, like the Knight, are strong enough to bear the truth and take responsibility for it and those who, as Aers puts it, will "feel relieved and consoled, latching on to the few brief assertions about the future of Palamon and Emily, feeling reassured at the role of official secular authority in the marital union, and abandoning the disturbing meditations stimulated by the complete work" (*Creative Imagination*, 14). The Knight's conviction that the former group is small and the latter large is attested by his use of the particular revisionist strategy I have described as well as by such things as the notable fact that there is finally only one "real" character in the tale: only Theseus is as penetrating, resourceful, and responsible as the Knight himself. However strong the grounds are in the Knight's experience for believing that most people cannot be trusted to control themselves and live with others without the carrot and stick of mystified institutions, and however uneasy he may feel about this belief, the fact of distrust remains, as does the elitism.

To look at the tale in this way is to become more aware of how it continues to participate in the dynamics of heroic society, and of course male domination, that it also analyzes. That is, heroic consciousness prereflectively *constitutes* the world as a chaos so as to give itself something to be heroic about and to order. Such a view involves a certain undervaluing of institutions and their permanence and power in the interests of heroic individualism; there is something aristocratic about it, appropriate to a class that is in control of the institutions in question.[13] The *Miller's Tale* does not disagree with either the awareness of injustice or the stress on human agency in the *Knight's Tale*. Rather, it concentrates attention on what the Knight seems to leave out—both the richness and opportunity for human expression af-

---

13. Given, as I have already remarked, that the institution most prominently featured here is the tale itself, with all its filiations to various generic and ideological processings of symbolic capital, an adjustment in the theoretical framework of a materialist analysis like Aers's suggests itself. Aers consistently treats the world of the poem as if it were the real world, a field in which substructure and superstructure are in conflict, where ideologies and material facts struggle. Both Chaucer and the Knight see it differently: for them, the romance and its associated conventions are already ideologically processed, and a tale is already a representation before ever it gets to a teller. It is the *story* that needs to be revalued as an item in the world, as the Knight does with his tale, and this revaluation is the process, in general, that Chaucer represents in the *Canterbury Tales*.

forded by complex and stable institutions, and their coercive power. The Miller's "quityng" of the *Knight's Tale* involves the full polarity of that word, whose various meanings coalesce around the notion of repaying a service or an injury. Thus, on the one hand, the "foyson" of institutional avenues for individual expression available in the world of the tale creates its cast of richly variegated characters with their multifarious projects and complex appeals to our sympathy and judgment. All the characters in the *Knight's Tale* are variously adequate or deficient versions of a single role, that of the hero.[14] The characters in the *Miller's Tale* are a counterdemonstration of the range of roles available in modern society, especially as embodied in the Miller himself, who plays them all with gusto. From this perspective the Miller's message to the Knight is something like, You built better than you know and gave us all a world that has become "hende," no longer in need of constant vigilance and defense against elemental chaos. On the other hand, the Miller is extremely sensitive to society's power, as he shows, for example, in his resentment that the Knight is ensured, simply by virtue of being who he is, of a kind of hearing for his lengthy old romance that the Miller has to work much harder to get. In the tale itself this perspective is sustained in such things as the rush of prying eyes into the tale at its conclusion and the power of the class solidarity of clerks in defining the situation at the end. (See above, p. 11.) This aspect of the tale might be read as the Miller's reproach to the Knight: You and your kind have built prisons for the rest of us that are stronger than any of stone and iron and are in the form of the structure of society itself. The *Miller's Tale* locates in human institutions both the opportunities and the threats that the *Knight's Tale* places in the individual heroic psyche and the nonhuman world.[15]

Because it both is and is not closed, because it ends but is not concluded, the *Knight's Tale* passes on to its various audiences the tensions it develops and embodies. As soon as we attempt to resolve

---

14. This may perhaps suggest how character itself, which is derived, as Warren Ginsberg points out in *The Cast of Character*, from a word meaning to cut or engrave a mark, is not only a social construction inscribed in individuals but also an institution one of whose functions is to make other persons comprehensible. As such, it is of course subject to the manipulations of practical consciousness, and in the *Knight's Tale* the characters of the characters, so to speak, are things the teller negotiates with the story.

15. The Knight's sensibility is thus in a certain sense antihistorical, according to the formula "Ther is no newe gyse that it nas old" (2125).

these tensions, we begin to compete with the text, in part because the text itself construes the assigning of meaning itself, in a Nietzschean way, as a matter of power and competing wills. This competition may take place either within the problematic the text proposes, in which case it is, as I have argued, dominated by the text, or outside it, in which case a new voice with its own aporias, like that of the Miller, is generated. Within the poem the meaning of a given tale is ongoing and shifting, redefined and continually reflected anew in the responses (or lack of them) of the other pilgrims. The same is of course true outside the poem in the community of interpreters, and my own characterization of that community has not escaped the grip of the tale. If I did not believe my interpretation to be superior to previous ones I would not be making it, and the fact that there is such a thing as academic machismo, or, to put it more benignly, that the world of literary criticism is an arena of civilized competition not unrelated to the Knight's world, is not necessarily altogether bad. Nonetheless, it is also true that my previous characterization of the critics as shrimps is an irresponsible caricature of my professional colleagues because it reduces them to a relatively arbitrary classification of what they maintain about the ending of the tale, one that impoverishes their various contributions to the institution we make and share—the ongoing discourse about the tale from which I have obviously learned a great deal and on which I depend. Further, I may not be able to get away with it when they read this. The reader will note that, like the Nun's Priest, I have apologized—"Taketh the fruyt, and lat the chaf be stille"—and that, also like the Nun's Priest, I have not rewritten my earlier comments, and I have more choice than he because I am not even pretending to perform orally. Does it help (you or me) to say that I am only trying to "quite" the Knight?

Pointing to this action of the tale in worlds beyond it not only indicates its participation in the larger discourses of an ancient masculinity that is still with us and of a modern criticism that may question what it does not always escape. It is a way of pointing as well to the specificity of both the Knight's tale and his personality. It calls attention to a certain sort of "presence," that of a consistent and specific voice of the text that we are justified in calling the Knight's voice and whose consistency throughout the tale my own "longe serye" has tried to demonstrate. But this voice should still not be confused with an external subject or "person," at least not in the sense of something that can be summed up once and for all and dismissed, especially since it is still at work in my own text and elsewhere. The Knight's subjectivity, like the Pardoner's and the Wife of Bath's, is constituted, as I have tried to show throughout, by a set of dialectical relations between antithetical terms, eros/aggression, psychological/social, "masculine"/"feminine," and so on, to which may now be added text/*hors-texte*. Thus from one point of view, for example, the characters are projections of the psychological makeup of the narrator and draw their life from his conscious and unconscious drives and investments of psychic energy. But insofar as the characters are also traditional, having a life in a story and a genre that is larger than the life of just this narrator, the same set of identifications can be viewed as a social construction: the individual self becomes a small society, the mediated reflection of the institutional structure that supports and constrains it. The "character" of Theseus (or of the Knight for that matter) can be seen as organized around a complex and unresolved ambivalence about his own aggressive impulses. But insofar as the institutionalized notion of masculinity and heroism central to the tale is so constructed as to generate both intense male bonding driven by feelings of loyalty and community in competitive endeavor, and at the same time encourage a competitive ferocity whose most glorious exemplar is the last man left alive on a field of corpses, what is legitimately viewed as an individual ambivalence at one level is just as accurately seen as an institutional contradiction at another.

In fact, to try to reify the *Knight's Tale*, and thereby the Knight, is to place oneself in the textual position that the text itself already undercuts, either as subordinate to the Knight or in competition with him. The question "What does the Knight mean?" does not, strictly speaking, have an answer, whether it is construed as a question about the speaker's intentions (does he wish to conceal or to reveal the nature of human institutions?) or as a question about the final significance of his character. The question always leads to an aporia, an undecidability, which can only be "resolved" by neglecting one or the other of the elements that make up the tension. What constitutes the specificity of the voice is that this particular set of tensions, rather than any others, cannot be decided. In so long and so detailed an interpretation based so much on questions of tone, I am certain to have sometimes gotten the tone wrong. But I hope I have succeeded in delineating accurately the limits within which the choice of tone can (or cannot) be fixed. As I suggested with the Pardoner, irony, the problem of tone or of the voicing of a given sentence, is not so unlocatable as is sometimes supposed because one can always, in principle, locate what a statement is or is not being ironic *about*. The advantage of a voice-oriented reading is that it allows us to propose the range of possibilities from serious to ironic on a given topic as a set of tensions not in the statement as a proposition but in the speaker, the proposer, construed as the site where they occur. This set of specific tensions, as elucidated by interpretation, can be said to *constitute* for Chaucer the personality or set of psychosocial processes that produce, and are produced by, a given pilgrim in his or her tale. It is in the nature of those processes, of that subjectivity, that they render closure—of text, person, or reading—impossible.

Conclusion: The Disenchanted Self

I was wondering myself if I know where I am going. So I would answer you by saying, first, that I am trying, precisely, to put myself at a point so that I do not know any longer where I am going.

Jacques Derrida, "Structure, Sign, and Play in the Discourse of the Human Sciences"

I am nat wont in no mirour to prie,
But swynke soore and lerne multiplie.
The Canon's Yeoman's Prologue
(VIII, 668–69)

As an institution, the author is dead: his civil status, his biographical person have disappeared; dispossessed, they no longer exercise over his work the formidable paternity whose account literary history, teaching, and public opinion had the responsibility of establishing and renewing; but in the text, in a way, I *desire* the author: I need his figure (which is neither his representation nor his projection), as he needs mine.

Roland Barthes, *The Pleasure of the Text*

What seem to me to be the two best treatments of the *General Prologue*, E. Talbot Donaldson's "Chaucer the Pilgrim" and Jill Mann's *Chaucer and Medieval Estates Satire*, between them outline the general structure of Chaucerian practice in the *Canterbury Tales*, the telling of tales as the interaction between a subject and an institution. Donaldson, of course, concentrated on the subject side of the interaction in his influential characterization of the naive narrator of the *General Prologue* and the links, who so often misses the point of the complex phenomena he describes in order that Chaucer the satirist or the poet or the man can make sure that *we* see how complex they are. Donaldson was the first to call attention to the issue of voicing in the prologue and the first to apply to the poem the dramatic method that had previously been used only on the tales.

By contrast, Mann, firmly established for the first time the genre of the *General Prologue* by demonstrating that the poem is an estates satire, one of a class of medieval treatments of the orders, or estates, of society. These works generally list the various members of society according to the traditional scheme of the estates and comment on their abuses—themselves stereotyped. Though she notes that Chaucer shows a freedom typical of him in the selection of the particular estates he presents, Mann proves that he "does cover the elements of social anatomisation made familiar by estates literature" as a means "to suggest society as a whole by way of [a] representative company of individuals" (*Medieval Estates Satire*, 4, 5). The traditional classification provides Chaucer with a conceptual framework shared with his audience (what I have been calling an institution) for organizing his observations of individuals in society, an underlying structure of common assumptions about what society is and the way it is put together. I shall briefly consider each of these approaches in turn before trying to combine their best features for a fuller reading of the poem.

CHAUCER THE PILGRIM

Donaldson's formulations of Chaucer the pilgrim are made with an awareness of the complexity of the actual performance situation, which he images as social: the author (Chaucer the man), reading aloud to a court audience, projects a fictional caricature of himself (Chaucer the pilgrim), which both masks and emphasizes the complex ironic sensibility Donaldson calls Chaucer the poet. When he asserts "the probability—or rather the certainty—that [the three Chaucers] bore a close resemblance to one another, and that indeed, they frequently got together in the same body" ("Chaucer the Pilgrim," 1), Donaldson is close to an image of the poet as subject, a site from which multiple selves, roles, and so on emerge simultaneously and undecidably. Such oxymoronical characterizations of the poet's "elusion of clarity"[1] as "that double vision that is his ironical essence" ("Chaucer the Pilgrim," 11) reflect similar intimations of the absence, in the last analysis, of a determinate Chaucer.

Nonetheless, Donaldson is concerned in "Chaucer the Pilgrim" and elsewhere to construct a self for the fictional pilgrim, a distinct, fin-

---

1. The phrase is taken from Donaldson, "Chaucer and the Elusion of Clarity."

ished personality whose attitudes toward all the other pilgrims he describes in the *General Prologue* can be made fully consistent with a set of root tendencies or traits in him: snobbishness, overreadiness to please, Babbittry, and the like. In "Chaucer the Pilgrim," at least, these traits again appear to be grounded in social typification. Donaldson is aware of the estates tradition as a general background of the poem, which he refers to in passing as "the ancient stock satirical characters" that "it was left to Chaucer to turn . . . into real people assembled for a pilgrimage" (9). For him, however, these classifications are of interest not as what lies behind the depiction of the *pilgrims* (as they are for Mann) but as a source of the attitudes of the *speaker,* whose membership in the third estate is loosely held to account for his personality, "a bourgeois exposed to the splendors of high society, whose values, such as they are, he eagerly accepts" (4). Though there is much to be said for this turn toward the historical and institutional situation of the poet (which he normally brackets out of his readings, often for good reasons),[2] Donaldson himself does not follow it out far, nor does he fully textualize the poet's self-representation. The idea of Chaucer the pilgrim requires that in any given passage we first decide what Chaucer the pilgrim means by what he says and then what Chaucer the poet means by what the pilgrim means, and this division of the speaker leaves a certain residual uncertainty about the distinction between the voice of the text and a presence behind and beyond it who somehow guarantees the meaning we find there. Some of Donaldson's characterizations of Chaucer the poet take on a distinctly metaphysical cast:

> Undoubtedly Chaucer the man would, like his fictional representative, have found [the Prioress] charming and looked on her with affection. To have got on so well in so changeable a world Chaucer must have got on well with the people in it, and it is doubtful that one may get on with people merely by pretending to like them: one's heart has to be in it. But the third entity, Chaucer the poet, operates in a realm which is above and subsumes those in which Chaucer the man and Chaucer the pilgrim have their being. In this realm prioresses may be simultaneously evaluated as marvellously amiable ladies and as prioresses.
>
> (11)

A moment's reflection establishes that this third realm can only be the text; that is where Donaldson reads the simultaneous double evalu-

---

2. See the quotation from Donaldson, *Chaucer's Poetry* above, p. 36.

ation. The text is here being hypostatized, in the New Critical fashion that locates Donaldson's own historical situation, as an "entity" that hovers in a paradoxical nonplace that is both in the text and outside it, somewhere between the two institutional sites called the work and the author.[3]

But even at the level Donaldson is working at, the representation of the self, I do not see the need to reify these tensions in the text into separate personalities of the same speaker, and I think this way of talking about the narrator of the General Prologue has proved misleading because it has promoted not just the detextualization but the oversimplification of the speaker as well. It has encouraged us not only to treat him as if we knew who he was apart from his utterances and could predict his responses but to treat him as more of a simpleton than the evidence warrants. The general personality traits of Chaucer the pilgrim have themselves become reified in the Chaucer criticism of the last thirty years, and this frozen concept of the character has fostered a carelessness in reading that Donaldson himself rarely committed. I suspect that the success of this reified partial object, despite a few attempts to put him back together,[4] has been due in large part to a natural desire on the part of critics to evade the feelings of contingency and responsibility that haunt the act of interpretation and the indeterminacy of the text.[5] The notion of Chaucer the pilgrim at least offers an homme moyen sensuel with whom we can feel we know where we are and whose apparent mistakes can serve as the stalking horses of our more accurate—though no less assured—moral judgments, which we authorize through the equally assured poet who must have "meant" us to see them. Chaucer the pilgrim thus becomes another version of the more general phenomenon of the self-betraying speaker already encountered in the criticism of the Wife's and Pardoner's tales. But I think that it is just this sense of knowing where we are and with whom we are dealing that the General Prologue, like those tales, deliberately and calculatedly denies us.

3. See Foucault, "What Is an Author?"
4. Most notable is the valuable and neglected article by John M. Major, "The Personality of Chaucer the Pilgrim," but see also Donald Howard, who makes the parsimonious Aristotelian move of putting the ideal form back into the matter in "Chaucer the Man."
5. See Donaldson's brilliant and humane critique of stemma editing on similar grounds in "The Psychology of Editors of Middle English Texts."

Consider, for instance, the following passage from the Monk's portrait, a notorious locus—and one fastened on by Donaldson—for the naiveté of the narrator:

> He yaf nat of that text a pulled hen,
> That seith that hunters ben nat hooly men,
> Ne that a monk, whan he is recchelees,
> Is likned til a fissh that is waterlees—
> This is to seyn, a monk out of his cloystre.
> But thilke text heeld he nat worth an oystre;
> And I seyde his opinion was good.
> What sholde he studie and make hymselven wood,
> Upon a book in cloystre alwey to poure,
> Or swynken with his handes, and laboure,
> As Austyn bit? How shal the world be served?
> Lat Austyn have his swynk to hym reserved!
> Therfore he was a prikasour aright.
>
> (I, 177–89)

If we think of these lines as the performance of a speaker who is blind to their "real" significance, as apparent praise of the Monk that actually dispraises him, we immediately run into the following difficulties. First, the Monk's own bluff manner is present in these lines. I agree with most commentators that he is being half-quoted and that we hear his style, for example, in a phrase like "nat worth an oystre."[6] This semicitation already introduces a measure of uncertainty as to who is speaking, or at least a question about the extent to which the narrator really does agree with what he cites. Second, the standards of the Monk's calling, against which, if we will, he may be measured, are also present. The social and moral worlds indeed display their tension here, but *who brought these issues up?* Who is responsible for the slightly suspended enjambment that turns the deadly precision of "As Austyn bit?" into a small firecracker? For the wicked specificity with which, at the beginning of the portrait, the Monk's bridle is said to jingle "as dooth the *chapel* belle" (171, emphasis added)? Who goes to such pains to explain the precise application of the proverb about the fish, "This is to seyn, . . ."? Who if not the speaker? The Monk? Given the quasi-citational character of the passage, it is possible to see not only

---

6. See, e.g., Charles A. Owen, Jr., "Development of the Art of Portraiture in Chaucer's *General Prologue*," *LeedsSE* 14 (1983): 125–27.

the narrator but also the Monk himself as a man who is aware of the discrepancy between the impression he makes and the ideals of his estate and whose no-nonsense utterances are attempts to face it directly, if not quite squarely. Who is talking here? Third, even if we confine this sort of awareness to the narrator, these observations do not permit us to say that he is only making a moral judgment or only poking fun at the Monk. Donaldson and Mann are surely right to point to the way the portrait registers the positive claims made by the pilgrim's vitality and "manliness."[7] The speaker's amused enjoyment of the Monk's forthrightness is too patent to let us see him as just a moralist. Fourth, the way the speaker's voice evokes complex possibilities of attitude is neatly caught by "And I seyde his opinion was good." The past tense reminds us that the *General Prologue* is a retrospective account of a meeting that took place at some unspecified time in the past, "in that seson on a day" (19). The virtual now of the prologue is situated not only after the first night at the Tabard but after the whole of the rest of the pilgrimage as well, including the telling of all the tales. It thus opens up a gap between the past of meeting and the now of telling that has room for any amount of reconsideration and revision of first impressions. "And I seyde his opinion was good": that is what he said when he and the Monk had their conversation, but is he saying the same thing now in this portrait? Did he really mean it at the time? Does he now? In what sense?

The point of this exercise is not merely to show that the speaker's attitude is complex and sophisticated but also to stress how obliquely expressed it is, all in ironic juxtapositions whose precise heft is hard to weigh, in part because we have no clear markers for tone as we might if we heard the prologue spoken. What we have, in fact, is a speaker who is not giving too much of himself away and who is not telling us, any more than he told the Monk, his whole mind in plain terms. The tensions among social, moral, and existential worlds are embodied in a single voice here, and they are embodied *as tensions,* not as a resolution or a synthesis. We cannot tell exactly what the speaker thinks of the Monk *or* of conventional morality, and it is not fully clear that he can tell either. One of the things that turning the speaker into Chaucer

7. See Donaldson, "Chaucer the Pilgrim," 5, and Mann, *Medieval Estates Satire,* 17–37, esp. 20. See also Sklute, "Catalogue Form and Catalogue Style," 43.

the pilgrim may deny him is his own ambivalence about the complexity of his own responses to the pilgrims. I will have more to say about this point later, but we can tell here that we are dealing with a speaker who withholds himself from us, with the textual traces of a presence that asserts its simultaneous absence. The speaker, even as a performer, a self, is present as uncomprehended and not to be seized all at once in his totality. He *displays his difference* (or, textually, his *différance*) from his externalizations, his speaking, in the act of externalizing himself.

Thus even at the level of self-presentation, before the issue of subjectivity is broached, the reification involved in making the speaker of the *General Prologue* into Chaucer the pilgrim seems unsatisfactory. At this level textuality manifests itself as the sort of humanist richness Donaldson locates only in Chaucer the poet as a quasi–*hors-texte* but which is in fact operating as the unspoken of the narrator's textual utterances to generate a kind of *effet du réel*. In literature (as in life, come to think of it), the "reality effect" of characters is a function of their mystery, the extent to which we are made to feel that there is more going on in regard to them than we know or can predict. Criseyde is a well-known and well-analyzed example elsewhere in Chaucer's poetry of this effect,[8] and the general narrator of the *Canterbury Tales* is another. His lack of definition may in fact explain why he can be taken for Chaucer the pilgrim. Because his "identity" is a function of what he leaves unspoken—that is, because it is derived from implication, irony, innuendo, and the potentialities of meaning and intention that occur in the gaps between observations drawn from radically different realms of discourse[9]—there is room for the temptation to reduce his uncomfortable indeterminacy by forcing the gaps shut and spelling out the connections. But suppressing the indeterminacy in this way involves reducing complex meanings to simpler ones

8. See Mizener, "Character and Action in the Case of Criseyde," and apRoberts, "Central Episode in Chaucer's *Troilus*."

9. This observation suggests that a paratactic style is conducive to producing the kind of effect I am describing because the information (syntax) that would *specify* the connection between statements is left out. See Auerbach, *Mimesis*, 83–107. Parataxis is one of the the main descriptive techniques of the *General Prologue*, particularly noticeable in the three central portraits of the Shipman, the Physician, and the Wife of Bath but widely employed throughout. Further, the structure of the prologue is itself paratactic (composed of juxtaposed, relatively independent portraits), and so is the poem as a whole (composed of juxtaposed tales).

that may not be "meant" (may not function in the discourse of the text) in the first place. One infers Chaucer the pilgrim by displacing the things the speaker does not say (since, after all, he does not *say* them but only suggests them) and by insisting that he "means" his statements in only the plainest, most literal sense. Such an interpretation does not fail to recognize that the displaced complexities are there; it simply relocates them in "the poem" or "Chaucer the poet," thus *choosing* to constitute from the manifold of the text a social (or moral, or intellectual) dope, a speaker who is unaware of the import of his own language, which is being fed to and through him by a "higher" entity.

"Chaucer the pilgrim" thus does function as a hedge against textuality and the play of semiosis: the construct both contains them and sets them free under controlled conditions. The pilgrim himself is the representative of determinate, communicative meaning, which is both preserved and criticized in him. At the same time textual, disseminated, ironic signification is displaced to the poet, who functions as a place where such literary effects can be acknowledged yet still treated as meant or authorized. But my first objection to this procedure is that once again it denies the speaker—who in this case seems clearly to be the maker as well—his agency in the production of the performance. It is not that there is no such thing as Chaucer the pilgrim, first of all in the sense that the text does represent a human agent who undertakes the project of describing a set of events that he represents as having actually happened to him. These events are in some important sense fictional, and that makes their protagonist some kind of a fiction as well. Nor would I want to deny that there is an issue in the poem about whether or not the speaker is always in complete command of the project. The trouble is that the notion of Chaucer the pilgrim as it has been used displaces what is complex or problematic about this activity to the author or the work, even before we bring our Foucaultian guns to bear on those notions. It has thus made it too easy to miss the ways in which the poem is itself a representation of the speaker's active encounter with the difficulties of judging and classifying others and the extent to which the question of his control of the description (including the play of semiosis) is an issue first and foremost for him. My problem with Chaucer the pilgrim, even before the question of the subject enters into the matter, is that he has not yet been sufficiently recognized as a self.

ESTATES SATIRE

One of the most valuable features of *Chaucer and Medieval Estates Satire* is the attention Mann pays to Chaucer's unique treatment of the estates form itself. The *General Prologue* is not, she argues, merely an example of estates satire but also an alteration and revision of estates techniques that produces a different, we might say a more "modern," image of society. As she shows, Chaucer consistently displaces or complicates the relatively straightforward moral judgments of traditional estates literature in favor of the more ambiguous details of the immediate social impression his pilgrims make. Whereas we are never in doubt about what we are to think of the monks, friars, or townsmen in other estates satires, we are almost always unsure of exactly how good or bad their counterparts in the *General Prologue* are. This uncertainty produces what Mann describes as the effect of an estates satire from which the purpose of moral classification has been removed and at least suggests a view of society as constituted more by the behavior and performances of individuals and groups than by an a priori scheme. Chaucer "ironically substitut[es] for the traditional moral view of social structure a vision of a world where morality becomes as specialized to the individual as his work-life" (*Medieval Estates Satire*, xi).[10]

Though I agree, Mann's way of formulating and presenting her case seems to me to go at once too far and not far enough: too far in that she applies her unquestionably valid insights too broadly and generally to all the portraits and the prologue as a whole; and not far enough in that in practice she, like Donaldson, neglects the ways the poem actively challenges not only the traditional assumptions of moral classification in general but also those of estates satire in particular. Both of these difficulties stem from a neglect of the poem's voicing and especially the temporal inflections of voice that are registered in, and as, its *sequence*. Thus in the first instance Mann's discussions of individual portraits take them out of sequence and relocate them in new groupings according to the various methods of characterization she analyzes in separate chapters: in chapter 4, the omission of the victim (the Man of Law, the Doctor, the Merchant, the Five Guildsmen); in chapter 7, portraits organized around scientific classifications (the Par-

---

10. See also the last chapter of *Medieval Estates Satire*, "Conclusions," 187–202.

doner, the Franklin, the Miller, the Reeve); and so on. As a result, in her treatment all the portraits make essentially the same point about the displacement from moral classification to social impression without registering differences of emphasis and degree. Mann frequently makes observations that cry out for further explanation. She notes, for instance, that one of Chaucer's techniques of complication involves the application of attractive images to characters who are also critically presented—the Friar's eyes twinkling like stars, for example. She goes on to note that sometimes "the imagery works *with* the moral comments. . . . The animal imagery in the portraits of the Miller, Pardoner, and Summoner persuades us that we are dealing with crude or unpleasant personalities" (*Medieval Estates Satire*, 193–94). What she does not notice is that all three of these pilgrims are closely bunched together in the cluster of five rogues that ends the portrait gallery in the prologue. That is, there is a conjunction of moral and social unpleasantness at this point in the poem, a locally consistent use of imagery to create negative moral comment at a structurally significant juncture in a way that works against the more global tendency in the poem to render such judgments problematic.

Similarly, Mann notes the undoing of determinate signification, "Chaucer's constant exploitation of the different semantic values of words," in the poem:

> The adjective "worthy" is used as the keyword of the Knight's portrait, where it has a profound and serious significance, indicating not only the Knight's social status, but also the ethical qualities appropriate to it. In the Friar's portrait, the word is ironically used to indicate the Friar's lack of these ethical qualities—but it can also be read non-ironically as a reference to social status.[11] . . . The reference to social status seems to be the only one in the portrait of the Merchant, who "was a worthy man with alle" (283). By the time we reach the Franklin's portrait, the word is used with a vague heartiness which seems to indicate little beside the narrator's approval: "Was nowher swich a worthy vavasour" (360).
>
> (*Medieval Estates Satire*, 195–96)

As this passage shows, Mann is not unaware of the sequential character of the process, and she sees that it has something to do with the narrator, whom she earlier calls "a representative for the rest of society

---

11. See Mann's discussion of the Friar's portrait, *Medieval Estates Satire*, 53.

in its relation to each estate" (*Medieval Estates Satire,* 194). The fact of sequence has no real significance for her argument, however, as it might if it were correlated with the parallel sequence through the estates—from Knight to Friar to Merchant and Franklin—that the poem also displays. That is, "worthy" becomes *progressively* less informative and more indeterminate as the narrator moves *through* the traditional estates classifications; the undoing of determinate meaning is connected to the categories of social classification and their progression in the text.

One thing that keeps these features of the text from pulling their weight in Mann's reading is her generally distant and unfocused treatment of the speaker: her inattention to sequence is an effect of her relative disinterest in the poem as a performance. Though she is aware of the Donaldsonian tradition and pays it lip service at points, she is more interested in the poem as a record of the poet's original use of estates conventions. As she sees it, this transaction takes place as it were behind the scenes of the poem. She is willing to accord the poet as maker a considerable range of independent authorial activity, including the deliberate deployment of intertextualities with both the *Decameron* and Langland,[12] but she sees the poem itself as the trace or product, rather than the depiction, of authorship. *Auctoritas* itself is not a problematic notion for her except at the level of large-scale historical process, the gradual drift of medieval society toward modernity that she seems to feel the poem registers. For Mann, the poet *uses* the institution of estates classification richly and often critically, and she has brought that institution into the center of the poem in a way Donaldson does not. What is missing from her reading that Donaldson supplies is an attention to how the text *represents* the act of description and classification itself in the person of its narrator.

In what follows I will combine the Donaldsonian emphasis on voice-oriented reading with Mann's institutional perspective to explore how the text itself represents and revises—at once uses and questions—both. I will begin by sketching a prospective reading of the

12. This is an interesting and suggestive feature of Mann's treatment of the poem, which appears to have gone unremarked, perhaps because she simply assumes the poet's knowledge of these works that an older generation of Chaucerians was inclined to deny. Her evidence is generally convincing because it is firmly textual and detailed. See *Medieval Estates Satire,* 46–47, 198, 208–12.

General Prologue that follows the sequence of the performance the poem depicts—the unfolding deployment of available conventions of social and moral classification by a speaker who attempts to use them to organize the practical task of making sense of his experience. Such a prospective reading is appropriate as a way of acknowledging the *specificity* of the prologue, its representation of a particular intentional agent, or self, under concrete institutional and social conditions of performance. I will end by considering the prologue as a disenchanted text that retrospectively identifies its own agency and its own textuality as central facts about itself, thereby undoing its own prospective ambitions to objectivity, completeness, and closure and opening itself to indefinite rereadings. This redefinition of the text necessarily entails a reevaluation of the "self" it has generated as only an effect of its prospective (or prologal) character, and this revision provides a model, I will suggest, for the representation of subjectivity in the *Canterbury Tales*.

THE PROLOGUE AS PERFORMANCE:
NOTES TOWARD A PROSPECTIVE READING

> But nathelees, whil I have tyme and space,
> Er that I ferther in this tale pace,
> Me thynketh it acordaunt to resoun
> To telle yow al the condicioun
> Of ech of hem, so as it semed me.
>
> (35–39)

The *General Prologue* presents itself prospectively as the record of an experience, but not the experience of meeting the pilgrims on the way to Canterbury. Rather, as Donald Howard has shown, the poem purports to represent the experience of the speaker in putting together the memory of that meeting, which took place at some time in the past, so as to give it to us reordered "acordaunt to resoun."[13] This is the task he undertakes *now*, in the present of narrating, "whil I have tyme and space / Er that I ferther in this tale pace," after the pilgrimage itself has been completed. The experience is of course a fiction, the textual representation of a virtual "I" addressing a virtual audience "To telle

13. Howard, *Idea of the Canterbury Tales*, 134–58.

yow al the condicioun / Of ech of hem." As I have suggested, the fiction is one of *performance,* the logocentric illusion, as we say nowadays, of a performer who unfolds his meaning to us as he speaks, but it is no less consistently presented for all of that. The poem keeps us aware of this fictional or virtual now of audience address from its beginning to its end, when "now is tyme to yow for to telle / . . . al the remenaunt of oure pilgrimage" (720, 724). The rational ordering of the pilgrims is thus a *project* the narrator proposes at the outset of the prologue, one we watch him enact as the poem unfolds.

If the ordering of the pilgrims is a project of the narrator's, it does not initially seem difficult or challenging to him or to us. Like the famous opening sentence, with its effortless progression from the impersonal cosmic eros of seasonal change through vegetable growth and animal (or at least avian) sexuality to the *amor spiritualis* that drove Saint Thomas, the presentation of the pilgrims in the first half of the *General Prologue* is a richly embroidered and elegantly varied expression of "what everybody knows" about the shape of society.[14] The progression of portraits from the Knight through the Wife of Bath is consistently, though complexly, structured on the time-honored model of the three estates. The tally of the pilgrims begins with a preeminent representative of the estate of *milites* and pauses for a moment to list the Knight's hierarchically ordered entourage—his son the Squire and his servant the Yeoman—before passing on to the second group, the three members of the regular clergy. As Mann notes (*Medieval Estates Satire,* 6), it would be more correct in conventional estates terms to place the clerical figures first, and this fact suggests that the estates organization is modified by hierarchical considerations of another sort: the Knight is in some sense the highest-ranking pilgrim. This displacement does not, however, affect the overall organization in estates terms. With the clerical figures too there is room for flexibility and play—the Prioress's entourage is also listed briefly at the end of her portrait. But here, as with the treatment of the Five Guildsmen as a single unit, the choice to stress the portrait as more basic than the individual person by brushing past the Second Nun and the Nun's Priest(s) points to the importance of estates classification over indi-

---

14. See the fine discussion of the organization of the poem in Hoffman, "Chaucer's Prologue to Pilgrimage."

viduality as such. In any case, the basic structural outline is clear: three religious presented in order of official rank, a prioress, a monk as monastery official ("kepere of the celle"), and an ordinary friar. This grouping is followed by the inevitably more miscellaneous list of the pilgrims of the third estate, which by the late Middle Ages had become a kind of catchall for those who were not knights or clergy and which is itself variously carved up by other estates satires.[15] The first part of the poem, viewed from a certain distance, displays a complex articulation of interrelated hierarchical schemata within a basic triadic structure continued through the Wife of Bath's portrait, at least in the sense that the portrait groupings continue to be divisible by three. The triad of the Franklin, the Five Guildsmen, and the Cook, for instance, outlines a modern, citified, bureaucratic, and competitive parallel—a knight of the shire, burgesses who aspire to rank,[16] and a proletarian craftsman in the temporary hire of his betters—to the more traditional and naturalized sociomoral hierarchy of the first triad, the Knight, the Squire, and the Yeoman, who are bound together by ties of blood and homage.

If there are problems with the order I have sketched so far—and there are—they are not allowed to emerge in the unfolding of the poem for some time. Like the opening sentence, the order of the pilgrims in the first half of the prologue, which is rooted in conventional and collective norms, reflects "what everybody knows" about the exfoliation of natural and spiritual energies in springtime and the relation of these energies to the shape of society and its estates. This is perhaps one reason why the portraits in this part of the poem exhibit the relatively relaxed tone and the lack of overt moralization that Mann notes. These descriptions draw easily on the shared framework of assumptions in whose name our representative, the narrator, speaks. That the kind of loving the Squire currently practices is more closely allied to the energies of the animal soul than to the rational love of *ecclesia* and *respublica* his father embodies need not be spelled out. It is carried in the implications of the image that links him to the sleep-

15. See Mann, *Medieval Estates Satire,* Appendix A, 203–6.
16. Sylvia L. Thrupp, in *The Merchant Class of Medieval London,* has demonstrated how typical was the desire, in men of the Five Guildsmen's class, to crown a career in the city by buying land, moving to the country, and becoming gentry. These pilgrims thus "belong" with the Franklin in part because they are trying to become him.

lessly amorous birds of the first eighteen lines—"He sleep namoore than dooth a nyghtyngale" (98)[17]—birds that are themselves balanced between the immanent "gravitational" love that moves the sun and the other stars through the round of the seasons and the focused and rational divine love that calls to and through the saint. Similarly, our common expectation that any literary friar will be a bad one makes it unnecessary for the narrator to condemn the pilgrim Friar explicitly. One reason the Friar's portrait is the longest in the prologue is the extreme popularity and ubiquity of antifraternal satire in the fourteenth century: there is a rich fund of conventional material to draw on, and the poet-narrator can count on this tacitly shared background to enforce his ironies.[18]

As Mann's discussion of "worthy" may suggest, however, the precise placing of these pilgrims does create some difficulties, and, as I want to insist, these difficulties are experienced by the speaker, and experienced progressively. An overview of the pilgrims of the third estate reveals an increasing strain between what the poet's common culture tells him he ought to be able to say about people ("what everybody knows") and what his actual experience of trying to describe them provides. It is preeminently in this section of the poem that technical and scientific jargon and the language of craft, for example, become conspicuous, with the effects Mann notes: the felt absence of more widely applicable and less specialized role definitions, and a sense of the disjunction between the moral and professional spheres that emphasizes the fundamentally amoral character of professional expertise; think of the Shipman's navigational skill, which appears to make him a more efficient pirate, or the learning of the Doctor, whose tag, "He was a verray, parfit praktisour" (422), calls attention to the difference between his *skills* and the Knight's *virtues* (72). Details of dress and appearance become less informative. The end of the Man of Law's portrait, with its abrupt dismissal "Of his array telle I no lenger tale" (330), stresses how little we can learn about him from his off-duty dress, especially compared to the amount of symbolic information about character carried by the estates uniform of the Knight with his armor-stained "gypon"; likewise the portrait of the Friar with his

17. See Hoffman, "Chaucer's Prologue to Pilgrimage."
18. See Bowden, *Commentary on the General Prologue,* 119–145, and my discussion of the Monk's portrait above.

double-worsted semicope. The same indefiniteness characterizes such things as the Cook's "mormal," the name of the Shipman's barge, the *Maudelayne* (what would that mean if it meant?), and most of the details of the Wife of Bath's portrait: her deafness, her complicated love life, and her big hat. The Wife's portrait is the culmination in the poem of the progressive tendency of particular qualities of individuals to shift their area of reference from the exemplary to the idiosyncratic. The often-noted excellence of each pilgrim becomes rooted more and more in the existential being and activity of the individual and less and less in his or her representative character as the symbol of a larger group. The individual's place in a hierarchy becomes less important than his or her performances; consider again the difference between a "verray, parfit gentil knyght" and a "verray, parfit praktisour." These are persons whose stories we would have to tell to understand them— or who would have to tell their stories.

This need for more information is overtly recognized in the Wife of Bath's portrait, the only place in the portraits that refers beyond them to the tale-telling to come:

> Housbondes at chirche dore she hadde fyve,
> Withouten oother compaignye in youthe—
> But thereof nedeth nat to speke as nowthe.
>   (460–62)

"What everybody knows" is not enough to account for the Wife either morally or socially, and the promise of more to come points to the narrator's awareness that she will have to do it herself later. As I have suggested, following Hoffman, the hierarchy of the opening lines of the prologue, in terms of which the pilgrims are organized and against which, broadly speaking, they are measured, is fundamentally a hierarchy of loves. It ought therefore to be possible "acordaunt to resoun" to place the Wife's loves in relation to that order. But that is just what the speaker does not do. The details of the Wife's portrait are as vibrant as the woman we sense behind them, but their vividness only stresses their lack of coherence in traditional terms. Prospectively neither we nor the speaker can arrange them in a hierarchy of significance with respect to the hierarchies of nature, society, and the divine order. It is clear that the question interests the speaker since he allows it to take over the latter part of the portrait. The list of the Wife's pilgrimages (463–66), a record of travel that competes with the Knight's, is made an excuse to remind us, with an elbow in the ribs, that "She koude muchel of wandrynge by the weye" (467)—unlike, no doubt, that proper father and head of an extended family unit. Her gap teeth and "hipes large" keep the issue before us, and the portrait ends "Of remedies of love she knew per chaunce, / For she koude of that art the olde daunce" (475–76). This continued fascination does not, however, allow the speaker to rest secure in a neutral, "objective" presentation of the Wife's love life and its place in the scheme of things, as his mildly chauvinist tone reveals. The Wife certainly raises the questions that gender and sexuality put to the standard, patriarchal hierarchies, questions of the relations between sensual love, "felaweshipe," marriage, *amor dei,* and *remedia amoris,* but these relations, as she will remind us in her prologue and tale, are matters of controversy, and the description of her here does not begin to resolve them.

It seems to me to be no accident that the portrait of the highly idealized and morally transparent Parson occurs at just this point, forming the strongest possible contrast to the ambiguities of the Wife of Bath. Even more significant, however, is the fact that now the organizing principle of the poem changes. After the closely linked Parson-Plowman grouping, the final five pilgrims are bunched together and announced in advance as completing the tally: "Ther was also a REVE, and a MILLERE, / A SOMNOUR, and a PARDONER also, / A MAUNCIPLE, and myself—ther were namo" (542–44). As opposed to the complex complementarity and hierarchy of the ordering of the portraits in the first half, we are here presented with rather simple oppositions: two against five, bad against good. If the initial organization of the poem is indeed that of the three estates, we obviously do well to ask why the Parson's portrait is not included with the second, clerical, triad and why it interrupts the account of the third estate (to which all the remaining pilgrims in the list belong) instead. In the sort of sequential or prospective reading I am urging here, the question does not arise until we reach the Parson's portrait, but it certainly does arise then. The effect is to make the initial three-estates ordering, *in retrospect,* look much more selective and ad hoc than it did at first, much more the product of tacit choices and decisions on the part of the narrator who now alters and abandons it.

The two most striking features of the final sequence of seven portraits from the Parson through the Pardoner are, first, a drive to ultimate moral clarification that I will call *apocalyptic,* in the etymological sense of the word as an unveiling, a stripping away of surface complexity to reveal the fundamental truth beneath it,[19] and second, the conspicuous emergence of the narrator as the source of this drive. The effect of the insertion of the Parson-Plowman dyad is to provide a golden "ensample" against which not only the remaining pilgrims but also the previous ones—the Parson's portrait contains a number of "snybbing" critical references to previous portraits such as those of the Monk and Friar—are measured and found wanting.[20] Besides the animal imagery cited by Mann (*Medieval Estates Satire*, 194–95), which is itself susceptible of typological and physiognomical interpretation *in malo,* as Curry, Robertson, and others have shown, there are other patterns that cut across the last portraits and produce the effect of a uniformly wicked and worsening world. The Miller, whose badness is qualified by the energy of his animal spirits, carries a sword and buckler. The more sinister-sounding Reeve, who does not just defraud a few village yokels but undermines a whole manor from lord to laborers, carries a *"rusty* blade" (618, emphasis added), and the Summoner's failure to sustain and defend ecclesiastical order is pinned down by the allegory of his armory: "A bokeleer hadde he maad hym of a cake" (668). Read across the portraits and, once more, against the image of hierarchy and vigilant order embodied in the first triad, where the Yeoman keeps the Knight's weapons "harneised wel" (114) for use at need, the symbolic progression of weapons here implies that as evil becomes more spiritual and intense, its outward signs become clearer and more concrete emblems of the inner state, and that such progressive evils are increasingly revealed as demonic parodies of the good. The Summoner and the Pardoner in particular have the *privatio boni* theory of evil written all over them.

At the same time the narrator moves forward out of the relatively anonymous "felaweshipe" of "what everybody knows" into a position of isolated prominence as he takes a God's-eye view more akin perhaps to the Parson's. He says "I" more often; he addresses us more overtly, breaking off description to do so; he warns and exhorts and judges:

---

19. And more or less in the sense that Morton W. Bloomfield uses it with respect to Langland in *Piers Plowman as a Fourteenth Century Apocalypse.*

20. For example, "He was a shepherde and noght a mercenarie" (514) or "He was to synful men nat despitous, / Ne of his speche daungerous ne digne, / . . . But it were any persone obstinat, / What so he were, of heigh or lough estat" (516–17, 521–22). See also Donaldson, "Adventures with the Adversative Conjunction," esp. 356.

"Wel I woot he lyed right in dede" (659). The effect is well represented by the Manciple's portrait, which is, notoriously, not about the Manciple but about the lawyers he works for. As the speaker moves toward the end of the portrait, he idealizes them more and more, stressing the power for social good bound up in them who are "able for to helpen al a shire" (584) and then managing to suggest that it is somehow the Manciple's fault that they do not help: "And yet this Manciple sette hir aller cappe" (586). Because the speaker so conspicuously wrenches us away from the Manciple, he calls attention to himself and his own social concerns. For this reason, among others, all this apocalyptic processing registers, I think, as a failure of vision on the narrator's part. In sequence and in context it looks like a reaction to the complexities and uncertainties of classification and judgment generated by the enterprise of the first half of the *General Prologue,* a retreat to simpler and more rigorous standards of moral classification that, because its psychological motives emerge so clearly, also looks like name-calling, a product less of objective appraisal of the pilgrims in question than of the speaker's own wishes and fears about the evils of society.

The pattern of this psychology is fairly precisely that of what I have called "masculine" disenchantment since it is focused on the ways human agents like the Manciple and the Summoner manipulate and subvert what should be a transcendent and stable order, and is marked by nostalgia for what it knows has been lost. The Summoner is an actively disenchanted cynic, whose perversion of what ought to be the justice of God is accompanied by an articulate conviction that it is only the justice of men as corrupt as himself: " 'Purs is the ercedekenes helle,' seyde he" (658). If the speaker protests this blatant assertion, he seems nonetheless to agree that it is all too often true, as the Pardoner's portrait affirms even more strongly:

> But with thise relikes, whan that he fond
> A povre person dwellynge upon lond,
> Upon a day he gat hym moore moneye
> Than that the person gat in monthes tweye;
> And thus, with feyned flaterye and japes,
> He made the person and the peple his apes.
>
> (701–6)

Like the pilgrims in their tales, the narrator of the *General Prologue* does not simply use categories to make neutral descriptions but also has attitudes toward the descriptions he makes and the things he describes. The pervasive symbolic processing of the end of the portrait gallery shows that there is more at stake for him here than the features and foibles of individuals. By the end of the prologue the pilgrims are being made aggressively to stand for estates as images of the state of society. Once again it seems no accident, in retrospect, that the tale of the pilgrims ends with the Pardoner, the darkest example and the most trenchant spokesman of an attitude the speaker here comes close to sharing.

This reading of the narrator's psychology is the more convincing, at least to me, because of the character of the passage that immediately follows the portraits. An address that begins confidently with a straightforward statement of what has been achieved, "Now have I toold you soothly, in a clause" (715), becomes more and more tentative and apologetic as it proceeds and more and more nervous about the *effect* not only of what remains to say but also of what has already been said:

> But first I pray yow, of youre curteisye,
> That ye n'arette it nat my vileynye,
> Thogh that I pleynly speke in this mateere,
> To telle yow hir wordes and hir cheere,
> Ne thogh I speke hir wordes proprely.
> For this ye knowen al so wel as I:
> Whoso shal telle a tale after a man,
> He moot reherce as ny as evere he kan
> Everich a word, if it be in his charge,
> Al speke he never so rudeliche and large,
> Or ellis he moot telle his tale untrewe,
> Or feyne thyng, or fynde wordes newe.
> He may nat spare, althogh he were his brother;
> He moot as wel seye o word as another.
> Crist spak hymself ful brode in hooly writ,
> And wel ye woot no vileynye is it.
> Eek Plato seith, whoso kan hym rede,
> The wordes moote be cosyn to the dede.
>
> (725–42)

The passage is dogged by the speaker's repetitions of the attempt to deny responsibility for the descriptions of the pilgrims he is about to give and haunted by his sense that the denials are not convincing because he is too clearly responsible for the descriptions he has already given. He ends oddly, after a discussion of the tales that are to come, where we might have expected him to begin, with an apology for having failed to order the pilgrims correctly, and this peculiarity suggests what is really on his mind: "Also I prey yow to foryeve it me, / Al have I nat set folk in hir degree / Heere in this tale, as that they sholde stonde" (743–45).[21] In strong contrast to the atmosphere of shared understandings and common agreements he projected at the beginning of the prologue, the speaker here appears nervously isolated, as if surrounded by an audience of Millers, Manciples, Reeves, Summoners, and Pardoners, whose accusation of "vileynye" he might have some cause to anticipate.

What seems to *happen* in the performance represented in the *General Prologue* is that two rather different procedures of classifying the pilgrims, which I have called hierarchical and apocalyptic and which seem to correspond in emphasis to the classificatory and the moralizing impulses respectively in estates satire, are adopted and then discarded by the speaker. In the final movement of the poem he turns to the pilgrims themselves, in part as a way of getting himself off the hook. The movement of the prologue is within two versions of "resoun," understood, as it can be in Middle English, as a translation of Latin *ratio*.[22] The distinction I have in mind is between, on the one hand, underlying cause, the reasons in things that are patterned on the *rationes seminales* in the mind of God, the basic rational structure of reality; and, on the other hand, account, argument, and especially opinion, as with the Merchant: "His resons he spak ful solempnely, / Sownynge alwey th'encrees of his wynnyng" (274–75). The poem goes from an account "acordaunt to resoun," which seems to want to claim the first definition, to the moment when the Knight begins his tale, "As was resoun, / By foreward and by composicioun" (847–48)—that is, according to an explicitly man-made, ad hoc, and open-ended *ratio* or plan, the tale-telling project, which will require the activity not of the narrator but of the pilgrims themselves in telling their tales and

---

21. Laura Kendrick notices the changing tone of this apology in *Chaucerian Play*, 144–45.

22. See the excellent account of the word and its medieval uses in McKeon, *Selections from the Medieval Philosophers*, 2:488–90.

of the reader in putting together and evaluating the various performances. This movement is paralleled by a shift in the meaning of the
word "tale" from "Er that I ferther in this tale pace" at the beginning
of the prologue to the force the word takes on contextually in the
apology just quoted. In the first instance the primary meaning would
seem to be "tally," "reckoning," in the sense of a completed list or
account, which is also one of the primary meanings of *ratio*. By the
time the end of the portrait gallery is reached, however, the developed
sense of the speaker's contribution to the way the list has unfolded lets
the meanings "Canterbury tale"—that is, traveler's tale, whopper—
and more generally "fiction," "story," such as the pilgrims will tell,
speak out. These transformations of "tale" and "resoun" have in
common the disenchanted view in the more technical sense that they
enforce of the enterprise of the poem and its speaker.

I began by suggesting that the *General Prologue* actively challenges
the traditional assumptions of estates satire. An analysis of the prologue's detailed representation of the practice of classifying establishes
that the poem is in fact not an estates satire but a critique of an estates
satire in the mode of deconstruction. That is, its narrator's gradual and
eventually conspicuous questioning of his own procedures operates as
a miming of traditional classifications so as to bring out gradually the
tensions and contradictions that underlie and constitute them. As the
representation of an unfolding experience, the poem is also a representation of the coming into something like discursive consciousness of
the problematic character of what begins as the relatively unreflective
practical activity of classifying people, and it presents that coming into
consciousness as an awakening to disenchantment. The speaker of the
poem eventually encounters his own agency, the inescapable likelihood that he has made use of estates conventions to *create rather than
discover* the order of society, so that the *General Prologue* turns out to
be, like the tales that follow, much more a representation of the voice
generated by a certain kind of activity in the moment-by-moment,
line-by-line process of describing than an objective narration. The
stalking horse of this enterprise is indeed the performing narrator, a
self-conscious version of Chaucer the pilgrim, who appears to find
himself enmeshed in the tensions and bedeviled by the impasses that
lead to what I take to be a central theme of the prologue, the question
of what it means to judge and classify one's fellows. If the speaker feels

and fears that he may have falsified the pilgrims in describing them, the corollary is that the poem is indeed a performance in exactly the way that the tales are. It is the self-presentation of a speaker, far more the Poet's portrait than an account of the other characters, who must now be expected to present themselves in their tales. What for the represented speaker is an experience of disenchantment is for the textualizing poet the representation of practical disenchantment.

It is one thing to have such an experience but quite another to write it down, in particular to make *a written representation of a failed performance*. If the aim is to give a satisfactory account of the pilgrims, one might start over on a different plan or, having learned one's lesson, discard the prologue. But to read the poem prospectively as a fictional performance—a reading it initially encourages—is finally to be made aware of the inadequacies of that mode of reading, and this awareness I take to be one of the aims of the representation. From this point of view, what the poem is criticizing, in estates satire and elsewhere, is the notion that once having heard what you say, I know what you mean and who you are. This is the assumption that seems to underlie the speaker's project to classify a group of pilgrims whose own performances he has already heard before we have gotten to them. It is the logocentric supposition that would make of the prologue a version of Derrida's characterization of Hegel's preface to *The Phenomenology of Mind:* something written last and put first, something meant, in an odd way, to do away with the need for the work itself.[23] What replaces this notion, what moves into the gap created by the undoing of definitive classification and interpretation, is the notion of reading and rereading, or to put it another way, the replacement of the poem as performance by the poem as text. The *General Prologue* ends, in a typically deconstructive move, with an act of *différance,* a deferring of

23. See "Outwork, prefacing," in *Dissemination, 2–59.* The supplementarity of prefacing is presented by Derrida pretty much as something Hegel encounters (or is oblivious of), outside his project, unwillingly, as an effect of a blindness. In this sense Chaucer's prologue is unlike one view of *The Phenomenology of Mind* because the poem is patently *not* finished and does not, therefore, form a completed system and because the prologue itself points conspicuously to the inadequacy of its prefacing. Hence it becomes, as I say in the text, an analysis of the impulse to such completion rather than an instance of it. What if these things were true of "Hegel" as well? Though de Man raised this question with respect to Derrida's reading of Rousseau in *Blindness and Insight,* and Harry Berger, Jr., has raised it about the reading of Plato in "Plato's Pharmacy," it has never to my knowledge been followed up.

the meaning of the pilgrims and the pilgrimage as something different from what the poem as performance achieved. The deferral is what makes the difference, and makes difference possible, because it frees up the prologue to be reread as a piece of writing in all sorts of new conjunctions with the tales. And of course it frees up the speaker too, who is not really, or at least not only, the somewhat more ambitious version of Chaucer the pilgrim that my performance analysis has been making him out to be, a matter to which I will now turn.

VOICE AND TEXT, PILGRIMS AND POET

A definitive version of the retrospective rereading that the prospective "failure" of the *General Prologue* opens up is in principle impossible and in practice impracticable—this book is only one version of a part of it. Nonetheless, a sketch of its implications will bring my own reading here to a close. I begin by observing that a prospective reading of the prologue, and the kind of reading of the poem as a whole that it encourages, is both overly traditional—perhaps even "establishment"—and overdominated by institutional perspectives at the expense of those of individuals. One index is the way the prospective unfolding of the prologue tries to control textuality by enforcing the importance of certain details in the portraits at the expense of others. The placing of the last five portraits over against the Parson-Plowman dyad and the stress given to patterns of imagery that run across portraits, like the weaponry pattern analyzed above, make such things as the Reeve's rusty blade, his top "dokked lyk a preest biforn" (590), or his governance of "His lordes sheep" (597) to his own advantage stand out as emblems of an estate and its responsibilities misused to the detriment of society. In doing so, they make other details, like the Reeve's actual trade of carpenter or his "wonyng . . . ful faire upon an heeth; / With grene trees yshadwed" (606–7), recede in importance or take on an anomalous feel, as in Mann's analysis of the Friar's twinkling eyes. Such details come into their own in a retrospective rereading, where the perspective of the tale can play back on the prologue to open up new lines of interpretation. The Reeve's assessment of the dignity owed his trade, as it combines with the generalized paranoia the portrait sketches and the tale confirms, motivates his attack on the Miller, for example, and the Friar's eyes twinkling "As doon the sterres in the frosty nyght" (268) are given point by the cold, distant, calculated way the Friar in his tale tries to watch and control his own performance before others, a kind of role-playing that brings out the element of technique and false heartiness in "rage he koude [that is, knew how], as it were right a whelp" (257).[24]

In a more general way, the institutional overdetermination of the prologue as performance and the repression of textual indeterminacy that rereading reveals are present in the portraits that go with the tales analyzed in this book. Prospectively the Knight's portrait is tied to an idealized image not only of the man but also of his estate and the place it occupies in a larger image of social hierarchy. The portrait has to do duty for so much in the way of symbolic support of estates hierarchies and the like that it makes less than it might of questions about the historical state of the institution of chivalry. The concreteness of the details of the description—all those named battles, for instance—has led disenchanted readers like Terry Jones to give them a weight of historical reference that many other critics have felt the portrait itself does not use or pushes to one side. Though I have yet to see a convincing argument that the portrait is ironic about the Knight, the more we know about the places he has been, the less confidence the institution of knighthood he seems so ideally to uphold inspires. This impression is in line with my reading of the prologue as a text that gradually reveals its own disenchantment. By its end the poem has become—or shown itself as—an analysis of the social and ideological commitments that are entailed in estates satire itself, in particular analysis of the form's "establishment" commitments to tradition, authority, and hierarchy such as might lead us—or the narrator—to try to make a "good" knight into an image of the health of knighthood. The tensions that make such commitments problematic are only present in the portrait as suppressed or latent textual possibilities that are not directly used in the prologue. Where they turn up, of course, is in the tale, as *problems about his estate that the Knight himself must engage,* and I have argued at length for the disenchanted realism of his portrayal of the temple of Mars as it bears on Theseus's chivalry, a portrayal that matches anything Froissart—or Jones—has to say about Peter of Cy-

---

24. See Leicester, " 'No Vileyns Word,' " and the discussion of the Physician's portrait above, Introduction, pp. 11–12.

prus at Atalia ("Satalye") or the siege of Alexandria. Thus it is probably accurate to think of the fundamental institutional grounding of character in the *Canterbury Tales* as the estate, and that this grounding holds for the pilgrims themselves as well as for the poet and the reader. Estates classification looks like a set of fundamentals about character in the sense of a foundation or a place to start, which is to say that such classifications represent not the *essences* of the pilgrims but *pre-texts,* ways of naming what they have to draw on, what they are confronted with about themselves socially, and what they have to enact, sustain, alter, and above all *negotiate* in their lives and their tales.

A rereading of this sort thus returns to both the prologue and the tales the historical and social, as well as personal, specificity of that negotiation, which the relatively abstract and idealizing thrust of the prospective reading initially denies them. To come back to the Knight's portrait after reading the tale is to see more readily how its details might support a reading of the Knight that is less idealized in the sense of less faded, unreal, and outmoded or late medieval than the criticism, or indeed the prospective thrust of the prologue itself, often allows.[25] For instance, the prospective encouragement the portrait unquestionably gives to a reading of "Ful worthy was he in his lordes werre" (47) as a shorthand representation of the Knight's crusading defense of God's Christendom in his numerous campaigns (as if he were himself a Peter of Cyprus) recedes in the light of the tale because of the tale's consistent and principled refusal of a providential interpretation of history. Despite the perennial temptation, reenunciated by A. J. Minnis, in *Chaucer and Pagan Antiquity,* to read the Knight's (and Chaucer's) awareness of historical difference as finally loaded in favor of modern Christianity over pagan antiquity, it will be clear by now that I see the tale and the Knight as deeply protohumanist in the credit they extend to the ancient world, a credit that is no doubt critical but far more in the emulative mode of the Renaissance than in some "medieval" theological one. Our own historical hindsight can locate the tale's undoing of such pieties precisely in historically conditioned disenchantment: the Knight's approval of olden times can be read as an index of his disenchanted failure to be convinced by a style of providential reading of historical process in relation to the kind of history

25. See, for example, Howard, *Idea of the Canterbury Tales,* 94–97.

making he knows best that had become increasingly ideologized and conspicuously political since at least the time of the investiture controversy. It is a style whose continuing use by the propagandists of two rival popes and a Holy Roman Emperor in the Knight's own time cannot have made it *more* convincing. The Knight thus joins Boccaccio and Chaucer as a progenitor of a project to restore and renew the epic that has, like a certain version of knighthood, a future; and if the English were not as quick as the Italians to make effective political and ideological use of this humanism, the fact that Chaucer thought a knight an appropriate voice for it suggests that he understood the social valence of the kind of change it represented.

From this retrospective angle the Pardoner too escapes the twin misrepresentations as contemptible body and apocalyptic symbol of social decay that the prologue's prospect foists on him. Out of place like the Parson in the estates structure of the prologue, the Pardoner is an "ecclesiaste" whose relation to both orders and degree is genuinely problematic and felt as such in the poet's voicing. But to read this problematic quality back to the prologue portrait from the Pardoner's assault in his tale on the church he represents is to see how these moments of strain in the classification project of the poem register more than the confusions of an inept performing speaker, as if such difficulties only beset comic unreliable narrators. What are from one point of view psychological tensions are from another registrations of a culture that is genuinely in tension with itself about its own structure and the adequacy of its own principles of classification— orders and estates—to its developing historical actuality. The Pardoner is an extension and complication of a relatively familiar type in the period, a radical-conservative social critic of the abuses of the church, the commodification of the sacramental system, and the secularization of the clergy, all of which are part of his own subjectivity since he is a site of them all. As such, he joins a chorus of disenchanted voices, from spiritual Franciscans to Lollards to satirical poets, chroniclers, and the Sultan of Turkey,[26] who condemn the debasement of what ought to be a divine institution by human manipulation and urge a revolutionary return to primitive gospel standards. From a longer perspective he participates as well in the Reformation project,

26. See above, chapter 9, note 2.

carried on by Luther, Calvin, and Kierkegaard, of reconceiving Christian subjectivity on neo-Donatist, individualistic, and psychological grounds whose radical conservatism might be summed up in the phrase *neo-Augustinian*—which is no doubt why modern exegetical neo-Augustinianism is so helpful in reading him.

In the case of the Wife of Bath there is a similar moment of social tension evident in the transition from her portrait to that of the Parson, reflected in the "feminine" questioning of various economic, social, and gender boundaries and categories that she and her description embody and in the "masculine" retrenchment of authority, orthodoxy, and male dominance that comes with the Parson. If the wider sociocultural sources and repercussions of this central moment are harder to evoke in the mode of glancing allusion I have adopted with the Knight and the Pardoner, I suspect that is due less to the absolute modernity of feminist gender theory than to the fact that the historical work needed to ground an understanding of the social and economic meaning of gender difference in the period, which needs to be directed by that theory as well as inform it, is only beginning to get done—and that I have only begun to read it. Certainly it is clear enough that the Wife's own prologue and tale are, among other things, an engagement with precisely the kind of authority the Parson is made to carry in the *General Prologue,* and it seems likely that read retrospectively, her portrait announces, and her prologue and tale carry out, her participation in a late medieval gynesis, or contribution to the discourse on woman, that such figures as Margery Kempe, Juliana of Norwich, and Christine de Pisan also have something to do with and that we are just beginning to learn to read.[27] For my purposes here, however, I want to use the issues the Wife raises about gender to return to the question of the subject, impersonation, and "Chaucer."

The three pilgrims whose tales occupy most of this book are situated at the beginning, middle, and end of the portrait gallery in the *General Prologue* (though I did not select them for that reason). They

27. For gynesis, "the putting into discourse of 'woman' as [a] *process* . . . neither a person nor a thing, but a horizon, that toward which the process is tending" (25), see Jardine, *Gynesis.* For bibliography on the developing study of this field in the Middle Ages, the reader might start with Burns and Krueger, eds., *Courtly Ideology,* and their "Selective Bibliography of Criticism: Women in Medieval French Literature," 375–90; Erler and Kowaleski, eds., *Women and Power in the Middle Ages;* Rose, ed., *Women in the Middle Ages and the Renaissance;* and *Medieval Feminist Newsletter.*

thus outline the sequence of the poem in a way that is particularly telling with respect to the themes of desire, gender, and the paternal law. The poem begins in an atmosphere of official hierarchy, plenitude, and male power ("vertu," from Latin *virtus*, "maleness," derived from *vir*, "man") that are specifically associated in the opening lines with phallic assertion. Those lines give, one might say, a very *gendered* representation of what April does to March to get the world moving in spring:

> Whan that Aprill with his shoures soote
> The droghte of March hath perced to the roote,
> And bathed every veyne in swich licour
> Of which vertu engendred is the flour . . .
>
> (1–4)[28]

Consistent with this opening, the first portrait, the Knight's, supplies the image of a powerful patriarch, worthy and vir-tuous. He is a victorious fighter, a defender of the church, and the legitimate father of a squire who will succeed legitimately to the paternal estate—the very person to justify the speaker's tacit faith in the links between authority, determinate transmissable meaning, and male gender dominance. By the time those assumptions have been put in question by the anomalies of the third estate and the breakdown of hierarchy associated with them, it seems more than fortuitously appropriate that the boundaries of the third estate, and of the project to order the performance hierarchically, should be marked by a woman, and a markedly competitive, combative, and threatening one at that. And just as it seems no accident that the Parson's portrait, which is a strident reaffirmation of male authority as well as ideal Christian order, follows the Wife's and initiates the last phase of the portraits, it seems even less of one that the gallery ends in an atmosphere of divine order undermined by human abuses, of active disenchantment, and with the Pardoner, the one pilgrim who is lacking the phallus, the embodiment of the not-masculine, castrated: "I trowe he were a geldyng or a mare" (691). His song "Com hider, love, to me!" (672) may even remind us, in context, that the opening paragraph itself ends not in stable order and fulfillment but in desire and lack: "The hooly blisful martir for to seke, / That hem hath holpen whan that they were seeke" (17–18).

28. See Fineman, "Structure of Allegorical Desire."

What a rereading of the prologue in terms of these gender themes reveals is the emergence of another kind of plot and a different sort of psychological structure for the poem. As I have been arguing, the disenchanted perspective on its own unfolding that characterizes the end of the prologue stresses retrospectively the extent to which the poem is the representation not of the objective reality of others but of the undeclared (and perhaps unconscious) motives that lie behind a particular attempt to classify them. The particular inflection of this general pattern that a focus on gender produces is the way the speaker associates gender and its vicissitudes (if that is the right word for the Pardoner's portrait) with order or the lack of it. But precisely because this way of reading brings the speaker out from behind the conceal- ment of "objective" description, it also reveals the extent to which these portraits are carriers of the speaker's projections. They are aspects of his own attitudes toward his undertaking, markers of his own "masculine" rage for order and its vicissitudes, apparently uncon- scious roles that he plays. They are also, of course, clues to his own instability of gender and his own proper (improper) subjectivity.

The reading of the *General Prologue* I have been calling prospec- tive is also masculine in the terms developed in this book. That read- ing traces a *project* of the speaker's to generate a decisive account of the pilgrims that will establish them as stable sources or origins of the tales they tell and which therefore encourages the kind of bad, old- fashioned, dominated-by-the-frame reading I have been continually fighting from the beginning of my own project here. It is important to see that a version of the speaker's project is fundamental to the poem and the poet—that it is what they begin with in one sense, and equally, given the prologue's claim to come after the pilgrimage, what they end with in another. The desire of this project is to find, establish, or make *selves* for the pilgrims that their tales will embody without alteration, and reflexively that desire makes the project a version of *the poet's desire to be and to have a self of his own.* The prologue and the links—the entire frame that punctuates the *Canterbury Tales,* as Lacan might say—testifies to its maker's desire to establish and inhabit stable structures of gender and genre, to record and preserve the social status quo and its workings, to delineate and maintain clear bounda- ries between the self and others, and to be a transmitter of the phallus, an authority, and what his culture calls a man. The poem *represents* this desire, and represents it as the poet's from beginning to end. It is particularly important to recognize this about the poem because the recognition supports the fundamental validity of the dramatic method in reading it. No textually responsible reading of the poem, including a deconstructive one, can ignore or factor out the pilgrim tellers, the issue of agency, and the problem of voice. These are things that must be read *through* rather than around. If the *Canterbury Tales* is, as I have maintained, one of the major explorations and analyses of subjectivity and its implications—of the escape of the self from itself—in the Western tradition, it founds that exploration and analysis in an understanding of the human fact of the self as that impossible thing, that insatiable desire, that ceaselessly escapes and returns.

Thus if we desire the author, as Barthes suggests, there is evidence in the poem that Chaucer did too. But that desire is of course only part of the story. There is further evidence that "Chaucer," the voice of that text, desires the other as well, and *that* desire speaks in the most characteristic act of the *Canterbury Tales,* impersonation. "Thereof nedeth nat to speke as nowthe" (462) in the Wife's portrait in effect allies the feminine with supplementarity, with what is *left out* of the "masculine" prospect, what has to come "after." The edge of masculine locker-room innuendo that dominates the portrait combines with this admission/promise of more to come to suggest just how inadequate a "masculine" (indeed a male) perspective is for understanding the Wife and the virtual necessity of finding a way to let her own point of view speak out even if it means dressing in drag to do it. Moments like this, or like the apology at the end of the portrait gallery, call attention to the fact that the *General Prologue* does not do justice to the pilgrims and therefore, by the same token and for the same reasons, does not do justice to the poet-speaker and his understanding of his world. From this point of view it can be said that the voice of the textual working we call "Chaucer" shares the Derridian desire to escape knowledge and certainty, to reach a point of not knowing any longer where he is going because of the constraints such "knowledge" imposes. Out of the dramatized insufficiency of traditional social, moral, and gender classifications, and the dramatized insufficiency of the kind of self that goes with them to deal with the complexity of individuals and their relations, the poet turns to the pilgrims, and turns to them as texts.

After all, one of the first things that is obvious about the voice-of-the-text of the *Canterbury Tales,* the agency or self we are led to construct for it, is that "he" is an impersonator in the conventional sense: he puts fictional others between himself and us. Each of the tales is, we know, Chaucer impersonating a pilgrim, the narrator speaking in the voice of the Knight or the Reeve or the Second Nun. They are his creatures; he gives them his life. One of the motives of this enterprise—certainly one of its effects—is to slow us down, to keep us from grasping the central consciousness, the author's self, too quickly and easily by directing our attention to the variety and complexity of the roles he plays and the voices he assumes. Though he is—he must be—each of the pilgrims and all of them, he seems to insist that we can only discover him by discovering who the Knight is, the Parson, the Pardoner, the Wife of Bath. But this self-protective motive is again only half the story. We might as easily say that the poet takes his own life from the pilgrims he impersonates, and the amount of time and effort spent on making the pilgrims independent, the sheer labor of consistent, unbroken impersonation to which the poem testifies, suggests that this perspective is at least as compelling for Chaucer as for us. The enterprise of the poem involves the continual attempt, continually repeated, to see from another's point of view, to stretch and extend the self by learning—and practicing—to speak in the voices of others.

This perspective seems not only opposed to the "masculine" reading of the prologue and the tales but also allied to the kind of impulses I have been calling feminine. It is associated with a fluidity of identity and identification: the desire and ability to appreciate and enact a variety of positions, including gender positions. It is allied with the desire and ability to see the "feminine" in men and the "masculine" in women and imagine how subjects who occupy those bodies within those social constructions might feel, act, desire, and "go on" practically in the circumstances. It seems allied as well with a preference for individuals over society, with private life as opposed to public life, and with the escape from self and the phallus called *jouissance.* It indeed has something to do with bisexuality, and it allows us to locate that feature of all the pilgrims/texts analyzed here in their putative maker as well. In fact Chaucerian impersonation itself has this consistently double or bisexual quality. It oscillates continually and simultaneously between, on the one hand, the desire and practice of dominating others and turning them into versions and extensions of the self that I have analyzed in the Pardoner and, on the other hand, the desire and practice of exploring new roles, possibilities, and personalities that I have examined in the Wife of Bath. Though one mode is dominant in those two pilgrims, each is constantly engaged in both modes, and how should the poet who makes, and is made by, them both escape the same fate and the same desire?

As the foregoing list may suggest, however, the pair "masculine"/ "feminine" begins to take on an allegorical reach at this point that is both a genuine and important fact about the symbolic ramifications of gender and a difficult opposition to work with in finishing up here. I have been playing with a number of (to me) dauntingly complex oppositions, most centrally perhaps "masculine"/"feminine" and self/ subject. Like Chaucer, I do not think I can control all their relations in my text (to say nothing of elsewhere), and I want now to veer again to the latter pair, remarking only that though the two sets of terms are intimately related, they are neither reducible to one another nor even always consistently parallel.

I have argued that the end of the *General Prologue* enacts a shift from the poem as performance to the poem as text. In doing so, it focuses attention on the speaker as performer in the act—prospectively—of giving way to what I have called the voice of the text. It thus identifies itself—retrospectively—as another instance of what the tales also are (and were first), a representation of the agency of an individual subject in its dealings with language, if language is considered as the most general instance of an institutional construct. That last formulation might do as a definition of the key term I have not defined in this book, *voice*. If so, however, the definition will have to be glossed so as to encompass the dynamics of self and subject, the undecidable play between the coalescence of the subject site into a shapely, self-mastering humanist agent, and the undoing of that position into the place of a fluid, multifarious polyvocality. Voice ought to be a term for that process, a way of referring to the tug toward undoing the self and letting loose the dance of the signifiers, and the complementary drive to contain the plurivocal unruliness of what goes on where subjectivity happens. This is the dynamic Chaucer's poem represents between "masculine" and "feminine," speaker and pilgrims, prologue and tales, self and subject. It is the dynamic as well of reading in general—

the movement between the "decoding" of meaning and the pleasure of the text—and of the kind of reading this particular text represents and invites.

The version of the opposition that seems most apposite for understanding voice, however, remains that between performance and text. This is so first of all because of the fairly obvious ways *performance* as a notion evokes location, the willed agency of the performer and the dominance of "his" voice in what is performed, the humanist self, embodiment, and the like, whereas *text,* as now understood, suggests dissemination, the deconstruction of the self in favor of larger, structural forms of agency, the ironing out of relations of dominance and recession among voices, loss of location or disembodiment, and so on. To make voice the swing term of this opposition, more or less in the way *estate* is the hinge between personal and social in the poem, is to make it the field within which those doings and undoings go on, that is, to make it the site of its own other and, as I have maintained, the central concern, along with estate, of the *Canterbury Tales.* Second, the appropriateness of thinking of voice as the site of the play between performance and text is enhanced if we recall again that the *Canterbury Tales* proposes and presents itself patently, right on the surface, as the textual representation of oral performance, that is, as something that represents the location of language in the agency of individuals but does so in a form that is also bound to undo that location and agency and put them in question.

Such a definition, or collocation of definitions, of voice allows us to respond to the rhythms of performing and textualizing, the doing and undoing of voice in the poem, as part of its larger structure and of what it represents—allows us to attend to them not simply as what the poem evinces or enacts because all uses of language do but also as a large part of what the poem is about. This response in turn helps draw attention to what I have been focusing on throughout this reading: those moments in the poem when its performing subjects encounter their own living-out of the condition I have tried to describe. These are the moments, and they come in every tale, when the subject represents and experiences itself as unselfed, textualized, and escaping itself at the same time that it continues to produce performance effects from its location in body and book. As one of the readers of an earlier version of this book, Paul Strohm, remarked, "I still believe that some uncertainty in the attribution of narrative perspective is a property of Chaucer's texts, and that at least some multiplication of narrative voices and perspectives loose within individual tales is inevitable." Exactly. This is a very Chaucerian predicament, one that is represented over and over in his poetry as the situation that poetry both represents and confronts, struggles with and exploits, and it is, not surprisingly, a predicament of his readers as well. The end of the *General Prologue* multiplies a performing self into a textual subjectivity, and the crucial feature of that subjectivity is impersonation. To appear as a disenchanted self in one sense—as one who is aware of the human construction of society and self—is to appear as a disenchanted self in another: as a self-constructing activity that continues into the rest of the poem *in the form* of an impersonation, a practice of voicing, that is always its own undoing and therefore demands continual rereading. The advent of the poem as text identifies the speaker of the *General Prologue,* like the pilgrim tellers of the tales, as simply one of the poet's many self-representations, a multiplicity he is no more (though no less) in control of than any of those other tellers or than any other human subject. That textualization sets the terms of both his writing and our reading and serves notice that we—all of us—will have to read his "real nature" differently, and keep reading.

Works Cited

Adelman, Janet. " 'That We May Leere Som Wit.' " In Dewey R. Faulkner, ed., *Twentieth Century Interpretations of The Pardoner's Tale*, 96–106. Englewood Cliffs, N.J.: Prentice-Hall, 1973.

Aers, David. *Chaucer, Langland and the Creative Imagination*. London: Routledge and Kegan Paul, 1980.

Albrecht, W. P. "The Sermon on 'Gentilesse.'" *College English* 12 (1951): 459.

Anonymous. "The Phallic Phase and the Subjective Import of the Castration Complex." *Scilicet* 1 (1968), 61–84. Reprinted in Juliet Mitchell and Jacqueline Rose, eds., *Feminine Sexuality: Jacques Lacan and the École Freudienne*, 99–122. New York: Norton, 1982.

apRoberts, Robert P. "The Central Episode in Chaucer's *Troilus*." *PMLA* 77 (1962): 373–85.

Aquinas, Saint Thomas. *Catena aurea quatuor evangelia. Opera Omnia*. Vols. 11–12. Parma: Fiaccadori, 1852–73. Reprint. New York: Musurgia, 1949.

Auerbach, Erich. *Mimesis: The Representation of Reality in Western Literature*. Translated by Willard Trask. Garden City, N.Y.: Doubleday, Anchor, 1953.

Augustine, Saint. *On Christian Doctrine*. Translated and with an introduction by D. W. Robertson, Jr. Indianapolis: Bobbs-Merrill, 1958.

Barthes, Roland. "Écrivains et écrivants." In *Essais critiques*, 147–54. Paris: Editions de Seuil, 1964. Translated by Richard Howard under the title "Authors and Writers," in *Critical Essays*, 143–50. Evanston, Ill.: Northwestern University Press, 1972.

———. "Introduction to the Structural Analysis of Narratives." In *Image, Music, Text*, translated by Stephen Heath, 74–124. New York: Hill and Wang, 1977.

———. *The Pleasure of the Text*. Translated by Richard Miller. New York: Hill and Wang, 1975.

———. *S/Z*. Translated by Richard Miller. New York: Hill and Wang, 1974.

———. "To Write, an Intransitive Verb?" In Richard Macksey and Eugenio Donato, eds., *The Structuralist Controversy: The Languages of Criticism and the Sciences of Man*, 134–45. Baltimore: Johns Hopkins University Press, 1972.

———. "Writers, Intellectuals, Teachers." In *Image, Music, Text*, translated by Stephen Heath, 190–215. New York: Hill and Wang, 1977.

Bede. *In Marci evangelium expositio.* In J.-P. Migne, ed., *Patrologia Cursus Completus . . . Series Latina,* vol. 92, cols. 134d–302c. Paris, 1862. Reprint. Turnhout, Belgium: Brepols, 1985.

Beichner, Paul E., "Confrontation, Contempt of Court, and Chaucer's Cecilia," *Chaucer Review* 8 (1974): 198–204.

Benveniste, Emile. *Problems in General Linguistics.* Translated by Mary Elizabeth Meek. Miami Linguistics Series, no. 8. Coral Gables, Fla.: University of Miami Press, 1971.

Berger, Harry, Jr., "Ecology of the Medieval Imagination: An Introductory Overview." *Centennial Review* 12 (1968): 279–313.

———. "The F-Fragment of the Canterbury Tales: Part II." *Chaucer Review* 1 (1967): 135–56.

———. "What Did the King Know, and When Did He Know It? Shakespearian Discourses and Psychoanalysis." *South Atlantic Quarterly* 88 (1989): 811–62.

Berger, Harry, Jr., and H. Marshall Leicester, Jr. "Social Structure as Doom: The Limits of Heroism in *Beowulf.*" In Robert B. Burlin and E. B. Irving, Jr., eds., *Old English Studies in Honour of John C. Pope,* 37–79. Toronto: University of Toronto Press, 1974.

Bethurum, Dorothy. "The Center of the *Parlement of Foules.*" In *Essays in Honor of Walter Clyde Curry,* 39–50. Nashville: Vanderbilt University Press, 1954.

Biggins, Dennis. "O Jankyn, Be Ye There?" In Beryl Rowland, ed., *Chaucer and Middle English Studies in Honor of Rossell Hope Robbins,* 249–54. Kent, Ohio: Kent State University Press, 1974.

Blake, Kathleen A. "Order and the Noble Life in Chaucer's *Knight's Tale?*" *Modern Language Quarterly* 34 (1973): 3–19.

Bloomfield, Morton W. *Piers Plowman as a Fourteenth Century Apocalypse.* New Brunswick, N.J.: Rutgers University Press, 1961.

Boccaccio, Giovanni. *The Book of Theseus (Teseide delle Nozze d'Emilia).* Translated by Bernadette Marie McCoy. New York: Medieval Text Association, 1974.

———. *Teseida, delle nozze d'Emilia.* Edited by Aurelio Roncaglia. Bari: Laterza, 1941.

Boethius, Anicius Manlius Severinus. *The Theological Tractates.* Translated by H. F. Stewart and E. K. Rand, with *The Consolation of Philosophy,* "I.T.," trans. and rev. H. F. Stewart. Loeb Classical Library. 1953.

Bourdieu, Pierre. *Outline of a Theory of Practice.* Translated by Richard Nice. Cambridge Studies in Social Anthropology, edited by Jack Goody, no. 16. New York: Cambridge University Press, 1977.

Bowden, Muriel. *A Commentary on the General Prologue to the Canterbury Tales.* 2d ed. New York: Macmillan, 1967.

Brandt, William. *The Shape of Medieval History.* 1966. Reprint. New York: Schocken Books, 1973.

Bronson, Bertrand H. *In Search of Chaucer.* Toronto: University of Toronto Press, 1960.

Brooks, Peter. *Reading for the Plot: Design and Intention in Narrative*. New York: Vintage, 1985.

Brown, Emerson, Jr., and Eren Hostetter Branch. Review of Terry Jones, *Chaucer's Knight: The Portrait of a Medieval Mercenary*. *Anglia* 102 (1984): 525–32.

Burlin, Robert B. *Chaucerian Fiction*. Princeton: Princeton University Press, 1977.

Burns, E. Jane, and Roberta L. Krueger, eds., *Courtly Ideology and Woman's Place in Medieval French Literature*. Special issue. *Romance Notes* 35, no. 3 (1985).

————. "Selective Bibliography of Criticism: Women in Medieval French Literature." *Romance Notes* 35, no. 3 (1985), 375–90.

Burton, T. L. "The Wife of Bath's Fourth and Fifth Husbands and Her Ideal Sixth: The Growth of a Marital Philosophy." *Chaucer Review* 13 (1978): 34–50.

Cameron, Allen Barry. "The Heroine in the Knight's Tale." *Studies in Short Fiction* 5 (1968): 119–27.

Campbell, A. P. "Chaucer's 'Retraction': Who Retracted What?" *Humanities Association Bulletin* 16, no. 1 (1965): 75–87.

Cappellanus, Andreas. *The Art of Courtly Love*. Translated by John Jay Parry. New York: Norton, 1941.

Carruthers, Mary. "The Wife of Bath and the Painting of Lions." *PMLA* 94 (1979): 209–22.

Cary, Meredith. "Sovereignty and the Old Wife." *Papers on Language and Literature* 5 (1969): 375–80.

De Certeau, Michel. *Heterologies: Discourse on the Other*. Translated by Brian Massumi. Theory and History of Literature, vol. 17. Minneapolis: University of Minnesota Press, 1986.

Chaucer, Geoffrey. *The Oxford Chaucer*. 5 vols. Edited by W. W. Skeat. 1894–97.

————. *The Riverside Chaucer*. 3d ed. Edited by Larry D. Benson, based on F. N. Robinson, ed., *The Works of Geoffrey Chaucer*, 2d ed. Boston: Houghton Mifflin, 1987.

Chodorow, Nancy. *The Reproduction of Mothering: Psychoanalysis and the Sociology of Gender*. Berkeley and Los Angeles: University of California Press, 1978.

Clément, Catherine. *The Lives and Legends of Jacques Lacan*. Translated by Arthur Goldhammer. New York: Columbia University Press, 1983.

Colmer, Dorothy. "Character and Class in the Wife of Bath's Tale." *Journal of English and Germanic Philology* 72 (1973): 329–39.

Condren, Edward I. "The Pardoner's Bid for Existence." *Viator* 41 (1973): 177–205.

Cook, Albert S. *The Historical Background of Chaucer's Knight*. New Haven: Yale University Press, 1916.

Cooper, Geoffrey. " 'Sely John' in the 'Legende' of the *Miller's Tale*." *Journal of English and Germanic Philology* 79 (1980): 1–12.

Cooper, Helen. *The Structure of the Canterbury Tales*. London: Duckworth, 1983.

Cotter, James Finn. "The Wife of Bath and the Conjugal Debt." *English Language Notes* 6 (1969): 169–72.

Crampton, Georgia Ronan. *The Condition of Creatures: Suffering and Action in Chaucer and Spenser*. New Haven: Yale University Press, 1974.

Culler, Jonathan. *On Deconstruction: Theory and Criticism After Structuralism*. Ithaca, N.Y.: Cornell University Press, 1982.

——— . *Structuralist Poetics: Structuralism, Linguistics, and the Study of Literature*. Ithaca, N.Y.: Cornell University Press, 1975.

Curry, Walter Clyde. *Chaucer and the Medieval Sciences*. 2d ed. New York: Barnes and Noble, 1960.

David, Alfred, *The Strumpet Muse: Art and Morals in Chaucer's Poetry*. Bloomington: Indiana University Press, 1976.

Deleuze, Gilles, and Felix Guattari. *Anti-Oedipus: Capitalism and Schizophrenia*. [Vol. 1.] Translated by Robert Hurley, Mark Seem, and Helen R. Lane. New York: Viking, 1977.

——— . *Mille plateaux: Capitalisme et schizophrénie*. [Vol. 2.] Paris: Editions de Minuit, 1980.

——— . *On the Line*. Translated by John Johnstone. New York: Semiotexte, 1983.

Derrida, Jacques. "Discussion," following "Structure, Sign, and Play in the Discourse of the Human Sciences." In Raymond Macksey and Eugenio Donato, eds. *The Structuralist Controversy: The Languages of Criticism and the Sciences of Man*, 265–72. Baltimore: Johns Hopkins University Press, 1972.

——— . *Dissemination*. Translated by Barbara Johnson. Chicago: University of Chicago Press, 1981.

——— . "FORS: The Anglish Words of Nicolas Abraham and Maria Torok." Translated by Barbara Johnson. *Georgia Review* 31 (1977): 64–116.

——— . "Living On / Border Lines." Translated by James Hulbert. In Harold Bloom et al., *Deconstruction and Criticism*, 75–176. New York: Seabury Press, 1979.

——— . *Of Grammatology*. Translated and with an introduction by Gayatri Chakravorty Spivak. Baltimore: Johns Hopkins University Press, 1976.

——— . *Spurs: Nietzsche's Styles = Épérons: les styles de Nietzsche*. Translated by Barbara Harlow. Introduction by Stefano Agosti. Drawings by François Loubrieu. Chicago: University of Chicago Press, 1978.

Donaldson, E. T. "Adventures with the Adversative Conjunction in the General Prologue to the *Canterbury Tales;* or, What's Before the But?" In Michael Benskin and M. L. Samuels, eds., *So Meny People Longages and Tonges: Philological Essays in Scots and Medieval English Presented to Angus McIntosh*, 355–60. Edinburgh: Benskin and Samuels, 1981.

——— . "Chaucer and the Elusion of Clarity." In T. E. Dorsch, ed., *Essays and Studies 1972 in Honor of Beatrice White*, 23–44. New York: Humanities Press, 1972.

————. *Chaucer's Poetry: An Anthology for the Modern Reader.* 2d ed. New York: Ronald Press, 1975.

————. "Chaucer the Pilgrim." *PMLA* 69 (1954). Reprinted in *Speaking of Chaucer*, 1–12. Durham, N.C.: Labyrinth Press, 1983.

————. "The Psychology of Editors of Middle English Texts." In *Speaking of Chaucer*, 102–18. Durham, N.C.: Labyrinth Press, 1983.

————. *The Swan at the Well: Shakespeare Reading Chaucer.* New Haven: Yale University Press, 1985.

DuBois, Page. *History, Rhetorical Description and the Epic from Homer to Spenser.* Cambridge: Brewer, 1982.

Duby, Georges. *The Three Orders: Feudal Society Imagined.* Translated by Arthur Goldhammer. Chicago: University of Chicago Press, 1980.

Ebner, Dean. "Chaucer's Precarious Knight." In Charles Adolph Huttar, ed., *Imagination and the Spirit: Essays in Literature and the Christian Faith Presented to Clyde S. Kilby*, 87–100. Grand Rapids, Mich.: Eerdmans, 1971.

Eggebroten, Anne. "Laughter in the *Second Nun's Tale:* A Redefinition of the Genre." *Chaucer Review* 19 (1984): 55–60.

Erler, Mary, and Maryanne Kowaleski, eds. *Women and Power in the Middle Ages.* Athens, Ga.: University of Georgia Press, 1988.

Felman, Shoshana. *The Literary Speech Act: Don Juan with Austin, or Seduction in Two Languages.* Translated by Catherine Porter. Ithaca, N.Y.: Cornell University Press, 1983.

Felman, Shoshana, ed., *Literature and Psychoanalysis, the Question of Reading: Otherwise.* Special issue. *Yale French Studies* 55–56 (1977).

Ferrante, Joan M. *Woman as Image in Medieval Literature.* New York: Columbia University Press, 1975.

Fichte, Joerg O. *Chaucer's "Art Poetical": A Study in Chaucerian Poetics.* Tübingen: Günter Narr, 1980.

Fifield, Merle. "The *Knight's Tale:* Incident, Idea, Incorporation." *Chaucer Review* 3 (1968): 95–106.

Fineman, Joel. "The Structure of Allegorical Desire." In Stephen Greenblatt, ed., *Allegory and Representation: Selected Papers from the English Institute*, 26–60. New Series, no. 5. Baltimore: Johns Hopkins University Press, 1981.

Fleischman, Suzanne. "Evaluation in Narrative: The Present Tense in Medieval 'Performed Stories.' " *Yale French Studies* 70 (1986): 199–251.

Fletcher, P. C. B. "The Role of Destiny in 'The Knight's Tale.' " *Theoria* 26 (1966): 43–50.

Foley, Barbara. "The Politics of Deconstruction." In Robert Con Davis and Ronald Schleifer, eds., *Rhetoric and Form: Deconstruction at Yale*, 135–58. Norman: University of Oklahoma Press, 1985.

Forshall, Josiah, and Sir Frederic Madden, eds. *The Holy Bible, Containing the Old and New Testaments, with the Apocryphal Books, in the Earliest English Versions Made from the Latin Vulgate by John Wycliffe and His Followers.* 2 vols. Oxford: Oxford University Press, 1850.

Foster, Edward E. "Humor in the *Knight's Tale*." *Chaucer Review* 3 (1968): 88–94.

Foucault, Michel. "What Is an Author?" Translated by Josué V. Harari. In Josué V. Harari, ed., *Textual Strategies: Perspectives in Post-Structuralist Criticism*, 141–60. Ithaca, N.Y.: Cornell University Press, 1979.

Freud, Sigmund. *Civilization and Its Discontents*. Translated by James Strachey. New York: Norton, 1961.

——— . *The Interpretation of Dreams*. Edited and translated by James Strachey. New York: Avon, 1965.

Froissart, Jean. *Chronicles of England, France, Spain and the Adjoining Countries, from the Latter Part of the Reign of Edward II to the Coronation of Henry IV*. 2 vols. Translated by Thomas Johnes. London: Bohn, 1849.

Frost, William. "An Interpretation of Chaucer's Knight's Tale." *Review of English Studies* 25 (1949): 290–304.

Frye, Northrop. *Anatomy of Criticism: Four Essays*. Princeton: Princeton University Press, 1957.

Fyler, John. *Chaucer and Ovid*. New Haven: Yale University Press, 1979.

Gaylord, Alan. "The Role of Saturn in the *Knight's Tale*." *Chaucer Review* 8 (1974): 172–90.

Gerould, G. H. "The Second Nun's Prologue and Tale." In W. F. Bryan and Germaine Dempster, eds., *Sources and Analogues of Chaucer's Canterbury Tales*, 664–84. Reprint. New York: Humanities Press, 1958.

Giddens, Anthony. *Central Problems in Social Theory: Action, Structure, and Contradiction in Social Analysis*. Berkeley and Los Angeles: University of California Press, 1979.

——— . *The Constitution of Society: Outline of the Theory of Structuration*. Cambridge: Polity Press, 1984.

Ginsberg, Warren. *The Cast of Character: The Representation of Personality in Ancient and Medieval Literature*. Toronto: University of Toronto Press, 1983.

Glossa Ordinaria, attributed to Walafrid Strabo. In J.-P. Migne, ed., *Patrologia Cursus Completus . . . Series Latina*, vols. 113–14, cols. 1a–752b. Paris, 1862. Reprint. Turnhout, Belgium: Brepols, 1985.

Gottfried, Barbara. "Conflict and Relationship, Sovereignty and Survival: Parables of Power in the *Wife of Bath's Prologue*." *Chaucer Review* 19 (1985): 202–24.

Green, John Martin. "World Views and Human Power: The Four Phases of Chaucer's Knight's Tale." Ph.D. diss., University of California, Santa Cruz, 1974.

Haller, Robert S. "The *Knight's Tale* and the Epic Tradition." *Chaucer Review* 1 (1966): 67–84.

——— . "The Wife of Bath and the Three Estates." *Annuale Medievale* 6 (1965): 47–64.

Hallisy, Margaret. "Poison Lore and Chaucer's Pardoner." *Massachusetts Studies in English* 9 (1983): 54–63.

Halverson, John. "Aspects of Order in the Knight's Tale." *Studies in Philology* 57 (1960): 606–21.

———. "Chaucer's Pardoner and the Progress of Criticism." *Chaucer Review* 4 (1970): 184–202.

Hamel, Mary. "The Wife of Bath and a Contemporary Murder." *Chaucer Review* 14 (1979): 132–39.

Hanning, Robert W. "Roasting a Friar, Mis-taking a Wife, and Other Acts of Textual Harassment in Chaucer's Canterbury Tales." *Studies in the Age of Chaucer* 7 (1985): 3–21.

———. " 'The Struggle Between Noble Designs and Chaos': The Literary Tradition of Chaucer's Knight's Tale." *The Literary Review* 23 (1980): 519–41.

Helterman, Jeffrey. "The Dehumanizing Metamorphoses of the *Knight's Tale.*" *ELH* 38 (1971): 493–511.

Hoffman, Arthur W. "Chaucer's Prologue to Pilgrimage: The Two Voices." *ELH* 21 (1954): 1–16.

Hoffman, Richard L. "Ovid and Chaucer's Myth of Theseus and Pirothoüs." *English Language Notes* 2 (1965): 252–57.

———. "The Wife of Bath and the Dunmow Bacon." *Notes and Queries* 10 (1963): 9–11.

Howard, Donald R. "Chaucer the Man." *PMLA* 80 (1965): 337–43.

———. *The Idea of the Canterbury Tales*. Berkeley and Los Angeles: University of California Press, 1976.

Huppé, Bernard F. *A Reading of the Canterbury Tales*. Rev. ed. Albany, N.Y.: State University of New York Press, 1967.

Irigaray, Luce. *This Sex Which Is Not One*. Translated by Catherine Porter with Carolyn Burke. Ithaca, N.Y.: Cornell University Press, 1985.

Jameson, Fredric. "Pleasure: A Political Issue." *Formations,* 1983 ("Formations of Pleasure"): 1–14.

———. *The Political Unconscious: Narrative as a Socially Symbolic Act*. Ithaca, N.Y.: Cornell University Press, 1981.

Jardine, Alice. *Gynesis: Configurations of Woman and Modernity*. Ithaca, N.Y.: Cornell University Press, 1985.

Jerome, Saint. *Commentaria in Evangelium Matthaei*. In J.-P. Migne, ed., *Patrologia Cursus Completus . . . Series Latina*, vol. 26, cols. 15a–228b. Paris, 1862. Reprint. Turnhout, Belgium: Brepols, 1985.

Johnson, Barbara. "Gender Theory and the Yale School." In Robert Con Davis and Ronald Schleifer, eds., *Rhetoric and Form: Deconstruction at Yale,* 101–12. Norman: University of Oklahoma Press, 1985.

Jones, Ernest. *The Life and Work of Sigmund Freud*. 3 vols. New York: Basic Books, 1955.

Jones, Terry. *Chaucer's Knight: The Portrait of a Medieval Mercenary*. Baton Rouge: Louisiana State University Press, 1980.

Jordan, Robert M. *Chaucer and the Shape of Creation*. Cambridge, Mass.: Harvard University Press, 1967.

———. "Chaucer's Sense of Illusion: Roadside Drama Reconsidered." *ELH* 29 (1962): 19–33.

Kaske, R. E. "Chaucer's Marriage Group." In Jerome Mitchell and William Provost, eds., *Chaucer the Love Poet,* 45–65. Athens, Ga.: University of Georgia Press, 1973.

Kean, P. M. *Chaucer and the Making of English Poetry.* 2 vols. Vol. 1, *Love Vision and Debate;* vol. 2, *The Art of Narrative.* London: Routledge and Kegan Paul, 1972.

Keene, J. M. *The Laws of War in the Later Middle Ages.* London: Methuen, 1965.

Kellogg, Alfred L., and Louis A. Haselmeyer. "Chaucer's Satire of the Pardoner." In Alfred L. Kellogg, *Chaucer, Langland, Arthur,* 212–244. New Brunswick, N.J.: Rutgers University Press, 1972.

Kempton, Daniel R. "Chaucer's Tale of Melibee: 'A Litel Thyng in Prose.' " *Genre* 21 (1988): 263–78.

———. "The *Physician's Tale:* The Doctor of Physic's Diplomatic 'Cure.' " *Chaucer Review* 19 (1984): 24–38.

Kendrick, Laura. *Chaucerian Play: Comedy and Control in the Canterbury Tales.* Berkeley and Los Angeles: University of California Press, 1988.

Kernan, Anne. "The Archwife and the Eunuch." *ELH* 41 (1974): 1–25.

Kierkegaard, Søren. *The Sickness unto Death.* Edited and translated by Howard V. Hong and Edna H. Hong. Princeton: Princeton University Press, 1980.

Kittredge, G. L. *Chaucer and His Poetry.* Cambridge, Mass.: Harvard University Press, 1915.

———. "Chaucer's Pardoner." 1893. Reprinted in Edward Wagenknecht, ed., *Chaucer: Modern Essays in Criticism,* 117–25. New York: Galaxy, 1959.

Kolve, V. A. *Chaucer and the Imagery of Narrative.* Stanford, Calif.: Stanford University Press, 1984.

Lacan, Jacques. "Aggressivity in Psychoanalysis" (1948). In *Écrits: A Selection,* translated by Alan Sheridan, 8–29. New York: Norton, 1977.

———. "God and the *Jouissance* of ~~The~~ Woman." Translated by Jacqueline Rose. In Juliet Mitchell and Jacqueline Rose, eds., *Feminine Sexuality: Jacques Lacan and the École Freudienne,* 137–48. New York: Norton, 1982.

———. "The Mirror Stage as Formative of the Function of the I." In *Écrits: A Selection,* translated by Alan Sheridan, 1–7. New York: Norton, 1977.

———. "Of the Gaze as *Objet Petit a.*" In *The Four Fundamental Concepts of Psycho-analysis,* edited by Jacques-Alain Miller and translated by Alan Sheridan, 67–122. New York: Norton, 1977.

———. "The Subversion of the Subject and the Dialectic of Desire in the Freudian Unconscious." In *Écrits: A Selection,* translated by Alan Sheridan, 292–325. New York: Norton, 1977.

————. "What Is A Picture." In *The Four Fundamental Concepts of Psycho-analysis,* edited by Jacques-Alain Miller and translated by Alan Sheridan, 105–19. New York: Norton, 1977.

Laplanche, J., and J.-B. Pontalis. *The Language of Psycho-analysis.* Translated by Donald Nicholson-Smith. New York: Norton, 1973.

Lawlor, John. *Chaucer.* New York: Harper, 1968.

Leicester, H. Marshall, Jr. "The Dialectic of Romantic Historiography: Prospect and Retrospect in *The French Revolution.*" *Victorian Studies* 5 (1971): 5–17.

————. "The Harmony of Chaucer's *Parlement*: A Dissonant Voice." *Chaucer Review* 9 (1974): 15–34.

————. " 'No Vileyn's Word': Social Context and Performance in Chaucer's *Friar's Tale.*" *Chaucer Review* 17 (1982): 24–25.

————. "Oure Tonges *Différance*: Textuality and Deconstruction in Chaucer." In Laurie A. Finke and Martin B. Schichtman, eds., *Medieval Texts and Contemporary Readers,* 15–26. Ithaca, N.Y.: Cornell University Press, 1987.

Levy, Bernard S. "The Wife of Bath, the Loathly Lady and Dante's Siren." *Symposium* 19 (1965): 359–73.

Lindberg, Conrad, ed. *MS. Bodley 959, Genesis-Baruch 3.20 in the Earlier Version of the Wycliffite Bible.* Vol. 2, Leviticus-Judges 7.13. Acta Universitatis Stockholmiensis: Stockholm Studies in English, vol. 8. Stockholm, 1961.

Lumiansky, R. M. *Of Sondry Folk: The Dramatic Principle of the Canterbury Tales.* Austin: University of Texas Press, 1955.

Magee, Patricia Anne. "The Wife of Bath and the Problem of Mastery." *Massachusetts Studies in English* 3 (1971): 40–45.

Major, John M. "The Personality of Chaucer the Pilgrim." *PMLA* 75 (1960): 160–62.

De Man, Paul. *Allegories of Reading: Figural Language in Rousseau, Nietzsche, Rilke, and Proust.* New Haven: Yale University Press, 1979.

————. *Blindness and Insight: Essays in the Rhetoric of Contemporary Criticism.* 2d ed. Minneapolis: University of Minnesota Press, 1983.

Mann, Jill. *Chaucer and Medieval Estates Satire: The Literature of Social Classes and the General Prologue to the Canterbury Tales.* Cambridge: Cambridge University Press, 1973.

Manning, Diane. "The Temple of Venus, Love, and the Knight—Their Interrelationship in Parts I and III of the Knight's Tale." Unpublished paper, University of California, Santa Cruz, 1978.

McCall, John P. *Chaucer Among the Gods.* University Park, Pa.: Pennsylvania State University Press, 1979.

McKeon, Richard. *Selections from the Medieval Philosophers.* 2 vols. New York: Scribners, 1930.

Middleton, Anne. "The *Physician's Tale* and Love's Martyrs: 'Ensamples Mo than Ten' in the *Canterbury Tales.*" *Chaucer Review* 8 (1973): 9–32.

Miller, J. Hillis. "The Critic as Host." In Harold Bloom et al., *Deconstruction and Criticism.* New York: Seabury Press, 1979.

Miller, Robert P. "Chaucer's Pardoner, the Scriptural Eunuch, and the *Pardoner's Tale." Speculum* 30 (1955): 180–99.

Minnis, A. J. *Chaucer and Pagan Antiquity.* Cambridge: Brewer, 1982.

Mitchell, Juliet, and Jacqueline Rose, eds. *Feminine Sexuality: Jacques Lacan and the École Freudienne.* New York: Norton, 1982.

Mizener, Arthur. "Character and Action in the Case of Criseyde." *PMLA* 54 (1939): 65–81.

Mogen, Joseph. "Chaucer and the *Bona Matrimonii." Chaucer Review* 4 (1970): 123–41.

Mulvey, Laura. "Visual Pleasure and Narrative Cinema." 1975. Reprinted in Bill Nichols, ed., *Movies and Methods,* 2:303–15. Berkeley and Los Angeles: University of California Press, 1985.

Muscatine, Charles. *Chaucer and the French Tradition: A Study in Style and Meaning.* Berkeley and Los Angeles: University of California Press, 1957.

——— . "Form, Texture, and Meaning in Chaucer's *Knight's Tale." PMLA* 65 (1950): 911–29.

Nelson, Lori. "The Temples in the *Knight's Tale."* Unpublished paper, University of California, Santa Cruz, 1978.

Neuse, Richard. "The Knight: The First Mover in Chaucer's Human Comedy." *University of Toronto Quarterly* 31 (1962): 299–315.

Nichols, Robert E., Jr. "The Pardoner's Ale and Cake." *PMLA* 82 (1967): 498–504.

Nietzsche, Friedrich. *Beyond Good and Evil.* Translated by Walter Kaufmann. New York: Vintage, 1966.

——— . *The Birth of Tragedy from the Spirit of Music.* Translated by Francis Golfing. Garden City, N.Y.: Doubleday, 1956.

——— . *The Will to Power.* Edited by Walter Kaufmann. Translated by Walter Kaufmann and R. J. Hollingdale. New York: Vintage, 1968.

Norris, Christopher. "Some Versions of Rhetoric: Empson and de Man." In Robert Con Davis and Ronald Schleifer, eds., *Rhetoric and Form: Deconstruction at Yale,* 191–214. Norman: University of Oklahoma Press, 1985.

North, J. D. "Kalenderes Enlumyned Ben They: Some Astronomical Themes in Chaucer." *Review of English Studies* 20 (1969): 129–54, 257–83.

Oberembt, Kenneth J., "Chaucer's Anti-misogynist Wife of Bath," *Chaucer Review* 10 (1976): 287–302.

Ovid. *Metamorphoses.* Translated by Frank Justin Miller. 2d ed. 2 vols. Loeb Classical Library. 1921.

Owen, Charles A., Jr. "The Crucial Passages in Five of the *Canterbury Tales:* A Study in Irony and Symbol." *Journal of English and Germanic Philology* 52 (1953): 294–311.

——— . "Development of the Art of Portraiture in Chaucer's *General Prologue." Leeds Studies in English* 14 (1983), 116–33.

——— . *Pilgrimage and Storytelling in the Canterbury Tales: The Dialectic of "Ernest" and "Game."* Norman: University of Oklahoma Press, 1977.

Palomo, Doris. "The Fate of the Wife of Bath's 'Bad Husbands.' " *Chaucer Review* 9 (1975): 303–19.

Pantin, W. A. *The English Church in the Fourteenth Century.* Cambridge: Cambridge University Press, 1955.

Parker, David. "Can We Trust the Wife of Bath?" *Chaucer Review* 4 (1970): 93.

Patterson, Lee W. "Chaucerian Confession: Penitential Literature and the Pardoner." *Medievalia et Humanistica,* n.s., 7 (1976): 153–73.

———. " 'For the Wyves Love of Bathe': Feminine Rhetoric and Poetic Resolution in the *Roman de la Rose* and the *Canterbury Tales." Speculum* 58 (1983): 656–95.

———. "The 'Parson's Tale' and the Quitting of the 'Canterbury Tales.' " *Traditio* 34 (1978): 333–380.

Payne, F. Anne. *Chaucer and Menippean Satire.* Madison, Wisc.: University of Wisconsin Press, 1981.

Pearsall, Derek. *The Canterbury Tales.* London: Allen and Unwin, 1985.

Pratt, Robert A. "The Development of the Wife of Bath." In MacEdward Leach, ed., *Studies in Medieval Literature in Honor of Professor Albert Croll Baugh,* 45–79. Philadelphia: University of Pennsylvania Press, 1961.

Robertson, D. W., Jr. *Chaucer's London.* New York: Wiley, 1968.

———. "The Doctrine of Charity in Medieval Literary Gardens: A Topical Approach Through Symbolism and Allegory." *Speculum* 26 (1951): 24–49.

———. *Essays in Medieval Culture.* Princeton: Princeton University Press, 1980.

———. *A Preface to Chaucer: Studies in Medieval Perspectives.* Princeton: Princeton University Press, 1962.

Robinson, Ian. *Chaucer and the English Tradition.* Cambridge: Cambridge University Press, 1972.

Ropollo, J. F. "The Converted Knight in Chaucer's 'Wife of Bath's Tale.' " *College English* 12 (1951): 263–69.

Rose, Mary Beth, ed. *Women in the Middle Ages and the Renaissance: Literary and Historical Perspectives.* Syracuse: Syracuse University Press, 1986.

Rowland, Beryl. "On the Timely Death of the Wife of Bath's Fourth Husband." *Archiv für das Studium der Neueren Sprachen und Literaturen* 209 (1972): 273–82.

Ruggiers, Paul G. "Some Philosophical Aspects of Chaucer's *The Knight's Tale." College English* 19 (1958): 296–302.

Salter, Elizabeth. Introduction to *The Knight's Tale and the Clerk's Tale,* by Geoffrey Chaucer, 7–36. London: Arnold, 1962.

Salter, F. M. "The Tragic Figure of the Wife of Bath." *Transactions of the Royal Society of Canada,* 3d ser., 48 (1954): 1–13.

Sands, Donald B. "The Non-Comic, Non-Tragic Wife: Chaucer's Dame Alys as Sociopath." *Chaucer Review* 12 (1978): 171–82.

Sartre, Jean-Paul. *Being and Nothingness.* Translated by Hazel E. Barnes. New York: Washington Square Press, 1966.

———. "Faces, Preceded by Official Portraits." Translated by Anne P. Jones.

In Maurice Natanson, ed., *Essays in Phenomenology*, 157–63. The Hague: Martinus Nijhoff, 1966.

———. *The Transcendence of the Ego*. Translated by Forrest Williams and Robert Kirkpatrick. New York: Noonday, 1957.

De Saussure, Ferdinand. *Course in General Linguistics*. Edited by Charles Bally and Albert Sechehaye with Albert Riedlinger. Translated by Wade Baskin. New York: McGraw-Hill, 1959.

Schauber, Ellen, and Ellen Spolsky. "The Consolation of Alison: The Speech Acts of the Wife of Bath." *Centrum* 5 (1977): 20–34.

Schmidt, A. V. C. "The Tragedy of Arcite: A Reconsideration of the *Knight's Tale*." *Essays in Criticism* 19 (1969): 107–16.

Schnur, Susan. "Hers" column. *New York Times*, July 18, 1985, C2.

Sedgwick, Eve Kosofsky. *Between Men: English Literature and Male Homosocial Desire*. New York: Columbia University Press, 1985.

Shapiro, Gloria K. "Dame Alice as Deceptive Narrator." *Chaucer Review* 6 (1971): 130–41.

Silva, D. S. "The Wife of Bath's Marital State." *Notes and Queries* 14 (1967): 9.

Silverman, Kaja. *The Subject of Semiotics*. New York: Oxford University Press, 1983.

Sklute, Larry. "Catalogue Form and Catalogue Style in the General Prologue of the *Canterbury Tales*." *Studia Neophilologica* 52 (1980): 35–46.

———. *Virtue of Necessity: Inconclusiveness and Narrative Form in Chaucer's Poetry*. Columbus: Ohio State University Press, 1984.

Slade, Tony. "Irony in the Wife of Bath's Tale." *Modern Language Review* 64 (1969): 241–47.

Sledd, James. "The *Clerk's Tale*: The Monsters and the Critics." *Modern Philology* 51 (1953–54): 73–92.

Smith, James. "Chaucer, Boethius and Recent Trends in Criticism." *Essays in Criticism* 22 (1972): 4–32.

Sontag, Susan. "On Style." *Partisan Review* 32 (1965): 546–47.

Spearing, A. C. *The Pardoner's Prologue and Tale*. Cambridge: Cambridge University Press, 1965.

———. *Selected Tales from Chaucer: The Knight's Tale*. Cambridge: Cambridge University Press, 1966.

Spiers, John. *Chaucer the Maker*. London: Faber and Faber, 1951.

Spitzer, Leo. "A Note on the Poetic and the Empirical 'I' in Medieval Authors." *Traditio* 4 (1946): 414–22.

Spivak, Gayatri Chakravorty. *In Other Worlds: Essays in Cultural Politics*. New York: Methuen, 1987.

———. "Translator's Preface." In Jacques Derrida, *Of Grammatology*, xiii–xx. Baltimore: Johns Hopkins University Press, 1976.

Statius, Publius Papinius. *Statius*. Translated by J. H. Mozley. 2 vols. Loeb Classical Library. 1928.

Stockton, Eric W. "The Deadliest Sin in the *Pardoner's Tale*." *Tennessee Studies in Literature* 6 (1961): 47–59.

Theweleit, Klaus. *Male Fantasies*. Vol. 1, *Women, Floods, Bodies, History*, translated by Stephen Conway. Minneapolis: University of Minnesota Press, 1987.

Thrupp, Sylvia L. *The Merchant Class of Medieval London (1300–1500)*. Chicago: University of Chicago Press, 1948.

Thurston, Paul T. *Artistic Ambivalence in Chaucer's Knight's Tale*. Gainsville, Fla.: University of Florida Press, 1968.

Twycross, Meg. *The Medieval Anadyomene: A Study in Chaucer's Mythography*. Medium Aevum Monographs, n.s. 1. Oxford: Blackwell, 1972.

Underwood, Dale. "The First of the Canterbury Tales." *ELH* 26 (1959): 455–69. Reprinted in Charles A. Owen, Jr., ed., *Discussions of the Canterbury Tales*, 37–44. Boston: Heath, 1961.

Vale, Malcolm. *War and Chivalry: Warfare and Aristocratic Culture in England, France, and Burgundy at the End of the Middle Ages*. Athens, Ga.: University of Georgia Press, 1981.

Van, Thomas A. "Second Meanings in Chaucer's *Knight's Tale*." *Chaucer Review* 3 (1968): 69–76.

——— . "Theseus and the 'Right Way' of the *Knight's Tale*." *Studies in the Literary Imagination* 4 (1971): 83–100.

Verdonk, P. " 'Sire Knyght, Heer Forth Ne Lith No Wey': A Reading of Chaucer's *The Wife of Bath's Tale*." *Neophilologus* 60 (1976): 305–7.

De Voragine, Jacobus. *The Golden Legend*. Translated by Granger Ryan and Helmut Ripperger. New York: Arno Press, 1969.

Webb, Henry J. "A Reinterpretation of Chaucer's Theseus." *Review of English Studies* 23 (1947): 289–96.

Weber, Max. "Religious Rejections of the World and Their Directions." In H. H. Gerth and C. Wright Mills, eds., *From Max Weber: Essays in Sociology*, 323–59. New York: Oxford University Press, 1946.

——— . "Science as a Vocation." In H. H. Gerth and C. Wright Mills, eds., *From Max Weber: Essays in Sociology*, 129–56. New York: Oxford University Press, 1946.

Westlund, Joseph. "The *Knight's Tale* as an Impetus for Pilgrimage." *Philological Quarterly* 43 (1964): 526–37.

Wetherbee, Winthrop. *Chaucer and the Poets: An Essay on Troilus and Criseyde*. Ithaca, N.Y.: Cornell University Press, 1984.

Whiting, Bartlett J. "The Wife of Bath's Prologue." In W. F. Bryan and Germaine Dempster, eds., *Sources and Analogues of Chaucer's Canterbury Tales*, 207–22. Reprint. New York: Humanities Press, 1958.

——— . "The Wife of Bath's Tale." In W. F. Bryan and Germaine Dempster, eds., *Sources and Analogues of Chaucer's Canterbury Tales*, 223–68. Reprint. New York: Humanities Press, 1958.

Whittock, Trevor. *A Reading of the Canterbury Tales*. Cambridge: Cambridge University Press, 1968.

Wood, Chauncey. *Chaucer and the Country of the Stars: Poetic Uses of Astrological Imagery*. Princeton: Princeton University Press, 1970.

Wright, Elizabeth. *Psychoanalytic Criticism: Theory in Practice*. New York: Methuen, 1984.

Zimbardo, Rose A. "Unity and Duality in the *Wife of Bath's Prologue and Tale*." *Tennessee Studies in Literature* 11 (1966): 11–18.

Index